ASCENT
CENTER FOR TECHNICAL KNOWLEDGE

Creo Parametric 3.0:
Introduction to Solid Modeling
Part 2

Student Guide
2nd Edition

ASCENT - Center for Technical Knowledge®
Creo Parametric 3.0: Introduction to Solid Modeling
Part 2
2nd Edition

Prepared and produced by:

ASCENT Center for Technical Knowledge
630 Peter Jefferson Parkway, Suite 175
Charlottesville, VA 22911

866-527-2368
www.ASCENTed.com

Lead Contributor: Scott Hendren

ASCENT - Center for Technical Knowledge is a division of Rand Worldwide, Inc., providing custom developed knowledge products and services for leading engineering software applications. ASCENT is focused on specializing in the creation of education programs that incorporate the best of classroom learning and technology-based training offerings.

We welcome any comments you may have regarding this student guide, or any of our products. To contact us please email: feedback@ASCENTed.com.

Contents
Part 1

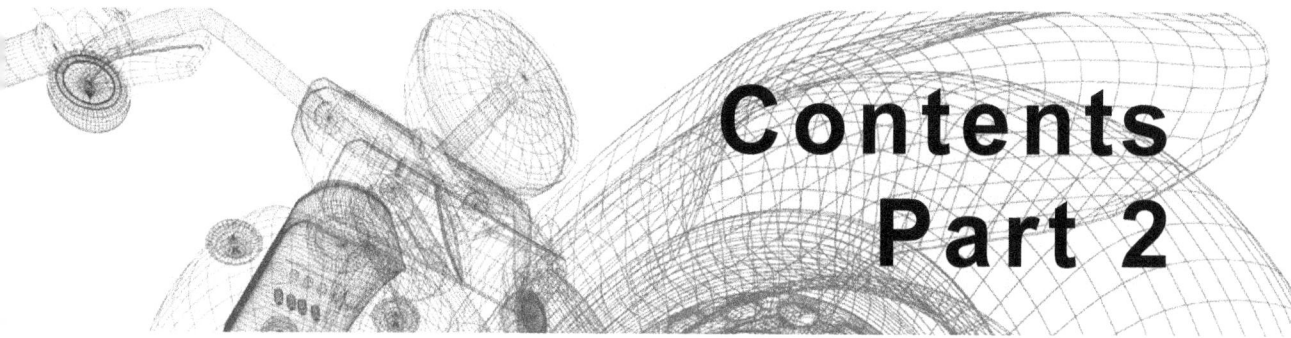

Contents
Part 2

Preface

The *Creo Parametric 3.0: Introduction to Solid Modeling* student guide provides you with an understanding of the process of designing models with Creo Parametric 3.0 through a hands-on, practice-intensive curriculum. You will learn the key skills and knowledge required to design models using Creo Parametric 3.0, starting with 2D sketching, through to solid part modeling, assembly creation, and drawing production.

Topics Covered:

- Creo Parametric fundamentals and interface
- Principles behind design intent
- Manipulating a model
- Creo Parametric file management
- Part creation and modification
- Sketching and creating geometry
- Sketcher mode functionality (sketching and dimensioning)
- Datum features
- Duplication techniques (patterns, mirroring)
- Creating relations to capture design intent
- Creo Parametric customization
- Design documentation and detailing
- Feature management
- Sweeps and blends
- Assembly creation and manipulation
- Parent/Child relationships in Creo Parametric models
- Model Analysis
- Feature failure resolution
- Effective modeling techniques

Note on Software Setup

This student guide assumes a standard installation of the software using the default preferences during installation. Lectures and practices use the standard software templates and default options for the Content Libraries.

Lead Contributor: Scott Hendren

Scott has been a trainer and curriculum developer in the PLM industry for almost 20 years, with experience on multiple CAD systems, including Creo Parametric, Creo Parametric, and CATIA. Trained in Instructional Design, Scott uses his skills to develop instructor-led and web-based training products.

Scott has held training and development positions with several high profile PLM companies, and has been with the Ascent team since 2013.

Scott holds a Bachelor of Mechanical Engineering Degree as well as a Bachelor of Science in Mathematics from Dalhousie University, Nova Scotia, Canada.

Scott Hendren has been the Lead Contributor for *Creo Parametric 3.0: Behavioral Modeling* since 2017.

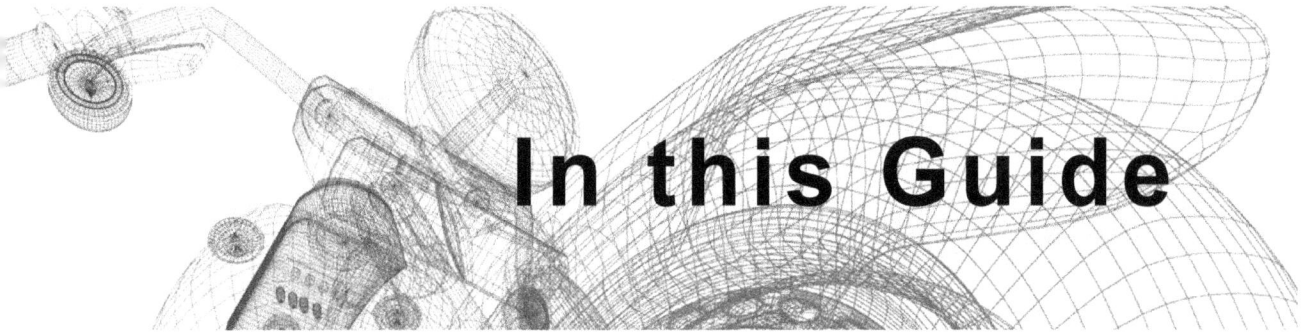

In this Guide

The following images highlight some of the features that can be found in this Student Guide.

Practice Files

Practice Files

The Practice Files page tells you how to download and install the practice files that are provided with this student guide.

FTP link for practice files

To download the practice files for this student guide, use the following steps:

1. Type the URL shown below into the address bar of your Internet browser. The URL must be typed **exactly as shown**. If you are using an ASCENT ebook, you can click on the link to download the file.

2. Press <Enter> to download the .ZIP file that contains the Practice Files.

3. Once the download is complete, unzip the file to a local folder. The unzipped file contains an .EXE file.

4. Double-click on the .EXE file and follow the instructions to automatically install the Practice Files on the C:\ drive of your computer.

   Do not change the location in which the Practice Files folder is installed. Doing so can cause errors when completing the practices in this student guide.

http://www.ASCENTed.com/getfile?id=xxxxxxxx

Chapter 1

Getting Started

In this chapter you learn how to start the AutoCAD® software, become familiar with the basic layout of the AutoCAD screen, how to access commands, use your pointing device, and understand the AutoCAD Cartesian workspace. You also learn how to open an existing drawing, view a drawing by zooming and panning, and save your work in the AutoCAD software.

Learning Objectives in this Chapter

Learning Objectives for the chapter

- Launch the AutoCAD software and complete a basic initial setup of the drawing environment.
- Identify the basic layout and features of AutoCAD interface including the Ribbon, Drawing Window, and Application Menu.
- Locate commands and launch them using the Ribbon, shortcut menus, Application Menu, and Quick Access Toolbar.
- Locate points in the AutoCAD Cartesian workspace.
- Open and close existing drawings and navigate to file locations.
- Move around a drawing using the mouse, the Zoom and Pan commands, and the Navigation Bar.
- Save drawings in various formats and set the automatic save options using the Save commands.

Chapters

Each chapter begins with a brief introduction and a list of the chapter's Learning Objectives.

Instructional Content

Each chapter is split into a series of sections of instructional content on specific topics. These lectures include the descriptions, step-by-step procedures, figures, hints, and information you need to achieve the chapter's Learning Objectives.

Side notes

Side notes are hints or additional information for the current topic.

Practice Objectives

Practices

Practices enable you to use the software to perform a hands-on review of a topic.

Some practices require you to use prepared practice files, which can be downloaded from the link found on the Practice Files page.

Chapter Review Questions

Chapter review questions, located at the end of each chapter, enable you to review the key concepts and learning objectives of the chapter.

Command Summary

The Command Summary is located at the end of each chapter. It contains a list of the software commands that are used throughout the chapter, and provides information on where the command is found in the software.

Getting Started

Command Summary

The following is a list of the commands that are used in this chapter, including details on how to access the command using the software's Ribbon, toolbars, or keyboard commands.

Button	Command	Location
	Close	• Drawing Window • Application Menu • Command Prompt: close
	Close Current Drawing	• Application Menu
	Close All Drawings	• Application Menu
NA	Dynamic Input	• Status Bar: expand Customization
Exit Autodesk AutoCAD	Exit AutoCAD	• Application Menu
	Open	• Quick Access Toolbar • Application Menu • Command Prompt: open, <Ctrl>+<O>
	Open Documents	• Application Menu
Options	Options	• Application Menu • Shortcut Menu: Options
	Pan	• Navigation Bar • Shortcut Menu: Pan • Command Prompt: pan or P
	Recent Documents	• Application Menu
	Save	• Quick Access Toolbar • Application Menu • Command Prompt: qsave, <Ctrl>+<S>
	Save As	• Quick Access Toolbar • Application Menu • Command Prompt: save
	Zoom Realtime	• Navigation Bar: Zoom Realtime • Shortcut Menu: Zoom

---

Practice Files

To download the practice files for this student guide, use the following steps:

1. Type the URL shown below into the address bar of your Internet browser. The URL must be typed **exactly as shown**. If you are using an ASCENT ebook, you can click on the link to download the file.

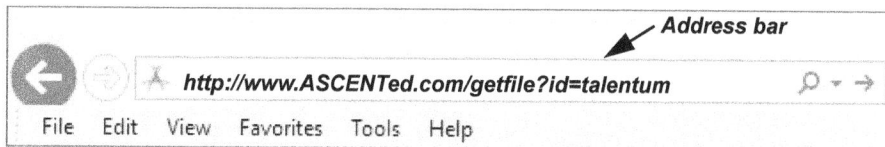

Address bar

http://www.ASCENTed.com/getfile?id=talentum

File   Edit   View   Favorites   Tools   Help

2. Press <Enter> to download the .ZIP file that contains the Practice Files.

3. Once the download is complete, unzip the file to a local folder. The unzipped file contains an .EXE file.

4. Double-click on the .EXE file and follow the instructions to automatically install the Practice Files on the C:\ drive of your computer.

   Do not change the location in which the Practice Files folder is installed. Doing so can cause errors when completing the practices in this student guide.

http://www.ASCENTed.com/getfile?id=talentum

Stay Informed!

Interested in receiving information about upcoming promotional offers, educational events, invitations to complimentary webcasts, and discounts? If so, please visit:

www.ASCENTed.com/updates/

Help us improve our product by completing the following survey:

www.ASCENTed.com/feedback

You can also contact us at: *feedback@ASCENTed.com*

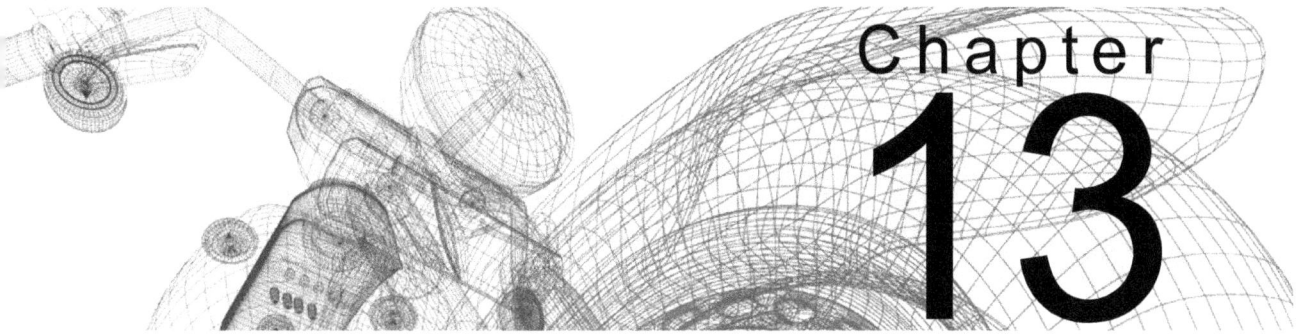

C h a p t e r

13

Display Control and Feature Order

As models become more complex, the number of features and/or components increases. You might want to display only pertinent features and/or components instead of everything at once while working with the model. Simplifying the process makes working with and visualizing a part easier. You can use tools such as Hide, Suppress, and Layers to simplify the model.

Learning Objectives in this Chapter

- Temporarily remove a non-solid feature from being included as part of the model geometry.
- Temporarily remove a feature from being included as part of the model geometry and regeneration sequence.
- Create a new layer, add features or components to that layer, and specify the display option (i.e. Hide, Unhide, or Isolate).
- Learn how to use default layers.
- Learn how to use layers as a selection tool to perform additional tasks.
- Understand how the order of feature creation affects the resulting model geometry.
- Change the order of features in the model tree by dragging and dropping them.
- Change the location of the new features that are added to a model using the Insert Here arrow.

© 2017, ASCENT - Center for Technical Knowledge®

13.1 Hiding Features

The **Hide** option enables you to quickly simplify the model. When you hide a feature or component, it remains in the model tree and in the regeneration sequence. When hiding features in a part, the solid geometry remains visible and only the datum features associated with the hidden features are removed from the display. When hiding components in an assembly, the selected components are entirely removed from the display. The **Hide** setting can be saved with the model when you ask the Creo Parametric software to save the display changes caused by the **Hide/Unhide** options. Once something is hidden, it is not shown again until it is unhidden.

Select the View tab and click 🔖 (Status), in the Visibility group to ensure that all hidden settings are saved when the model is saved. You can also click 🔖 (Reset Status) in the flyout menu, to reset your settings.

- Note that, although the default behavior of the software is to have the datum tags toggled off for points, planes and axes, the examples in this chapter will show the tags enabled to make it easier to refer to specific entities.

- Select the feature or component to be hidden, from the model tree or directly in the model. Parent/child relationships do not affect children of hidden parents because they remain in the regeneration sequence.

- To hide a feature or component, right-click and select **Hide** or select the *View* tab and click ✎ (Hide) in the Visibility group. Hidden features are identified in the model tree with a gray box that surrounds the feature or component symbol, as shown in Figure 13–1.

Axis A-1, used to create the coaxial hole (hole 1), is hidden. This feature was hidden by default when it was created on the fly with the hole.

The axis generated with Hole 2 is removed from the display because the hole is hidden.

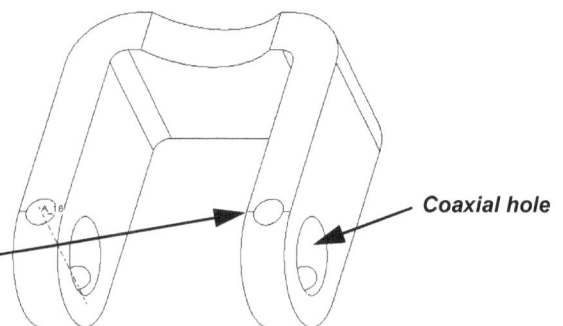

Coaxial hole

Figure 13–1

- To unhide a feature (or component), select it, right-click, and select **Unhide.** You can also select the *View* tab and click

    👁 (Unhide) in the Visibility group. The Unhide flyout icon also enables you to unhide all hidden features at once by clicking 👁 (Unhide All).

You can also access the layer tree by selecting the View tab and click

≡ (Layers) in the Visibility group.

- You can obtain a list of hidden features in the layer tree. To access the layer tree, click 📋 ▾ (Show) in the model tree and select **Layer Tree**. Figure 13–2 shows the same model and its associated layer tree. Select the **Hidden Items** row to highlight the hidden items.

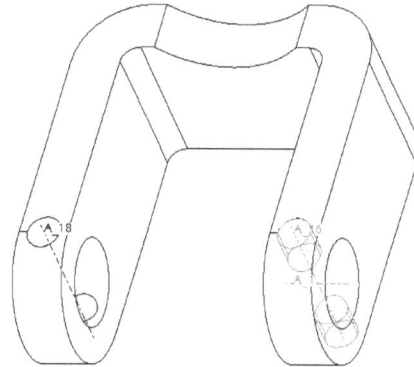

Figure 13–2

13.2 Suppressing Features

Suppressed features and/or components are temporarily removed from the display and the regeneration sequence. This simplifies the appearance of the model and decreases the amount of time it takes to regenerate. In Figure 13–3 the cut is suppressed and is therefore removed from the model tree and regeneration sequence.

The extruded feature is suppressed.

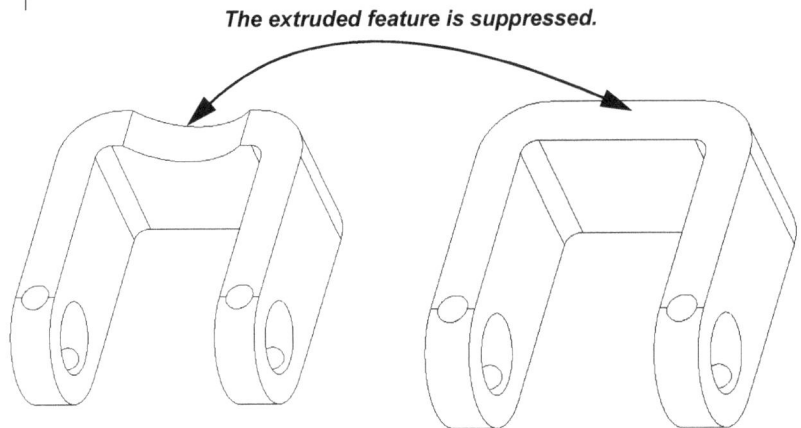

Figure 13–3

Select the feature or component to be suppressed from the model tree or directly on the model. Careful consideration must be taken with regard to parent/child relationships. By default, all children are suppressed with their parents.

All suppressed settings are saved when the model is saved.

To suppress the selected feature, right-click and select **Suppress.** You can also select **Operation>Suppress> Suppress** in the *Model* tab, as shown in Figure 13–4. The two options are available in the **Operations** menu are as follows:

- **Suppress to End of Model:** suppresses the selected feature and any feature that was created after it

- **Suppress Unrelated Items:** suppresses the selected feature and any feature that is not related.

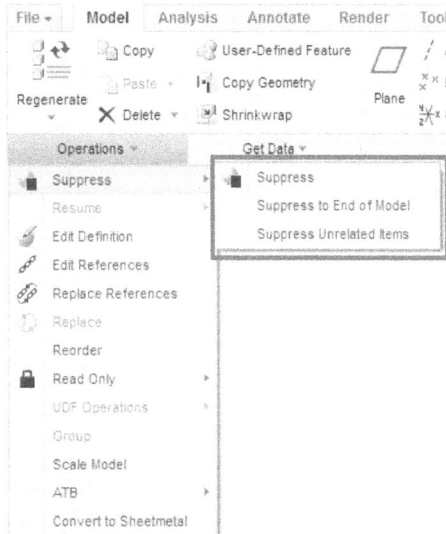

Figure 13–4

When suppressing a feature with children, all children are subsequently selected and the Suppress dialog box opens, as shown in Figure 13–5.

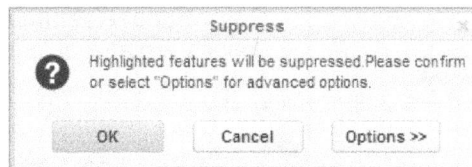

Figure 13–5

You can click **OK** to confirm suppression of the feature and all of its children or you can click **Cancel** to cancel the operation. For advanced options for controlling children, click **Options**. The Children Handling dialog box opens as shown in Figure 13–6.

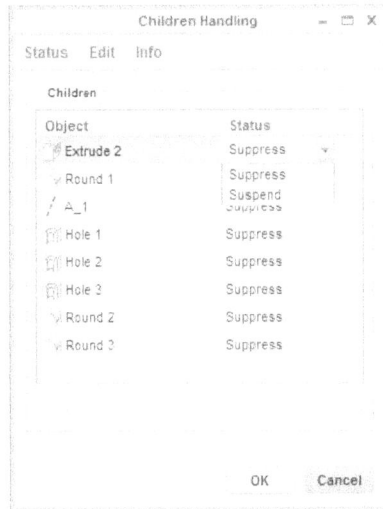

Figure 13–6

*In the Assembly mode, **Freeze** can also be assigned when suppressing a parent component or feature. Freezing enables you to lock the item in its current location.*

You can set the status of any of the children to **Suppress** (suppresses the child with the parent) or to **Suspend** (does not suppress the child). By default, the status is set to **Suppress**. However, the feature cannot be regenerated with its parent missing. If you attempt to regenerate the model, it fails and an Information window opens indicating that the parents of the feature are missing. Suspending the feature enables you to edit it so that you can remove the parent/child relationship between the suppressed parent and suspended child.

Suppressed features can be restored to the display by selecting **Operations>Resume>Resume** in the *Model* tab. The following options are available to resume previously suppressed features:

- Resume

- Resume Last Set

- Resume All

*The **Resume** option is only available if a suppressed feature is selected in the model tree before you select **Operations>Resume> Resume**.*

If the suppressed feature displays in the model tree you can resume it by selecting it and selecting **Resume**. A selected item can also be resumed by selecting **Operations>Resume> Resume** in the *Model* tab. By default, all suppressed features are removed from the model tree display when they are suppressed.

To display the suppressed features, click 📝 ˅ (Settings) and select **Tree Filters>Suppressed Objects** in the *Display* area in the Model Tree Items dialog box. Suppressed features display in the model tree with a black dot, as shown in Figure 13–7.

*Resuming individual features using the **Resume** option can cause failures if the resumed feature references a feature that is still suppressed. Consider this when resuming individual features.*

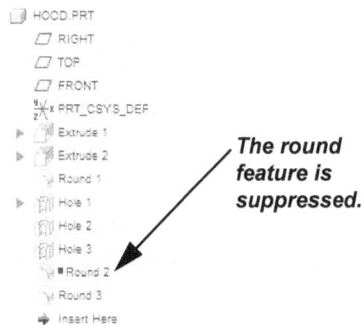

The round feature is suppressed.

Figure 13–7

The **Resume Last Set** option restores the last set of suppressed features, while the **Resume All** option restores all of the features that are currently suppressed in the model. If suppressed features display in the model tree, they can be resumed by selecting them, right-clicking and selecting **Resume**.

13.3 Adding Layers

Layers enable you to organize model items (e.g., solid features, datum features, and components) in a model so that you can perform operations, such as displaying or hiding them collectively. A layer can contain any number of features and components, and any one item can exist on more than one layer. For example, several datum features could be placed together on a layer, and then be hidden. All other datum features would still be visible.

- Similar to hiding features, only the datum feature associated with a solid feature is removed from the display and the solid geometry remains.

*The layer tree can be disconnected from the Navigator window using the Configuration option floating_layer_tree. By default, it is set to **no** and the layer tree displays inside the Navigator window. When you change the Configuration option to **yes**, the layer tree is disconnected from the Navigator window and displayed in a separate window.*

- All Layer information can be found in the layer tree. To access the layer tree, click ⊜ (Layers) in the *View* tab or click ⊟ ▾ (Show) in the model tree and select **Layer Tree**. The layer tree replaces the model tree, as shown in Figure 13–8.

Figure 13–8

- By default, all models created using the default template contain default layers. These are set up to include the datum features (planes, axes, curves, points, and coordinate systems) and surfaces that are added to the model.

General Steps

Use the following general steps to create a layer:

1. Create the layer.
2. Add features or components to the layer.
3. Set and save the display status of the layer, as required.
4. Modify the layer, as required.

Step 1 - Create the layer.

To display the layer tree you can also click

(Layers) in the View tab.

To create a new layer, click ▭ ▾ (Layer) and select **New Layer** in the drop-down list. The Layer Properties dialog box opens, as shown in Figure 13–9.

Figure 13–9

The default name of a new layer is LAY#, where # represents the number of layers that are created in the model. For example, the first layer that is created in the model is by default named **LAY0001**. It is recommended that you replace this name with one that describes the contents of the layer. Layer names can be numeric or alphanumeric, with a maximum of 31 characters. Names cannot consist of special characters (i.e., !, %, or &) or spaces. If a space is required, consider using an underscore (_).

Step 2 - Add features or components to the layer.

You can use the selection filter at the bottom of the main window to help select the correct item on the model.

Select features or components in the model tree or directly on the model to populate the layer. The Layer Properties dialog box opens as shown in Figure 13–10, with all of the items listed in the *Contents* tab. Click **Include** to add items to the layer. Once added, the status updates to display $+$. Click **Exclude** to exclude an item from the layer without actually removing it. Once removed, the status updates to $-$.

*Clicking **Pause** enables you to pause the selection of items without closing the Layer Properties dialog box. This button is useful if you want to review features before adding them to the layer.*

Figure 13–10

To remove an item from the layer, select it in the *Contents* tab in the dialog box and click **Remove**. To complete adding items to the layer, click **OK**.

Step 3 - Set and save the display status of the layer, as required.

The display status of a layer can include the following settings:

- Hide

- Unhide

- Isolate

Hide

The Hide status removes items in the layer from the display. To set the Hide status, select a layer in the layer tree, right-click, and select **Hide**. Another method is to select the layer, click

≣ ▾ (Layer) in the layer tree and select **Hide**.

When hiding layers in a part, only the datum items in the layer are hidden. If you must remove a solid feature from the display, consider using the **Suppress** option. When hiding layers in an assembly, the solid components placed on a layer are hidden.

Unhide

The Unhide status sets all items on the layer to be visible. This is the default display status for all new layers.

Isolate

The Isolate status enables you to show the items on the isolated layers, while all other layers are hidden. To set the display status of a layer to **Isolate**, click ≣ ▾ (Layer) and select **Isolate** in the drop-down list.

To display the current display status of a layer, right-click and select **Layer Info**. The Information window for the selected layer opens, as shown in Figure 13–11.

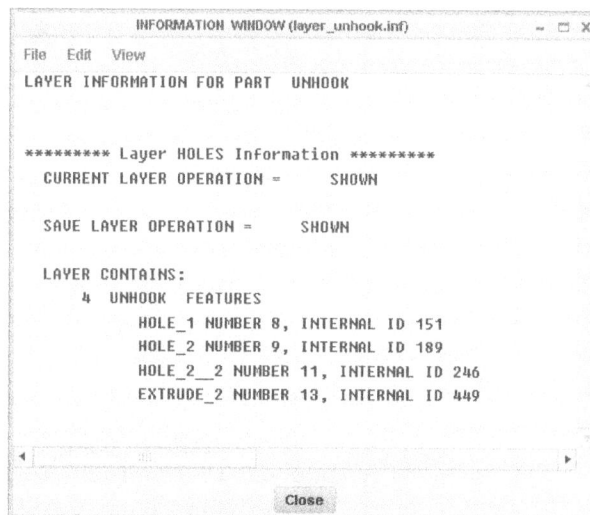

```
INFORMATION WINDOW (layer_unhook.inf)          – □ X
 File   Edit   View
 LAYER INFORMATION FOR PART   UNHOOK


 ********* Layer HOLES Information *********
   CURRENT LAYER OPERATION =       SHOWN

   SAVE LAYER OPERATION =       SHOWN

   LAYER CONTAINS:
       4   UNHOOK   FEATURES
             HOLE_1 NUMBER 8, INTERNAL ID 151
             HOLE_2 NUMBER 9, INTERNAL ID 189
             HOLE_2__2 NUMBER 11, INTERNAL ID 246
             EXTRUDE_2 NUMBER 13, INTERNAL ID 449


                        Close
```

Figure 13–11

The following two lines in the Information window identify the layer's display status:

*   Current Layer Operation

*   Save Layer Operation

The Current Layer Operation line identifies the display status of the layer in the current session of Creo Parametric. The Save Layer Operation line identifies the saved status of the layer. The model always opens using the saved display status for each layer. To save the display status for all layers in the model, right-click and select **Save Status**. To reset the layer display status to that which was previously saved, right-click and select **Reset Status**. You can also click 🔧 (Save Status) and

🔄 (Reset Status) in the Visibility group in the *View* tab.

Step 4 - Modify the layer, as required.

The following actions can be performed on a layer using the layer tree:

- Add items to a layer

- Remove items from a layer

- Delete a layer

- Copy and paste items between layers

To display the layer tree, click ☰ (Layers) in the Visibility group in the View tab.

To perform actions on a layer, the layer tree must be displayed. You can add and remove items by right-clicking in the layer tree. You can also use the original Layer Properties dialog box by right-clicking and selecting **Layer Properties**.

To select multiple items in the layer tree, press and hold <Ctrl> while selecting the items. To select all items between two selected items, press and hold <Shift> while selecting the first and last items in the selection.

To delete all items from the layer without using the Layer Properties dialog box, select the layer, right-click, and select the **Select Items** option to select all of the layer items. Right-click again and select **Remove Item**. All items on the layer are removed. However, the layer remains in the model. To delete an entire layer, select the layer, right-click, and select **Delete Layer**.

Items from one layer can be copied and pasted to another layer using the options in the ☰ ▾ (Layer) flyout or in the contextual menu. To copy an item, select it in the layer tree and select the **Copy Item** option. To paste an item, select the new layer and select the **Paste Item** option. The **Cut Item** option is also available.

Activate/ Deactivate Layers

You can activate a layer by selecting it, right-clicking and selecting **Activate**. When you activate a layer, any newly created 3D elements are added to it. This can be a tremendous time saver over creating features and manually adding them to layers.

Remember to deactivate layers when you no longer want items automatically added to them. An active layer remains active for the duration of your session, unless you select it, right-click and select **Deactivate**.

Default Layers

Default layers, each containing a different type of feature, are created when you use the default template. A default layer automatically associates features of the same type to itself. Using default layers prevents you from having to manually add items to the layer once the feature has been created.

The models and Layer Trees shown in Figure 13–12 display items that were added to layers in the part, and the display status that was set for the layers.

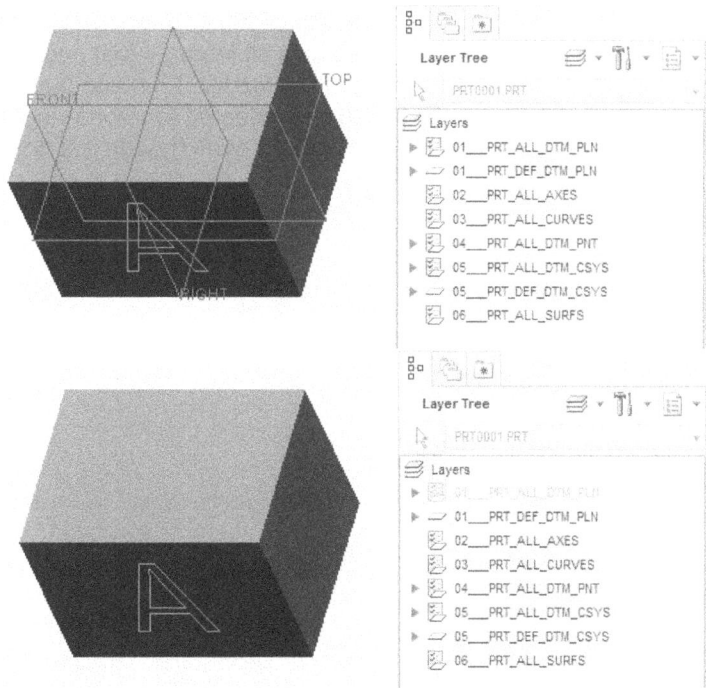

Figure 13–12

Layers as a Selection Tool

*Layers as a selection tool can also be used for operations, such as **Delete**, **Suppress**, or **Resume**.*

Layers can be used as a selection tool for feature operations. To select features, open the layer tree, select the layer(s), right-click, and select the **Select Items** option. Then apply the feature operation by selecting the option in the Ribbon or right-clicking and selecting the option.

The following feature operations, accessible through selecting **Operations>Feature Operations**, enable you to use the **Layer** option directly:

- Copy

- Reorder

For each operation (**Copy** or **Reorder**), the **Layer** option displays in the **SELECT FEAT** menu. This option opens the **LAYER SEL** menu, from which any current layer name can be selected. All features on the selected layer can then be selected for the feature operation. Note that they must display in consecutive order in the feature list when you are selecting multiple features to reorder at the same time. If you use a layer to select multiple features for this operation, the software also selects all features that occur between members of the layer on the feature list. For example, if features 4, 5, and 7 are on a layer that is selected for reordering, Creo Parametric also selects feature 6 even though it is not on that layer.

13.4 Reordering Features

Models are regenerated in the order in which the features display in the model tree. In certain situations, the resulting geometry can vary greatly depending on the order of feature creation. The **Reorder** option can be used to rearrange the creation sequence of the features to achieve the required geometry.

To reorder features on your model, select the feature and drag and drop it directly in the model tree. Note that features cannot be reordered before their parent features. The examples in Figure 13–13 and Figure 13–14 show the use of the reorder tool.

A Shell feature leaves a wall thickness on all surfaces. Therefore, a hole becomes a pipe when a shell is applied to it.

Shell surfaces to remove

A wall thickness is applied to the remaining surfaces, including surfaces on the hole.

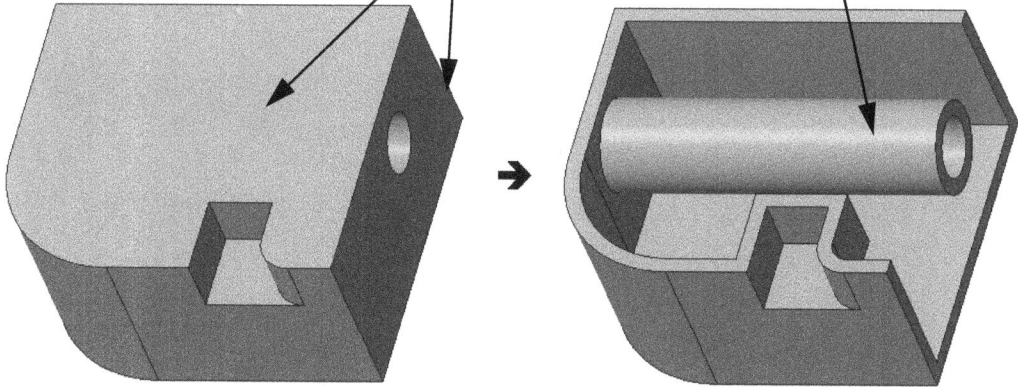

Figure 13–13

A Round placed after a shell might not have the required results.

The shell is not applied to features that display after it in the feature list.

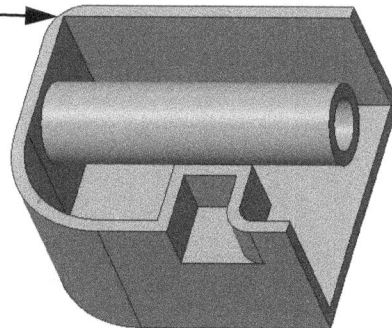

Figure 13–14

The reorder function can be used to rearrange the order in which features are regenerated. Figure 13–15 shows a part created with the feature sequence displayed in the model tree. Note that **Hole 1** displays before **Shell 1** in the model tree, because **Hole 1** is regenerated before **Shell 1**. The surfaces of the hole exist when the shell is created, so a thickness is applied to the hole surface.

The opposite is true for **Round 3**. It regenerates after the shell, so the shell does not apply a thickness to it.

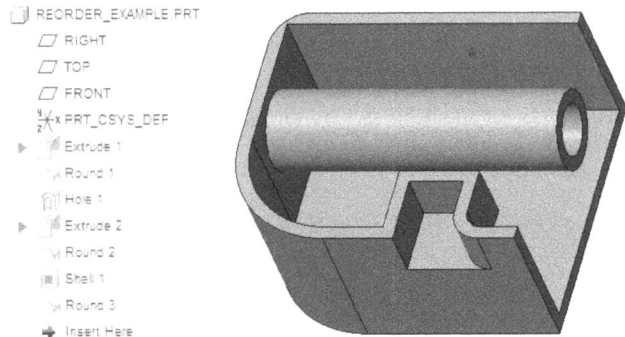

Figure 13–15

Reordering **Hole 1** after the shell, and **Round 3** before the shell, results in the part shown in Figure 13–16.

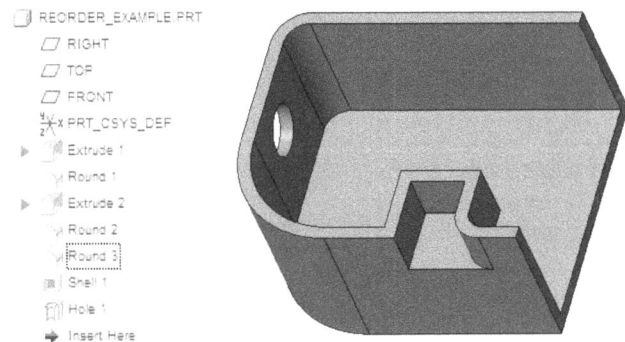

Figure 13–16

Complicated models might result in difficult parent/child relationships. If a feature depends on another feature for regeneration, a parent/child relationship exists. For example, if you create an extrusion and use an edge of the extrusion to create a round, the extrusion is a parent of the round. You cannot reorder the round to come before the extrusion.

In addition, although you may want to reorder a single feature, it is sometimes required to also reorder children of that feature. In Figure 13–17, **Round 2** is created on the edge of **Extrude 2**. To reorder **Extrude 2** and make it come later in the regeneration sequence, you would have to move the round as well.

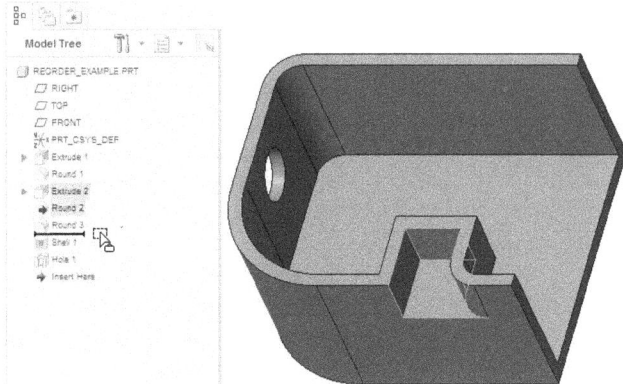

Figure 13–17

When you drag and drop to reorder, it can sometime not be obvious that additional features are also being moved. You can click the **Operations** option in the *Model* tab and select **Reorder** to open the Reorder dialog box, shown in Figure 13–18.

Select the feature you want to reorder, select the new location as **After** or **Before**, and select the *Target Feature*. Any dependent features that have to be moved will be listed in the *Dependent Features* area, as shown in Figure 13–19.

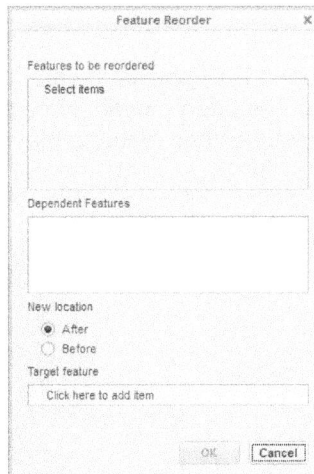

Figure 13–18

Figure 13–19

13.5 Inserting Features

When features are added to a model, they are added by default at the end of the feature list. Insert Mode is used to insert new features between existing features.

Insert Mode can be used in situations in which a design change occurs and you would like to create a feature earlier in the design process. It *rolls back* the model to the location in which you want to place the feature. This ensures that you only use references that exist at that point in the model. On occasion, features might abort during creation due to existing features on the part. In these cases, Insert Mode might enable the feature to be created.

To activate Insert Mode, click and drag **Insert Here** at the bottom of the model tree to the location at which you want to insert a feature(s). Figure 13–20 shows a model and its model tree before inserting a feature.

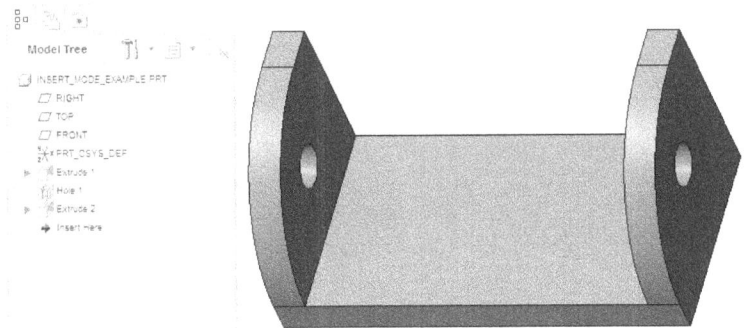

Figure 13–20

Figure 13–21 shows the model and its model tree once **Insert Here** has been moved. Note that the system temporarily suppresses any features that regenerate after the insertion point.

*Once **Insert Here** has been moved, the part is rolled back to the point at which you are inserting a feature.*

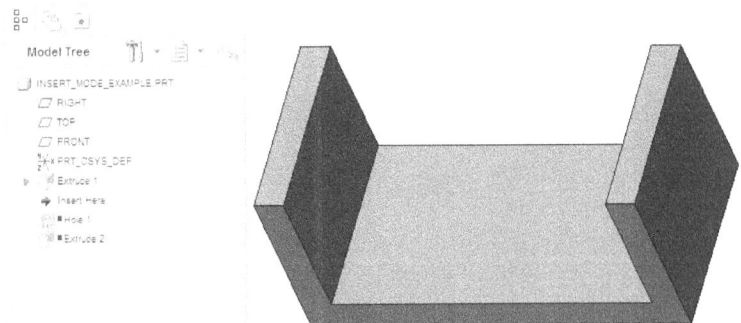

Figure 13–21

Once **Insert Here** has been moved to the required location in the model tree, you can start using the standard feature creation tools to insert one or more features. An extruded protrusion has been added to the model, as shown in Figure 13–22.

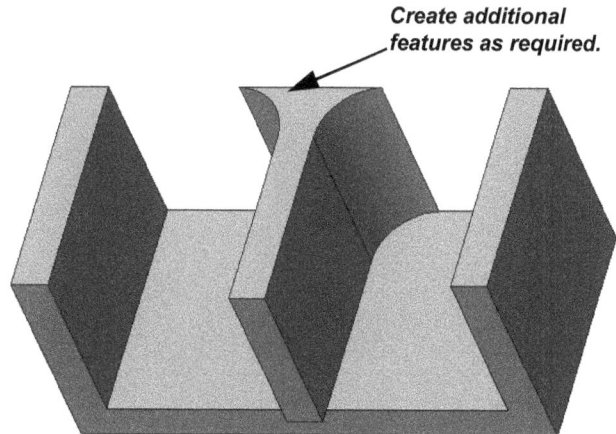

Create additional features as required.

Figure 13–22

When you have finished inserting features, select and drag **Insert Here** back to the bottom of the feature list, or right-click it and select **Exit Insert Mode**. Click **Yes** when prompted to resume suppressed features. All of the features are then regenerated, as shown in Figure 13–23.

Note that the same result could be accomplished by creating the extrude, then reordering it, but using Insert Mode can help reduce inadvertent parent/child relationships by temporarily removing features you might accidentally reference.

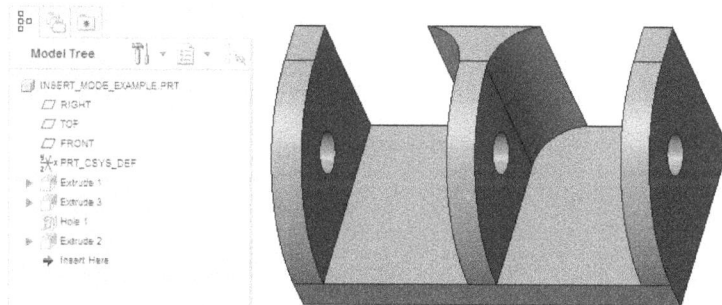

Figure 13–23

Practice 13a | Feature Order

Practice Objective

- Change the order of features in the model tree to obtain required geometry.

In this practice, you will explore the impact of the feature order on part geometry. You will create the switch plate part shown in Figure 13–24 with limited instructions. Once complete, you will reorder two holes, an extrude, and a shell feature.

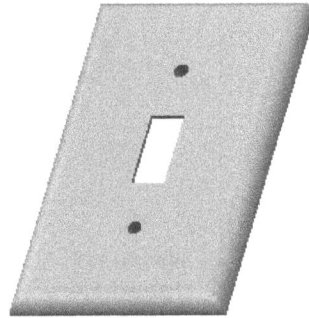

Figure 13–24

Task 1 - Create a new part.

1. Set the working directory to the *Chapter13\practice 13a* folder.

2. Create a new part and set the *Name* to **switch_plate**.

3. Set the model display as follows:

   - ✳ *(Datum Display Filters)*: All Off

   - ⌖ *(Spin Center)*: Off

   - ◢ *(Display Style)*: ⬜ (Shading With Edges)

4. Create the sketch shown in Figure 13–25 using datum **TOP** as the sketch plane.

5. Extrude the sketch to a *Depth* of **0.25**, as shown in Figure 13–26.

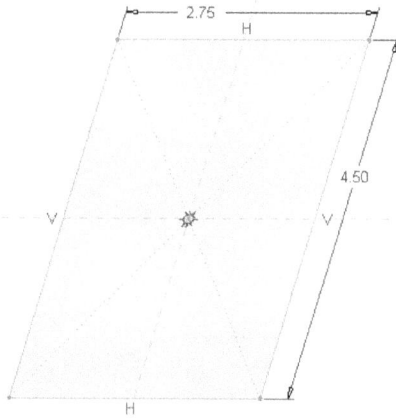

Figure 13–25

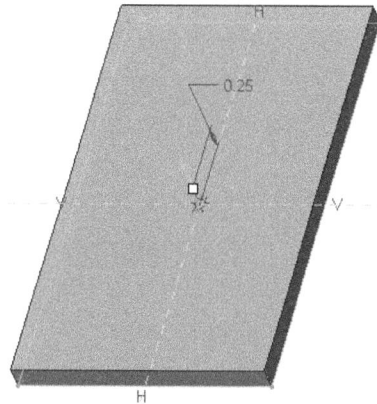

Figure 13–26

Task 2 - Create a hole.

---

1. In the In-graphics toolbar, click ⁺⁄⁎ (Datum Display Filters) and enable ⬙ (Plane Display).

2. Create a hole in the location shown in Figure 13–27 and set the following:

   • *Diameter:* **0.188**
   • *Offset* from datum **FRONT: 1.150**
   • Align to datum **RIGHT**
   • *Depth:* ⊒ ⊑ (Through All)

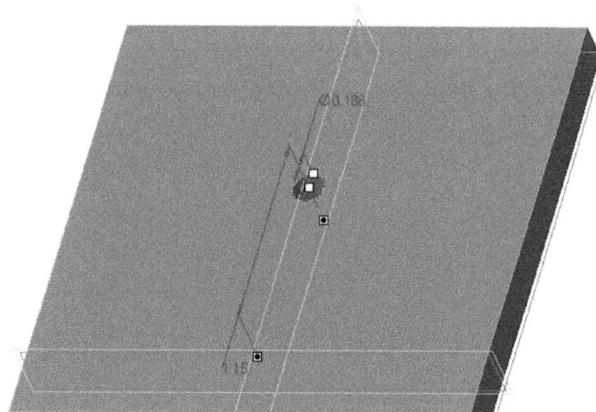

Figure 13–27

Task 3 - Create a second hole.

1. Create a second hole as shown in Figure 13–28, using the same references and dimensional values as the previous hole.

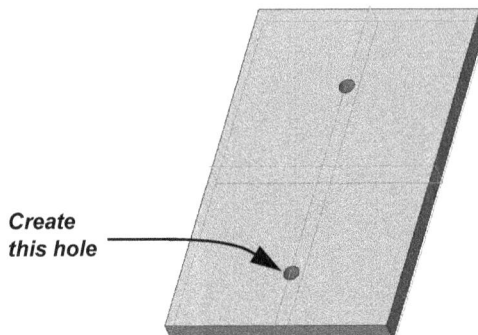

Create
this hole

Figure 13–28

2. Click ⁺⁄⁎ (Datum Display Filters) and disable ⊿ (Plane Display).

Task 4 - Create a round.

1. Create a round with a *Radius* of **0.25**, on the four edges shown in Figure 13–29.

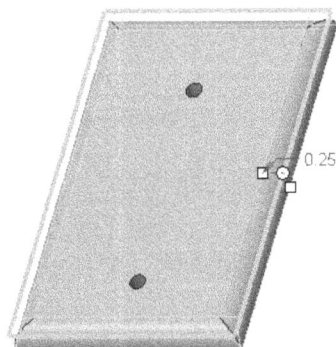

0.25

Figure 13–29

Task 5 - Shell the part.

1. Shell the part with a *Thickness* of **0.063** and select the bottom surface to remove, as shown in Figure 13–30. Once the shell is complete, the part displays as shown in Figure 13–31.

Figure 13–30

Figure 13–31

Task 6 - Create an extruded cut.

1. Create an extrude using the surface shown in Figure 13–32 as the sketch plane.

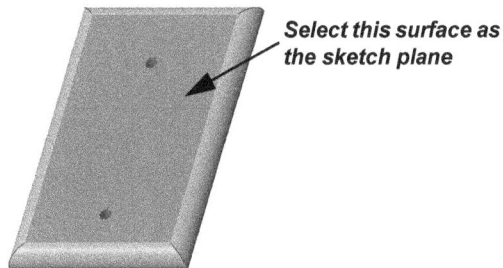

Figure 13–32

2. Sketch and dimension the section shown in Figure 13–33.

3. Extrude the sketch to cut through the part. The part should display as shown in Figure 13–34.

Figure 13–33

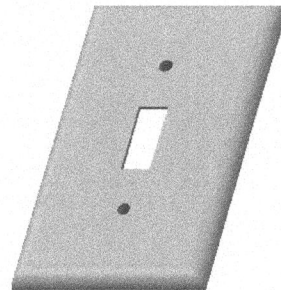

Figure 13–34

Task 7 - Reorder features.

1. Ensure that the part is oriented as shown in Figure 13–35.

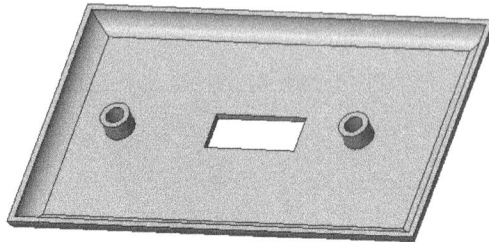

Figure 13–35

2. Display the model tree and note the order in which the features are listed. Note that the **Shell 1** feature comes before the **Extrude 2** feature, as shown in Figure 13–36.

Figure 13–36

3. Select **Shell 1** from the model tree and drag it below **Extrude 2**, as shown in Figure 13–37.

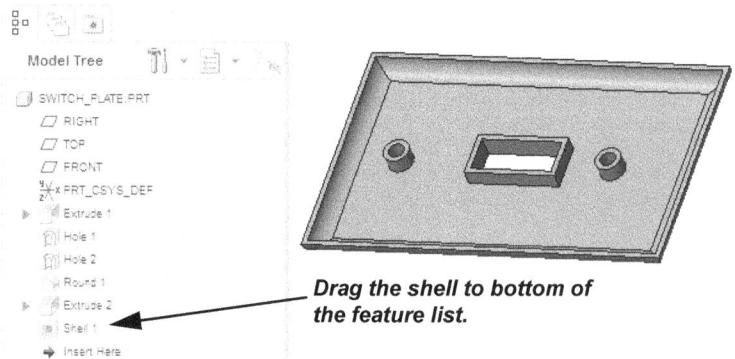

Drag the shell to bottom of the feature list.

Figure 13–37

4. Hold <Ctrl>, select the two holes, and drag them to after the shell to obtain the geometry shown in Figure 13–38.

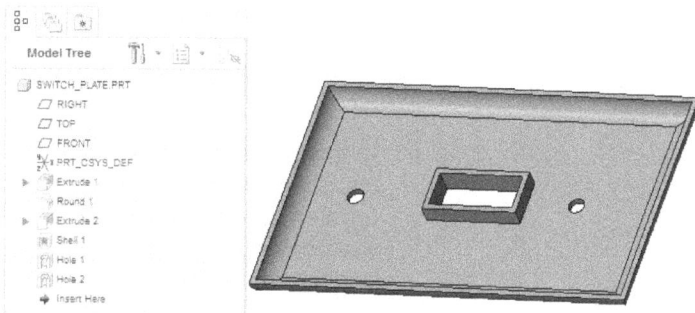

Figure 13–38

5. Make the appropriate changes to obtain the geometry shown in Figure 13–39.

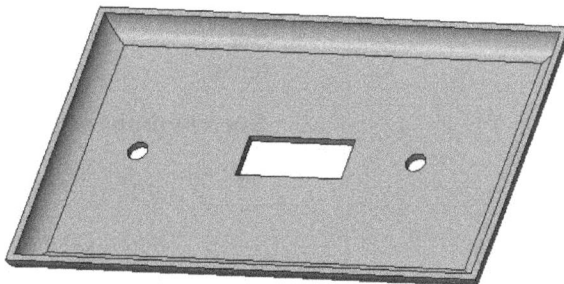

Figure 13–39

6. Save the part and erase it from memory.

Practice 13b | Insert Mode

Practice Objective

- Insert a new feature at a point other than the end of the feature list using the **Insert Here** arrow.

In this practice, you will use Insert Mode to insert an auto round into the feature list. When an auto round is created, a round is created on all edges of a part, except for the ones that are excluded by user input. The design intent of this part includes adding rounds to all edges (except excluded edges) that are on the outside of the part. Rounds are not required on any of the edges of the internal geometry. Insert Mode will be used to achieve this design intent.

Task 1 - Open a part file.

1. Set the working directory to the *Chapter 13\practice 13b* folder.

2. Open **hydrant.prt**.

3. Set the model display as follows:

   - ⁎ *(Datum Display Filters)*: All Off

   - *(Spin Center)*: Off

   - *(Display Style)*: ⬚ (Shading With Edges)

Task 2 - Investigate the part.

1. Orient the part to display the internal geometry. Display the model tree as well, as shown in Figure 13–40.

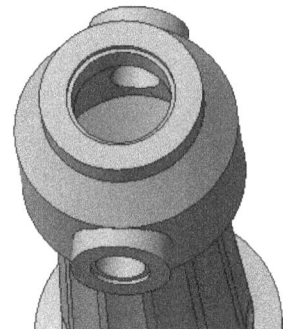

Figure 13–40

Task 3 - Activate Insert Mode.

1. In the model tree, click **Insert Here** and drag and drop it after **Pattern 1 of Cut**, as shown in Figure 13–41.

HYDRANT.PRT
  RIGHT
  BOTTOM
  FRONT
  x CS0
▶ Revolve 1
▶ Extrude 1
▶ Pattern 1 of Cut
  ➔ Insert Here
   ■ CUT1
   ■ THREAD1
   ■ CUT2
   ■ THREAD2A
   ■ THREAD2B

Figure 13–41

Task 4 - Create an auto round feature.

1. In the Engineering group, click the (Round) fly-out and select (Auto Round).

2. In the *Auto Round* tab, for the convex edges, set the *Radius* to **20.0**. For the concave edges, select **Same**.

3. Exclude the four edges shown in Figure 13–42.

4. Click (Complete Feature) to complete the feature. The completed model displays as shown in Figure 13–43.

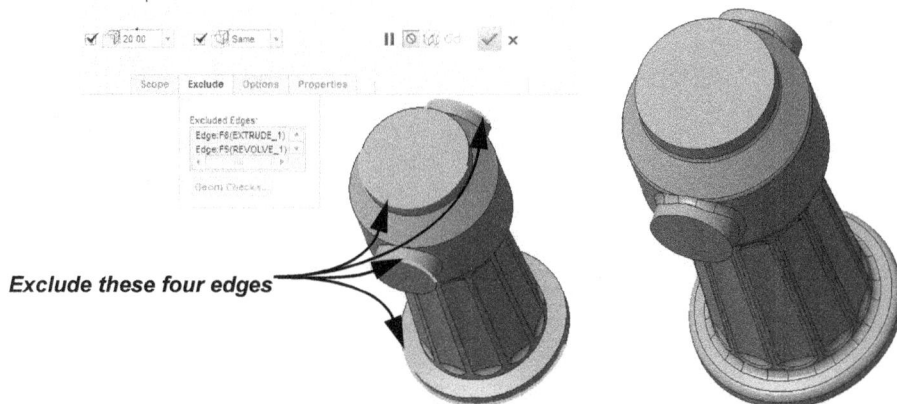

Exclude these four edges

| Figure 13–42 | Figure 13–43 |

Note that it may take some time to regenerate.

Task 5 - Deactivate Insert Mode.

1. In the model tree, click **Insert Here** and drag and drop it at the bottom of the feature list, as shown in Figure 13–44.

HYDRANT.PRT
   RIGHT
   BOTTOM
   FRONT
   x CSO
   Revolve 1
   Extrude 1
   Pattern 1 of Cut
   Auto Round 2
   CUT1
   THREAD1
   CUT2
   THREAD2A
   THREAD2B
   Insert Here

Figure 13–44

The completed model displays as shown in Figure 13–45. Note that the internal geometry has not been affected by the auto round.

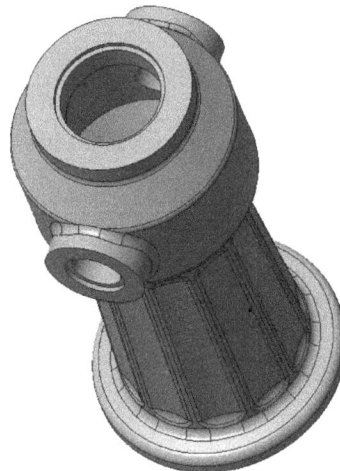

Figure 13–45

2. Save the model and erase it from memory.

Practice 13c | Feature Management

Practice Objectives

- Temporarily hide a datum plane and a hole from being included as part of the model geometry.
- Temporarily remove features and their children from being included as part of the model geometry and regeneration sequence.

In this practice, you will open an existing model and use the **Hide**, **Suppress**, and **Layers** tools to control the display of features in the model. You will learn how to switch between the model tree and layer tree by hiding and unhiding geometry using layers. You will also, specify the display options to a newly created layer. The complete model is shown in Figure 13–46.

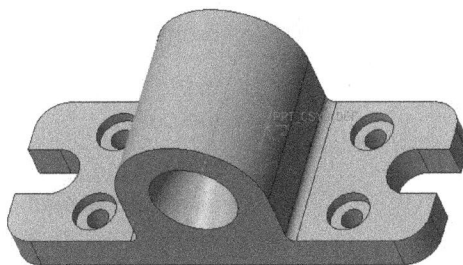

Figure 13–46

Task 1 - Open a part file.

1. Set the working directory to the *Chapter 13\practice 13c* folder.

2. Open **chamber.prt**.

3. Set the model display as follows:

   - *(Datum Display Filters)*: All On
   - *(Spin Center)*: Off
   - *(Display Style)*: (Shading With Edges)

Task 2 - Hide DTM1 from the display.

You can also select the View tab and click

(Hide) in the Visibility group.

1. Select **DTM1** from the model tree or directly on the model.

2. Right-click and select **Hide**. The datum plane is removed from the display.

3. Select **HOLE** in the model tree. Right-click and select **Hide**. The datum axis in that hole is removed from the display. However, the solid feature remains displayed.

You can also select the View tab to access the Unhide and Unhide All icons.

4. Select **HOLE** from the model tree. Right-click and select **Unhide**. Its axis displays on the model again.

   The **Hide** option enables you to remove datum features from the display without using the datum feature display icons that affect all like features. The **Hide** option cannot be used to control the display of solid geometry.

Task 3 - Suppress all features except for the base feature and rounds.

1. Select **NOTCH**, as shown in Figure 13–47.

You can also select Operations>Suppress in the Model tab.

2. Right-click and select **Suppress**.

3. In the Suppress dialog box, click **OK** to confirm suppressing the cut.

You can click Options>> and suspend children. Suspending enables you to retain the feature. However, it cannot be regenerated because its parent is missing. You can edit the feature to remove parent/child relationships.

4. Select **HOLE**, as shown in Figure 13–47. Right-click and select **Suppress**. A Warning dialog box opens prompting you to confirm suppression of all highlighted features. The highlighted features are all children of **HOLE**. To suppress this feature you must deal with the children.

5. Click **OK** to suppress the hole and its children.

6. Suppress **Revolve 1** and all of its children, as shown in Figure 13–47. The model, with its non-hidden datum features, displays as shown in Figure 13–48.

Suppress NOTCH and its children.

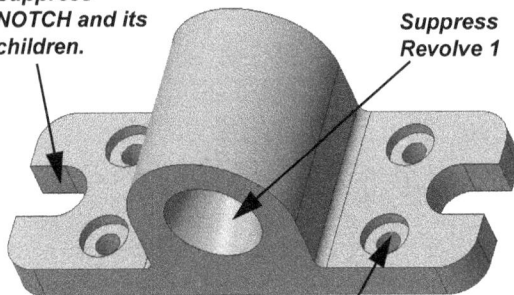

Suppress Revolve 1

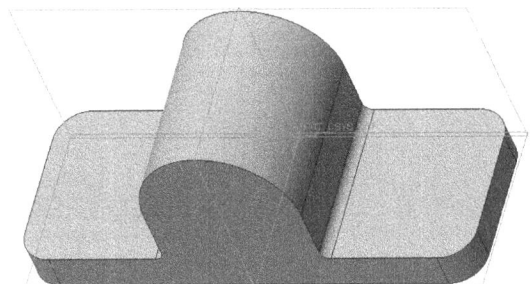

Suppress HOLE and all mirrored.

Figure 13–47

Figure 13–48

Task 4 - Review the feature list of the part.

1. Select the *Tools* tab in the Investigate group and click
   ⬚ (Feature List). The Feature List displays in the Creo
   Parametric Browser window listing all of the features in the
   model, including those that have been suppressed, as shown
   in Figure 13–49.

*Suppressed features
are easily identified in
the Status column in the
Browser, which lists the
features as Suppressed
rather then
Regenerated.
Suppressed features do
not have a feature
number because they
have been removed
from the regeneration
list.*

**Click ✕ to close the Browser
window**

No.	ID	Name	Type	Actions		Sup Order
1	1	RIGHT	DATUM PLANE	⟁⁺	⬚	---
2	3	TOP	DATUM PLANE	⟁⁺	⬚	---
3	5	FRONT	DATUM PLANE	⟁⁺	⬚	---
4	7	PRT_CSYS_DEF	COORDINATE SYSTEM	⟁⁺	⬚	---
5	40	---	PROTRUSION	⟁⁺	⬚	---
6	83	DTM1	DATUM PLANE	⟁⁺	⬚	---
---	85	NOTCH	CUT		⬚	1
---	130	NOTCH_MIRROR	MIRROR		⬚	1
---	133	---	CUT		⬚	1
---	174	HOLE	HOLE		⬚	2
---	241	HOLE_MIRROR_1	MIRROR		⬚	2
---	242	---	HOLE		⬚	2
---	309	HOLE_MIRROR_2	MIRROR		⬚	2
---	310	---	HOLE		⬚	2
---	367	---	HOLE		⬚	2

Figure 13–49

2. Close the Browser window.

Task 5 - Attempt to suppress datum plane FRONT.

1. Select datum plane **FRONT**. Right-click and select
   Suppress. The base feature and all subsequent features
   highlight on the model and in the model tree because they
   are children of datum plane **FRONT**. If you suppress this
   datum you also have to suppress or suspend all of the
   additional features. Suspending these features would not be
   recommended because it would require extensive work to
   reroute the parent/child references.

2. In the Suppress dialog box, click **Cancel**.

   If datum plane **FRONT** must be removed from the display,
   consider using the **Hide** option or adding the datum plane to
   a layer and hiding the layer.

Task 6 - Show all of the suppressed features in the model tree.

By default, all suppressed features are removed from the model tree display.

1. Expand the 🎛 ▾ (Settings) flyout and select **Tree Filters**. The Model Tree Items dialog box opens.

2. Select **Suppressed objects** and click **OK**. The model tree updates and displays all of the suppressed features. The suppressed features are identified by ■ next to their names.

Task 7 - Resume all the features.

1. In the model tree, select **HOLE**. Right-click and select **Resume** to resume the suppressed feature.

2. Resume the Hole's copied groups.

3. Select the *Model* tab. Select **Operations>Resume>Resume Last Set**. This resumes the last feature or group of features that were suppressed. In this case it resumes **SLOT**.

You must select the suppressed features in the model tree to access the Operations> Resume>Resume option.

4. Select **Operations>Resume>Resume All** to resume the remaining suppressed features.

Task 8 - Hide a layer.

You can also expand the ▤ ▾ flyout and select Layer Tree to display the layer tree.

1. In the model tree, click ▤ ▾ (Show) and select **Layer Tree**.

2. In the layer tree, select **01__PRT_DEF_DTM_PLN**.

3. By default, the display status for the layer is set to unhide. Right-click and select **Hide**. All of the default datum planes (**RIGHT**, **TOP**, and **FRONT**) are hidden. Click anywhere in the main window to repaint the screen.

4. Click ▤ ▾ (Show) and select **Model Tree** to toggle off the display of the layer tree and return to the model tree.

5. Unhide **DTM1**. This datum plane is not a default datum plane and was therefore not hidden from the display when you hid the default datum plane layer. The model displays as shown in Figure 13–50.

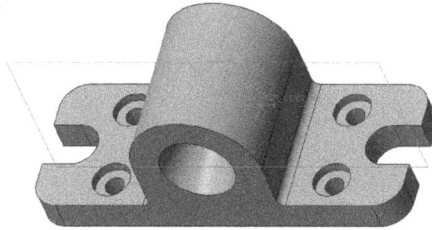

Figure 13–50

Task 9 - Unhide a layer.
---

1. Click ⊞ ▾ (Show)>**Layer Tree** to display the layer tree.

2. Select the **01__PRT_DEF_DTM_PLN** layer.

3. Right-click and select **Unhide**.

4. Click on the screen to update the display. All of the datum planes are now displayed on the model.

Task 10 - Create a new layer and hide it.

You can also right-click and select New Layer.

1. Expand ⊟ ▾ (Layer) and select **New Layer**. The Layer Properties dialog box opens.

2. Set the *Name* to **mounting_holes**. DO NOT press <Enter>.

3. Set the selection filter to **Feature** to select the hole features. The selection filter is located at the bottom right of the window as shown in Figure 13–51.

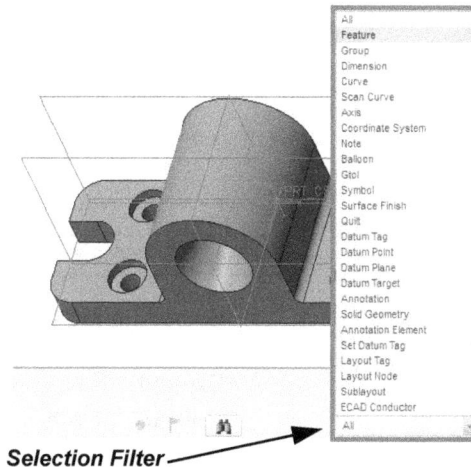

Selection Filter

Figure 13–51

---

4. Select the four countersunk holes. The contents of the layer update in the Layer Properties dialog box, as shown in Figure 13–52.

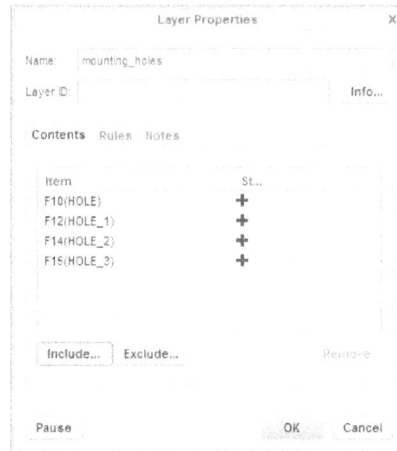

Figure 13–52

Note that the axes are removed from display, but the features are not. Hiding features does not hide solid geometry.

5. Click **OK** to close the Layer Properties dialog box.

6. In the Layer tree, select the **MOUNTING_HOLES** layer. Right-click and select **Hide**.

7. Click on the screen to update the display. The axes of the four countersunk sketched holes are hidden, as shown in Figure 13–53.

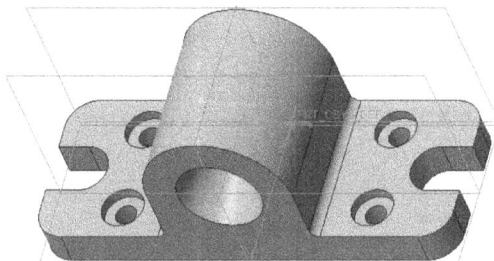

Figure 13–53

Task 11 - Isolate the MOUNTING_HOLES layer.

1. Select the **MOUNTING_HOLES** layer.

*The **Isolate** option is helpful when you are using several layers and you only need a few of them to be visible. The isolated layers are shown and all others are automatically hidden.*

2. Expand ⬚ ˅ (Layer) and select **Isolate** to change the layer status to isolate. The part displays as shown in Figure 13–54. Note that the only datum entities now visible are the axes in the counterbore holes.

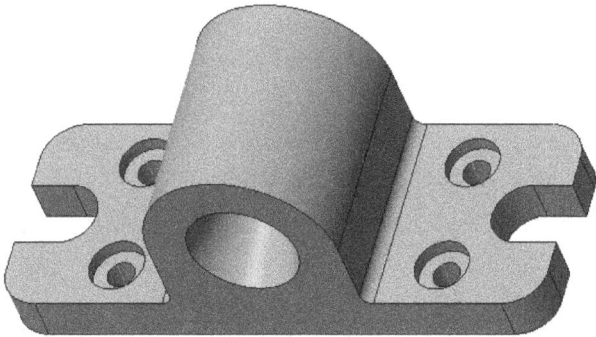

Figure 13–54

Task 12 - Create a layer for defeaturing the model.

Design Considerations

When conducting an finite element analysis, it is common practice to simplify the model by temporarily removing machined features such as rounds and holes. Create a layer for defeaturing the model.

1. Right-click in the layer tree and select **Reset Status**.

2. Click on the screen to update the display. Click ⬙ ▾ (Layer)> **New Layer**.

3. Set the layer *Name* to **Defeature** but do not press <Enter>.

4. Set the *Selection Feature* to **Features**.

5. Select the four counterbore holes and the two round features, as shown in Figure 13–55.

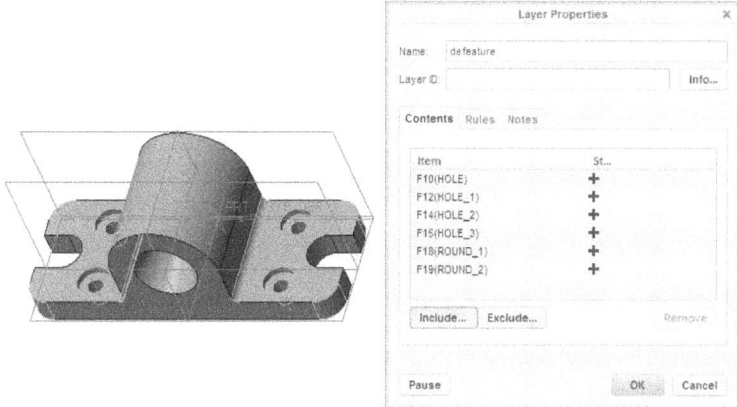

Figure 13–55

You cannot directly suppress a layer, but it can be used to quickly select features which can then be suppressed.

6. Click **OK**.

7. Right-click the **DEFEATURE** layer, and select **Select Items**.

8. Right-click in the main window, select **Suppress** and click **OK** in the Suppress dialog box. The model displays as shown in Figure 13–56.

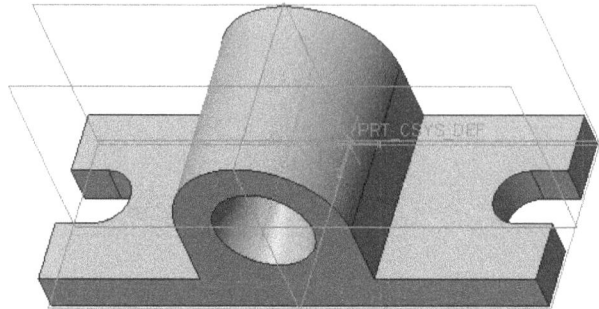

Figure 13–56

9. Use the layer to select the feature again, right-click in the main window, select **Resume**.

Task 13 - Obtain information on the layers.

1. Select a layer, right-click, and select **Layer Info**. An Information window opens displaying the layer operation and layer contents.

2. Close the Information window.

3. Select the **MOUNTING_HOLES** and **01__PRT_ALL_DTM_PLN** layers, right-click and select **Hide**.

4. Save the part and erase it from memory.

Task 14 - Open and investigate the model display status.

1. Open **chamber.prt**. Note that the layer settings that were set before saving the part have been lost.

Layer information is saved with the part, but the layer display status is only saved if the Save Status option is selected.

2. Click ⬚ ˅ (Show)>**Layer Tree**.

3. Select the **MOUNTING_HOLES** and **01__PRT_ALL_DTM_PLN** layers, right-click and select **Hide**.

4. Right-click and select **Save Status** to save the display status of the layer with the part.

5. Save the part and erase it from memory.

6. Open **chamber.prt**. Note that the layer settings that were set before saving the part have been retained in the model, as shown in Figure 13–57.

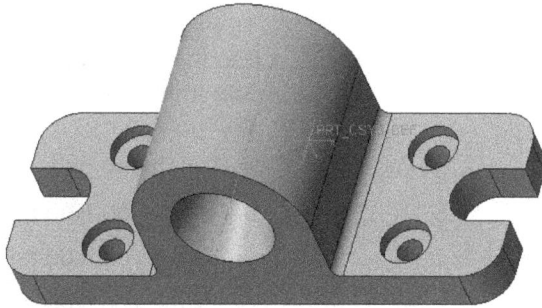

Figure 13–57

7. Close the part and erase it from memory.

Chapter Review Questions

1. Parent/child relationships do not affect the children of hidden parents.

    a. True

    b. False

2. The easiest technique for simplifying a model's display is to use the **Hide** option. Which of the following statements are true regarding hiding a feature in a model? (Select all that apply.)

    a. When you hide a feature, it remains in the model tree.

    b. When you hide a feature, it continues to regenerate.

    c. When you hide a feature, solid geometry remains visible.

    d. When you hide a feature, datum features associated with it are hidden.

3. Which of the following statements are true regarding Figure 13–58? (Select all that apply.)

Figure 13–58

    a. The **Hole 2** geometry is removed from the display.

    b. The axis generated with **Hole 1** is removed from the display.

    c. The axis created with **Hole 2** is removed from the display.

    d. Datum planes **RIGHT**, **TOP**, and **FRONT** are hidden.

4. Which of the following statements are true regarding suppressing a feature in a model?

   a. When you suppress a feature, it displays in the model tree with ■ next to its name.

   b. When you suppress a feature, it continues to regenerate.

   c. When you suppress a feature, solid geometry remains visible.

   d. When you suppress a feature, only datum features associated with it are suppressed.

5. Which feature(s) in Figure 13–59 are suppressed?

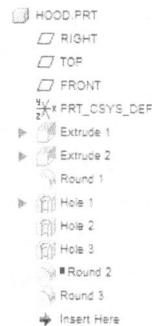

Figure 13–59

   a. Datum planes **RIGHT**, **TOP** and **FRONT**.

   b. **Hole 3**

   c. **A_1**

   d. **Round 2**

6. How do you display suppressed features in the model tree?

   a. Expand ⊤ ▾ and select **Tree Filters>Suppressed objects**.

   b. Expand ⊤ ▾ and select **Tree Columns>Suppressed objects**.

   c. Expand ▤ ▾ and select **Tree Filters>Suppressed objects**.

   d. Expand ▤ ▾ and select **Tree Columns>Suppressed objects**.

7. Which of the following statements are true regarding adding a feature to a layer and hiding it? (Select all that apply.)

   a. When you add a feature to a layer and hide it, it is removed from the model tree.

   b. When you add a feature to a layer and hide it, it continues to regenerate.

   c. When you add a feature to a layer and hide it, solid geometry remains visible.

   d. When you add a feature to a layer and hide it, only datum features associated with it are hidden.

8. Which of the following settings are valid display statuses for a layer?

   a. Hide

   b. Unhide

   c. Suppress

   d. Isolate

9. Which of the following statements are true regarding Hide, Suppress, and Layers? (Select all that apply.)

   a. All hidden settings are saved when the model is saved to disk.

   b. All suppressed settings are saved when the model is saved to disk.

   c. All layers are saved when the model is saved to disk.

   d. All layer display settings are saved when the model is saved to disk.

10. Which of the following statements is true regarding reordering and inserting features in a model?

    a. Reordering enables you to drag and drop features so that you can rearrange the feature creation order.

    b. When reordering, features can be moved anywhere in the model.

    c. Insert Mode enables you to rearrange features to change their order.

    d. Insert Mode is activated by selecting and dragging **Insert Here** in the model tree.

Command Summary

Button	Command	Location
	Hide	• **Ribbon:** *View* tab in the Visibility group
	Save Status	• **Ribbon:** *View* tab in the Visibility group
	Unhide	• **Ribbon:** *View* tab in the Visibility group
	Unhide All	• **Ribbon:** *View* tab in the Visibility group
	Layers	• **Ribbon:** *View* tab in the Visibility group
	Show	• Model Tree
	Settings	• Model Tree
	Layer	• Layer Tree

Duplication Tools

The Creo Parametric software provides many tools for duplicating model geometry and for creating dimensional patterns These tools enable you to model more efficiently without having to recreate identical geometry and to reuse design data through simple Copy/Paste and Paste Special actions. Additionally, mirroring enables you to quickly create symmetric models.

Learning Objectives in this Chapter

- Learn to quickly duplicate features in the same or different models using the Copy and Paste commands.
- Learn to paste features in the same model or between two different models using the Paste Special command.
- Mirror a solid part to duplicate all the geometry.
- Mirror select features in a model to create required geometry.

14.1 Copy and Paste

The **Copy** and **Paste** options enable you to quickly duplicate features in a model or between different models. This technique copies the exact options and elements that have been defined in the original feature. However, the placement references are lost and must be redefined in the new instance using the feature dashboard.

- To avoid lengthy redefinition of references when copying single features, use the **Copy** and **Paste** functionality.

- To copy multiple features at the same time, you can use the **Paste Special** option.

The **Copy** and **Paste** operation is considered an object action technique. Therefore, the object must be selected before you select the action that is to be performed. The action (i.e., **Copy**) remains unavailable unless the feature is selected first.

- You can select the feature from the model or in the model tree. To select multiple features, press and hold <Ctrl> while selecting the items.

Additionally, you can use <Ctrl>+<C> and <Ctrl>+<V>.

- Once a feature has been selected, click 🗋 (Copy) and then click 🗋 (Paste) in the *Model* tab.

- If pasting between models, you must click on the new window and then paste the feature. You are prompted to specify the scale of the feature in the new model. The options include: **Keep dimension values**, **Keep feature sizes**, and **Scale by value**.

- Once copied to the clipboard, the feature remains there. This enables you to paste it many times and to quickly reproduce multiple copies.

- Once pasted, the dashboard for the feature displays. Depending on the type of feature and whether or not references were selected before pasting the feature, you might still be required to select additional references. Any panel that displays in red in the dashboard requires references to place the feature. For example, when copying and pasting an **Extrude** feature, you must select a new sketching plane and place the sketch on that plane before the feature can be completed.

- To complete the feature, select ✓ (Complete Feature) when it displays in the dashboard.

- When a feature is pasted, it does not maintain a parent-child relationship with the source feature.

14.2 Copy and Paste Special

The **Paste Special** option provides additional pasting options when copying features. This option is useful in the following situations:

- To copy features with dimension dependency.

- To move or rotate features.

- To easily identify references and select new references when copying complex or multiple features.

- To copy dimension patterns.

To paste feature(s), expand ⬚ (Paste) in the *Model* tab and click ⬚ (Paste Special). The Paste Special dialog box opens, as shown in Figure 14–1.

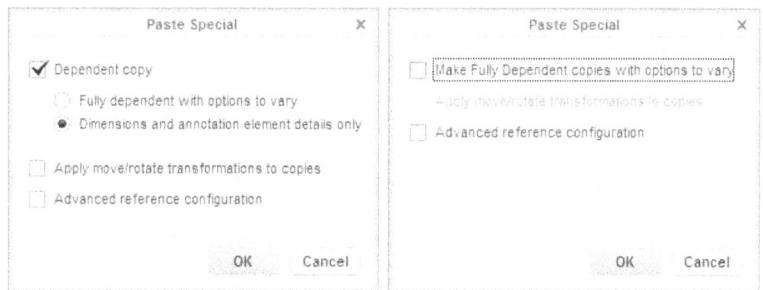

Copy/Paste Special inside the same model

Copy/Paste Special between two models

Figure 14–1

Dependent Copy (in the Same Model)

To maintain dependency between the source and the copied feature when pasting features, ensure that the **Dependent copy** option is selected. (By default, this option is selected.)

- **Dimensions and annotation element details only:** Enables you to create a copy of the feature with dependent dimensions, annotations, and sketches. You can change the dependency of dimensions, annotations, and sketches. (By default, this option is selected.)

- **Fully dependent with options to vary:** Enables you to create a copy of the feature with dependent dimensions, annotations, parameters, sketches, and references. You can change the dependency of dimensions, annotations, parameters, sketches, and references. This option can be set as the default by setting the **config.pro** option **default_dep_copy_option** to **full_dep**.

- **Make copies dependent on dimensions of original:** Enables you to maintain dependency between the source and the copied feature. This option is used when the **Dependent copy** option is not available in some situations (e.g., for patterns).

Dependent Copy (Between Models)

Features copied inside the same model are dependent by default.

To paste a feature in a new model so that it maintains dependency between the source and the copied feature, ensure that the **Make Fully Dependent copies with options to vary** option is selected. By default, this option is cleared.

For example, the features in the boss shown in Figure 14–2 are copied to a new location so that they are independent (**Dependent copy** has been cleared). The copied features are independent of the original. In Figure 14–3, the changes to the parent boss do not affect the copy.

All features in the Boss are copied in the model as independent.

The copy is independent of its parent. Changes made to the parent are not reflected in the copy.

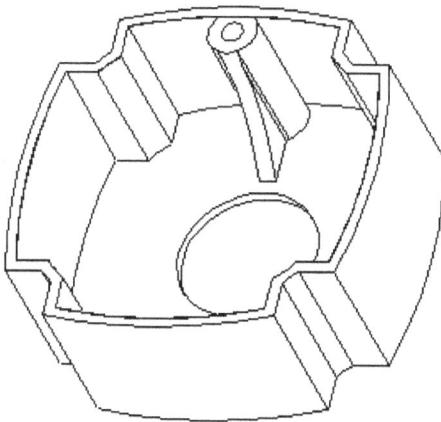

Figure 14–2

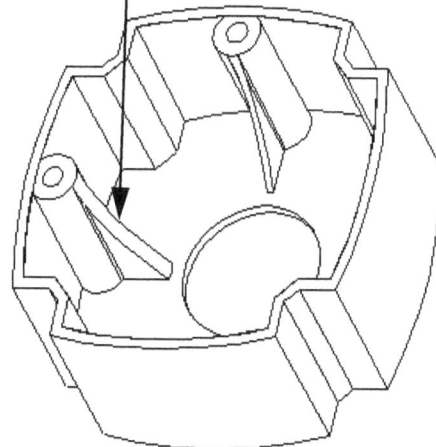

Figure 14–3

Features copied from a different model or a different version are independent by default.

In this example, the boss feature is copied, this time maintaining the dependency (**Dependent copy** has been enabled). When changes are made to the parent, the copied feature updates to reflect the changes, as shown in Figure 14–4.

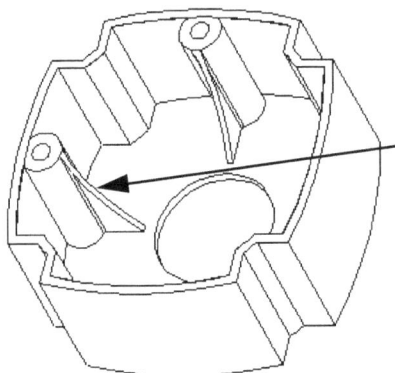

The copy is dependent on its parent. Changes made to the parent are reflected in the copy.

Figure 14–4

How To: Make an Individual Dimension in a Feature Independent, using the Dimensions and Annotation Element Details Only Option

1. Select the copied feature in the model or model tree.
2. Right-click and select **Edit**.
3. Select the specific feature dimension(s), right-click, and select **Make Dimension Independent**.

How To: Make an Individual Dimension in a Feature Independent, using the Fully Dependent with options to vary Option

1. Select the copied feature in the model or model tree.
2. Right-click and select **Edit**.
3. Double-click on the dimension in the Graphics window. The dialog box opens as shown in Figure 14–5.

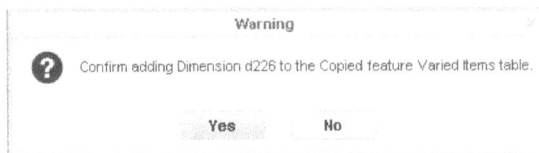

Figure 14–5

4. Click **Yes** to confirm the requested action.
5. Modify the dimension value, if required.

How To: Maintain and Browse a List of Varied Items (e.g. independent dimensions), when the Fully Dependent with options to vary Option Was Selected

1. Select the copied feature in the model or model tree.
2. Right-click and select **Copied Feature>Varied items**. The Varied Items dialog box opens, as shown in Figure 14–6.

The Varied Items dialog box enables you to maintain references, annotations (3D Notes), and parameters, as well.

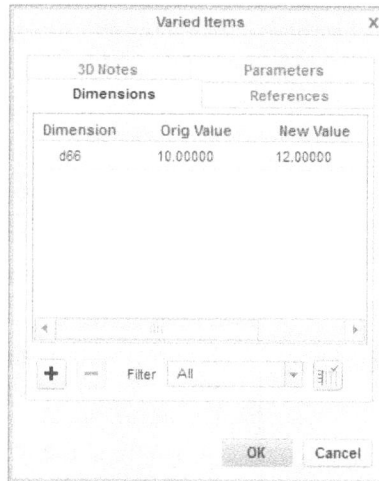

Figure 14–6

3. Enter new values for the dimensions in the *New Value* column.
4. To remove dimension independency, select the dimension and remove it from the list by clicking ▬ .

How To: Temporarily Suspend the Dependency of a Copied Feature on the Original Feature, when the Fully Dependent with options to vary Option Was Selected

1. Select the copied feature in the model or model tree.
2. Right-click and select **Copied feature>Break dependence**.
3. To restore the dependence, right-click and select **Copied feature>Restore dependence**.

How To: Completely Remove the Dependency of a Copied Feature on the Original Feature, when the Fully Dependent with options to vary Option Was Selected

1. Select the copied feature in the model or model tree.
2. Right-click and select **Copied feature>Remove dependence**. The dialog box opens as shown in Figure 14–7.

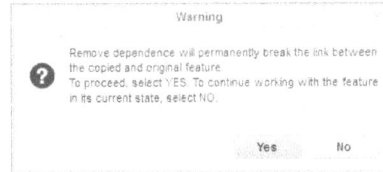

Figure 14–7

3. Click **Yes** to confirm the requested action.

Move/Rotate

The **Apply move/rotate transformations to copies** option enables you to translate or rotate the copied item in the model. For example, in Figure 14–8 the features shown at the bottom right side of the model are translated and rotated to create the copy at the top right side of the model.

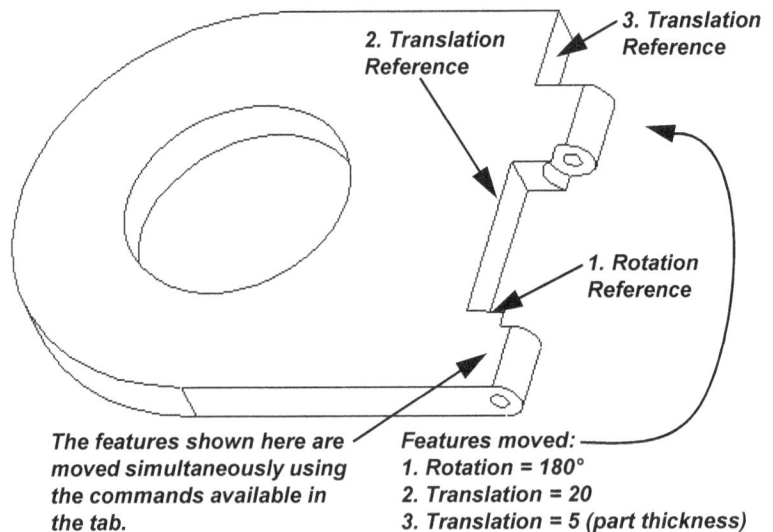

Figure 14–8

When moving a copied feature, you can also maintain dependency on the original dimensions.

Use the *Move (Copy)* dashboard shown in Figure 14–9 to move the copied items.

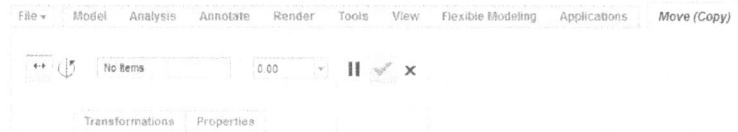

Figure 14–9

How To: Move Copied Items

1. Click ↔ (Translate Features) and ↺ (Rotate Features) to translate or rotate the copied item. Only one **Move** operation can be performed at a time.
2. Select a reference, such as a straight curve, edge, plane, or axis to translate along or rotate about.
3. Enter the translation or rotation value along or about the selected reference. You can also select and drag the handles on the model.
4. To create additional **Move** operations, right-click and select **New Move** or use the Transformations panel. Repeat Steps 1 to 3 to define the new **Move** operation.

Reference Definition

When using the **Copy** and **Paste** commands, you are placed in the tab and must locate the copied feature by redefining the original placement references. These commands can be confusing when copying multiple features, therefore, you can select the **Advanced reference configuration** option, which enables you to review all of the references that were used to place the original feature(s), as shown in Figure 14–10.

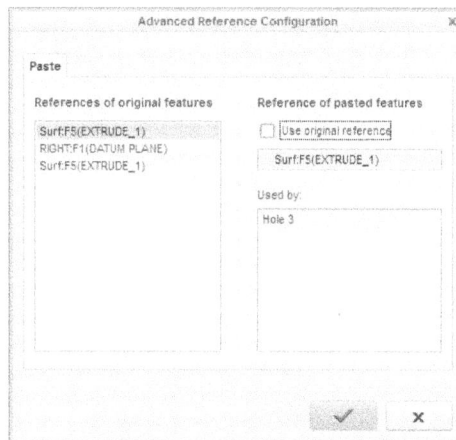

Figure 14–10

This dialog box lists all of the references that were used in the original feature(s) and enables you to maintain the original reference or select a new one. If you are copying multiple features, all of the references are listed on the left in the dialog box. As each reference is selected, the *Used By* area updates to list the copied features that use this reference.

Once all of the references have been redefined, complete the **Copy** operation.

14.3 Mirroring

In Creo Parametric, you can mirror selected features or the entire model geometry about a specified plane. This option is useful when designing symmetric parts.

Use one of the following methods to select geometry to mirror:

- To mirror the entire model, select the model name in the model tree, as shown on the left in Figure 14–11.

- To mirror the set of features, select the features in the model tree or on the model, as shown on the right in Figure 14–11.

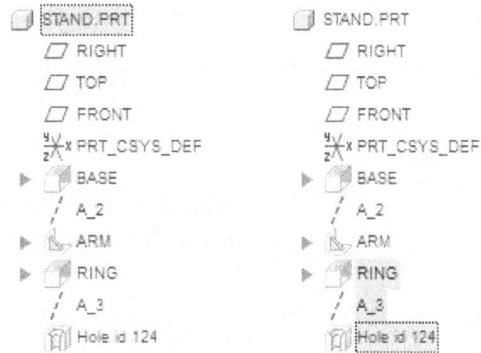

Figure 14–11

Click ⊃⊂ (Mirror) in the Editing group in the *Model* tab. The *Mirror* dashboard displays as shown in Figure 14–12.

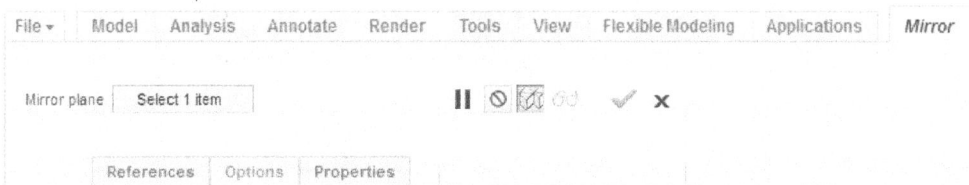

Figure 14–12

To mirror the model or individual features, select the plane that you want to mirror about. The mirroring plane can be a planar surface or a datum plane. Once selected, the mirroring plane is listed in the References panel, as shown in Figure 14–13.

If you mirror selected features, you can also determine whether the mirrored geometry is dependent or independent of the original. By default, the features are dependent with the **Partial dependent - Dimensions and AE Details only** option selected. To make them independent, clear the **Copy as dependent** option in the Options panel, as shown in Figure 14–14. If you mirror the entire model, this panel is not available.

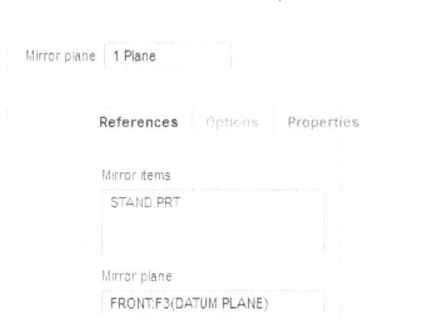

Figure 14–13

Figure 14–14

You can also make some dimensions independent by selecting the **Fully dependent with options to vary** option. This enables you to make the selected dimensions independent.

Click ✓ (Complete Feature) to complete the **Mirror** operation. The geometry displays in the model tree as a mirror feature once it has been mirrored, as shown in Figure 14–15. The independent mirrored feature displays a different icon in the model tree.

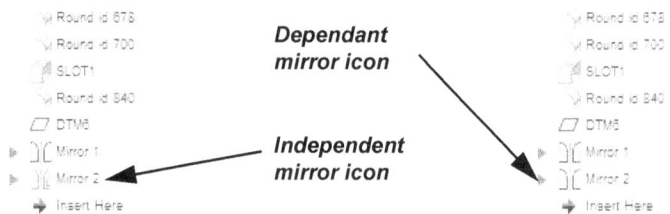

Figure 14–15

Individually mirrored features can be edited by selecting them in the model or model tree and right-clicking to display the contextual options.

Entire models that are mirrored cannot be edited. However, you can edit their definitions to change the mirroring plane.

Practice 14a | Copying Features

Practice Objective

- Use the Paste Special command to paste features using the Advance reference configuration option, and select new references to place the features in the same model.

In this practice, you will copy a group of features in a model using Copy and Paste commands to quickly duplicate them. By copying the features rather than recreating them, you can reduce modeling time. The boss shown in Figure 14–16, consists of five features. All of these features will be copied to new locations on the model.

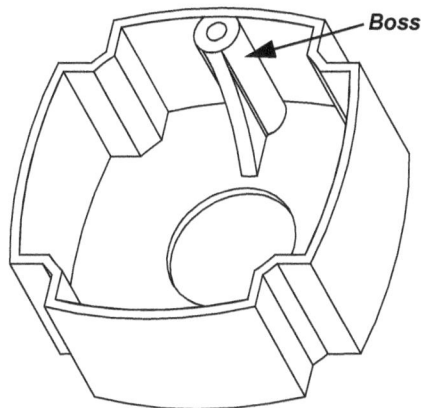

Figure 14–16

Task 1 - Open a part file.

1. Set the working directory to the *Chapter 14\practice 14a* folder.

2. Open **cover.prt**.

3. Set the model display as follows:

- *(Datum Display Filters)*: All Off

- *(Spin Center)*: Off

- *(Display Style)*: (No Hidden)

4. Investigate how the part was created by selecting the *Tools* tab and clicking ![] (Model Player). Which features is the boss made from? How many features make up the boss?

Task 2 - Copy Extrude 1.

Design Considerations

In this task, you will copy a single feature in the boss using the **Copy** and **Paste** functionality. In Task 3, you will use an alternate technique that will enable you to copy multiple features at once and avoid the use of the feature's tab.

1. Select the *Model* tab, and select **Extrude 1** in the model tree.

2. Click ![] (Copy) and then click ![] (Paste) or press <Ctrl>+<C> and <Ctrl>+<V>.

3. The *Extrude* dashboard for this feature displays. Note that two of the panels are displayed in red, indicating that references are missing in both sections.

4. Right-click and select **Edit internal Sketch** to edit the section of the sketch.

5. Select the surface shown in Figure 14–17 as the sketching plane for the sketch.

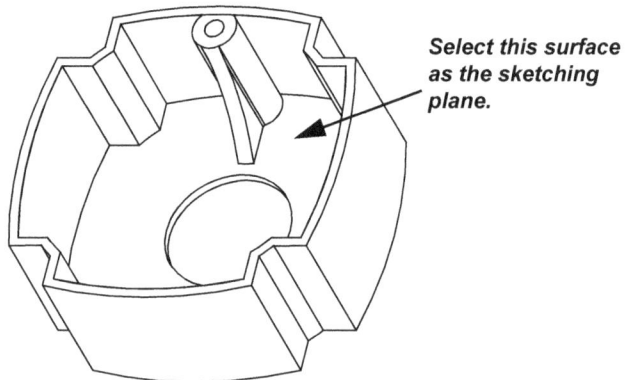

Select this surface as the sketching plane.

Figure 14–17

6. Change the orientation of the **RIGHT** orientation reference to face **Bottom**.

7. Click **Sketch** to activate the *Sketch* tab. The section displayed in red is attached to the cursor, as shown in Figure 14–18.

8. Place the sketch by clicking the left mouse button on the approximate location shown in Figure 14–19. Constrain and dimension the geometry.

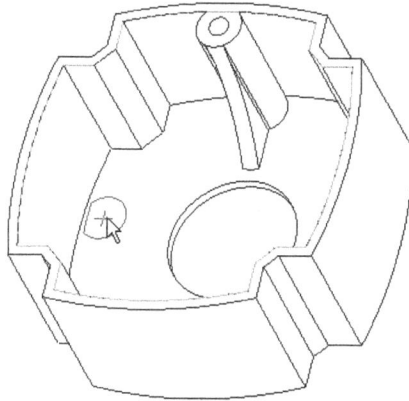

Figure 14–18

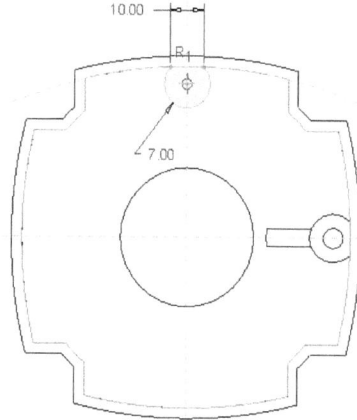

Figure 14–19

9. Complete the sketch.

10. Open the Options panel. The reference for the **To Selected depth** option is missing. As reference for the depth option, select the surface shown in Figure 14–20.

11. Complete the feature. The model displays as shown in Figure 14–21.

Select this surface as the depth reference.

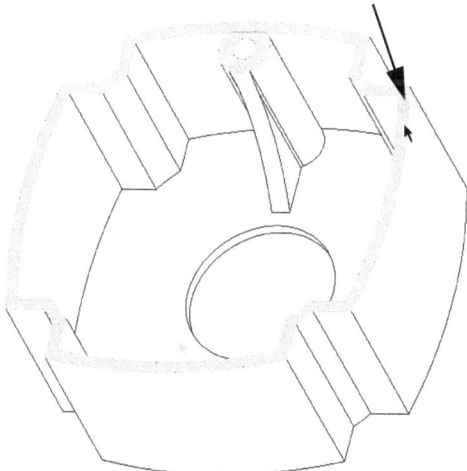

Figure 14–20

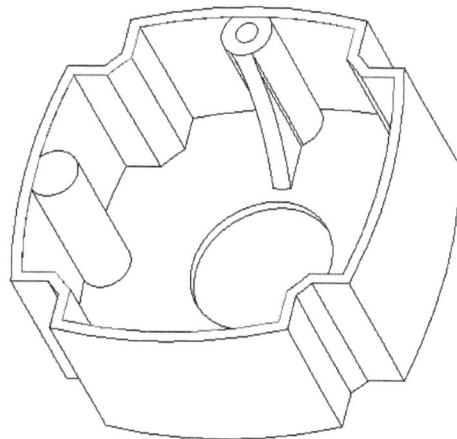

Figure 14–21

Task 3 - Copy the boss.

Design Considerations

If you had copied all five features that make up the boss using the **Copy/Paste** operation in Task 2, you would have been required to redefine the missing references for each feature. In this task, you will copy all of the boss features shown in Figure 14–22, in a single operation using the **Paste Special** option. This option provides one convenient interface to define all of the missing references.

Create this new copy of the Boss.

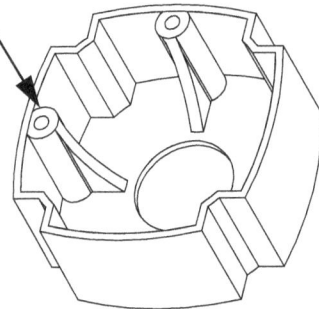

Figure 14–22

1. Delete the feature that you just duplicated in the model.

2. Select the last five features in the model tree (**Extrude 1**, **A_2**, **Hole 1**, **Rib 1**, and **Round 1**). These five features combine to make the boss.

3. Click ☐ (Copy).

4. In the *Model* tab, expand ☐ (Paste) and click ☐ (Paste Special). The Paste Special dialog box opens as shown in Figure 14–23.

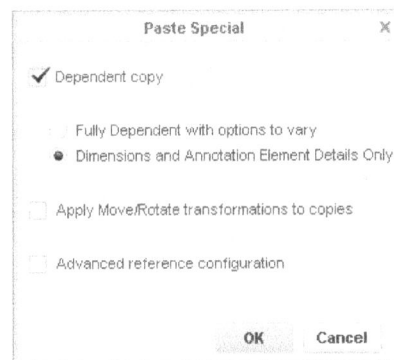

Paste Special ✕
✓ Dependent copy
Fully Dependent with options to vary
● Dimensions and Annotation Element Details Only
☐ Apply Move/Rotate transformations to copies
☐ Advanced reference configuration
OK   Cancel

Figure 14–23

5. Ensure that the **Dependent copy** and **Dimensions and annotation element details only** options are selected. This ensures that the dimensions on the copied boss are driven by the original.

6. Select the **Advanced reference configuration** option.

7. Click **OK**. The Advanced Reference Configuration dialog box opens as shown in Figure 14–24. All of the missing references required to place the feature are listed in the *References of Original Features* area.

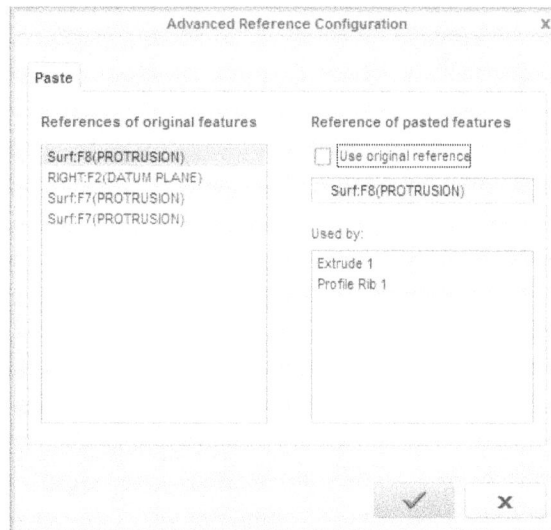

Advanced Reference Configuration	X
Paste	

References of original features
Surf:F8(PROTRUSION)
RIGHT:F2(DATUM PLANE)
Surf:F7(PROTRUSION)
Surf:F7(PROTRUSION)

Reference of pasted features
☐ Use original reference

Surf:F8(PROTRUSION)

Used by:
Extrude 1
Profile Rib 1

Figure 14–24

8. Select the first reference **(Surf:F7(PROTRUSION))**. It is used by both **Extrude 1** and **Rib 1**. It will remain the same for both features when they are copied. Select the **Use Original Reference** option.

9. Select the second reference **(RIGHT:F2(DATUM PLANE))**. Select **TOP** as the replacement reference.

10. Select the third reference **(Surf:F7(PROTRUSION))**. It remains the same for all features when they are copied. Select the **Use Original Reference** option.

11. Select the fourth reference **(Surf:F7(PROTRUSION))**. Select the reference shown in Figure 14–25 as the new reference.

Select this surface when redefining the fourth reference.

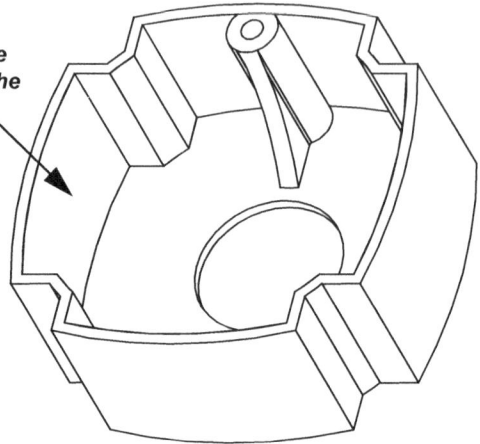

Figure 14–25

12. Click ✔ (Apply) to close the dialog box and place the features.

13. In the **Preview** dialog box, click ✔ (Apply) to accept the default direction of the vertical plane.

14. The copied features are listed in the model tree, as shown in Figure 14–26. Note that the names of the new features mimic the names of their dependent parents. This makes tracking dependencies much easier in the model tree.

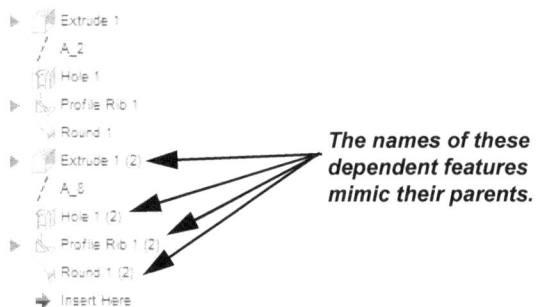

The names of these dependent features mimic their parents.

Figure 14–26

Task 4 - Copy the boss a second time and make one of the dimensions independent.

You can select original features or copied features created in the previous task.

1. Click 🗐 (Paste Special) again to create another dependent copy of the same features using the required references to place the boss as shown in Figure 14–27. Ensure that the arrow is pointed in the correct direction. Click **Flip** to flip the direction reference.

In this task you will create this new copy of the Boss.

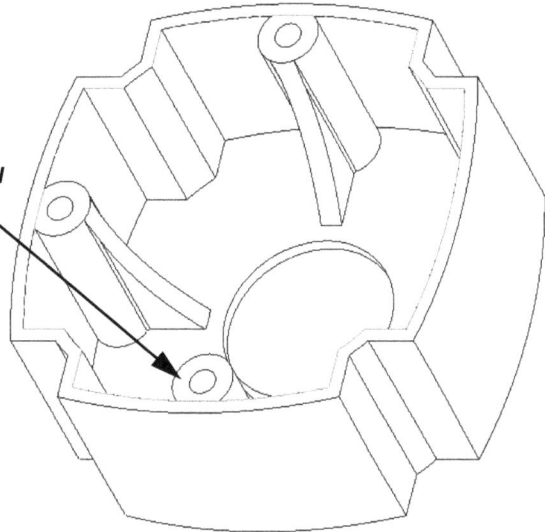

Figure 14–27

2. Once the boss has been placed, double-click on the original hole feature to display its dimensions. Select the **25** dimension, right-click and select **Make Dimension Independent**.

3. Select the new hole to specify the hole that you want to make independent and click **OK**.

4. Edit the new hole, set the *Depth* to **40**, and regenerate the model. Note that this hole has a different depth than the others.

5. Save the part.

Design
Considerations

Task 5 - Copy the boss into a different model.

In this task, you will copy the boss from **cover.prt** into the part shown on the left in Figure 14–28. This is done because the boss consists of a standard set of features, which are used for fixings in multiple plastic models. To copy between two different models, you must first have the source and target parts open in Creo Parametric. When pasting between models, the features are independent by default.

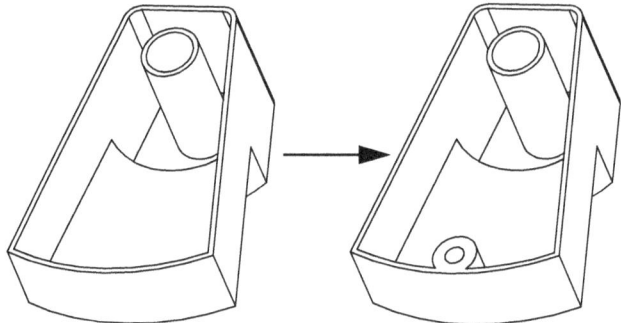

Figure 14–28

1. Open **cover2.prt** in the *Chapter 14/practice 14a* folder.

2. Click in the **cover.prt** window.

3. Select all of the features that combine to make the original boss.

4. Click ⬚ (Copy).

5. Select the **cover2.prt** window.

6. Click ⬚ (Paste Special). The Paste Special dialog box opens as shown in Figure 14–29.

Figure 14–29

7. Leave the **Make Fully Dependent copies with options to vary** option cleared to create an independent copy.

8. Select the **Advanced reference configuration** option.

9. Click **OK**. The Scale dialog box opens as shown in Figure 14–30. This dialog box enables you define how the size of the new features varies to fit the new part.

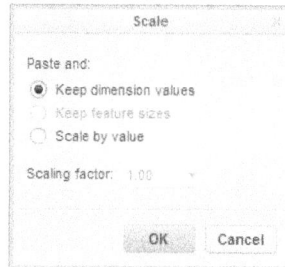

Figure 14–30

10. Select **Scale by value**, set the *Scaling factor* to **3**, and click **OK**.

Design Considerations

The Advanced Reference Configuration dialog box opens. Similar to selecting the new references in the same model, select references to place the boss in the new model. When you select the reference in the Advanced Reference Configuration dialog box, the Creo Parametric software automatically highlights the original references used in **cover.prt**. This enables you to see the original highlighted reference. You have to select the appropriate reference for **cover2.prt**.

11. The first reference is highlighted. Select the surface shown in Figure 14–31.

Select the bottom surface.

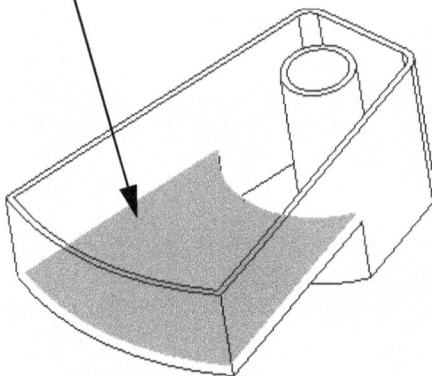

Figure 14–31

12. For the second reference, select **DTM1**, as shown in Figure 14–32.

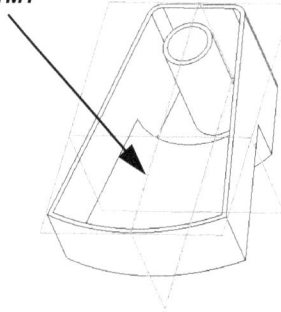

Select DTM1

Figure 14–32

13. For the third reference, select the surface shown in Figure 14–33.

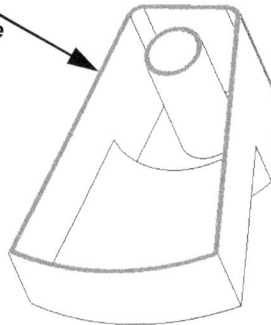

Select the top surface

Figure 14–33

14. For the last reference, select the surface shown in Figure 14–34.

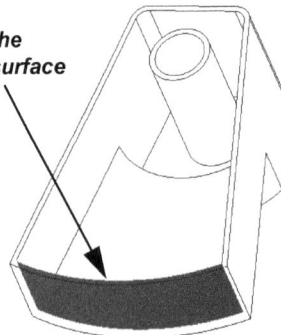

Select the inside surface

Figure 14–34

15. Click ✔ (Apply) to close the dialog box and place the features.

16. The Preview dialog box opens, in which you can change the arrow direction, as shown in Figure 14–35. Click ✔ (Apply) and place the features. The completed model displays as shown in Figure 14–36.

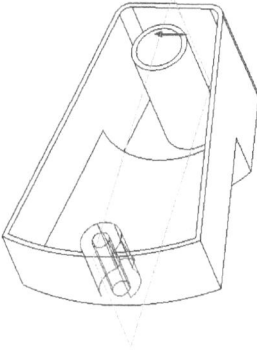

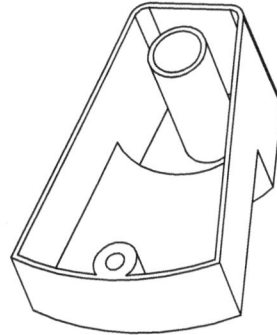

Figure 14–35   **Figure 14–36**

17. Review the model tree. The copied features are listed as individual features in the model tree.

18. Save the part and erase it from memory.

Practice 14b | Mirroring Features

Practice Objectives

- Mirror a solid part to duplicate all of its geometry.
- Edit parent features in the model and ensure that all mirrored geometry update as expected.

In this practice, you will start by opening the model shown on the left in Figure 14–37. This model will be mirrored using its existing planar surfaces to create the final model shown on the right in Figure 14–37.

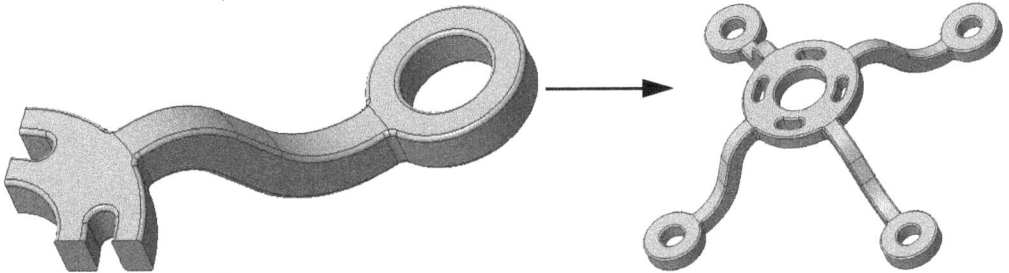

Figure 14–37

Task 1 - Open a part file.

1. Set the working directory to the *Chapter 14\practice 14b* folder.

2. Open **stand.prt**.

3. Set the model display as follows:

   - ⚹ *(Datum Display Filters)*: All Off

   - ⟶ *(Spin Center)*: Off

   - ⬚ *(Display Style)*: ⬚ (Shading With Edges)

Task 2 - Mirror the geometry.

1. Select **stand.prt** at the top of the model tree, as shown in Figure 14–38.

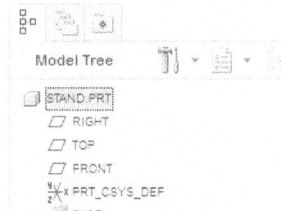

Figure 14–38

2. In the Editing group in the *Model* tab, click)((Mirror), to display the *Mirror* dashboard.

3. For the mirror reference, select the surface shown in Figure 14–39.

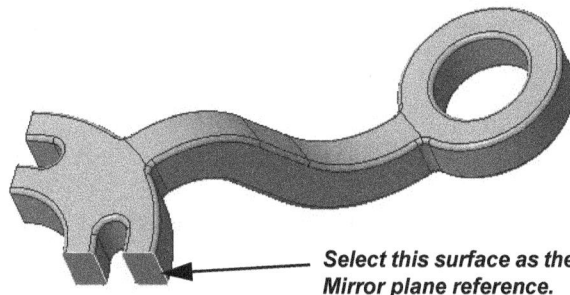

Select this surface as the Mirror plane reference.

Figure 14–39

4. The mirrored part previews on the screen. Click ✓ (Complete Feature) to complete the mirror. The new mirror feature is now available in the model tree.

*Select **Stand.prt** at the top of the model tree.*

5. Complete the part by creating another mirror feature in the model, as shown in Figure 14–40.

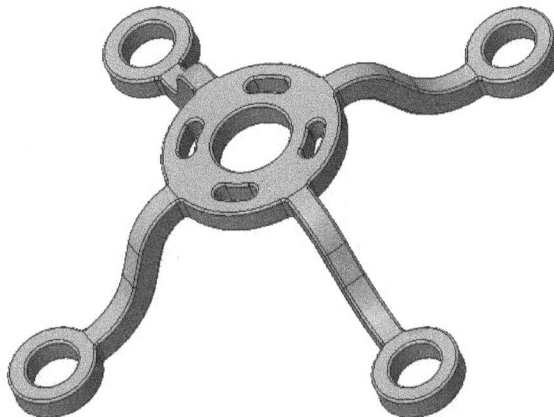

Figure 14–40

Task 3 - Modify the part.

1. Set the hole *Diameter* to **70**, as shown in Figure 14–41.

2. Regenerate the model. Because of their dependency on the original section, all of the holes update as shown in Figure 14–42.

Edit the diameter value of this hole.

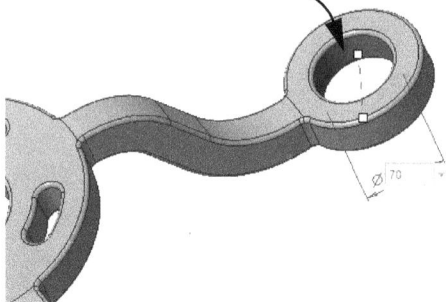

Figure 14–41

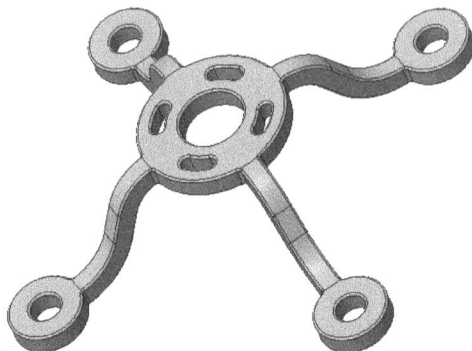

Figure 14–42

3. Save the part and erase it from memory.

Practice 14c | (Optional) Moving Features

Practice Objective

- Use the Paste Special command to paste features while using the Apply Move/Rotate transformations to copy option to place the features in the same model.

In this practice, you will be provided with a model of a partially completed hook spring, as shown in Figure 14–43. To complete the model you will use the **Paste Special** option to duplicate the hook end by defining **Move** operations to place it on the other end of the spring. The completed model is shown in Figure 14–44.

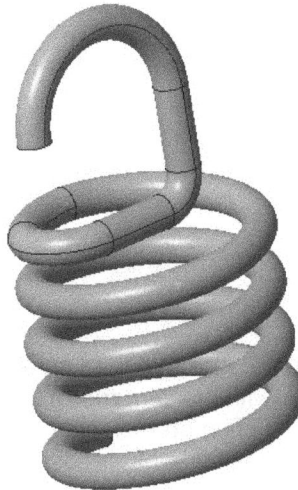

Original Model

Figure 14–43

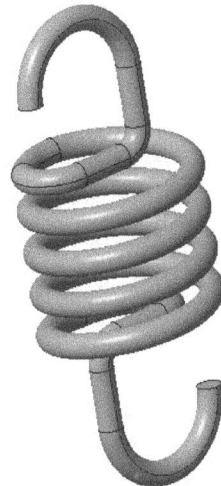

Completed Model

Figure 14–44

Task 1 - Open a part file.

1. Set the working directory to the *Chapter 14\practice 14c* folder.

2. Open **hook_spring.prt**.

3. Set the model display as follows:

   - ⚡ *(Datum Display Filters)*: Only 🔷 (Plane Display)

   - ⌁ *(Spin Center)*: Off

   - 🔲 *(Display Style)*: ⬜ (Shading With Edges)

Task 2 - Duplicate the hook end of the spring.

1. In the model tree, select **HOOK**.

Design Considerations

The design intent for the model requires that the hook must be duplicated so that any changes to the original reflect in the copied instance. To copy, you will move the instance using the **Paste Special** functionality. To define the movements, you will use two rotations and one translation.

2. In the *Model* tab, click (Copy). Expand the (Paste) flyout, and click (Paste Special). The Paste Special dialog box opens as shown in Figure 14–45.

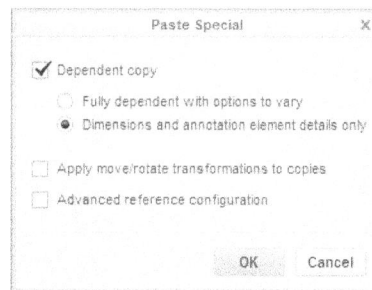

Figure 14–45

3. Ensure that the **Dependent copy** option remains selected with the **Dimensions and annotation element details only** option are selected. This ensures that the dimensions on the copied hook are driven by the original.

4. Select the **Apply move/rotate transformations to copies** option.

5. Click **OK**. The *Move (Copy)* tab displays as shown in Figure 14–46. It enables you to apply rotation and translation to copy the feature.

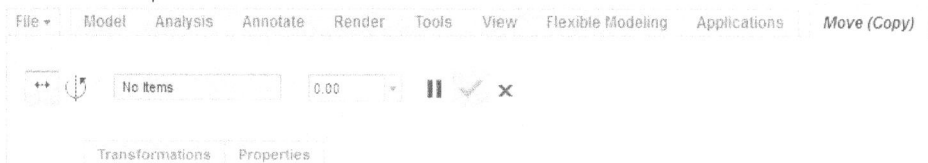

Figure 14–46

6. In the dashboard, click (Rotate Features) to define a rotation.

7. Currently, a reference does not exist that can be used to obtain the required rotation movement. In the dashboard, expand ⬚ (Datum) and click ╱ (Axis) to create a datum axis at the intersection of datum planes **RIGHT** and **FRONT**.

8. Click ▶ (Resume) in the dashboard to resume feature creation.

9. Set the *Rotation* to **180**.

10. Right-click on the main window and select **New Move**.

11. Click ↻ (Rotate Features).

12. Expand ⬚ (Datum) and click ╱ (Axis) to create a datum axis at the intersection of datum planes **RIGHT** and **TOP**.

13. Set the *Rotation* to **180**.

14. Right-click on the main window and select **New Move**.

15. Leave the default selection of ↔ (Translate Features).

16. Select the datum **TOP** and set the *Translation* distance to **40**.

17. Click ✓ (Complete Feature) to complete the feature.

18. In the In-graphics toolbar, click ╳╱╲ (Datum Display Filters) and select ⬚ (Plane Display). The model displays as shown in Figure 14–47.

Figure 14–47

19. Save the part and erase it from memory.

Chapter Review Questions

1. The **Paste Special** option is useful in which of the following situations? (Select all that apply.)

    a. To copy features with dimension dependency.

    b. To move or rotate features.

    c. To easily identify references and select new references when copying complex or multiple features.

    d. To copy dimension patterns.

2. Which option should be selected to paste a feature in a new model so that it maintains dependency between the source and the copied feature?

    a. **Dimensions and Annotation Element Details Only**

    b. **Apply Move/Rotate transformations to copies**

    c. **Advance reference configuration**

    d. **Make Fully Dependent copies with options to vary**

Command Summary

Button	Command	Location
	Mirror	• **Ribbon:** *Model* tab in the *Editing* group

Patterns

Patterning enables you to quickly duplicate features in a model. Dimension patterns are created when you select dimensions associated with a feature to create a pattern. Additional advanced pattern options enable you to expand on dimension patterns so that you can just select a patterning direction. Using these options, you no longer need to select a dimension directly from the pattern leader. Therefore, you can pattern features that do not explicitly have a dimension to use to create the required pattern.

Learning Objectives in this Chapter

- Create a dimensional pattern by selecting dimensions in one or two directions.
- Specify the type of pattern in the Options panel (i.e. Identical, Variable, and General).
- Make changes to the patterned features using the editing tools.
- Pattern a feature using a direction pattern that translates along one or two directions.
- Create an axis pattern by selecting an axis for rotation.
- Specify the dimension increment, number of instances, and rotational options for the pattern.
- Use various editing tools to make changes to the patterned features.

15.1 Dimension Patterns

Patterning enables you to quickly duplicate features in a model. The initial feature in a pattern is called the pattern leader. Figure 15–1 shows a pattern leader in a rectangular cut. The pattern is created from the pattern leader by referencing its dimensions. Dimension patterns are the most basic pattern type.

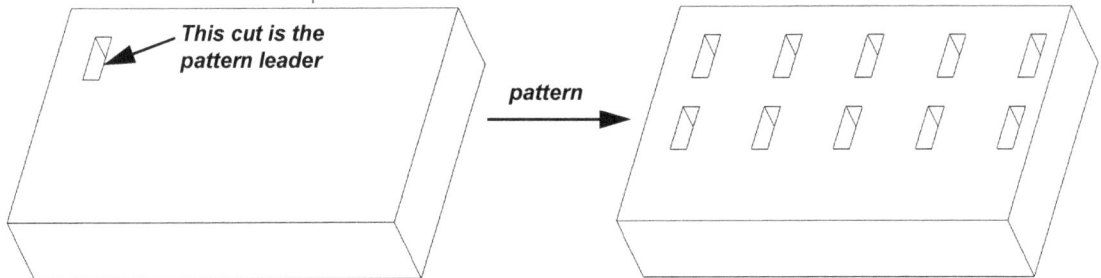

This cut is the pattern leader

pattern

Figure 15–1

Patterned features can vary in size, as shown in Figure 15–2.

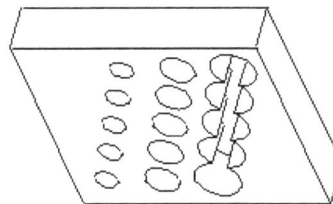

Figure 15–2

General Steps

Use the following general steps to create a dimension pattern:

1. Start the creation of the pattern.
2. Specify the dimensions in one or two direction(s).
3. Specify the number of pattern instances.
4. Define how to generate the pattern.
5. Modify the pattern, as required.

Step 1 - Start the creation of the pattern.

*You can also right-click and select **Pattern**.*

To start the creation of a pattern, select the feature to pattern in the model tree or directly from the model. In the Editing group in the *Model* tab, click ▦ (Pattern), as shown in Figure 15–19.

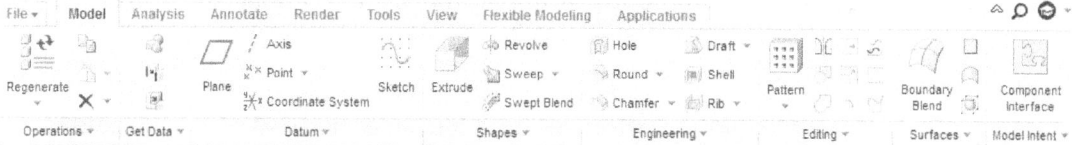

Figure 15–3

Step 2 - Specify the dimensions in one or two direction(s).

Dimensions are used to drive patterns in a model, as shown in Figure 15–4.

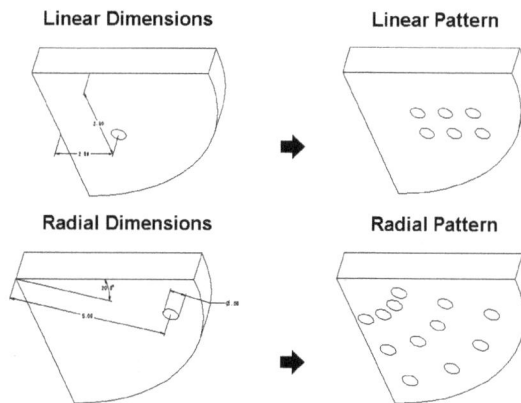

Linear Dimensions   Linear Pattern

Radial Dimensions   Radial Pattern

Figure 15–4

When creating a pattern, you are prompted to select the pattern dimension in the first direction and to specify an increment between instances. It is also possible to select a pattern dimension and specify an increment for the second direction. The uni-directional pattern shown on the left in Figure 15–5 is a pattern that was only created in the first direction. The bi-directional pattern shown on the right was created in the first and second directions.

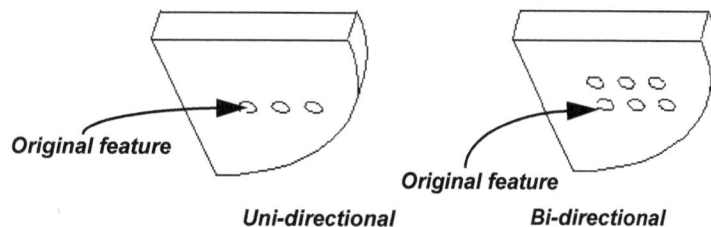

Original feature   *Original feature*

Uni-directional   **Bi-directional**

Figure 15–5

First Direction

When you create a pattern, the tab prompts you to select a dimension for the first direction. This dimension can be in the X-, Y-, or Z-direction, or it can be an angular dimension. The selected dimension drives the direction for the pattern. In Figure 15–6, selecting the dimension **d41** drives the pattern horizontally.

*Selecting **d40** would have caused the pattern to be driven vertically.*

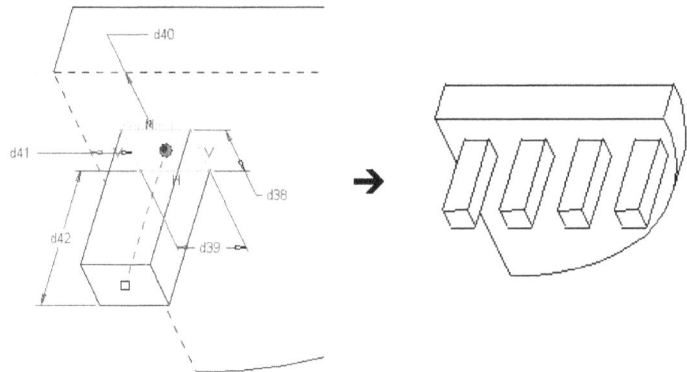

Figure 15–6

Once the first pattern dimension has been specified, you must specify a dimension increment. The increment is measured from the feature, not its placement reference (i.e., where **d19** meets the protrusion). The dimension increment can be entered in the value field that displays on the model or you can use the Dimensions panel, as shown in Figure 15–7.

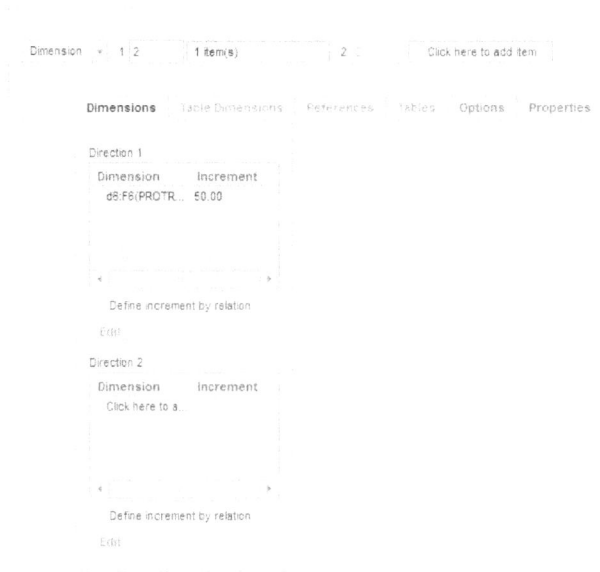

Figure 15–7

You can select multiple dimensions to drive the first direction of the pattern. To select multiple dimensions, press and hold <Ctrl> and select another dimension to vary.

Second Direction

To specify a dimension in the second direction to drive the pattern, right-click on the model and select **Direction 2 Dimensions**. The system prompts you to select the dimensions to vary in the second direction. Alternatively, you can select the *Direction 2* collector in the Dimensions panel. Similar to the first direction, you can select multiple dimensions using <Ctrl>.

Step 3 - Specify the number of pattern instances.

Once the first and second direction dimensions and their increments have been defined, you must enter the number of instances in the pattern. This indicates the number of times that the pattern is duplicated in the first and second directions. The number of pattern instances is defined in the *Pattern* dashboard, as shown in Figure 15–8. The number of instances must include the original pattern leader feature. The second is not selectable if the direction has not been defined.

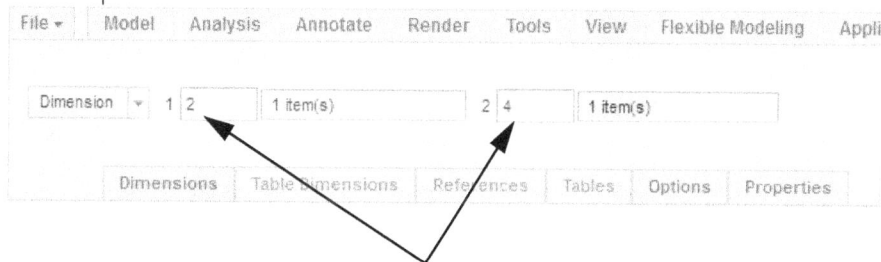

| File ▾ | Model | Analysis | Annotate | Render | Tools | View | Flexible Modeling | Appli |

| Dimension | ▾ | 1 | 2 | | 1 item(s) | | 2 | 4 | | 1 item(s) | |

| Dimensions | Table Dimensions | References | Tables | Options | Properties |

The number of instances in the first and second directions can be specified here.

Figure 15–8

Step 4 - Specify the dimensions in one or two direction(s).

The following three regeneration options are available for creating dimension patterns:

- Identical

- Variable

- General

Identical

Identical patterns are the most restrictive but also have the fastest regeneration time. An example of an identical pattern is shown in Figure 15–9.

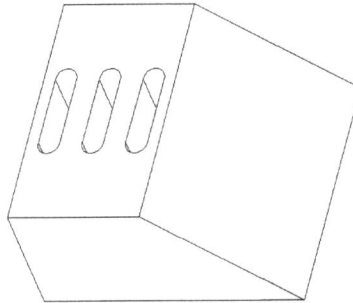

Figure 15–9

Identical patterns have the following restrictions:

- Features cannot vary in size.

- Features cannot lie on different surfaces.

- Features cannot break the edges of the part.

- Features cannot intersect with each other.

Variable

Variable patterns are less restrictive than identical patterns, but they still have some restrictions. Their regeneration times are moderate. An example of a Variable pattern is shown in Figure 15–10.

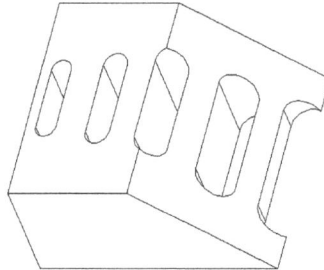

Figure 15–10

Variable patterns have the following capabilities/restrictions:

- Features can vary in size.

- Features can lie on different surfaces.

- Features can break the edge of the part.

- Features cannot intersect with each other.

General

General patterns are the most complex and also require the most regeneration time. An example of a General pattern is shown in Figure 15–11.

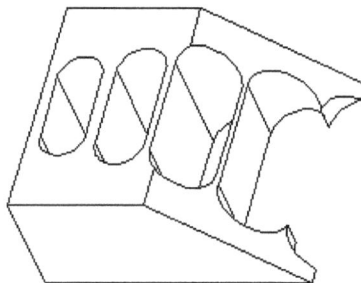

Figure 15–11

General patterns have the following capabilities:

- Features can vary in size.

- Features can lie on different surfaces.

- Features can break the edge of the part.

- Features can interfere with each other.

To minimize regeneration time, select the regeneration option that best suits the design. It might be helpful to initially create all of the patterns as **General**. By doing so, any errors that might have occurred during patterning are visible. The **Regeneration** option can be redefined later.

Consider the example shown in Figure 15–12. If the pattern had been created as **Identical**, it would abort without explanation. This is because one of the patterned instances intersects two different surfaces. By creating the pattern in Figure 15–12 as **General**, the error would have been detected visually once the pattern was created, and modifications could be made. Once the pattern has been modified to fit the rules for an identical pattern, it can be redefined from *General* to **Identical** to save regeneration time.

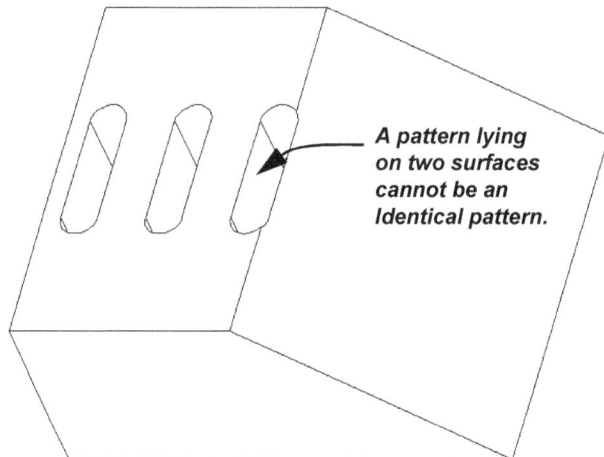

A pattern lying on two surfaces cannot be an Identical pattern.

Figure 15–12

*By default, the regeneration option is set to **General**.*

To change the regeneration option, open the Options panel, as shown in Figure 15–13.

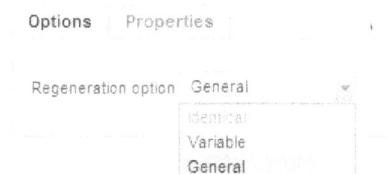

Figure 15–13

Click ✓ (Complete Feature) to complete the pattern.

Step 5 - Define how to generate the pattern.

Once the pattern has been created, you can perform any of the following operations:

- ⟼dı⟻ (Edit)

- 🥄 (Edit Definition)

- Delete Pattern

Edit

To modify pattern dimensions, select one of the pattern instances in the model or model tree, right-click, and select ⟼dı⟻ (Edit). Any of the pattern dimensions can be modified, including the number of instances in the pattern, as shown in Figure 15–14.

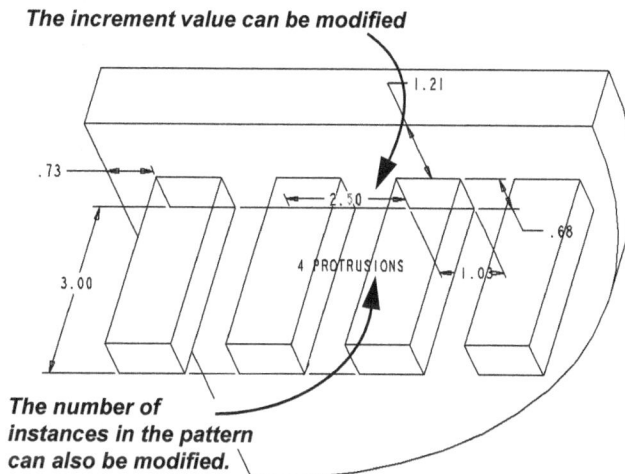

The increment value can be modified

The number of instances in the pattern can also be modified.

Figure 15–14

Edit Definition

To display the original *Pattern* tab that was used to create the pattern, select the pattern in the model tree, right-click, and select 🥄 (Edit Definition). You can make changes to the pattern using any of the *Pattern* dashboard options.

Delete Pattern

To delete the pattern, select the pattern in the model tree, right-click and select **Delete Pattern**. All instances of the pattern are deleted but the pattern leader still remains. Note that using the **Delete** option removes all of the pattern features including the pattern leader.

15.2 Direction Patterns

Directional patterns differ from dimension patterns in that you just select the patterning direction. Because you no longer need to select a dimension directly from the pattern leader, this pattern type can help you pattern features that do not explicitly have a dimension for the required pattern.

General Steps

Use the following general steps to create a directional pattern:

1. Start the creation of the pattern.
2. Select a direction to drive the pattern.
3. Specify the pattern increment and number of instances.
4. (Optional) Drive the pattern in a second direction.
5. Remove instances, as required.
6. Complete the pattern.
7. Edit the pattern, as required.

Step 1 - Start the creation of the pattern.

Select the feature to be patterned. To start the creation of the pattern, use one of the following methods to display the *Pattern* tab.

- In the Editing group in the *Model* tab, click ⚄ (Pattern).

- Right-click and select **Pattern**.

In the *Pattern* dashboard, expand the Pattern Type drop-down list and select **Direction**. The *Pattern* tab updates, as shown in Figure 15–15.

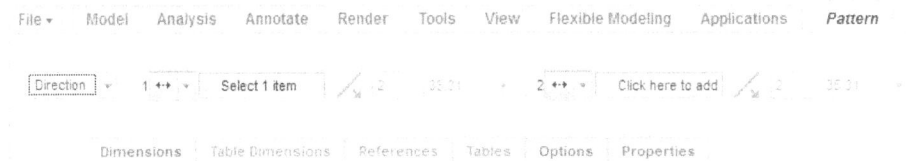

| File ▾ | Model | Analysis | Annotate | Render | Tools | View | Flexible Modeling | Applications | *Pattern* |

| Direction ▾ | 1 ↔ ▾ | Select 1 item | ⟋ | | | ▾ | 2 ↔ ▾ | Click here to add | ⟋ | |

Dimensions | Table Dimensions | References | Tables | Options | Properties

Figure 15–15

Step 2 - Select a direction to drive the pattern.

The coordinate system axis must be selected directly on the model.

Select a direction to use to drive the pattern in the first direction. A plane (surface or datum plane), linear curve, coordinate system axis, or axis can be selected.

Step 3 - Specify the pattern increment and number of instances.

You can enter an increment directly on the model, in the *Pattern* dashboard, or using the drag handle. Enter the number of instances by entering a value in the collector, as shown in Figure 15–16.

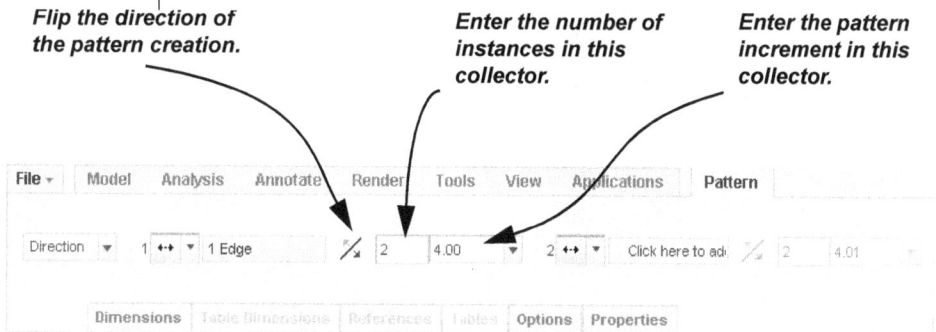

Flip the direction of the pattern creation.

Enter the number of instances in this collector.

Enter the pattern increment in this collector.

| File ▾ | Model | Analysis | Annotate | Render | Tools | View | Applications | Pattern |

| Direction ▾ | 1 ↔ ▾ | 1 Edge | ⁄ | 2 | 4.00 | ▾ | 2 ↔ ▾ | Click here to ad | ⁄ | 2 | 4.01 |

Dimensions | Table Dimensions | References | Tables | **Options** | Properties

Figure 15–16

Step 4 - (Optional) Drive the pattern in a second direction.

The coordinate system axis must be selected directly on the model.

You can drive the pattern in a second direction. To activate the second direction, select the collector in the second direction reference, or right-click and select **Direction 2 Reference**. Select a plane (surface or datum plane), linear curve, coordinate system axis, or axis to drive the second direction.

Enter the increment directly on the model, in the tab, or using the drag handle. Enter the number of instances for the second direction.

The pattern preview updates to include the second direction.

Step 5 - Remove instances, as required.

As with dimensional patterns, you can clear any unwanted instances by selecting the black hotspots that represent them.

Step 6 - Complete the pattern.

Click ✔ (Complete Feature) to complete the pattern. Figure 15–17 shows a preview and completed directional pattern. **A_3** was used as the direction reference to drive the pattern in one direction.

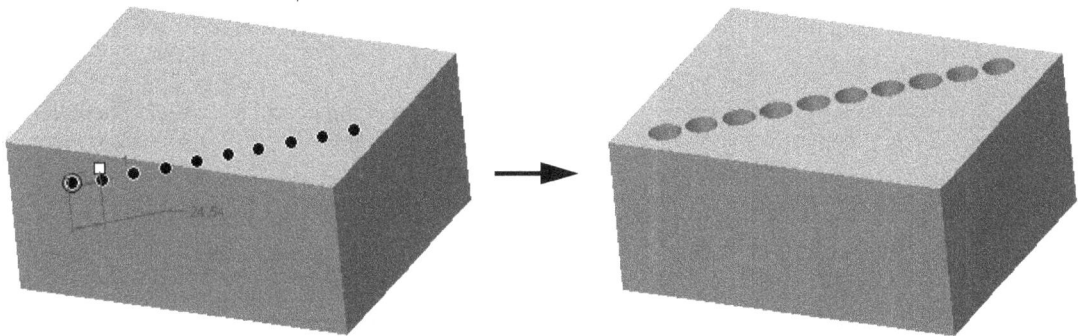

Figure 15–17

Step 7 - Edit the pattern, as required.

The pattern can be modified in the same manner as dimension patterns.

15.3 Axis Patterns

Axis pattern types enable you to create a rotational pattern around a selected datum axis. No angular dimension is required to create the feature. Figure 15–18 shows two examples of axis patterns.

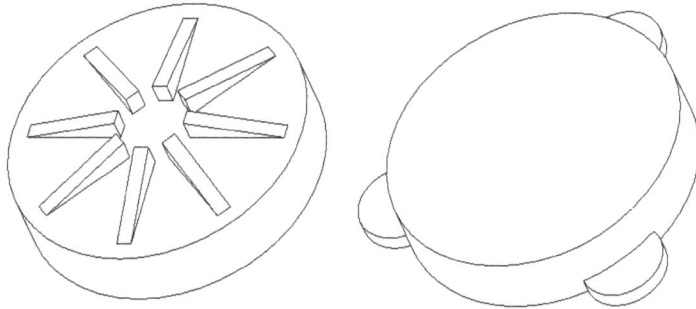

Figure 15–18

General Steps

Use the following general steps to create an Axis pattern:

1. Start the creation of the pattern.
2. Select the axis to pattern about.
3. Specify the pattern increment and number of instances.
4. (Optional) Drive the pattern in a second direction.
5. (Optional) Set the orientation of instances.
6. Remove instances, as required.
7. Complete the pattern.
8. Edit the pattern, as required.

Step 1 - Start the creation of the pattern.

An angular dimension does not need to be associated with the feature to drive a radial pattern.

Select the feature to be patterned. To start the creation of the pattern, use one of the following methods to display the *Pattern* tab shown in Figure 15–19:

- In the Editing group in the *Model* tab, click ⬚ (Pattern).

- Right-click and select **Pattern**.

Once the *Pattern* dashboard displays, expand the Pattern Type drop-down list and select **Axis**. The *Pattern* tab updates, as shown in Figure 15–19.

File ▾   Model   Analysis   Annotate   Render   Tools   View   Flexible Modeling   Applications   *Pattern*

Axis ▾   1 ● Select 1 item   ╱ ⬚   90.0   ▾   ╲ 360.0   ▾   2 ▸   85.01   ▾

Dimensions   Table Dimensions   References   Tables   Options   Properties

Figure 15–19

Step 2 - Select the axis to pattern about.

Select or create a datum axis to use as the center of the pattern. The system creates a default pattern in the angular direction. The pattern members are indicated by black dots, as shown in Figure 15–20.

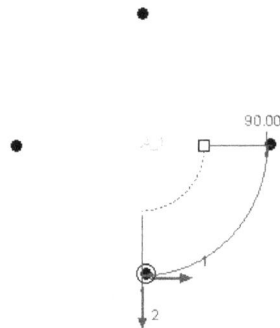

Figure 15–20

Step 3 - Specify the pattern increment and number of instances.

You can enter an increment directly on the model, in the *Pattern* tab, or using the drag handle.

Enter the number of instances by entering a value in the collector, as shown in Figure 15–21.

Enter the user-defined angle increment in this collector.

This icon toggles off the user-defined angle increment collector and activates the Angular Extent collector.

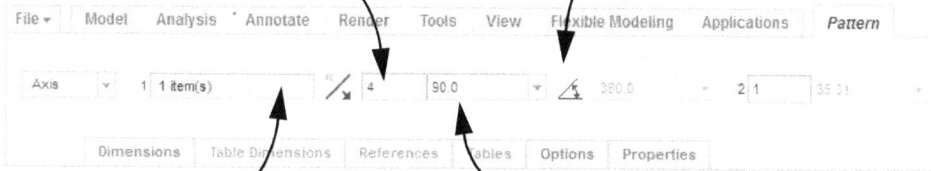

File ▾   Model   Analysis ˙ Annotate   Render   Tools   View   Flexible Modeling   Applications   *Pattern*

Axis   ▾   1 1 item(s)   4   90.0   ▾   380.0   ▾   2|1   35 31   ▾

Dimensions   Table Dimensions   References   Tables   Options   Properties

Enter the number of instances in this collector.

If the Angular Extent collector is active, the angle between instances is calculated using the following formula:
angle increment = angular extent/number of instances.

Figure 15–21

Step 4 - (Optional) Drive the pattern in a second direction.

You can drive the pattern in a second direction. To activate the second direction, select the collector in the *Second Direction Reference* area, and enter a value for the increment and number of instances. The second direction collectors are shown in Figure 15–22.

File ▾   Model   Analysis   Annotate   Render   Tools   View   Flexible Modeling   Applications   *Pattern*

Axis   ▾   1 1 item(s)   4   90.0   ▾   350.0   ▾   2|3   36.00   ▾

Dimensions   Table Dimensions   References   Tables   Options   Properties

Second direction collectors

Figure 15–22

The pattern preview updates to include the second direction.

Step 5 - (Optional) Set the orientation of instances.

The Options panel contains options that enable you to set the orientation of pattern instances, as shown in Figure 15–23.

Instance orientation options

Figure 15–23

- **Follow Rotation**: Produces a pattern whose instances are rotated around a selected axis, as shown on the left in Figure 15–24.

- **Constant**: Produces a pattern whose instances are not rotated - all instances have the same orientation as the patterned feature, as shown on the right in Figure 15–24.

Follow axis rotation enabled   Follow axis rotation disabled

Figure 15–24

Step 6 - Remove instances, as required.

As with dimensional patterns, you can clear any unwanted instances by selecting the black hotspots representing each of the instances. To restore a removed instance, select the white hotspot.

Step 7 - Complete the pattern.

Click ✔ (Complete Feature) to complete the pattern.
Figure 15–25 shows a preview and completed axis pattern. **A_3**
was used as the direction reference to drive this pattern in one
direction, and some instances have been removed.

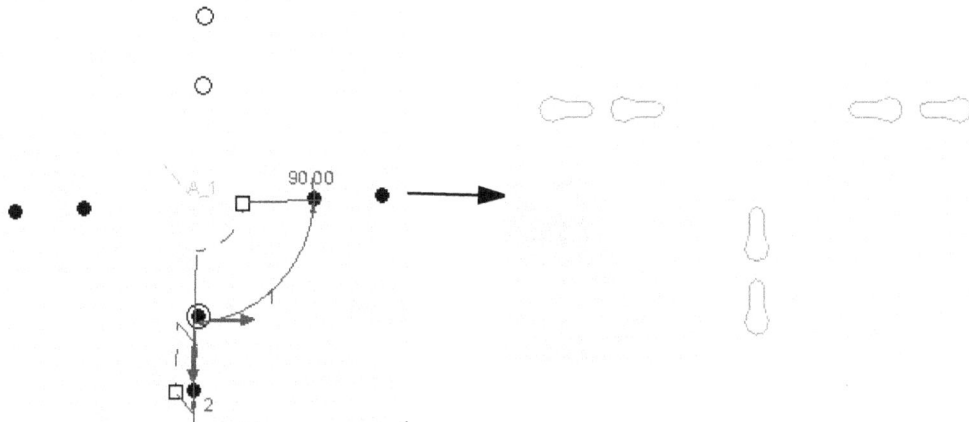

Figure 15–25

Step 8 - Edit the pattern, as required.

The pattern can be modified in the same manner as dimension
patterns.

Practice 15a | Linear Dimension Pattern

Practice Objectives

- Create a dimensional pattern using the general pattern type.
- Select a dimension for the first direction, enter the increment value, and number of pattern instances.
- Change the pattern type to Identical using Edit Definition.

In this practice, you will pattern the protrusion using a dimensional pattern in one direction to complete a heat sink part, as shown in Figure 15–26.

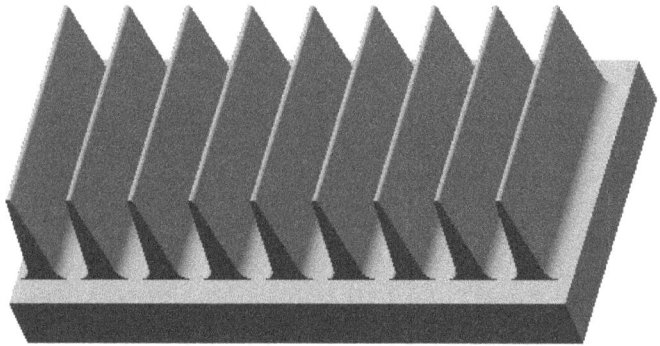

Figure 15–26

Task 1 - Open a part file.

1. Set the working directory to the *Chapter 15\practice 15a* folder.

2. Open **heat_sink.prt**.

3. Set the model display as follows:

   - *(Datum Display Filters)*: All Off
   - *(Spin Center)*: Off
   - *(Display Style)*: ☐ (Shading With Edges)

Task 2 - Pattern the protrusion.

*You can also right-click and select **Pattern** to start the pattern.*

1. Select the protrusion shown in Figure 15–27. In the Editing group in the *Model* tab, click ⣿ (Pattern) to display the *Pattern* dashboard.

2. As the first direction for the pattern, select the **0.03** dimension shown in Figure 15–28.

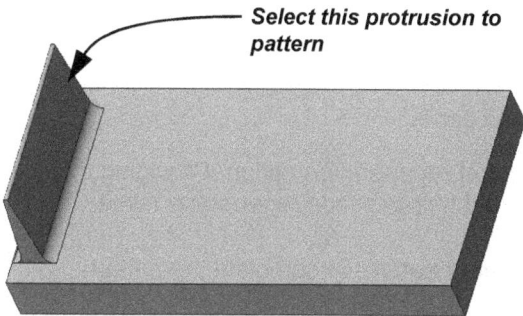

Figure 15–27

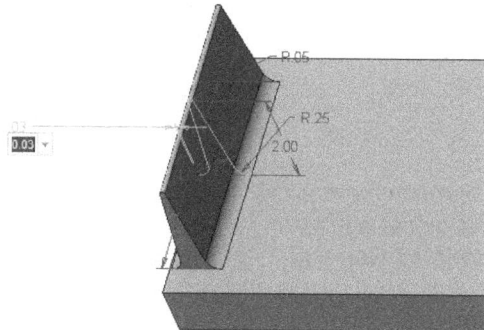

Figure 15–28

3. In the field that displays, set the *Dimension* increment to **1.1**.

4. Press <Enter>.

5. Set the number of pattern instances in the first direction to **9**, as shown in Figure 15–29.

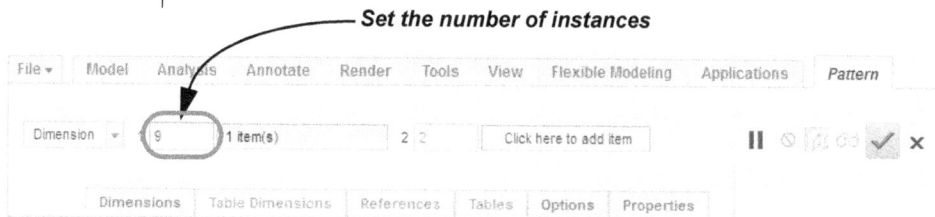

Set the number of instances

Figure 15–29

6. Click ✓ (Complete Feature) to complete the pattern. The model displays as shown in Figure 15–30.

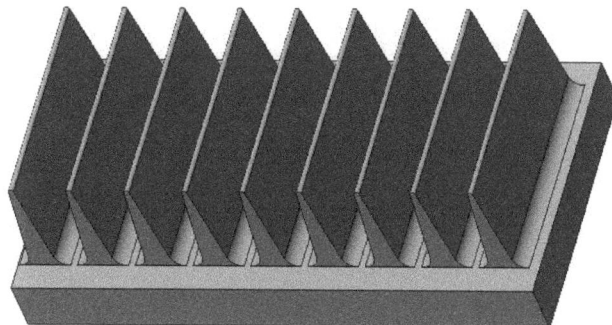

Figure 15–30

Task 3 - Redefine the pattern to improve regeneration time.

1. Select the pattern in the model tree.

2. Right-click and select ✐ (Edit Definition). The *Pattern* dashboard displays.

3. Open the Options panel.

*It is recommended to first create a pattern using the **General** regeneration option and then redefine it once the pattern has been successfully created. This helps you resolve any pattern creation problems.*

4. Select the **Identical** regeneration option. Changing the pattern to **Identical** helps reduce regeneration time.

5. Click ✔ (Complete Feature) to complete the pattern redefinition.

6. Save the part and erase it from memory.

Practice 15b

Bi-Directional Dimension Pattern

Practice Objectives

- Create a dimensional pattern using the general pattern type.
- Select a dimension for the first and second direction.
- Enter the increment value and number of pattern instances.

In this practice, you will pattern the cuts in the model in two directions using a dimensional pattern, as shown in Figure 15–31.

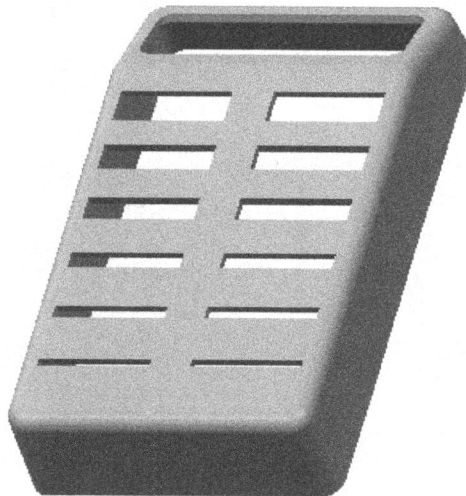

Figure 15–31

Task 1 - Open a part file for patterning.

1. Set the working directory to the *Chapter 15\practice 15b* folder.

2. Open **humidifier_cover.prt.**

3. Set the model display as follows:

   - ⚹ *(Datum Display Filters)*: All Off

   - ⤙ *(Spin Center)*: Off

   - ⬛ *(Display Style)*: ⬜ (Shading With Edges)

Task 2 - Pattern the feature in two directions.

1. Click ⬚ (Pattern) to pattern the **VENTS** extrude shown in Figure 15–32.

**Select the VENTS
extrude to be patterned**

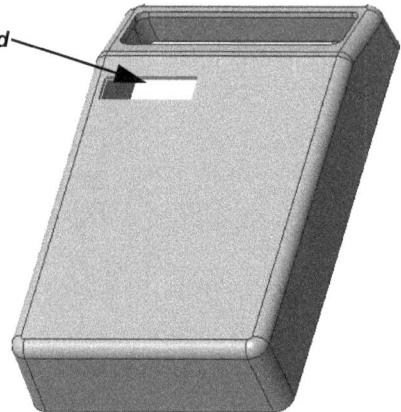

HUMIDIFIER_COVER.PRT
  RIGHT
  TOP
  FRONT
  PRT_CSYS_DEF
▶ Extrude 1
  Draft 1

  Round 1
  Round 2
  Shell 1
▶ CONTROL_INTERFACE
▶ VENTS
  ➔ Insert Here

Figure 15–32

2. As the first direction for the pattern, select the **2.00** dimension and set the *Dimension* increment to **-15**, as shown in Figure 15–33.

**Select this
dimension**

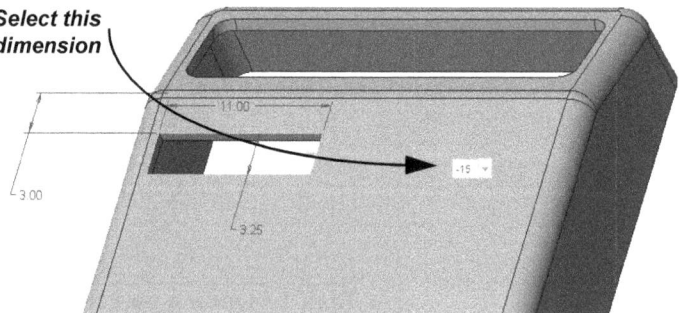

11.00

3.00

3.25

-15

Figure 15–33

3. Press <Enter>.

4. Hover the cursor on the model, right-click and select **Direction 2 Dimensions**, as shown in Figure 15–34.

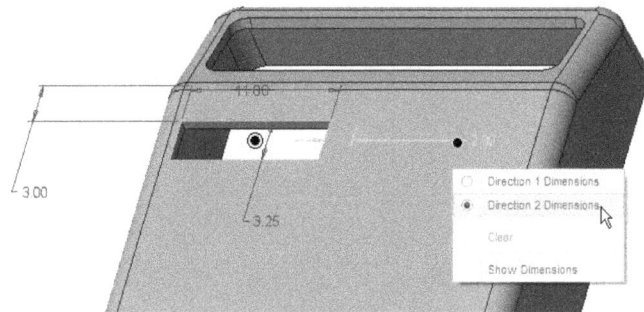

Figure 15–34

5. As the second direction for the pattern, select the **3.00** dimension and set the *Dimension* increment to **6**, as shown in Figure 15–35.

Select this dimension

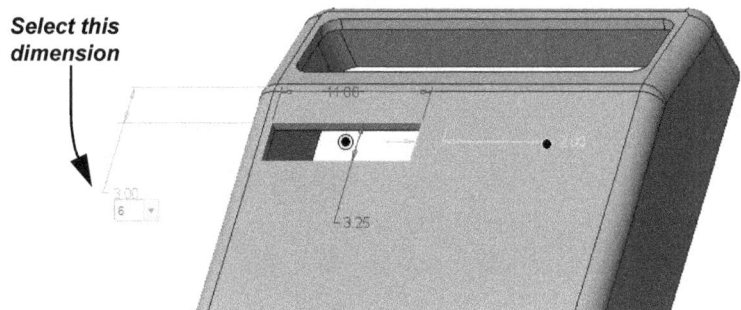

Figure 15–35

6. Press <Enter>.

7. Press <Ctrl>, select the **3.25** dimension, and set the *Dimension* to **-0.5**, as shown in Figure 15–36. This dimension becomes a variable dimension that changes with each instance of the pattern.

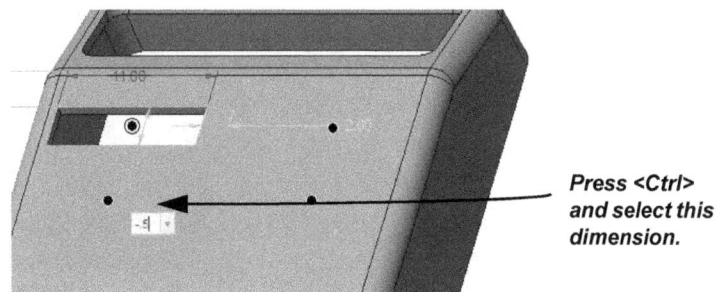

Press <Ctrl> and select this dimension.

Figure 15–36

8. Press <Enter>.

Task 3 - Specify the number of instances in each direction.

1. In the tab, set the first direction to **2** and the second direction to **6**, as shown in Figure 15–37.

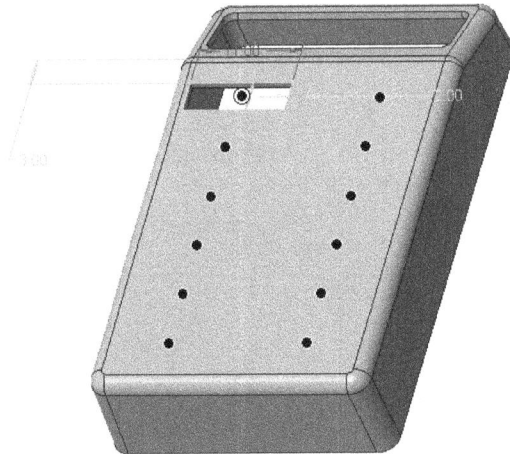

Figure 15–37

2. Click ✔ (Complete Feature) to complete the pattern. The model displays as shown in Figure 15–38.

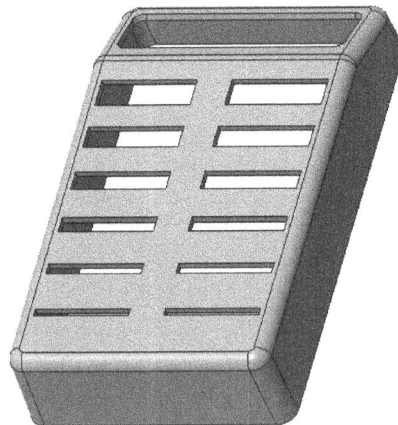

Figure 15–38

3. Save the part and erase it from memory.

Practice 15c | Direction Pattern

Practice Objectives

- Create a directional pattern by selecting the first and second directional references.
- Change the number of instances to compare the three different pattern types using the editing tools.

In this practice, you will create a directional pattern of an extruded protrusion. The completed model is shown in Figure 15–39.

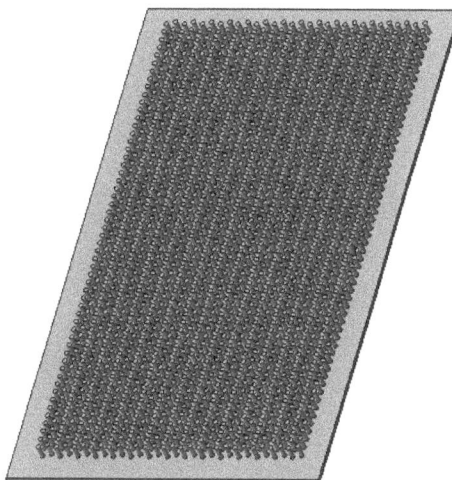

Figure 15–39

Task 1 - Open a part file.

1. Set the working directory to the *Chapter 15\practice 15c* folder.

2. Open **doormat.prt.**

3. Set the model display as follows:

    - ⁂ *(Datum Display Filters)*: All Off

    - ⊱ *(Spin Center)*: Off

    - ▢ *(Display Style)*: ▢ (Shading With Edges)

4. Investigate the dimension scheme of the **EXTRUDE_1** protrusion.

Task 2 - Pattern the EXTRUDE_1.

1. Select the **EXTRUDE_1** and click ⊞ (Pattern) in the *Model* tab. The *Pattern* dashboard displays.

2. Expand the Pattern Type drop-down list and select **Direction** as shown in Figure 15–40.

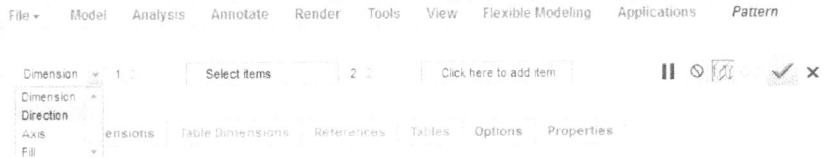

Figure 15–40

3. For the reference for the first direction, select datum plane **FRONT**.

4. Set the number of instances for the first direction to **3**. Set the distance between instances for the first direction to **10**. The *Pattern* dashboard displays as shown in Figure 15–41.

Figure 15–41

5. For the first direction, click ⁄▪ (Flip First Direction) to flip the patterned features on the **BASE** feature, if required.

6. Right-click and select the **Direction 2 Reference** option.

7. For the reference for the second direction, select datum plane **RIGHT**.

8. Set the number of instances for the second direction to **2**. Set the distance between instances for the second direction to **20**. The *Pattern* dashboard displays as shown in Figure 15–42.

Figure 15–42

The bottom left corner of the model displays as shown in Figure 15–43.

9. Click ✓ (Complete Feature) to complete the pattern. The model displays as shown in Figure 15–44.

Click ✗ to change the direction, if required.

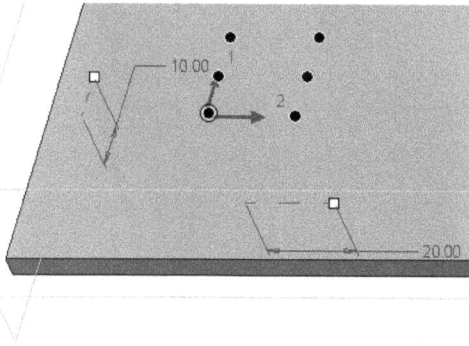

Figure 15–43

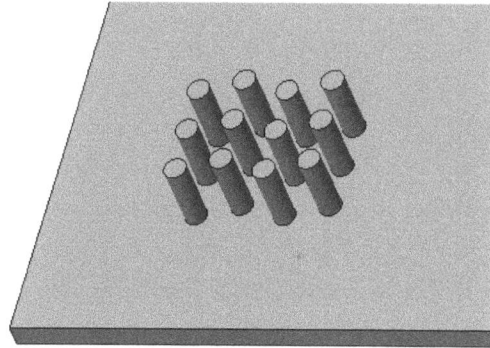

Figure 15–44

Task 3 - Modify the number of pattern instances.

1. In the model tree, select the pattern, right-click, and select ⟷ (Edit).

2. Change the number of **EXTRUDES** in the first direction to **20**.

3. Change the number of **EXTRUDES** in the second direction to **7**.

4. Click (Regenerate). Note that the regeneration takes a long time.

5. Try to reduce the regeneration time. Remember the three pattern types, their advantages, and disadvantages.

Task 4 - Modify the number of pattern instances again.

1. In the model tree, select the pattern, right-click and select ⟷ (Edit).

2. Change the number of instances in the first direction to **55**.

3. Change the number of instances in the second direction to **15**.

4. Regenerate the model. The model displays as shown in Figure 15–45.

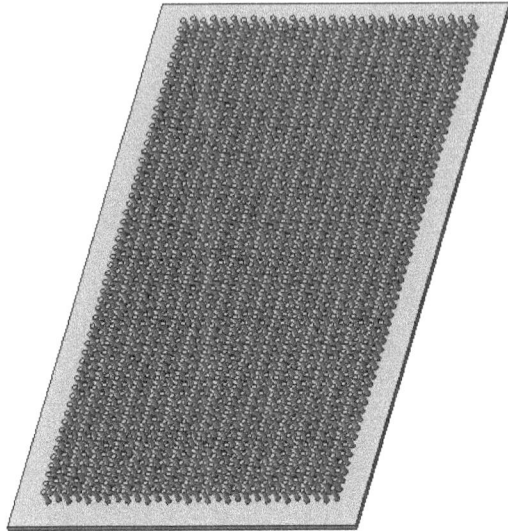

Figure 15–45

5. Save the part and erase it from memory.

Practice 15d | Axis Pattern

Practice Objective

• Create an axis pattern by selecting an axis for rotation.

In this practice, you will create a pattern of an extruded cut. You will use the Axis pattern type to create the required rotational pattern. Once the extrude has been created and patterned, the model displays as shown in Figure 15–46.

Figure 15–46

Task 1 - Open a part file.

1. Set the working directory to the *Chapter 15\practice 15d* folder.

2. Open **lamp.prt**.

3. Set the model display as follows:

   • ⁎⁎⁎ *(Datum Display Filters)*: Only ⁄∘ (Axis Display)

   • ⅀ *(Spin Center)*: Off

   • ▢ *(Display Style)*: ▢ (Shading With Edges)

Task 2 - Create a cut feature to be patterned radially.

1. Click ▱ (Extrude) to create an extruded feature.

2. For the sketching plane, select datum plane **FRONT** from the model tree. Click ⁺▯ (Sketch View).

3. Press and hold <Alt> and select the top of the base protrusion. Right-click and select **Add references** to add the surface as a sketcher reference, as shown in Figure 15–47.

4. Sketch the section shown in Figure 15–48.

Add this sketcher reference —

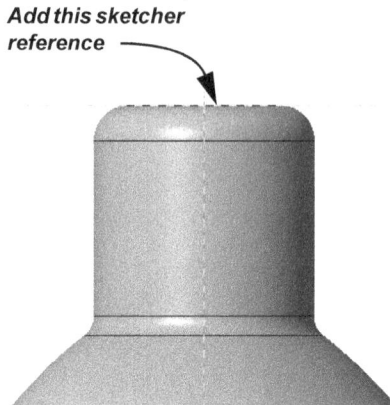

Figure 15–47

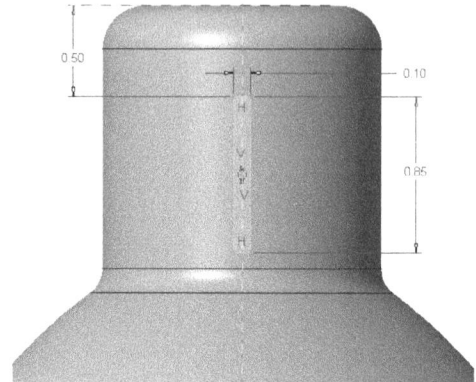

Figure 15–48

5. Complete the sketch.

6. Click ◿ (Remove Material) and extrude through all surfaces.

Click ✎ to flip the direction of feature creation, if required.

7. Click ✔ (Complete Feature) to complete the feature. The model displays as shown in Figure 15–49.

Figure 15–49

Task 3 - Create an Axis pattern on the extrusion.

1. Select the extrude that was just created, right-click and select **Pattern**.

2. Expand the Pattern Type drop-down list and select **Axis**.

3. Select the axis running through the center of the model as the reference to pattern about, as shown in Figure 15–50.

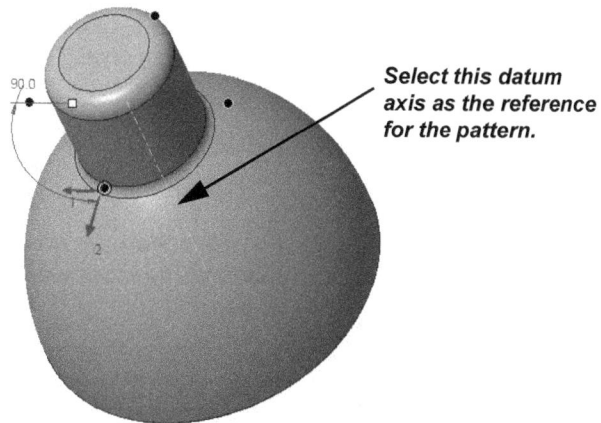

Select this datum axis as the reference for the pattern.

Figure 15–50

4. In the *Pattern* dashboard, click ⚄ (Equal Spacing) to ensure that instances are equally spaced. Accept the default angular extent value of **360** degrees.

5. Set the number of instances in the first direction to **18**. The pattern preview displays as shown in Figure 15–51.

6. Click ✓ (Complete Feature) to complete the pattern.

7. In the In-graphics toolbar, click ✳ (Datum Display Filters) and select ⦿ (Axis Display). The model displays as shown in Figure 15–52.

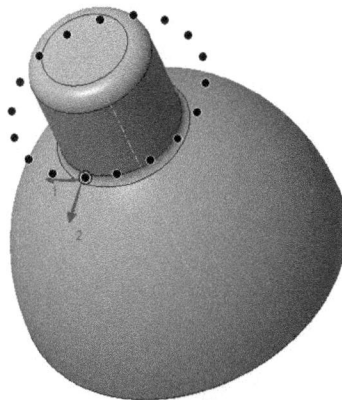

Figure 15–51

Figure 15–52

8. Save the part and erase it from memory.

Chapter Review Questions

1. Which type(s) of dimension pattern requires the shortest regeneration time?

   a. Identical

   b. Variable

   c. General

2. For the pattern shown in Figure 15–53, which dimension of the pattern leader was selected to drive the direction of the pattern?

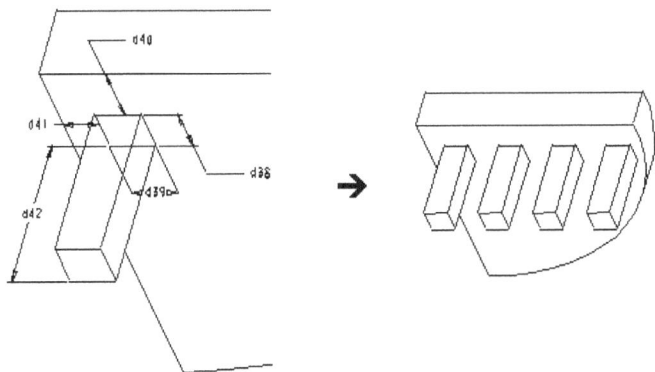

Figure 15–53

   a. d38

   b. d39

   c. d40

   d. d41

   e. d42

3. The model shown in Figure 15–54 has a pattern of extruded holes that were created in one direction. What was the number of pattern instances that were defined in the *Pattern dashboard*?

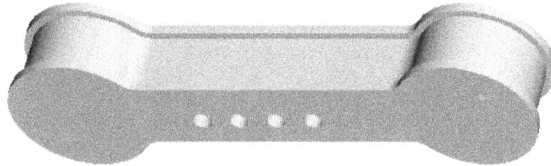

Figure 15–54

a. 1

b. 2

c. 3

d. 4

4. How do you remove an instance from a pattern?

a. Right-click and select **Delete Pattern Instance**.

b. Select the black hot spot.

c. Right-click and select **Suppress**.

d. Right-click and select **Hide**.

5. How do you restore a previously removed instance from a pattern?

a. Right-click and select **Undelete Pattern Instance**.

b. Select the white hot spot.

c. Right-click and select **Resume**.

d. Right-click and select **Unhide**.

6. Which of the following occurs if you select the pattern leader for a radial pattern, right-click, and select **Delete**?

a. The pattern leader is deleted and the second instance becomes the pattern leader.

b. The system prompts you to enter the instances to be deleted.

c. The pattern leader is deleted and all instances are also removed from the model.

d. All of the instances are deleted from the model. However, the pattern leader remains in the model.

7. Which of the following references can be used to drive a Directional pattern? (Select all that apply.)

   a. A plane (surface or datum plane)

   b. Linear curve

   c. 3D curve

   d. Coordinate System Axis

   e. Axis

8. Which pattern types can be used to pattern a Radial Hole? (Select all that apply.)

   a. Axial Pattern

   b. Dimensional Pattern

   c. Directional Pattern

   d. Fill Pattern

9. To create the radial pattern of cuts shown in Figure 15–55, you need a central _____.

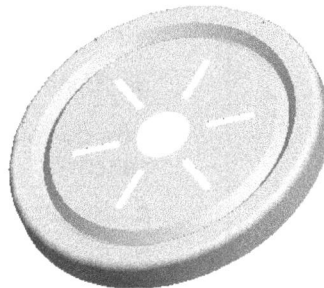

Figure 15–55

   a. Axis

   b. Plane

   c. Coordinate system

Command Summary

Button	Command	Location
	Pattern	• **Ribbon:** *Model* tab in the *Editing* group

Chapter 16

Creating Relations

In this chapter, you learn about creating relationships between parameters and dimensions using relations. This functionality, along with knowledge about the creation and verification of relations, enables you to build design intent into your model.

Learning Objectives in this Chapter

- Start the creation of a relation and change the dimension display type so that you can identify the symbols associated with a dimension.
- Enter the equations to capture required design intent.
- Edit and create equations between the model and the user-defined parameters.
- Create user-defined parameters in a model for driving the model geometry or providing additional model information.
- Edit model dimension that drive the geometry to ensure that the model updates as required.

16.1 Creating Relations

Adding relations incorporates design intent into a model by ensuring that the model behaves as intended if changes occur. Relations are established by creating mathematical relationships between dimensions and/or parameters in a specific feature, or between features.

General Steps

Use the following general steps to add a relation:

1. Start the creation of the relation.
2. Determine the required dimension symbols.
3. Enter the relation.
4. Complete the relation and flex the model.

Step 1 - Start the creation of the relation.

*You can also select Model tab>**Model Intent>Relations**.*

Relations can be added to a model by selecting the *Tools* tab and clicking ᵈ= (Relations). The Relations dialog box opens as shown in Figure 16–1.

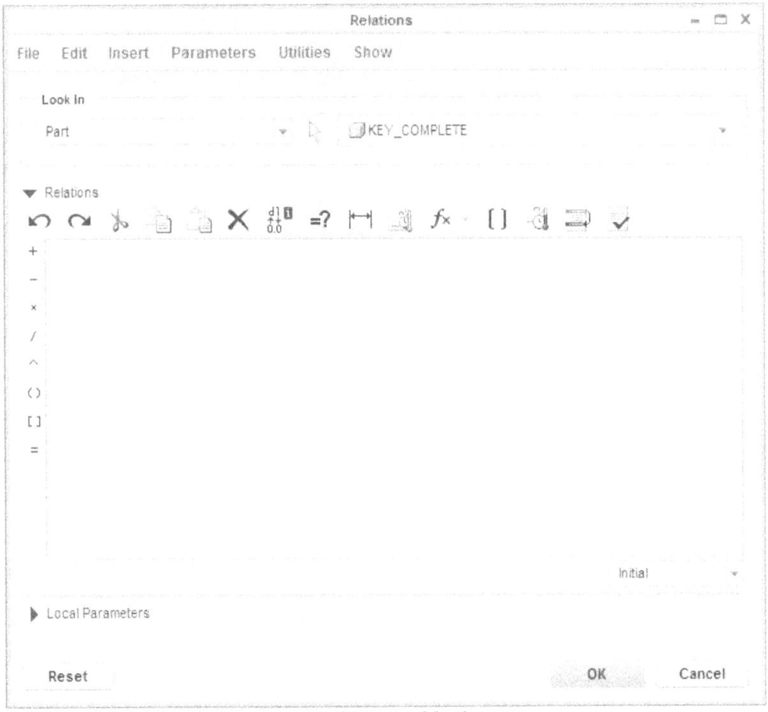

Figure 16–1

Step 2 - Determine the required dimension symbols.

All Creo Parametric dimensions have a unique symbol that identifies them. Symbols, in combination with mathematical operators, are used to write an equation. Dimension symbols display as **d#**, where the # indicates the specific dimension. Each number is unique in the model.

To display dimension symbols while editing, the model, click

(Switch Dimensions) in the Model Intent group in the Tools tab. You can also select the Model tab>Model Intent>Switch Symbols.

- To display the dimension symbol for a feature, select the required features on the model or in the model tree.

- Each dimension value associated with the selected feature displays and is automatically displayed in its symbolic form, similar to those shown in Figure 16–2. Click (Switch Dimensions) to toggle the dimension values between their symbolic and numeric forms.

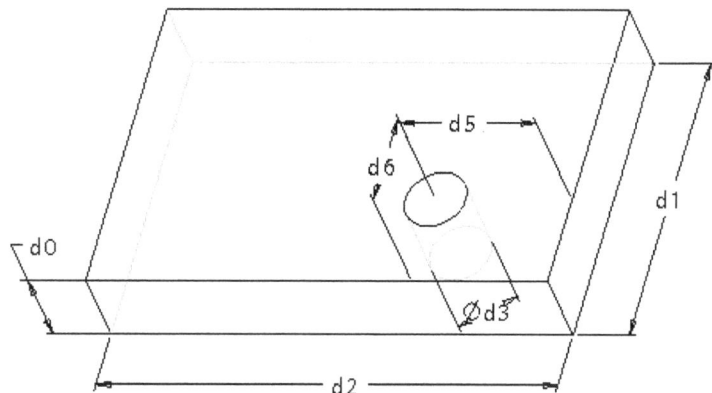

Figure 16–2

Step 3 - Enter the relation.

Alternatively, you can add a relation to the model by entering the equation directly in the main graphic window when modifying a driven dimension value.

Relations are entered in the main area in the Relations dialog box. You can type the equation manually or insert the symbols directly from the model. To insert a dimension symbol from the model, place the text cursor at the location in which the dimension symbol is to be placed in the relation and select the dimension on the model. The Creo Parametric software provides additional tools for defining relations.

Relation Types

The two types of relations that can be used are described as follows:

Relation Type	Description
Equality	Equates one parameter or dimension symbol as a function of another, as shown in Figure 16–3. Example: d36 = 2.75 + d20 * (1 - d42)

Conditional	Use IF/ELSE/ENDIF statements to equate one parameter or dimension symbol based on a specified condition, as shown in Figure 16–5.
	
	Example:
	
	IF (d12 + d16) <= 10
	
	d3=d6
	
	ELSE
	
	d4=d6
	
	ENDIF

The type of relation used should be based on the design intent. For example, if the design intent for the model shown in Figure 16–2 is to center the hole on the block, an equality relation is used. Figure 16–3 shows an example of an equality relation.

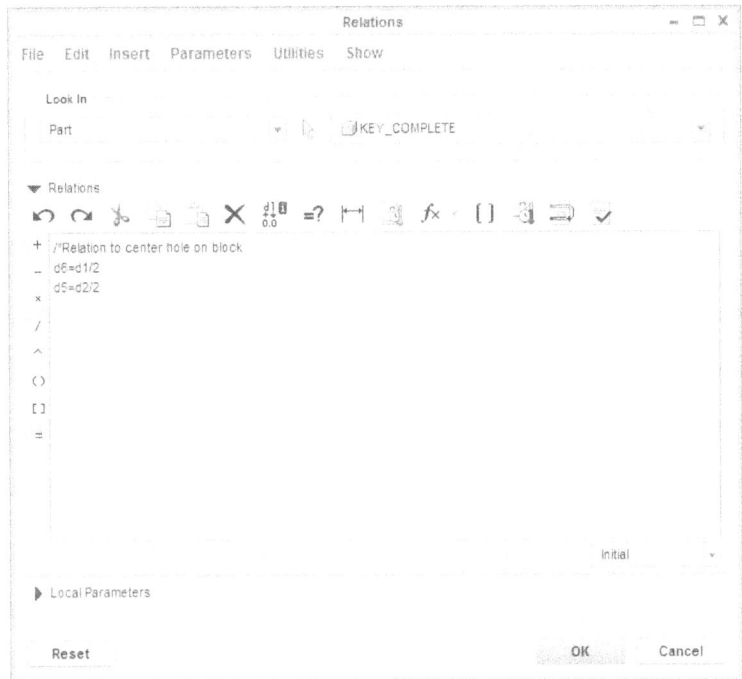

Figure 16–3

After adding the relation and regenerating the model, it displays with the hole positioned in the center, as shown in Figure 16–4.

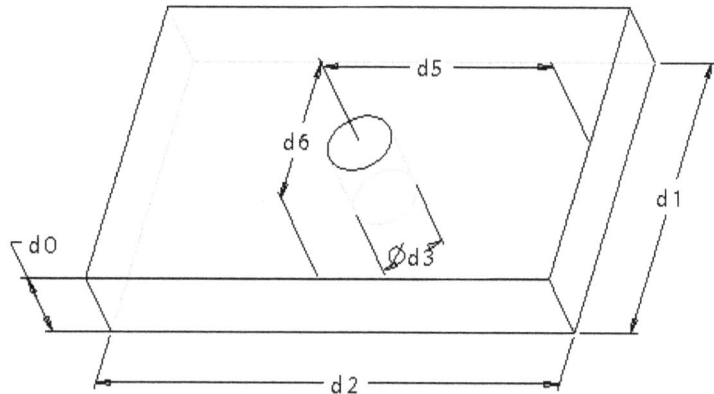

Figure 16–4

You can also use a conditional relation to drive the model shown in Figure 16–4. The conditional relation shown in Figure 16–5 defines two possible block sizes, **10x12** or **6x8**. If the diameter of the hole is greater or equal to **5.25**, the box size is **10x12**. Otherwise, it is **6x8**.

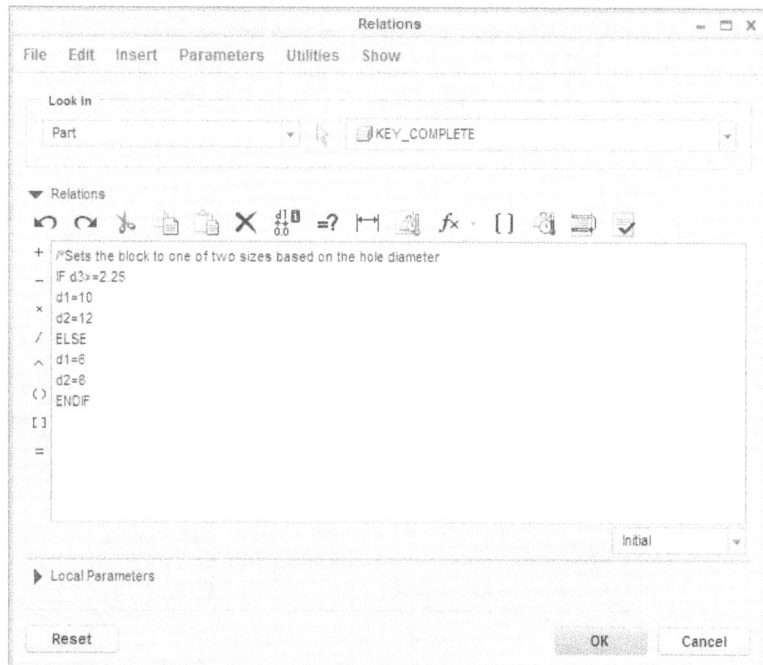

Figure 16–5

Comments

Comments are used to describe the intent of the relation. Comments are recommended because they are helpful for others using the model and/or for you if time has passed since the relation was added to the model. To add a comment to the relation, the characters /* must precede the statement.

For example:

> /* Relations to center hole
> d6=d1/2
>
> d5=d2/2
> /* Relations to control height
> d0=d2*0.25

Operators

The operators that can be used in relations are described as follows:

Operator	Description
+	Addition
-	Subtraction
*	Multiplication
/	Division
^	Exponentiation
()	Grouping
[]	Grouping
=	Equality
>	Greater than
>=	Greater than or equal
<	Less than
<=	Less than or equal
==	Equal to
!=, <>, ~=	Not equal to
&	And
|	Or
!, ~	Not

Functions

You can enter functions directly or select them from a list using

$f\times$ *(Insert Function).*

Some of functions that can be used in relations are described as follows:

Mathematical Functions

sin( )	tanh( )
cos( )	sqrt( )
tan( )	log( )
asin( )	ln( )
acos( )	exp( )
atan( )	abs( )
sinh( )	ceil( ) - the smallest integer not less than the real value
cosh( )	floor( ) - the largest integer not greater than the real value

Parameters

You can enter these parameters directly or select them using

$f\times$ *(Insert Function).*

System-defined parameters and user-defined parameters can be used to define the relation.

System-Defined Parameters

System-defined parameters are described as follows:

Predefined parameters

PI (= 3.1415...)	Mathematical constant, π.
G (= 9.8 m/sec2)	Gravity constant.
C1, C2, C3, C4 (= 1.0, 2.0, 3.0, 4.0)	Common parameters for all models in the current session that can be modified by relations.

Mass Property	Description	Mass Property	Description
mp_mass	Mass	mp_cg_x	X of center gravity
mp_density	Density	mp_cg_y	Y of center gravity
mp_volume	Volume	mp_cg_z	Z of center gravity
mp_surf_area	Surface area		

User-Defined Parameters

User-defined parameters can be created and added by expanding the *Local Parameters* area at the bottom of the

Relations dialog box. To create a new parameter, click ✚ (Add New Parameter) and enter the *Name*, *Type*, and *Value* of the parameter. The parameter types are listed in the Type drop-down list, as shown in Figure 16–6.

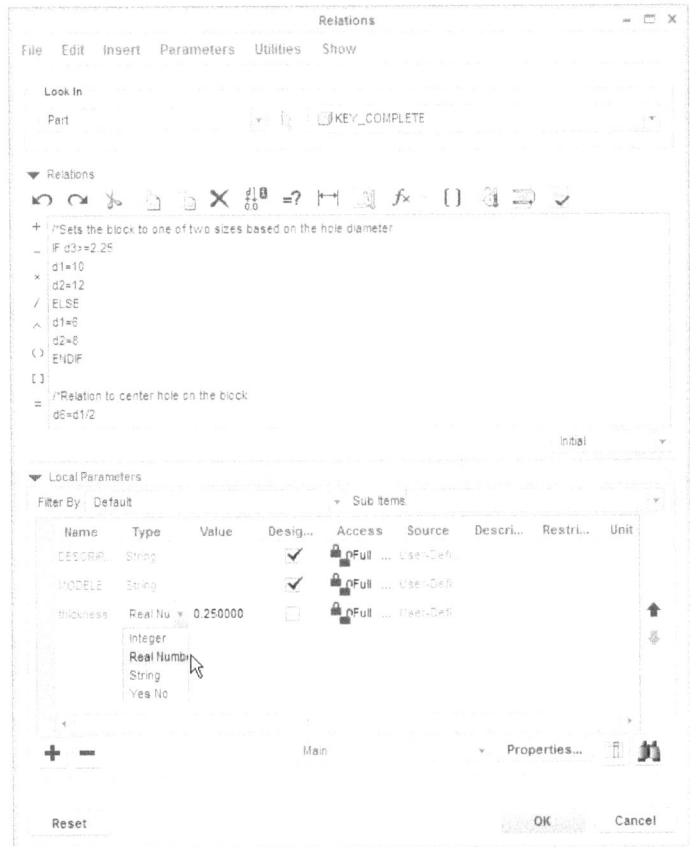

Figure 16–6

To insert the parameter into the relation, you can enter the name manually or select the parameter name in the *Local Parameters* area in the dialog box, right-click, and select **Insert to Relations**, as shown in Figure 16–7.

The parameter is inserted where the cursor was last placed in the Relations area in the dialog box.

Alternatively, you can click [ ] (Insert Parameter) in the Relations dialog box to open the Select Parameter dialog box, as shown in Figure 16–8. Select the parameter and click **Insert Selected** to insert the parameter at the cursor location in the relation.

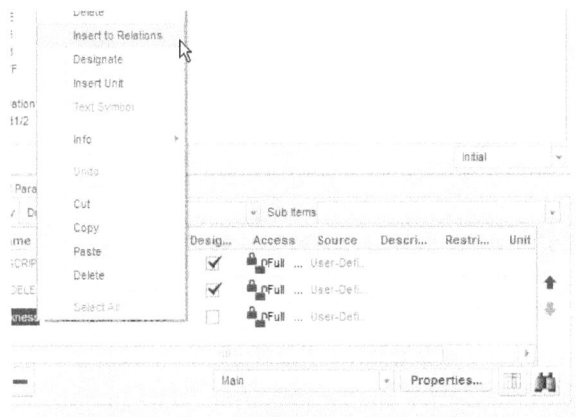

Figure 16–7

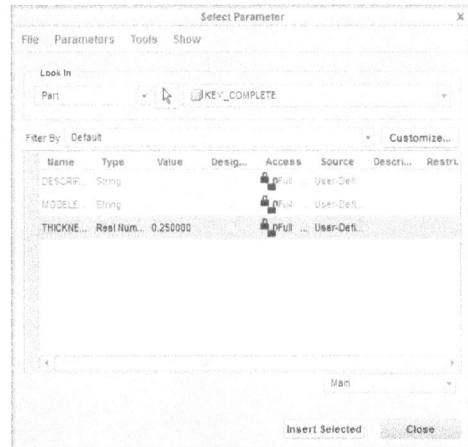

Figure 16–8

Sort Relation

Sorting relations enables you to change the order in which the relations are listed in the Relations dialog box. The order in which they are added to a model is important because it defines the order of regeneration. Checking and considering the order is important to ensure that the relations work in the way that they are intended.

For example, models can contain relations that are dependent on the values of other relations. You can use the **Sort Order** option to ensure that dependent relations follow the correct relations.

For example:

    /* Relation to drive the diameter of the hole
    d2=d5/2
    d5=d6*1.2

According to this relation, the first line is dependent on the second. When the model is regenerated, an error in the *Message* area prompts you that: *Some relations are no longer satisfied in PART for D2.* Regenerating the model again temporarily corrects the problem. However, to permanently correct it, the order of relations needs to be changed.

To change the sort order, you can manually cut and paste the relation lines as required, or have the system sort them by clicking ▦ (Sort Relations).

After sorting the relation, it displays as follows:

/* Relation to drive the diameter of the hole

d5=d6*1.2
d2=d5/2

With the new sort order, the model regenerates successfully each time.

Step 4 - Complete the relation and flex the model.

Once you finish adding the relation in the Relation dialog box, click **OK** and regenerate the model. Once regenerated, it is recommended to test or *flex* the model to verify that the relation captures the required design intent. You can test the model by editing the driving dimension values to see that it changes as required.

For the relation that centers the hole on the block, test it by modifying the block's overall dimensions. Verify that the hole remains centered regardless of model size, as shown in Figure 16-9.

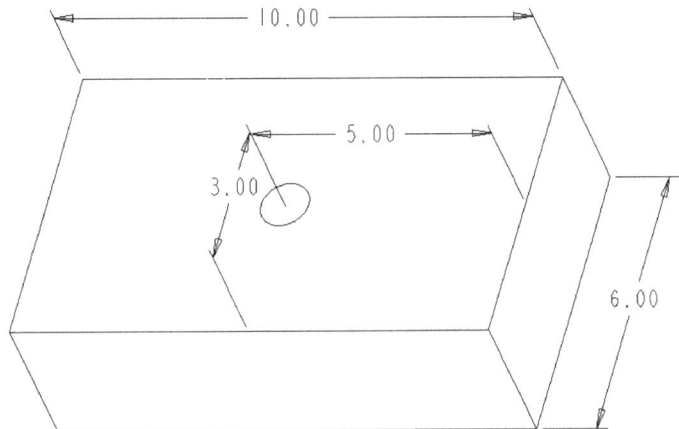

Figure 16-9

Practice 16a | Storage Bin

Practice Objectives

- Start the creation of the relation, show dimensions in the model, and obtain their symbolic value for use in an equation.
- Add a comment line and add an equation using the Relation dialog box.
- Edit model dimension that drives the geometry to ensure that the model updates as required.

In this practice, you will open an existing part, investigate the part to become familiar with it, and then write a relation to capture the design intent. The design intent that you need to capture is to ensure that the thickness of the part changes relative to the height so that structural integrity is maintained.

Task 1 - Open a part file.

1. Set the working directory to the *Chapter 16/practice 16a* folder.

2. Open **storage_bin.prt**. Investigate the part.

3. Edit the **Shell 1** feature. Note that the shell *Thickness* is set to **0.125**, as shown in Figure 16–10.

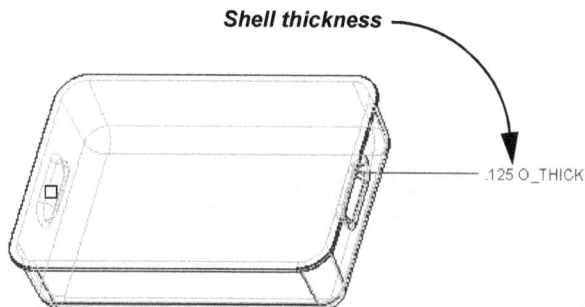

Shell thickness

.125 O_THICK

Figure 16–10

4. Repaint the screen.

5. Edit the **Extrude 1** feature. Display the dimensions and note that the *Height* is set to **4.00**, as shown in Figure 16–11.

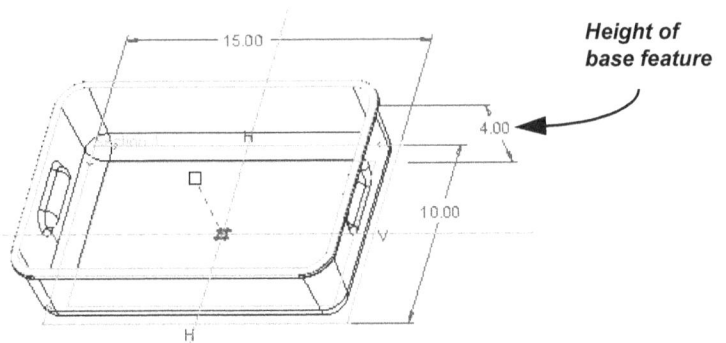

Height of base feature

Figure 16–11

Task 2 - Modify the part.

1. Change the *4.00* value of **Extrude 1** to **8.0**.

2. Regenerate the part.

3. Edit **Shell 1** and note that the *Thickness* is still set to **0.125**, as shown in Figure 16–12.

4. Set the *Height* of **Extrude 1** back to **4.00**, as shown in Figure 16–14.

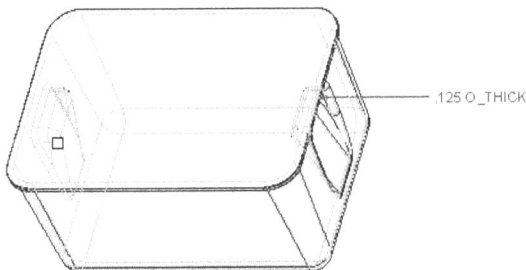

Figure 16–12

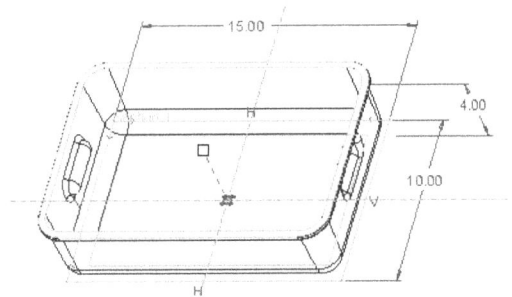

Figure 16–13

Task 3 - Write a relation.

Design Considerations

The analysis department reports that the wall thickness of this part must always be a ratio of 1/16:1 relative to the height of the part to maintain structural integrity. In this task, you will write a relation to capture this design intent.

*You can also select the Model tab>**Model Intent>Relations** to open the Relation Editor.*

1. Select the *Tools* tab and in the Model Intent group, click d= (Relations). The Relations editor opens.

2. Enter the following comment line: */*This relation sets the shell thickness to be 1/16 of the height*, as shown in Figure 16–14.

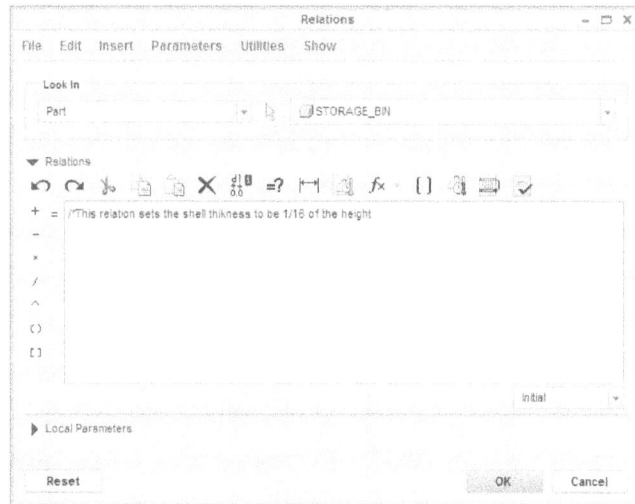

Figure 16–14

3. In the model tree, select **Extrude 1** and **Shell 1**. The symbolic dimensions display as shown in Figure 16–15.

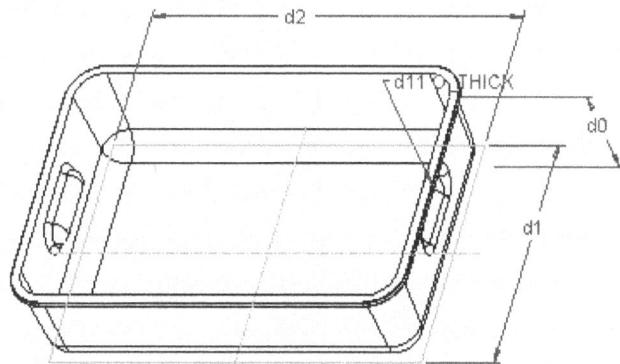

Figure 16–15

4. Enter the relation **d11=d0*0.063**. You can select **d11** and **d0** from the view window to insert them into the relation. The completed relation is entered into the editor, as shown in Figure 16–16.

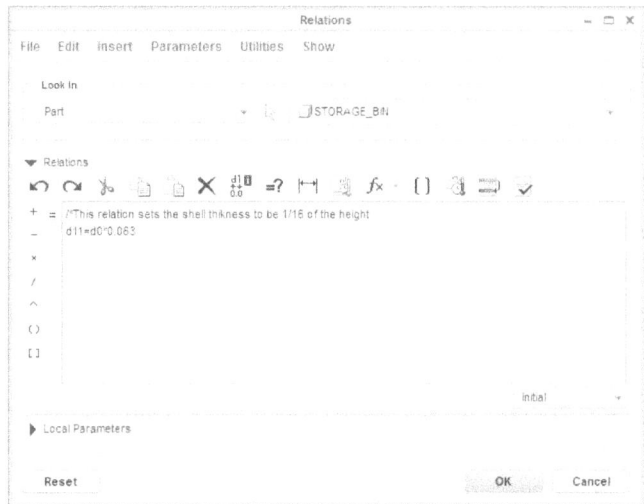

Figure 16–16

5. Click **OK** to close the Relations dialog box and regenerate the model.

6. Change the *4.00* value of **Extrude 1** to **8.0** and regenerate the part.

7. Edit **Shell 1** and note that the *Thickness* value has changed relative the *Height*, as shown in Figure 16–17.

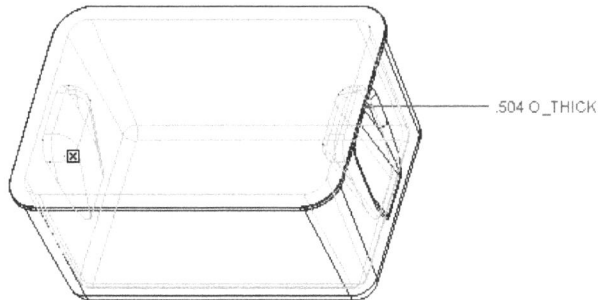

.504 O_THICK

Figure 16–17

8. Save the part and erase it from memory.

Practice 16b | Relations

Practice Objectives

- Create user-defined parameters for use in equations.
- Add a comment line and add an equation using the Relation dialog box.
- Insert the user-defined parameter to use in the relation.
- Edit model dimension that drives the geometry to ensure that the model updates as required.

In this practice, you will write relations so that the model shown in Figure 16–18, conforms to the following design intent:

- The outside diameter of the center protrusion is driven by a thickness parameter.

- The position of the bolt circle diameter of the mounting holes is always centered on the flat surface of the flange, regardless of the flange size.

Figure 16–18

Task 1 - Add a relation that drives the outside diameter of the center protrusion based on the thickness.

1. Set the working directory to the *Chapter 16\practice 16b* folder.

2. Open **coupling.prt**.

3. Model the inside diameter of the center hole from *15* to **10**. Note that the wall thickness of the center protrusion changes. The design intent requires the wall thickness to remain constant and the outside diameter to change.

4. Select the *Tools* tab and click d= (Relations) in the Model Intent group.

5. Expand the *Local Parameters* area, near the bottom of the dialog box, as shown in Figure 16–19.

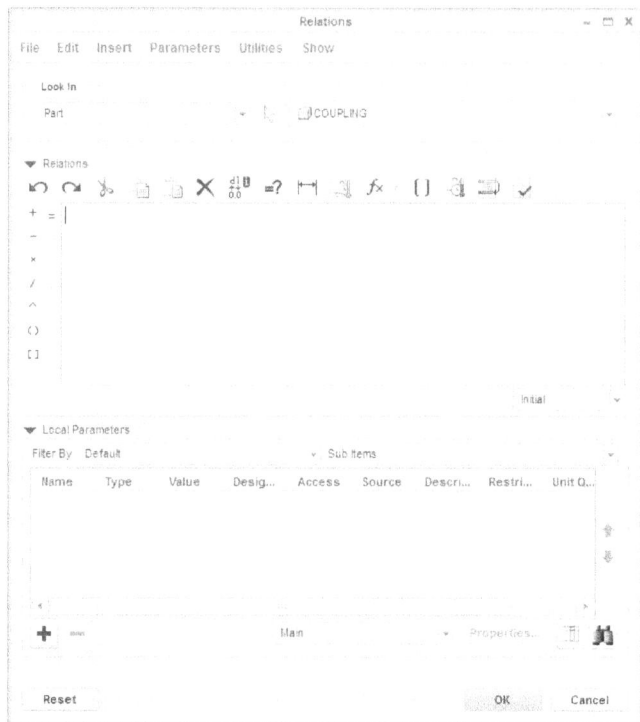

Figure 16–19

6. Click ✚ (Add New Parameter) to create a new parameter.

7. Set the following:

    - *Name:* **THICKNESS**
    - *Type:* **Real Number**
    - *Value:* **5.0**
    - *Relations* area: **/* This relation sets the OD to be driven by the thickness**

8. Press <Enter>.

Repaint the graphic window if the dimensions are not displayed.

9. Select the base protrusion and the center hole in the model or model tree.

10. Select the dimension for the outside diameter, **d24**, on the model. Enter **=**.

11. Select the dimension on the model for the center hole diameter, **d8**. Enter **+2***.

12. In the *Local Parameters* area, select **THICKNESS**, right-click, and select **Insert to Relations**. The dialog box displays as shown in Figure 16–20.

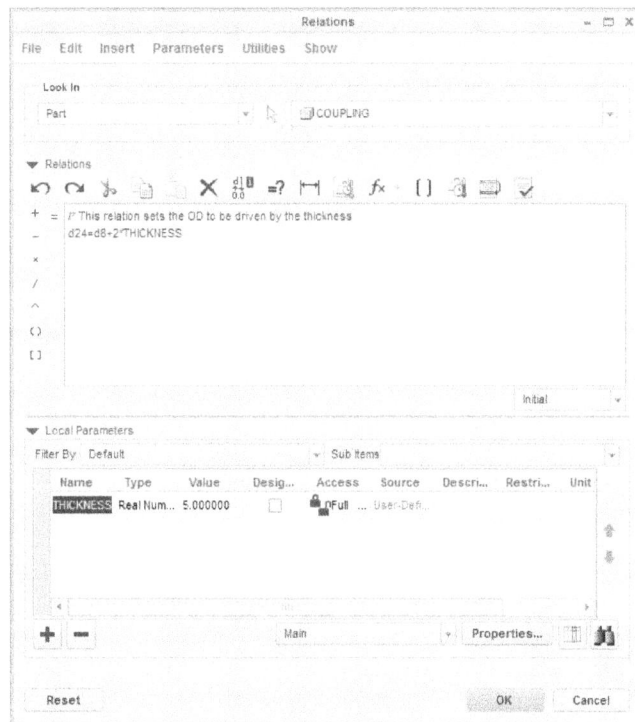

Figure 16–20

13. Click **OK** to close the Relations dialog box and regenerate the model.

14. Change the center hole *Diameter* from *10* to **20** and regenerate the part to test the relation. The model displays, as shown in Figure 16–21.

Figure 16–21

Task 2 - Add a relation to position the mounting holes to always remain in the center of the flat surface of the flange.

1. Open the Relations dialog box.

2. Click ⊢—⊣ (Display Specified Dimension), enter **d12** and press <Enter>. Dimension **d12** displays on the model. Repeat the procedure for dimensions **d2** and **d24**. The dimensions display in the graphic window, enabling you to understand the following relation.

3. Enter the following relation:

   **/* This relation centers the mounting holes radially on the flange
   d12=(d2+d24)/2**

4. Click **OK** to close the Relations dialog box and regenerate the model.

5. Change the enter hole *Diameter* from *20* to **10** and regenerate the model. Note that the position of the mounting holes remains radially centered on the flange, as shown in Figure 16–22.

Figure 16–22

6. Save the part and erase it from memory.

Chapter Review Questions

1. You can use the Relations dialog box to add a relation to a model. Select the *Model* tab and click d= (Relations) to open the dialog box.

   a. True

   b. False

2. Which of the following statements are true regarding relations? (Select all that apply.)

   a. Dimensions and parameters can be used in a relation to drive a value.

   b. Equations can be manually entered in the Relations dialog box.

   c. Equations can be created using a combination of manual entry and selecting dimensions directly from the model.

   d. Creo Parametric enables you to create both equality and conditional relations.

3. Which of the following is the correct syntax that must be used to precede a comment statement for a relation?

   a. */

   b. !

   c. /*

   d. #

4. Which of the following relations only centers the hole if the length and width are equivalent as shown in Figure 16–23?

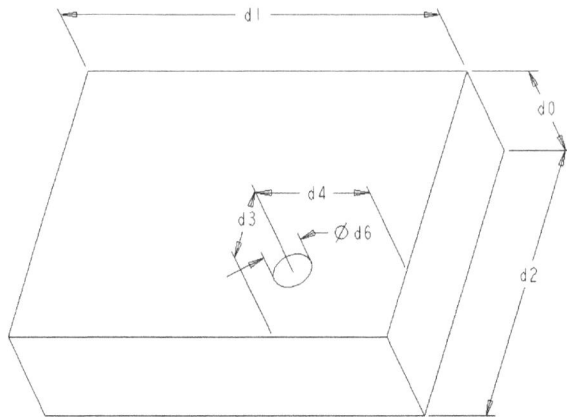

Figure 16–23

a. /*relation to center the hole if the length and width are equivalent

d4=d1/2

d3=d2/2

b. /*relation to center the hole if the length and width are equivalent

d1=d4/2

d2=d3/2

c. /*relation to center the hole if the length and width are equivalent

d1=d2

d4=d1/2

d3=d2/2

d. /*relation to center the hole if the length and width are equivalent

if d1=d2

d4=d1/2

d3=d2/2

endif

5. Which of the following statements is true regarding the following relation? (Select all that apply.)

/*relation to control the thickness of the model

THICKNESS=(d2+d15)/2

a. The relation is a conditional.

b. A comment is associated to the relation.

c. A parameter is being driven in this relation.

d. d2 and d15 are driven dimensions.

6. Which of the following icons enables you to select a function from a predefined list?

a.

b. $f\times$

c. [ ]

d.

7. Relations can be added to the model by entering an equation in the main graphic window when modifying a driven dimension.

a. True

b. False

8. Which of the following are valid operators that can be used in a relation? (Select all that apply.)

a. ^

b. !

c. ( )

d. #

9. Which of the following best describes how the following relation affects the model as shown in Figure 16–24?

d0=3*d6

d3=d4

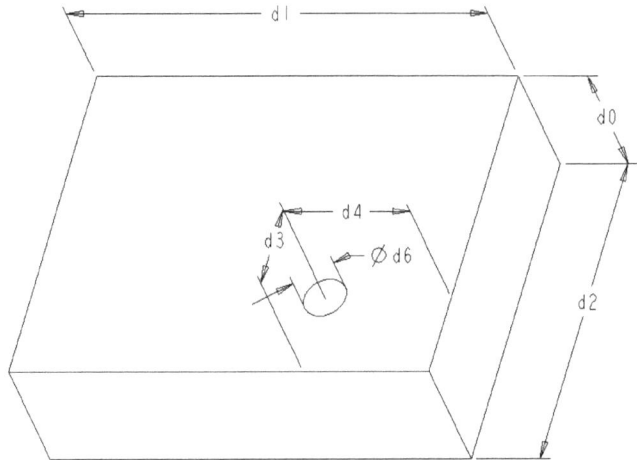

Figure 16–24

a. The depth of the base protrusion is equal to the diameter of the hole and the hole is centered on the base protrusion.

b. The depth of the base protrusion is equal to three times the diameter of the hole and the hole is centered on the base protrusion.

c. The depth of the base protrusion is equal to three times the diameter of the hole and the values for the horizontal and vertical hole dimensions are equivalent.

d. The depth of the base protrusion is equal to three times the diameter of the hole and the values for the horizontal and vertical hole dimensions are equivalent. In addition, d1 and d2 are equivalent.

Command Summary

Button	Command	Location
d=	**Relation**	• **Ribbon:** *Tools* tab in the *Model Intent* group • **Ribbon:** *Model* tab in the *Model Intent* group
¹⁵fx	**Switch Symbol**	• **Ribbon:** *Sketch* tab in the *Model Intent* group • Relations dialog box
[ ]	**Parameters**	• **Ribbon:** *Tools* tab in the *Model Intent* group • Relations dialog box

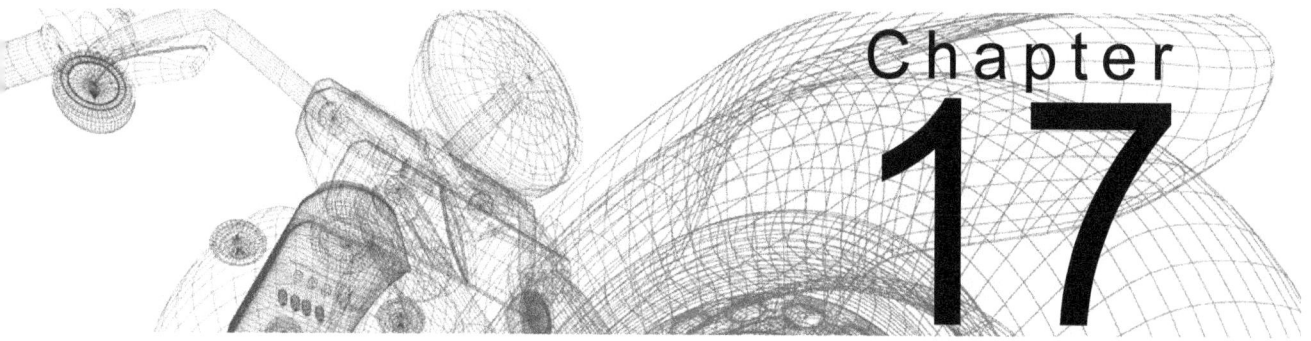

Customizing Creo Parametric

Customizing the Creo Parametric software enables you to change the system's default appearance and options to meet specific needs or preferences. Customization settings can be set to affect the entire company or can be user-specific.Customizing enables you to create and follow a more efficient workflow. This chapter covers some basic customization requirements.

Learning Objectives in this Chapter

- Understand how the categories in the Options dialog box can be used to globally customize the modeling environment.
- Customize the graphic and geometry colors using the Creo Parametric Options dialog box.
- Assign command aliases using keyboard keys for commonly used commands.
- Customize the ribbon using the shortcut menu or the Creo Parametric Options dialog box.
- Customize and add commands to the Quick Access Toolbar.
- Customize the system to meet preferences and requirements.
- Search the configuration options using keywords.
- Implement the changes set in the Configuration Editor.
- Modify the appearance and colors of parts, assemblies, and surfaces.
- Customize the model tree by specifying what items are displayed and by adding columns.

17.1 Customizing the Interface

You can customize almost any part of the Creo Parametric interface, including the window display, toolbar icons, and the tabs. The icons in the toolbars and ribbons provide shortcuts to commonly used commands. These commands can be added or removed to customize the toolbar or ribbon area. You can also place user-defined icons representing mapkeys.

• To customize the Creo Parametric interface, select **File> Options**. The Creo Parametric Options dialog box opens as shown in Figure 17–1. The dialog box enables you to customize toolbars, commands, navigation options, browser settings, and other interface options.

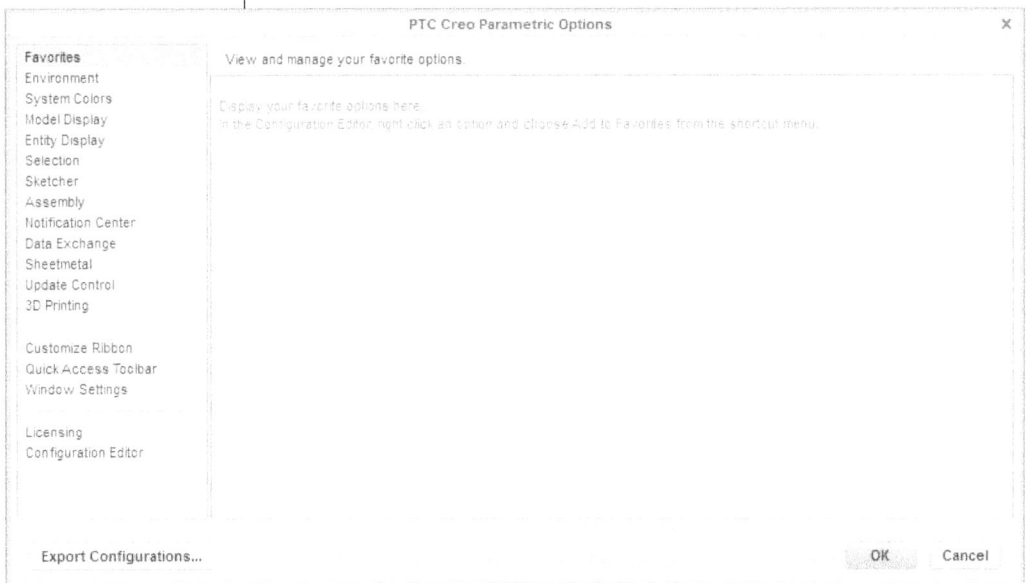

Figure 17–1

• The Customize dialog box is divided into multiple categories for customization.

Favorites

The *Favorites* category enables you to add and remove frequently used configuration options, as shown Figure 17–2.

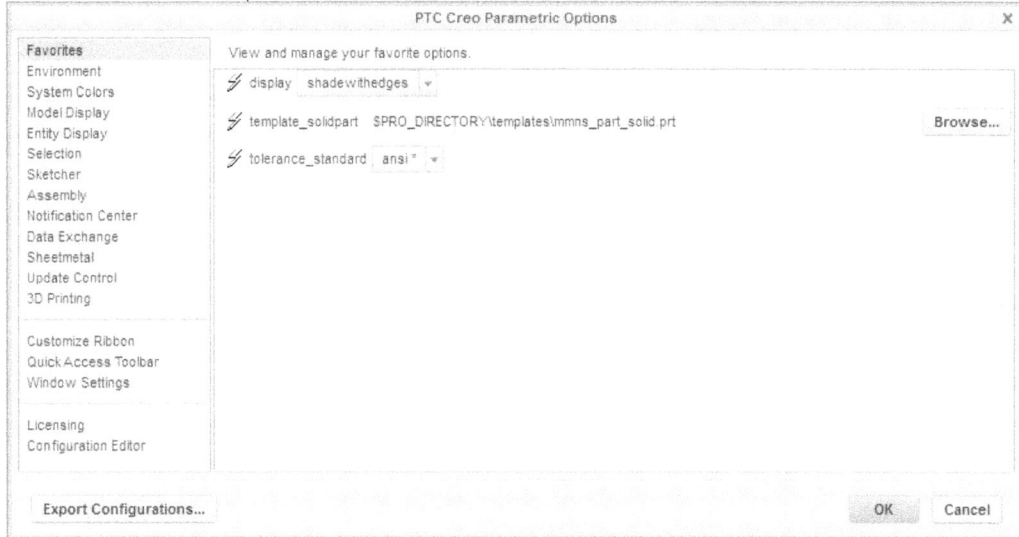

Figure 17–2

How To: Add the Configuration Option to the Favorites Category

1. In the Creo Parametric Options dialog box, select **Configuration Editor**.
2. Select the configuration option, right-click on the option, and select **Add to Favorites**.
3. Click **Export Configurations** to save the changes.

Environment

The Environment options in Creo Parametric enable you the set various settings. For example, you can set the working directory, save the display with the model, and create mapkeys.

System Colors

The Creo Parametric software has assigned specific colors to entities, but you can customize the default system colors. This ability is useful for adding contrast and definition to presentation materials and other purposes. You can modify the overall color scheme, interface colors, or individual feature types.

Model Display

The Creo Parametric software enables you to customize the orientation, display, and rendering of the model in the Creo Options dialog box, as shown in Figure 17–3.

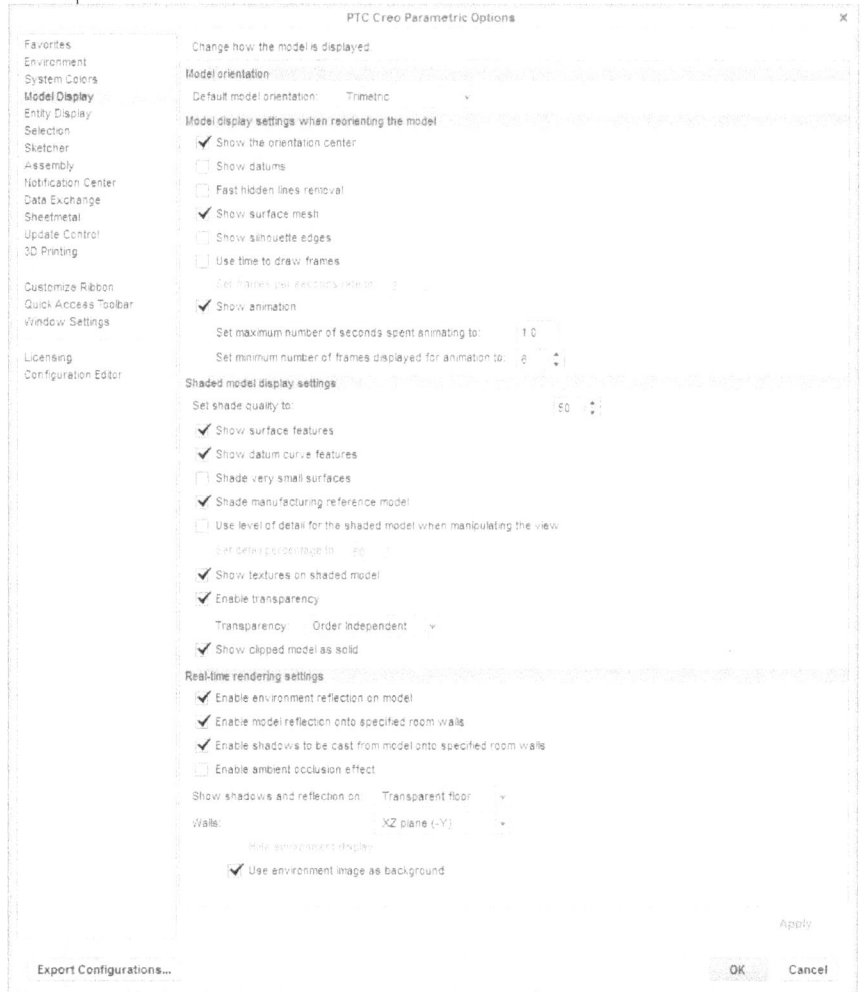

Figure 17–3

Entity Display

The **Entity Display** option enables you to change the display of geometry, show/hide datums, and show/hide annotations. These options, along with several others, are shown in Figure 17–4.

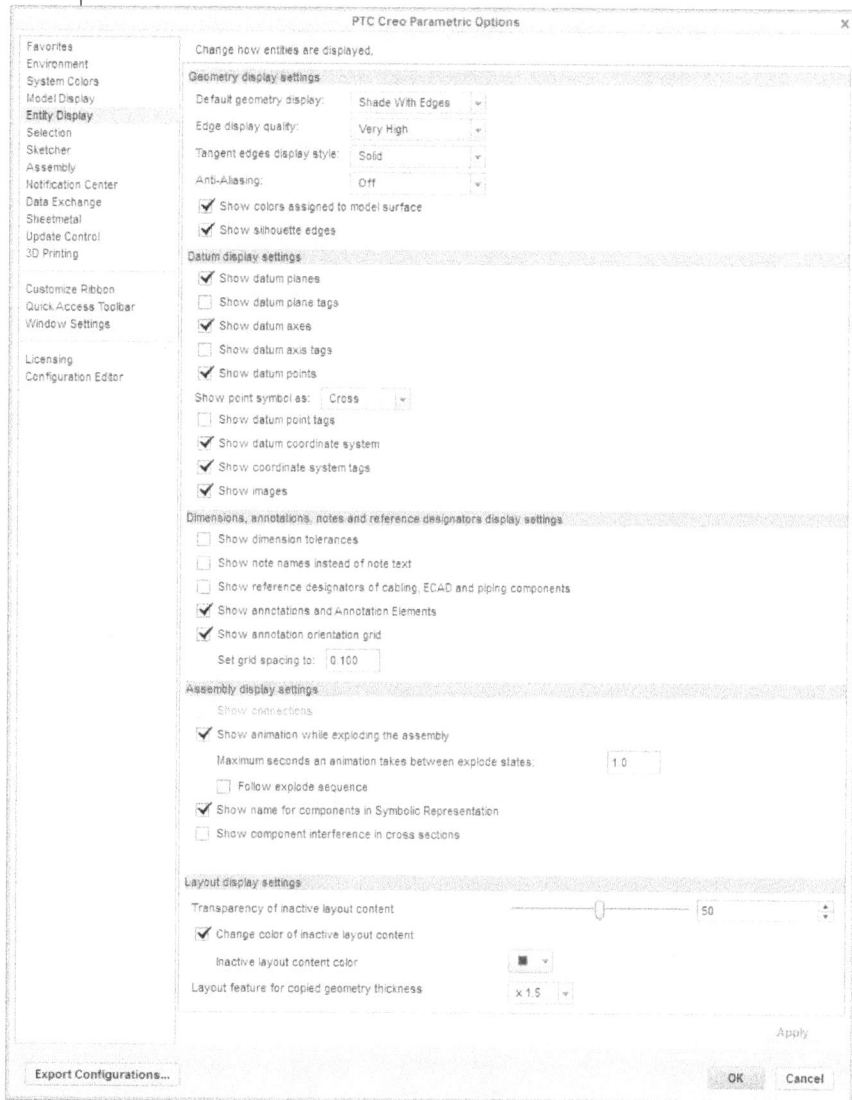

Figure 17–4

Selection

The selection filter is located in the bottom right of the view window. The options in the Filter drop-down list enable you to refine what you can select in the model. This filter changes depending on the operation you are performing. For example, if you are in the *Model* tab, the default option is set to **smart**. The Creo Parametric Options dialog box enables you to specify the options that are located in the selection filter, as shown in Figure 17–5.

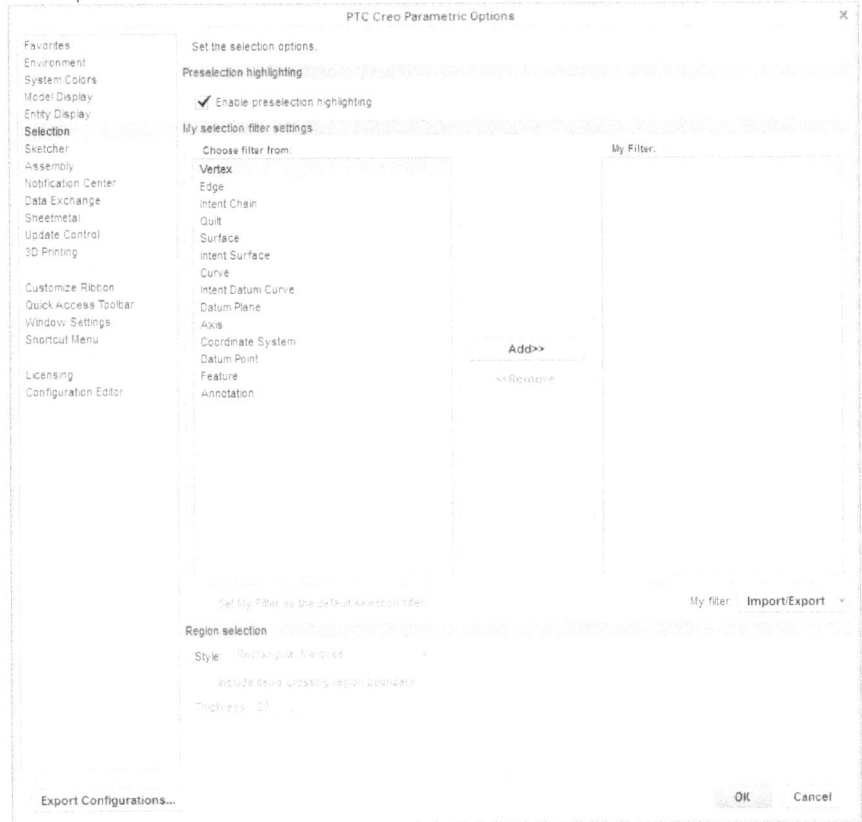

Figure 17–5

The changes that you make to the settings are only used for the current session. The default settings are defined by the configuration file. To save the changes that you have made to the configuration file, click **Export Configurations**, specify the location, and click **OK**.

17.2 System Colors

For complex assemblies, you can change the colors of parts and/or features to easily distinguish them from one another and to add contrast and definition to presentation materials. The Creo Parametric software enables you to customize the default system colors for such purposes and to modify the overall color scheme, interface colors, or individual feature types.

- To customize the colors, select **File> Options** and select the **System Colors** option. The System Colors options are available, as shown in Figure 17–6. The options enable you to customize the colors of datum features, geometry, graphics, sketched features, and/or the interface.

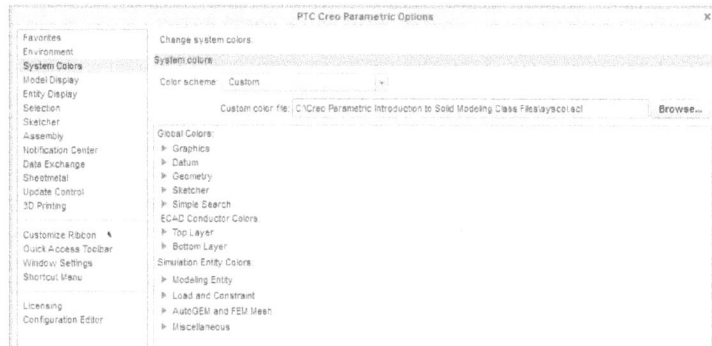

Figure 17–6

- The Global Colors section of the System Colors group is divided in various categories for customization.

Graphics

The *Graphics* category enables you to modify the colors of certain features on your models. Click **Graphics** to expand and show the items in the *Graphics* category as shown in Figure 17–7. Click a color swatch to change the color of any item.

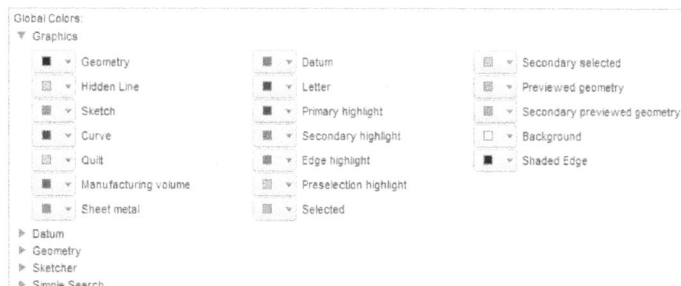

Figure 17–7

Datum	The *Datum* category enables you to modify the colors of all of the datum features, including datum planes, axes, points, and coordinate systems.
Geometry	The *Geometry* category enables you to modify the colors of sheetmetal geometry, surface geometry, cables, model and cast surfaces.
Sketcher	The *Sketcher* category enables you to modify the colors of all the sketched features, including centerlines, construction geometry, and dimensions.
Simple Search	The *Simple* search category enables you to modify the colors of miscellaneous items including failed items, frozen components, and packaged items.
Color Scheme	The Color Scheme drop-down list that displays at the top of the dialog box also enables you to change the color scheme. This builds contrast in the appearance of your models. Figure 17–8 shows the **Color Scheme** menu.

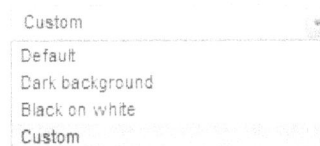

Custom

Default
Dark background
Black on white
Custom

Figure 17–8

To save your changes, click **Export**. The Creo Parametric interface displays with the new selected colors for the duration of the session. If you want to apply your new settings to the following sessions, you must point to the file with the saved settings in the config file option **system_colors_file**.

17.3 Creating Mapkeys

A mapkey is a keyboard macro that executes a series of menu selections. For operations that are used regularly, a mapkey is useful instead of going through multiple menu selections.

How To: Create Mapkeys

1. Select **File>Options>Environment**. Click **Mapkeys Settings** to open the Mapkeys dialog box as shown in Figure 17–9. The dialog box enables you to create, modify, delete, and save mapkeys.

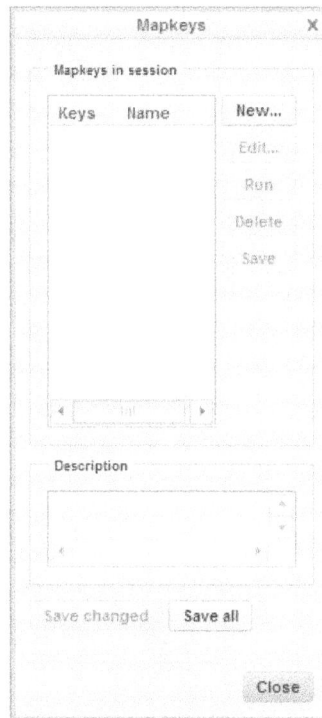

Figure 17–9

2. Click **New** to create a new mapkey. The Record Mapkey dialog box opens as shown in Figure 17–10. Then, select a key sequence in the top drop-down list, to be used to activate the macro. It can be a sequence of numbers or letters or a function key. Select **$F#** to use a function key, where # is the required function key number.

The name and description are optional. However, it is useful to name the mapkey if it is going to be added as a toolbar option. Naming the mapkey also enables you remember its functionality at a later date. For example, in Figure 17–10 a mapkey is being defined that advances you to sketching an extruded feature by pressing <F2>.

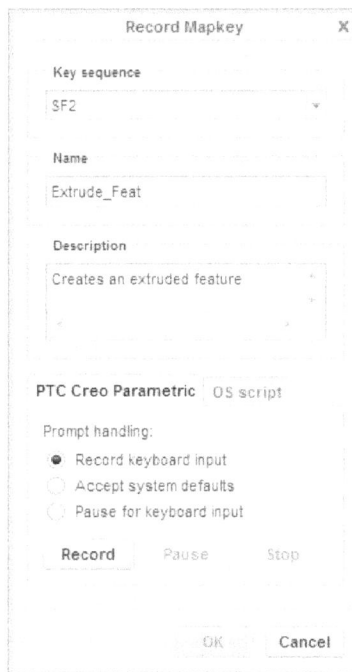

Figure 17–10

3. You can begin recording the mapkey once the key sequence, name, and description have been defined. For details on how to record a sequence, follow the steps further below.
4. A mapkey initially only applies to the current session. However, when saved, it is stored to the **config.pro** option and can be used when the **config.pro** is loaded.

The Mapkeys dialog box also enables you to modify, run, or delete existing mapkeys.

To save any individual mapkey, select it in the Mapkeys dialog box and click **Save**. To save all of the mapkeys or all changed mapkeys, click **All** or **Changed**, respectively. When saving, you are prompted to select the configuration file to which you want to save the mapkeys.

When recording a mapkey, it is recommended that you only select the required options, to create as efficient a mapkey as possible.

How To: Record the Sequence

1. Click **Record** to start recording and select the required menu options. Additional options enable you to pause the recording and customize how the mapkey handles keyboard entry and operating system commands. For example, to create a mapkey that opens the Creo Parametric Options dialog box, select **File>Options**.
2. Click **Stop** to stop the recording. You can resume the mapkey creation by clicking **Resume**.
3. Once you have completed the mapkey, click **OK**.

17.4 Customize the Ribbon, Toolbars, and Window Settings

You can customize the toolbars and ribbons in the Creo Parametric software. Customizing your interface provides shortcuts for accessing commonly used commands. These commands can be added or removed to customize the ribbon and toolbar area. You can also add and remove tabs and place user-defined icons representing mapkeys.

Ribbon

To customize the ribbons, right-click on the ribbon and select **Customize the Ribbon**, as shown in Figure 17–11. You can also select **File>Options** and select **Customize Ribbon**.

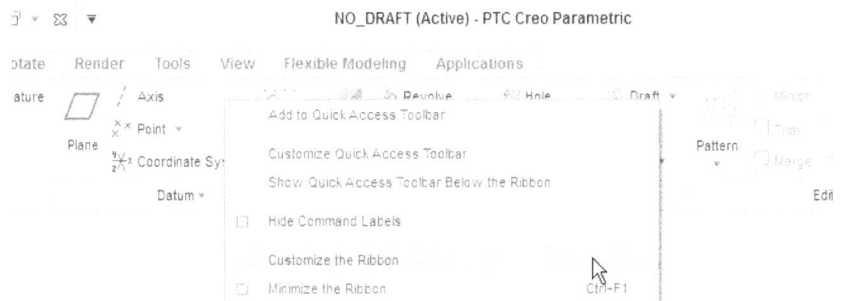

Figure 17–11

The *Customize Ribbon* category enables you to select the tabs that display in the Creo Parametric window. Select the checkboxes next to each ribbon that is to be displayed.

You can also click ▶ to expand the list and determine the groups and icons you want to display in the tab as shown in Figure 17–12.

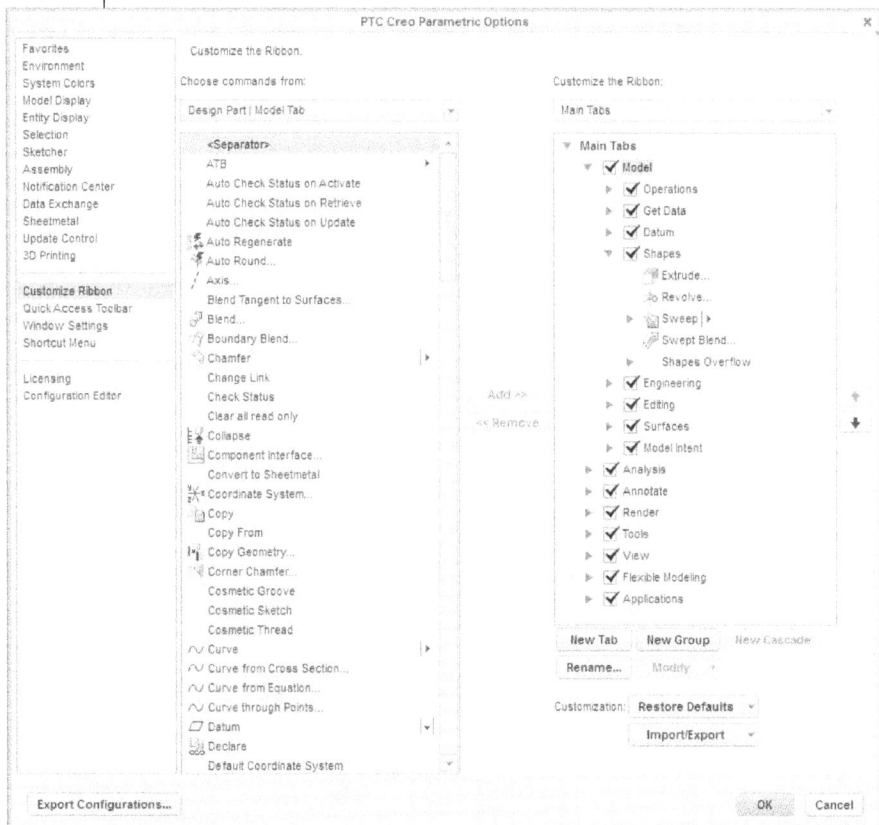

Figure 17–12

In addition to adding and removing tabs, you can use the Customize Ribbon command do perform the following:

- Create new tabs, groups, and group overflow menus (cascades).

- Rename buttons, tabs, and groups.

- Add and remove icons.

- Change the size of the icons.

- Change the order of icons and groups.

Quick Access Toolbar

The Quick Access Toolbar option enables you to customize the command in the toolbar by adding system- or user-defined icons, as shown in Figure 17–13. You can also specify to display the toolbar below or above the ribbon. You can open the dialog box using the following methods:

- Select **File>Options>Quick Access Toolbar**.

- Right-click on the toolbar and select **Customize Quick Access Toolbar**.

The shortcut menu also enables you to remove the toolbar and display it below the ribbon.

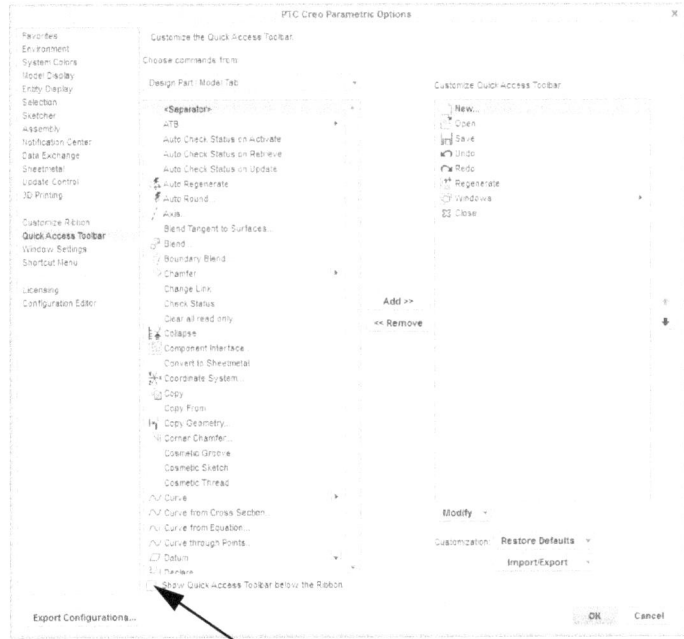

Toggle to display the toolbar below or above the Ribbon.

Figure 17–13

The commands are listed alphabetically and sub-divided into categories based on their function. You can sort them using the flyout menu at the top. By default, some of these commands are already located in the toolbar or the tabs.

How To: Add Additional Commands to the Quick Access Toolbar

1. Select the category to locate the command.
2. Press and hold the left mouse button over the required icon.
3. Drag the icon to the required location until the vertical or horizontal sash displays and release the left mouse button to place the icon.

Figure 17–14 shows a command being added to the toolbar.

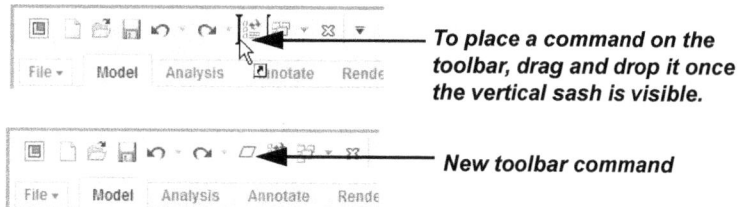

To place a command on the toolbar, drag and drop it once the vertical sash is visible.

New toolbar command

Figure 17–14

To delete a toolbar icon or menu bar option, select the item, right-click, and select **Remove**. You can also remove the icon by dragging it out of the toolbar or menu.

Mapkeys Category

Once created, a mapkey displays as an icon in the *Mapkeys* category. The default icon image for all mapkeys is identical and can be customized to better identify their intent. As with all other icons, mapkeys can be added to the toolbar using drag and drop. Add the mapkey to the *Customize Quick Access Toolbar* area and use the options in the Modify drop-down list to customize the mapkey image, as shown in Figure 17–15.

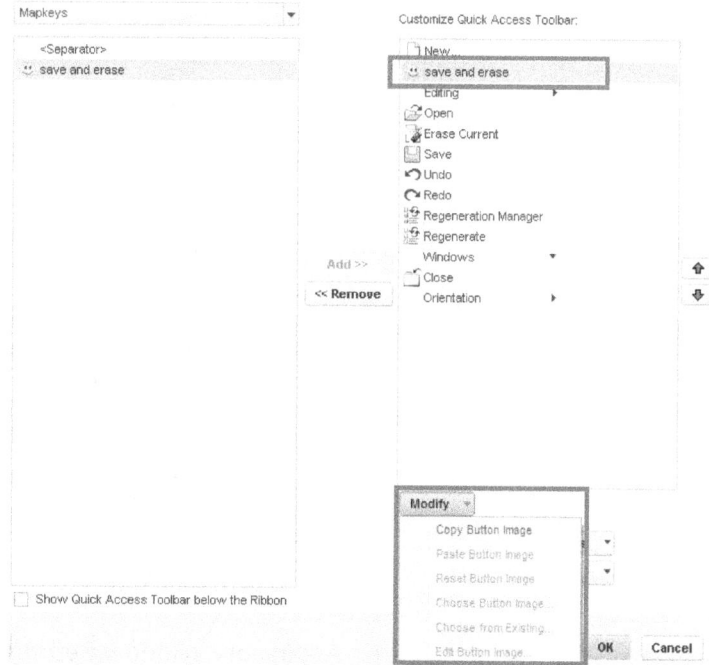

Figure 17–15

Window Settings

The *Window Settings* category enables you to configure settings for the Navigation tab, Model Tree, Browser, Accessory Window, and In-graphics toolbar, as shown in Figure 17–16.

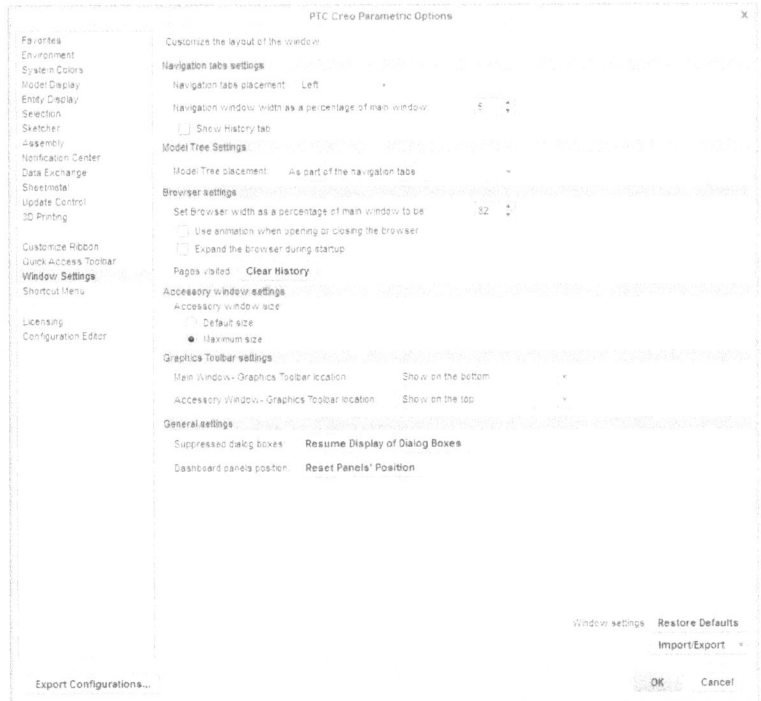

Figure 17–16

- **Navigation Tabs Settings:** The Placement drop-down list enables you to place the window on the left or right side of the *Graphics* area. Its width can be set as a percentage of the overall window or by entering the appropriate value. To access the *History* tab in the Navigator, enable the **Show History tab** option.

- **Model Tree Settings:** Enables you to customize the model tree display so that it is part of, or separate from, the navigation window. The default setting for the model tree is to be a part of the navigation window. If separate, the model tree can be placed above or below the graphics area and its height can be set to suit you requirements.

- **Browser Settings:** Enables you to customize the size and settings for the web browser.

- **Accessory Window Settings:** Enables you to specify your preferences for the secondary windows and menu icons.

- **Graphics Toolbar Settings:** Contains icons that control the display of the model. You can move the toolbar to various locations, add and remove icons, resize the icons to be small, medium, or large. You can customize the toolbar in the Creo Parametric Options dialog box, or by right-clicking and selecting options as shown in Figure 17–17.

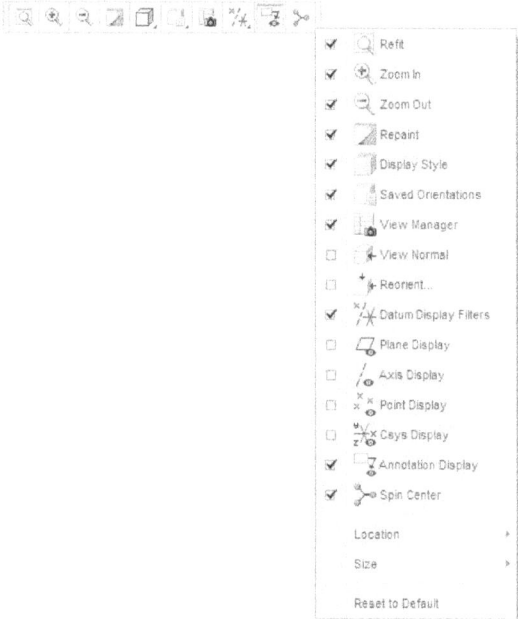

Figure 17–17

- **General Settings:** The panels in the dashboard for any feature type can be dragged and undocked from the dashboard so they can be located anywhere in the graphics area, as shown in Figure 17–18.

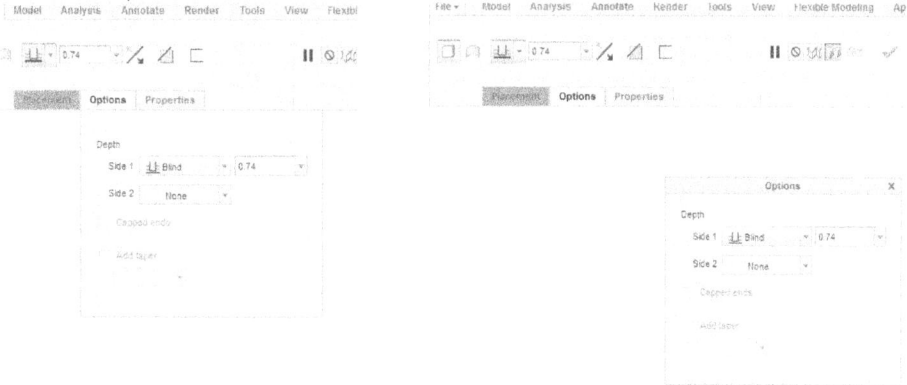

Options Panel　　　　　　　*Options Panel*

Figure 17–18

17.5 Customize the Configuration File

The main configuration file that is used in Creo Parametric is **config.pro**. It is used to customize the system to meet your preferences and requirements. A significant number of options can be customized in **config.pro**, which can save you modeling time and help to ensure the use of modeling standards. The most frequently customized settings include display settings, model decimal places, model standards, and file storage and retrieval standards.

General Steps

Use the following general steps to customize the **config.pro** file:

1. Open the **config.pro** configuration file.
2. Set the options and values.
3. Implement the changes.
4. Restart the Creo Parametric session, as required.

> ## Step 1 - Open the config.pro configuration file.

The **config.pro** file can be accessed by selecting **File>Options> Configuration Editor**. The PTC Creo Parametric Options dialog box opens, enabling you to set your preferences in the **config.pro** file, as shown in Figure 17–19.

The dialog box consists of two frames:

- The left frame, which contains all of the options.

- The right frame, which contains the value, status, and description for each option.

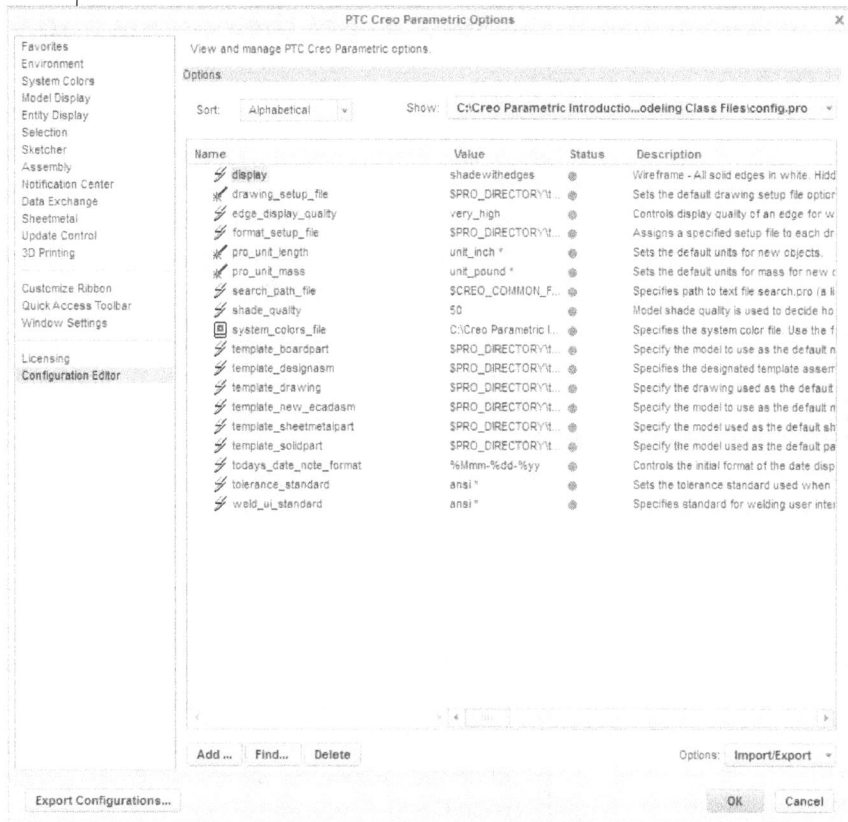

Figure 17–19

By default, only the options that exist in the current file display in the Creo Parametric Options dialog box. To display all of the options, click the Show drop-down list and click **All options**. It is recommended to use the **Sort** options to group the options, when reviewing them.

When Creo Parametric is launched, the system automatically looks for a **config.pro** file in the following locations:

- The */loadpoint/text* directory in the Creo Parametric software.

- Your home directory.

- Startup directory of the Creo Parametric software.

If an option is listed in more than one configuration file in any of these directories, the last value loaded is the one used by the system. Therefore, it is important to know the **config.pro** file that is being displayed in the PTC Creo Parametric Options dialog box.

Step 2 - Set the options and values.

Changes are made to the **config.pro** file by adding options or changing the value for the options that are currently set. An option can be added by clicking **Add**. The Add Options dialog box opens and you can change an option by entering its name in the *Option name* field in the dialog box. The appropriate value for the option can be set using the *Option value* field. Depending on the option, you can select the entry for the value or you might be required to enter a value. Figure 17–20 shows a value being selected from a predefined list of model display settings (i.e., **shade**, **wireframe**, **hiddenvis**, or **hiddeninvis**). To add the option to the configuration file, click **OK**.

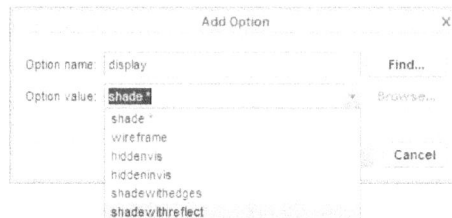

Figure 17–20

If an option has already been added and only the value is to be changed, select the value from the list, change the value, and click **OK**.

Searching for Configuration Options

If the name of the option is not known, you can search for it by clicking **Find**. The Find Option dialog box opens as shown in Figure 17–21.

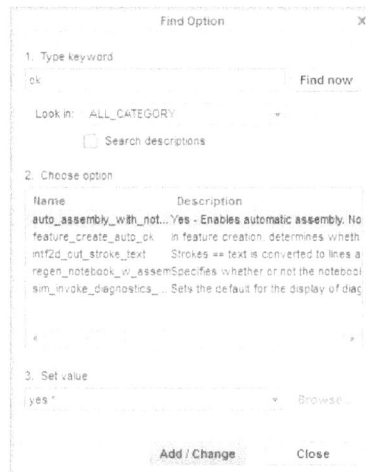

Figure 17–21

To search for an option name, enter the keyword and click **Find Now**. The system searches all of the option names and descriptions (if enabled) and returns a list of results. Select the required option in the *Choose option* area, set the value and click **Add / Change** to add it to the **config.pro**. To narrow your search results, consider selecting a category in the Look In drop-down list.

Step 3 - Implement the changes.

When all of the required options and values are set, the **config.pro** file should be applied to the current Creo Parametric session. To apply the option(s), click **OK**. The status symbol changes from ✳ to a ● . A dialog box opens as shown in Figure 17–22. It enables you to decide whether the changes are only applied to the current session or if they are saved and applied in the next session.

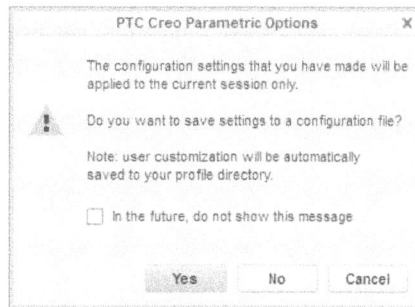

Figure 17–22

- Click **Yes** to save the settings in the PTC Creo Parametric Options dialog box. This applies the changes that were made. If you click **No** instead, it applies all of the changes that were done, but does not save the changes.

- The **Import/Export** option at the bottom of the PTC Creo Parametric Options dialog box enables you to import or export the **config.pro** file in the current location or store it in a new directory.

- For example, the software is started from */USER/PEOPLE/ TRAINING*, and the **config.pro** in the *TRAINING* directory is used. If the working directory for Creo Parametric is changed to */USER/PEOPLE*, the **config.pro** in the *PEOPLE* directory must be manually loaded. Otherwise, the file in the *TRAINING* directory still applies.

Step 4 - Restart the Creo Parametric session, as required.

In most cases, changes to the configuration file are applied to the current session immediately. However, options that affect the graphical display of Creo Parametric require you to restart the software to implement them, as shown in Figure 17–23. It is recommended that you restart the session as soon as it is convenient to ensure that all of the options are being used.

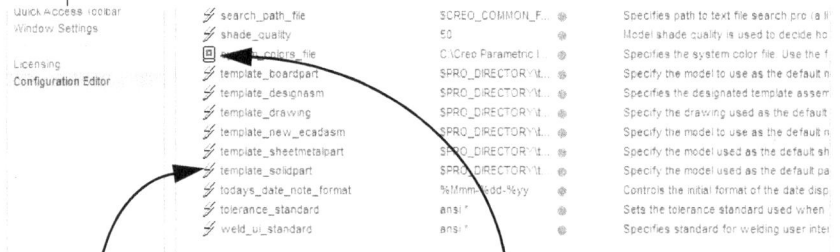

Indicates an option that has been applied without restarting Creo Parametric.

Indicates that Creo Parametric must be restarted to apply the option.

Figure 17–23

17.6 Assigning Colors to Parts and Surfaces

For complex assemblies, you might want to change the colors of parts and/or features to distinguish them from one another. Creo Parametric enables you to customize the default system colors for such purposes. The **Appearance Gallery** icon is used to create, delete, save, and modify the appearance of parts and surfaces.

- Select the part in the model tree or individual surfaces on the model to apply the color.

- Select the **Appearance Gallery** icon flyout in the *View* tab to pick a color as shown in Figure 17–24.

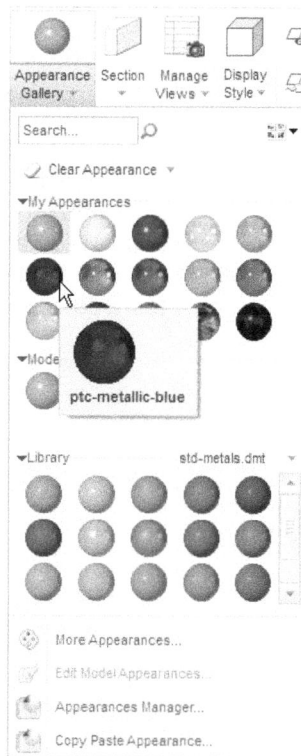

Figure 17–24

17.7 Configuring the Model Tree

In an earlier chapter, you looked at controlling the items and columns that display in the model tree. This section will focus on how to make changes to the model tree load automatically. To change the model tree settings, expand the ⬚ ⌄ (Settings) flyout at the top of the model tree, as shown in Figure 17–25.

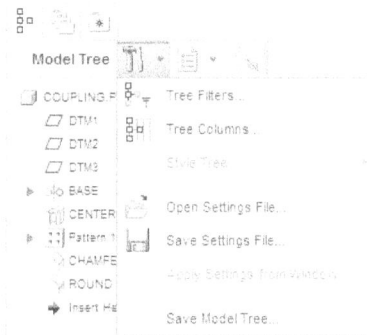

Figure 17–25

As a quick review, you can use the following the **Tree Filters** and **Tree Columns** options to control the model tree settings. Select **Tree Filters** in the Settings drop-down list to filter items open the Model Tree Items dialog box shown in Figure 17–26. Clear or select items in the dialog box to customize the display of items in the model tree.

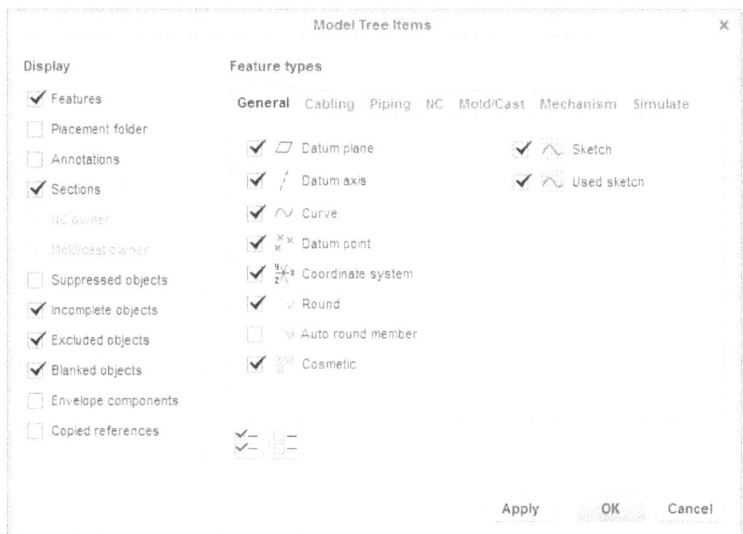

Figure 17–26

The model tree can also be customized to include additional columns of information. To manipulate columns in the model tree, select **Tree Columns** in the Settings drop-down list. The Model Tree Columns dialog box opens as shown in Figure 17–27.

Add columns to the Displayed list. Figure 17–28 shows a model tree that is configured to display the feature number and feature ID columns.

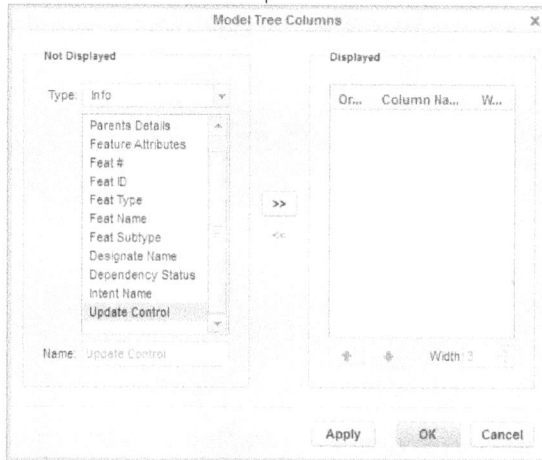

Figure 17–27

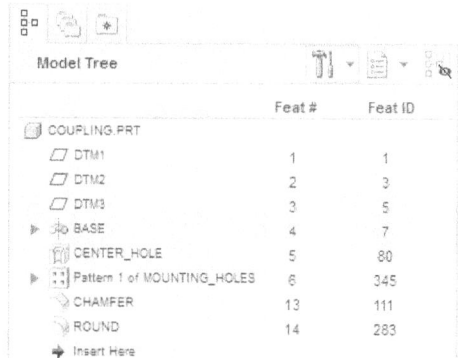

Figure 17–28

To avoid making changes with every new session, it is recommended to have the changes made to the model persist throughout.

How To: Save the Model Tree Settings and Set the config.pro to Use Them for all Sessions

1. Expand the ⫟⁾ ▾ (Settings) flyout and select **Save Settings File**.
2. Enter a name and location for the file containing model tree settings. By default, the model tree filter and column settings are stored in the **tree.cfg** file. The extension .CFG is mandatory.
3. Select **File>Preferences>Options** to open the **config.pro** file.
4. Set the c**onfig.pro** option **mdl_tree_cfg_file** to point to the file containing model tree settings.

Practice 17a | Customization

Practice Objectives

- Set and save the configuration options for the Creo Parametric system.
- Assign and test a command alias, referred to as a Mapkey, using keyboard keys to save and erase a file with one click.
- Customize the Quick Access Toolbar and the model tree with user preferences.

In this practice, you will customize the system's default settings to be user-specific.

Task 1 - Make changes to the config.pro file.

1. Set the working directory to the *Chapter 17\practice 17a* folder.

2. Select **File>Options**.

3. Select the *Configuration Editor* category.

4. Click **Add**. The Add Option dialog box opens.

5. Set the *Option name* collector to **display**. Note that you do not need to type the entire name. When the system matches an option, it completes the collector. If the provided option is not correct, continue typing.

6. For the value, select **hiddenvis** as shown in Figure 17–29.

7. Click **OK** to apply the option to the list.

8. Click **OK** in the PTC Creo Parametric Options dialog box.

9. A dialog box opens, as shown in Figure 17–30. Click **Yes** to save the settings.

Figure 17–29

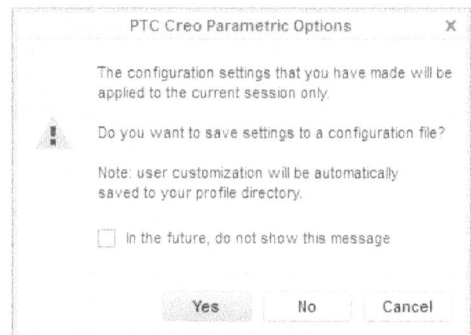

Figure 17–30

10. Maintain the default name of **config.pro** and click **OK**.

11. Open any model and note that the model has now been set to **Hidden Line**. This is now the default display setting. Erase the file from session.

Task 2 - Set another config option.

---

1. Select **File>Options>Configuration Editor**.

2. Click **Add**. The PTC Creo Parametric Options dialog box opens.

3. Enter **prompt_on_erase_not_disp**. This configuration option prompts you to save the files that are to be erased when you select **Erase>Not Displayed**.

4. For the value, select **Yes** and click **OK**.

5. Add another configuration option. Enter **prompt_on_exit** and select a value of **Yes**. This option prompts you to save the files in session when you exit.

6. Click **OK**.

7. Click **Yes** to save the settings. Maintain the default name of **config.pro** and click **OK**.

8. Click **OK** to close the PTC Creo Parametric Options dialog box.

Task 3 - Test the config.pro

---

1. Create a new part and set the *Name* to **test**.

2. Select **File>Close**. **Test.prt** is still in session but has not been saved to the hard drive.

3. Click (Erase Not Displayed). **Test.prt** is now in the list of objects to be deleted.

4. Click **OK**.

5. Press <Enter> to save the file to the hard drive. You might be prompted a few times if you have other files in session. The *Message* area now displays the *All the objects which were not displayed have been erased* prompt.

6. Create another new part and name it **exit**.

---

7. Select **File>Exit** and select **Yes** to exit.

8. The *Message* area again displays a prompt to save the **exit.prt** file.

9. Enter **No** and press <Enter>.

Task 4 - Create a mapkey.

---

1. Open another session of Creo Parametric.

2. Open any part, then select **File>Options>Environment** and click **Mapkeys Settings**.

3. Click **New**. The Record Mapkey dialog box opens. Set the following, as shown in Figure 17–31:

   - *Key Sequence:* **se**
   - *Name:* **SaveErase**
   - *Description:* **Saves the current file and erases**

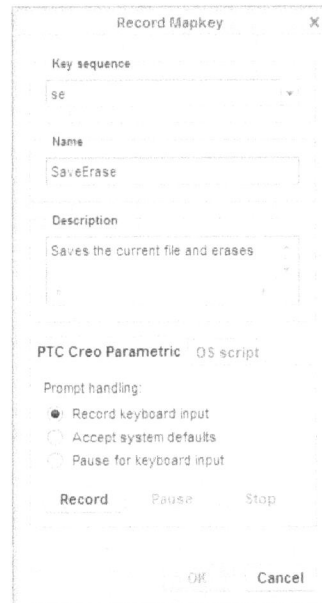

Figure 17–31

4. Click **Record**.

5. Select **File>Save** and press <Enter>.

6. Select **File>Manage Session>Erase Current** and click **Yes**.

7. Click **Stop** to finish the mapkey creation and click **OK**.

8. Click **Save** to save the mapkey. Click **OK** to accept the default name of **config.pro**.

9. Click **Close** to close the Mapkeys dialog box.

10. Save the mapkey definition to the **config.pro**.

Task 5 - Test the mapkey.

1. Open any part.

2. Press the letter sequence **se** to activate and test the mapkey.

Task 6 - Customize the Creo Parametric interface.

1. Open any part.

2. Select **File>Options>Quick Access Toolbar**. Scroll down to the **Suppress** command, as shown in Figure 17–32.

Figure 17–32

3. Drag the command to the toolbar, as shown in Figure 17–33.

Drag and drop the icon into the toolbar.

Figure 17–33

4. Scroll through the categories in the drop-down list and select **Mapkeys**, as shown in Figure 17–34.

5. Select the **Save Erase** mapkey that you created earlier. Drag the command to the Quick Access Toolbar, as shown in Figure 17–35.

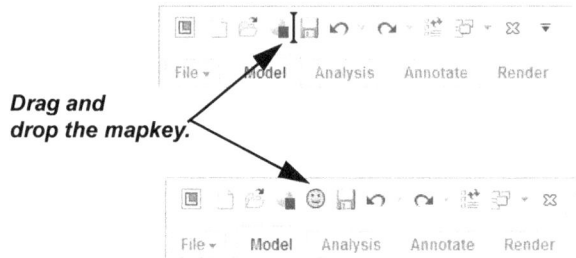

Drag and drop the mapkey.

Figure 17–34   **Figure 17–35**

6. In the PTC Creo Parametric Options dialog box, click **OK** to accept the changes.

Task 7 - Customize the model tree.

---

1. Ensure you have a model open.

2. Expand (Settings) in the model tree and select **Tree Filters**.

3. Select **Suppressed Object** to display the suppressed objects in the model tree.

4. Click **OK** to save the changes.

5. Expand (Settings) in the model tree and select **Tree Columns**.

6. In the Not Displayed list, select **Feat #** as shown in Figure 17–36.

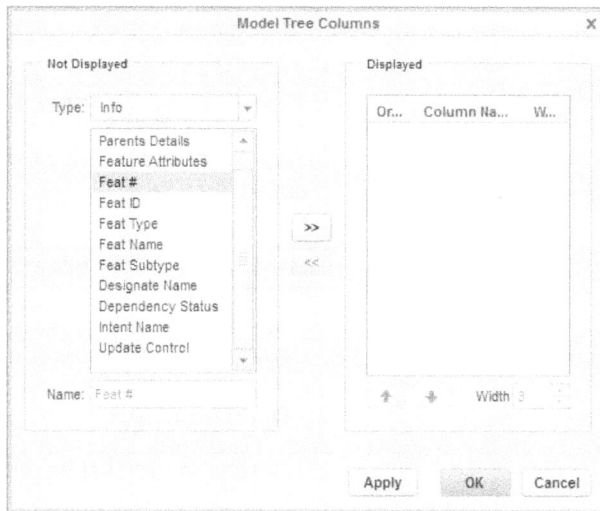

Figure 17–36

7. Click ⟫ (Add Column) to move it to the *Displayed* area.

8. Repeat the steps to move **Feat ID** and **Feat Name** to the *Displayed* area.

9. Click **OK**. Note that the three columns have been added to the model tree.

10. Click 🗊 ▾ (Settings)**>Save Settings File** to save the changes you made to the model tree. Note the location/directory the file is being saved to and accept the default name (**tree.cfg**). Click **Save**.

11. Select **File>Options>Configuration Editor**. Click **Add**. The Options dialog box opens. Enter the configuration option **mdl_tree_cfg_file**. Click **Browse** and browse to the new saved tree configuration from the previous step. Select **tree.cfg**. and click **Open**. The new path is added to the Options value.

12. Click **OK**. Click **OK** in the Creo Parametric Options dialog box. Click **Yes** to save the settings. When restarting Creo Parametric, the added column and suppressed features still display in the model tree.

13. Click ☺ to save and erase the current file.

Practice 17b | (Optional) Favorites

Practice Objectives

- Discover and set favorite configuration files that are commonly used.
- Create and add commands to a new tab in the Ribbon.

In this practice, you will customize the *Favorites* category and create a new tab.

Task 1 - Add configuration options to Favorites.

1. Set the working directory to the *Chapter 17\practice 17b* folder.

2. Open **block.prt**.

3. Set the model display as follows:

   - ⁎⁄⁎ *(Datum Display Filters)*: Only ⬚ (Plane Display)

   - ⅔ *(Spin Center)*: Off

   - ⌐ *(Display Style)*: ⬚ (Shading With Edges)

4. Select **File>Options**.

5. Select the *Favorites* category. Note that there are no current options in the dialog box.

6. Select the *Configuration Editor* category. There are several config options that are changed often. It is a good idea to list these in the *Favorites* category for quick access.

7. Click **Add**. The PTC Creo Parametric Options dialog box opens.

8. In the *Option name* collector, add the following configuration options that are listed as follows:

Configuration Option	Value
sketcher_starts_in_2d	yes
show_axes_for_extr_arcs	yes
allow_move_view_with_move	yes
spin_with_part_entities	yes
auto_add_remove	yes

9. Select the **auto_add_remove** configuration option, right-click, and select **Add to favorites**, as shown in Figure 17–37.

10. Repeat Step 8 for the configuration options listed.

11. Select the *Favorites* category. Note that the options are now added to the list as shown in Figure 17–38. You can quickly change their values by selecting and clearing the option.

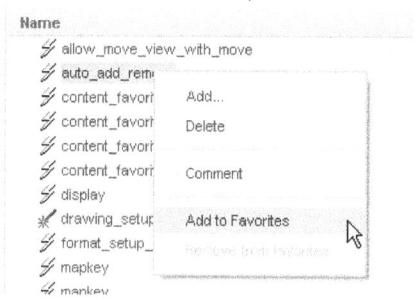

Figure 17–37

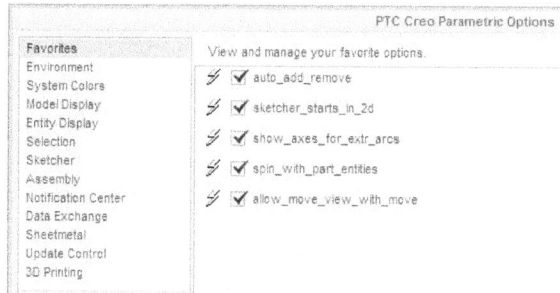

Figure 17–38

12. Click **OK** in the Creo Parametric Options dialog box.

13. Click **Yes** to save the settings. Maintain the default name of **config.pro** and click **OK**.

Task 2 - Create an extruded cut.

1. Spin the part and note that the datum planes remain displayed while the model is spinning.

2. Click (Extrude).

3. Use the top surface to create the sketch. Note that your sketch starts in the 2D orientation. Select the appropriate references and sketch the section as shown in Figure 17–39.

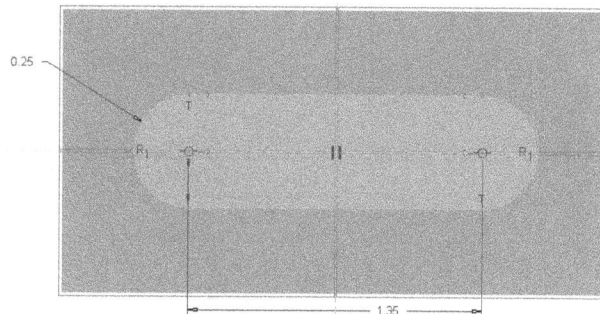

Figure 17–39

4. Complete the sketch.

5. Drag the depth handle into the model, then set the *Depth* to **.2**, as shown in Figure 17–40.

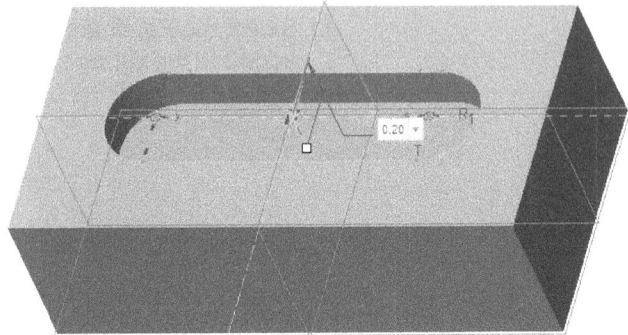

Figure 17–40

6. Complete the feature.

7. In the In-graphics toolbar, click ⅍ (Datum Display Filters) and select ⟋ₒ (Axis Display).

8. Note that the system automatically created axes for the sketched arcs as shown in Figure 17–41.

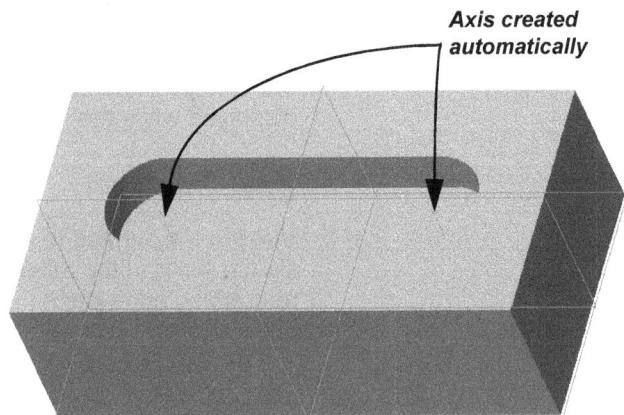

Axis created automatically

Figure 17–41

Task 3 - Create a new tab.

1. Select **File>Options**.

2. Select **Customize Ribbon** in the PTC Creo Parametric Options dialog box.

3. Right-click in the *Customize the Ribbon* area and select **Add New Tab** as shown in Figure 17–42.

4. Right-click on the new tab and select **Rename** as shown in Figure 17–43.

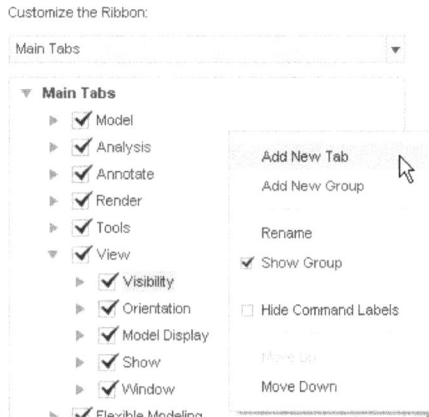

Figure 17–42

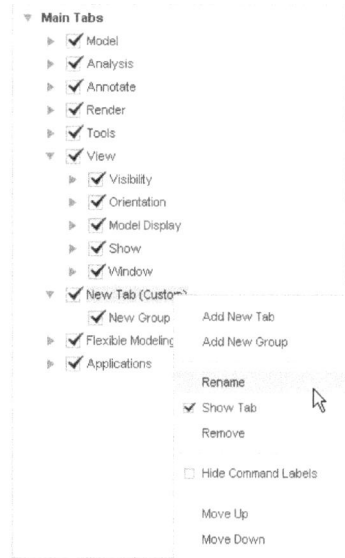

Figure 17–43

5. Set the new *Name* to **Edit** and press <Enter>.

6. If required, click ▶ to expand the *Edit* tab and select **New Group** as shown in Figure 17–44.

7. Select the **Edit Definition** command and click **Add** as shown in Figure 17–45.

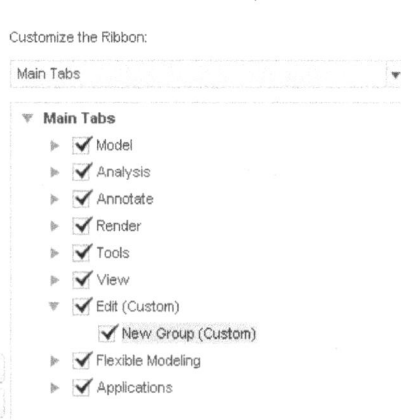

Figure 17–44

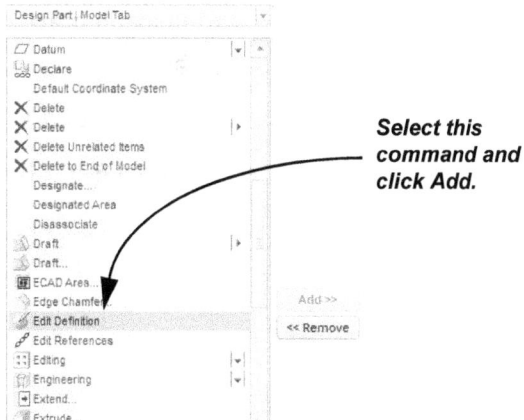

Figure 17–45

Select this command and click Add.

8. Repeat Step 6 for **Edit References**, **Suppress**, and **Resume**.

9. The *Customize the Ribbon* area display look as shown in Figure 17–46.

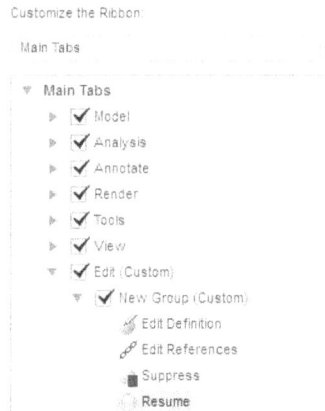

Figure 17–46

10. Click **OK**.

11. Select **Extrude 2**. Then, select the *Edit* tab and click ⬛ (Suppress).

12. Click **OK**.

13. Resume the feature.

Task 4 - Change the color of the model and of individual surfaces.

---

1. In the In-graphics toolbar, click ⁘ (Datum Display Filters) and toggle off ⌀ (Axis Display) and ▱ (Plane Display).

2. Select the *View* tab.

3. Select **BLOCK.PRT** in the model tree.

4. In the Model Display group, click the ◉ (Appearance Gallery) drop-down list.

5. Select the ● (ptc-painted-red) color swatch. The model updates as shown in Figure 17–47.

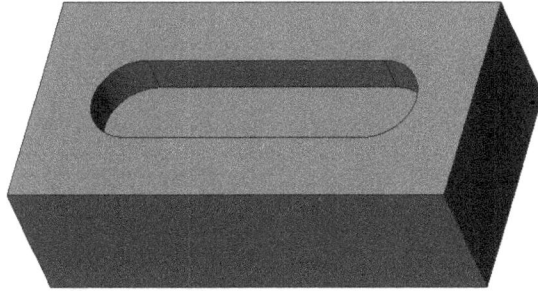

Figure 17–47

6. Select the internal surfaces highlighted in Figure 17–48.

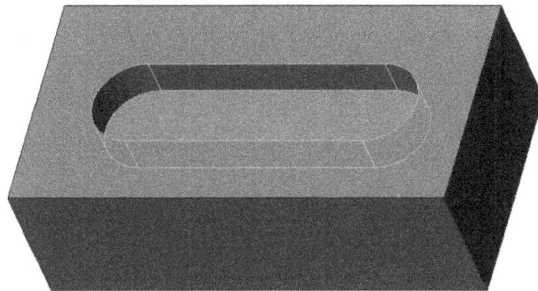

Figure 17–48

7. Click ● (Appearance Gallery) and select the ● (ptc-painted-green) swatch. The model updates as shown in Figure 17–49.

Figure 17–49

8. Save and erase the file.

9. Exit Creo Parametric and restart it, so that it no longer loads the customizations made.

Chapter Review Questions

1. What is the name of the configuration file that is used to customize your user preferences?

   a. config.pro

   b. configuation_file.pro

   c. preferences.pro

2. The Configuration Editor is divided into two frames. The left frame defines the _____ and the right frame defines its value, status, and description.

   a. Name

   b. License

   c. Favorite

   d. Display

3. Values for the configuration file options can be selected or entered in the value collector.

   a. True

   b. False

4. The color of Datum planes can be changed in the Creo Parametric Options dialog box.

   a. True

   b. False

5. Which of the following statements are true regarding mapkeys? (Select all that apply.)

   a. Mapkeys enable you to record a series of menu selections that can be executed together as one keystroke.

   b. To create a mapkey, select **File>Mapkey**.

   c. Function keys cannot be used for the key sequence of a mapkey.

   d. Mapkeys can be paused during definition.

6. You can show assembly constraints in the model tree.

   a. True

   b. False

7. Which of the following statements are true regarding customizing the Creo Parametric interface? (Select all that apply.)

   a. The In-graphics toolbar can be displayed at the top, left, or right side of the main window.

   b. Command icons can be added to the Quick Access Toolbar.

   c. Mapkey icons cannot be added to the Quick Access Toolbar. You must activate the mapkey using the assigned keystroke.

   d. Tabs can be added and removed.

8. The display of the model tree can be independent of the Navigation window.

   a. True

   b. False

9. Which of the following statements are true regarding customizing the model tree? (Select all that apply.)

   a. Select the Settings drop-down list in the model tree to access the customization options.

   b. The **Tree Filters** option enables you to filter the display of feature types.

   c. The **Tree Columns** option enables you to customize the display of columns in the model tree.

   d. All changes made to the model tree are stored in the **config.pro**.

Command Summary

Button	Command	Location
	Appearance Gallery	• **Ribbon:** *View* tab in the *Model Display* group

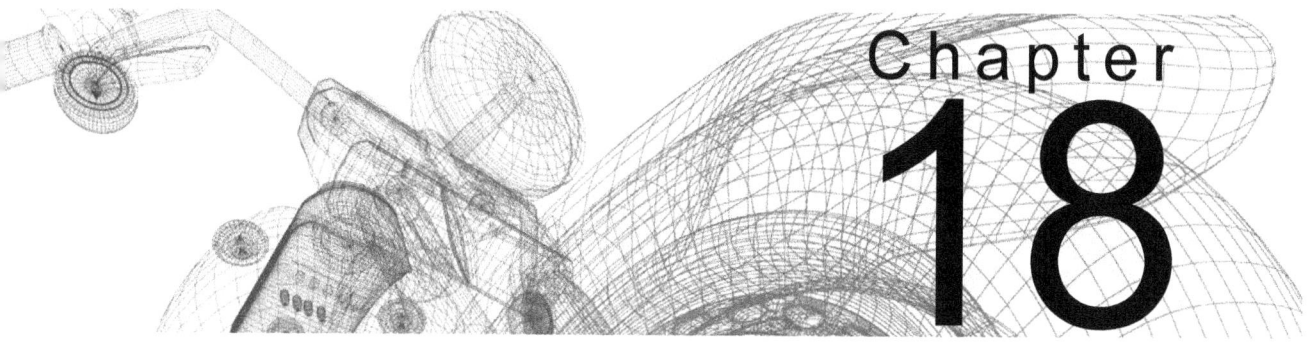

Feature Relationships and Resolving Failures

Parent/child relationships are defined as a dependency between features. They are established as you add each additional features to the model. If the parent feature is modified or deleted, the child feature(s) are affected. Parent/child relationships are a very powerful aspect of Creo Parametric.

As discussed in previous chapters, features can fail during feature creation. The failures can be resolved while you remain in the feature creation dashboard. Failures sometimes occur due to the options or elements selected while creating the feature or when changes are made. The resolution for regeneration failures might not be as obvious as for feature creation failures.

Learning Objectives in this Chapter

- Understand the parent/child relationships that are established when creating Engineering features.
- Understand the parent/child relationships that are established when creating sketched features.
- Understand how parent/child relationships are established between features and how to best control them.
- Recognize the possible relationships between features in the model using the model tree or model player.
- Identify all equations that have been established in a model using the Relations or Parameters dialog box.
- Identify relationships between features in the model using the commands in the Tools tab.
- Change an existing parent/child relationship in a model using the editing tools.
- Identify when most failures occur and learn the how to correct a feature failure.
- Diagnose and correct failures that occur using the appropriate tools.

18.1 Establishing Parent/Child Relationships

Parent/child relationships are created as a result of dependency between features. The independent feature is referred to as the parent and the dependent feature is the child. When such a dependency exists, Creo Parametric uses the parent feature to place or locate the child feature. Parent/child relationships can be created when either Engineering or sketched features are used.

Engineering Features

The shape of Engineering Features (e.g., holes, rounds, or chamfers) is predefined. Therefore, you are not required to sketch the section. You only need to select the placement references to locate the feature on the model. The placement references that you select establish parent/child relationships between the new feature and the existing features that were used for placement. Figure 18–1 shows an example of a coaxial hole. The placement references establish the parent/child relationships.

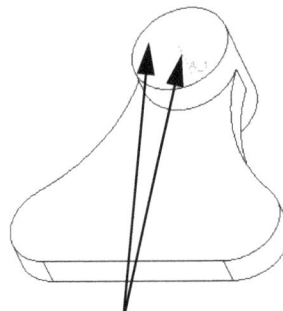

Hole references: axis A_1 and the planar surface of the cylindrical extrusion.

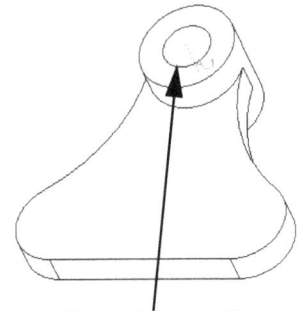

The hole is a child of this extrusion.

Figure 18–1

Figure 18–2 shows an example of a round created by referencing the indicated edge. The edge reference establishes a parent/child relationship with a previous protrusion.

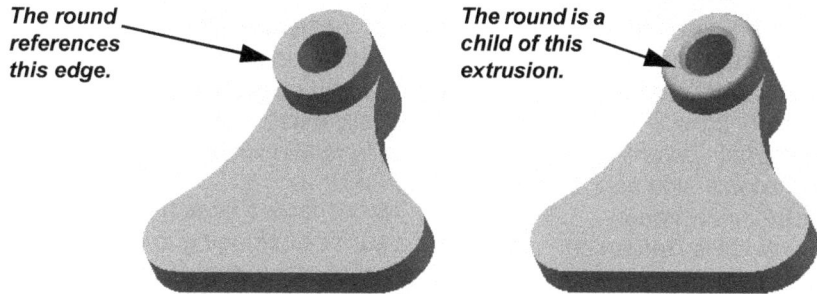

The round references this edge.

The round is a child of this extrusion.

Figure 18–2

The chamfer in the model shown on the right in Figure 18–3 is created by referencing the indicated edge. The edge reference establishes a parent/child relationship with the previous protrusion.

The chamfer references this edge.

The chamfer is a child of the hole.

Figure 18–3

Sketched Features

The process of creating a sketched feature results in the creation of parent/child relationships. Relationships are established for the following:

- Sketching and orientation plane references

- Section selection

- Sketching References

- Depth options

Sketching and Orientation Plane References

The sketch plane defines a planar reference on which a 2D section is sketched. The orientation plane defines the reference required to orient the sketch plane for sketching. The sketch and orientation references are then established as parents of the sketched feature.

*Creo Parametric might select an orientation reference plane by default. If this reference does not provide an appropriate parent/child relationship, you can create a new one by selecting the Reference field in the dialog box and selecting the new reference in the model. You can also change the **Orientation** option.*

If the sketch or orientation reference is created during the creation of the feature, the references used to create the required reference also establish a parent/child relationship. Note that if you select a sketch plane, and the system automatically establishes the orientation, that also creates a parent/child relationship.

Figure 18–4 shows a sketch plane for a new sketched feature that is a surface belonging to a protrusion. This makes the new feature a child of the protrusion. The sketch orientation reference is datum plane **FRONT**. This makes the new feature a child of datum plane **FRONT**. The Section dialog box displays the references that were selected for the sketch, as shown in Figure 18–4.

Sketch Plane   **Sketch Orientation**

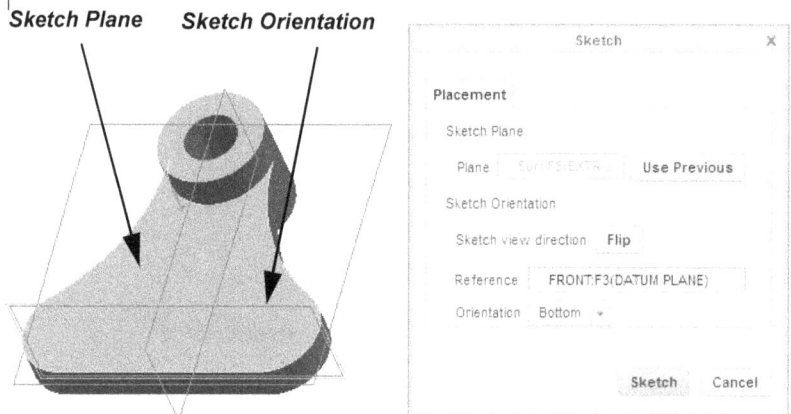

Figure 18–4

Section Selection

The section for a sketched feature can be sketched in the feature, or you can select an existing sketch in the model to reference. If an existing sketch is selected, it is copied into the current sketch and maintains an associative link to the original sketch. This establishes a parent/child relationship between the sketch and the sketched feature. Any changes to the sketch are reflected in the solid geometry.

Sketching References

Sketching references, such as entities, model edges, surfaces, and features are used to locate sketched geometry. When you select sketching references, parent/child relationships are established. The sketched geometry is located with respect to these entities using dimensions and constraints.

To review sketcher

references, click ☐
(References) while you
are in the Sketch tab.

Sketching references
display in the sketch as
cyan dashed lines.

Sketching references are provided in the References dialog box
as shown in Figure 18–5. The default references include a
horizontal and vertical reference for locating the sketch on the
model. These references might be datums or model surfaces,
and create a parent/child relationship with the referenced entity.

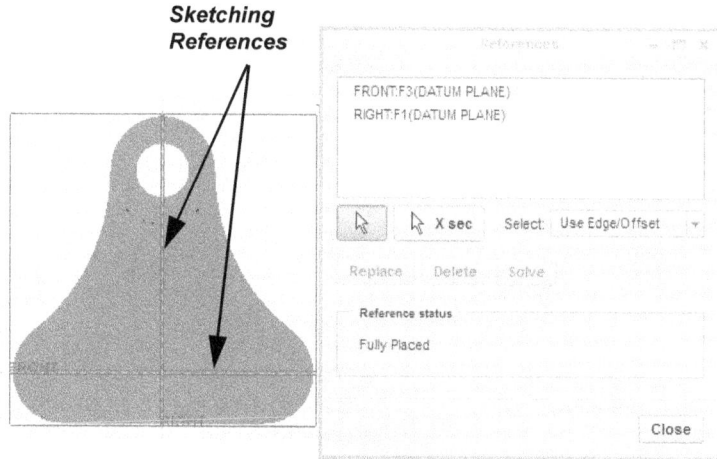

Figure 18–5

The default references might not provide you with the references
you need to meet your design intent. Additional references, such
as edges, surfaces, axes, or coordinate systems can also be
selected to establish parent/child relationships.

In Figure 18–6, the cut is located by selecting the surface of the
square extrusion as a reference and sketching the cut using the
point on entity constraint. The reference between the two
ensures that the cut is a child of the extrusion and that they
always remain in alignment.

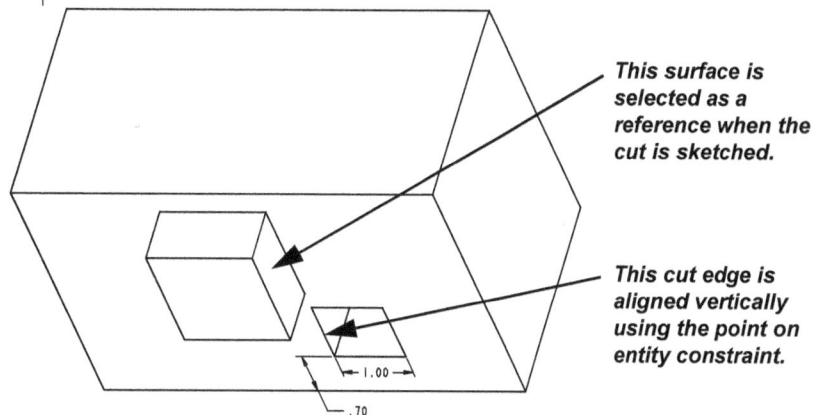

Figure 18–6

In Figure 18–7, the square cut was located by dimensioning it to the hole and the chamfer. The cut is now a child of both the hole and the chamfer.

It is not recommended that you dimension a feature to another one that could change later in the design (e.g., rounds or chamfers). If the reference feature is changed or deleted, the new feature can no longer be positioned correctly or might lose its reference and fail.

The cut is dimensioned to the center of the hole and the chamfer edge.

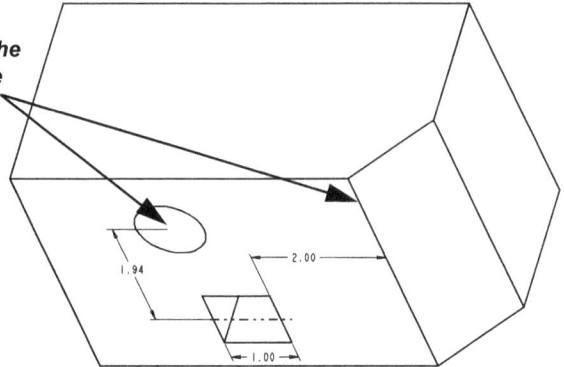

Figure 18–7

Certain geometry creation operations, such as projecting or offsetting an existing edge, create an implicit alignment and therefore establish parent/child relationships. In Figure 18–8, the entities at the bottom of the base protrusion are selected as edge references for offsetting. The new feature is a child of the base feature. Once the sketching references have been selected for offsetting, they are automatically added to the References dialog box.

A parent/child relationship would have also been established if concentric arcs were used to create the feature.

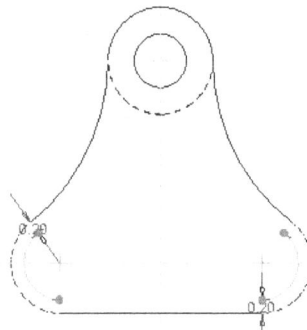

Figure 18–8

If you select a sketcher reference and it is not used (i.e., geometry is not located with respect to the reference with either a dimension or constraint), the reference is deleted when the sketch is complete and a parent/child relationship is not established.

Depth Options

It is recommended that you select surfaces instead of edges as references because an edge is more likely to change than a surface.

Some **Depth** options establish parent/child relationships. These options, as shown in Figure 18–9, establish parent/child relationships because a point, curve, plane, or surface is required as a reference to define the depth. These options include the following:

- Extrude to Selected Point, Curve, Plane, or Surface

- Extrude to Intersect with selected Surface or Plane

Extrude to Intersect with selected Surface or Plane Depth option

Extrude to Selected Point Curve, Plane or Surface Depth option

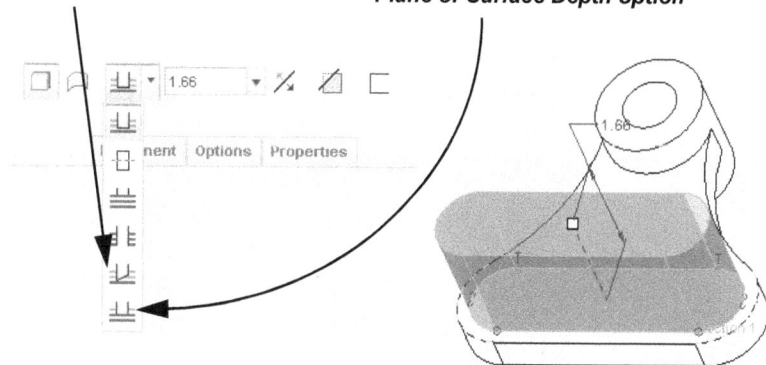

Figure 18–9

18.2 Controlling Parent/Child Relationships

Parent/child relationships can make models more robust and powerful. Use the following tips for controlling parent/child relationships:

- Create and use default datum planes. Since these are never deleted, they are useful as sketching and orientation plane selections. This establishes the datums, rather than a geometric feature, as parents of the sketched feature.

- Think about the surface you are selecting as a sketching or reference plane. Is this surface the best selection as a parent for this feature?

- When in the *Sketch* tab, select references with the model in a 3D orientation to ensure that you are selecting the correct references (i.e. surfaces, not edges).

- Use the hidden feature selection techniques to identify what is being selected. The help line describes the selected entity and the system highlights the reference and displays a message.

- When in the *Sketch* tab, consider the references used with tools such as project and offsetting edges as well as sketching concentric arcs and circles.

- Think about the references (points, curves, planes, or surfaces) that you are selecting when using the **Extrude to Selected Point, Curve, Plane or Surface** and **Extrude to Intersect with selected Surface or Plane Depth** options. Is this reference the best selection of a parent for this feature?

- Once a Engineering or sketched feature has been created you can also establish a parent/child relationship using relations. It is good practice to ensure that all of the relations contain a comment statement explaining the purpose of the relation.

18.3 Investigating Parent/Child Relationships

It is not practical to assume that you are always creating new models. In many cases you are required to continue someone else's design or make modifications to a previously completed model. In these cases, always investigate the model to understand the existing design and parent/child relationships. You can use the following review techniques:

- Model tree

- Relations

- Tools tab

- Model player

Model Tree

The model tree displays all of the features in the model. By reviewing the model tree, you can understand the hierarchy of the model and understand which feature can reference others.

Show Relations

Relations are used in models to control the design intent. In doing so, they establish parent/child relationships. To investigate existing relations in a model, select the *Tools* tab>**Model Intent>Relations and Parameters**. Any existing relations display in the viewer. You can also click ^{d=} (Relations) in the *Tools* tab and click ⊢⊣ (Display Specified Dimension) to review which dimensions are affected by the relation.

Tools tab

[Model Information] (Model Information) in the *Tools* tab, is used to obtain model information as shown in Figure 18–10.

Model Info : BRACKET

PART NAME :		BRACKET					
Units:		Length:	Mass:	Force:		Time:	Temperature:
Inch lbm Second (Creo Parametric Default)		in	lbm	in lbm / sec^2		sec	F

Feature List

No	ID	Name	Type	Actions		Sup Order	Status
1	1	RIGHT	DATUM PLANE	⊿	◻	---	Regenerated
2	3	TOP	DATUM PLANE	⊿	◻	---	Regenerated
3	5	FRONT	DATUM PLANE	⊿	◻	---	Regenerated
4	7	PRT_CSYS_DEF	COORDINATE SYSTEM	⊿	◻	---	Regenerated
5	39	---	PROTRUSION	⊿	◻	---	Regenerated
6	74	---	PROTRUSION	⊿	◻	---	Regenerated
7	114	---	HOLE	⊿	◻	---	Regenerated

Figure 18–10

The following icons in the *Tools* tab can be used to investigate parent/child relationships in the model.

- [icon] (Feature Information)

- [icon] (Reference Viewer)

- **Model Intent>Relations and Parameters**

Feature Information

The **Feature Information** option displays all of the information on a selected feature. Figure 18–11 shows all of the information for feature number 7. All parents of the selected feature are listed in the *Parents* area in the Creo Parametric Browser.

The **Feature List** and **Model Information** options display all of the features in the model. The feature number, id, name, type, suppression order and regeneration status of each feature is reported in the Browser window.

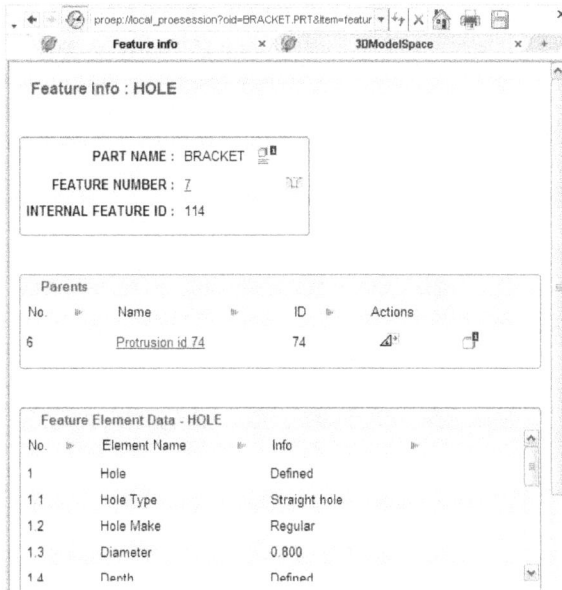

Figure 18–11

Reference Viewer

The Reference Viewer is available to display the parent/child relationships for selected features. To open it, select the required feature and click ✎ (Reference Viewer). The Reference Viewer dialog box opens as shown in Figure 18–12.

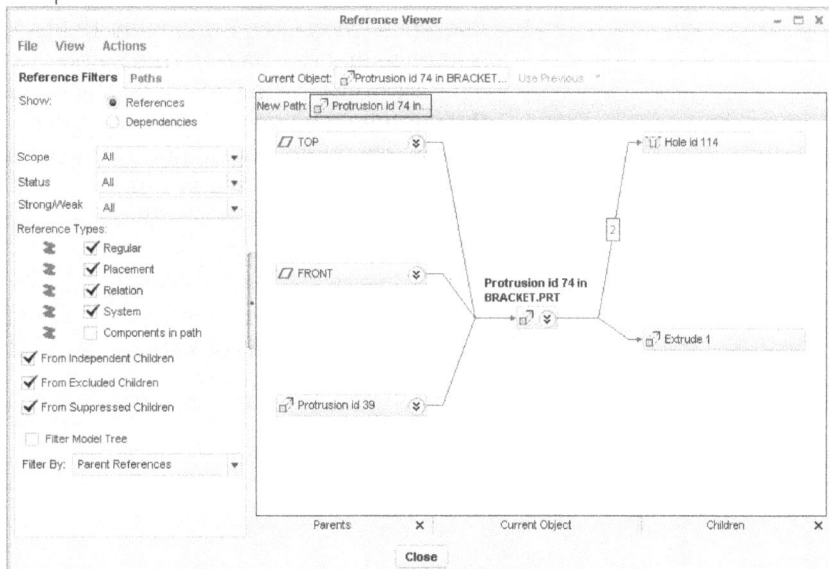

Figure 18–12

An arrow between two objects indicates a reference. When multiple references exist, a number displays on the arrow, indicating the exact number of references. Right-click on a reference arrow and select **Display Full Path** to display the full reference path between objects. The Full Path Display dialog box opens as shown in Figure 18–13.

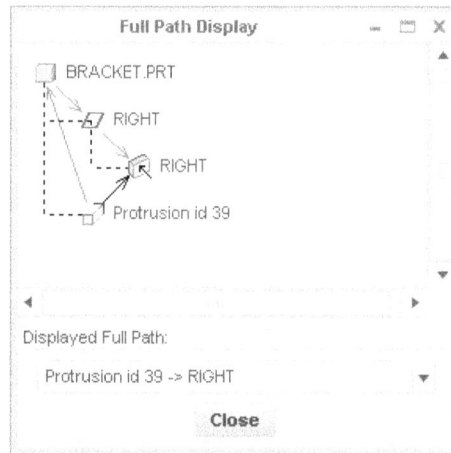

Figure 18–13

You can filter the Reference Viewer to display objects with parents only or objects with children only. To display objects with parents only, select **Parent References** in the Filter By drop-down list.

Using the Reference Viewer dialog box, you can only delete a reference when Creo Parametric identifies it as an additional reference that can be removed safely. To delete a reference, right-click on it in the Reference Viewer and select **Delete Reference**. You can use this option to delete references to rounds, chamfers, copied geometry, published geometry, annotation features, and thru-point datum curves.

Relations and Parameters

The Relations and Parameters option, in the Model Intent group drop-down list, lists all of the relations and parameters in the part as shown in Figure 18–14.

You can also select ***Relations and Parameters*** *in the Model Intent group in the Model tab.*

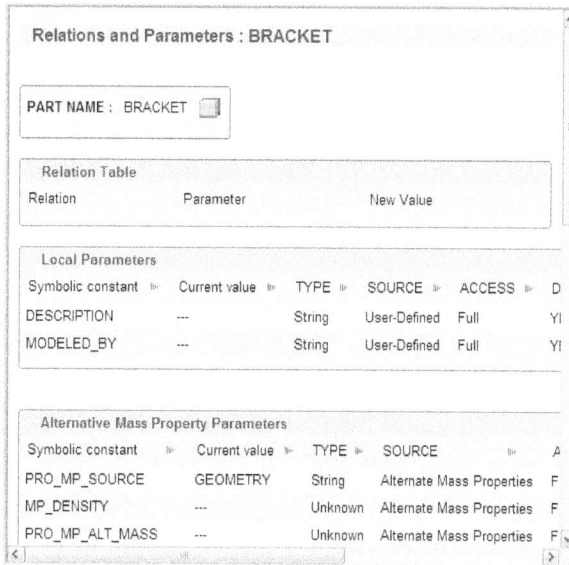

Figure 18–14

Model Player

(Model Player) in the Investigate group, in the *Tools* tab, reviews the construction history of a model, one feature at a time. This option is especially helpful when working with models created by other users. The model player can give you an idea of the modeler's design intent and modeling techniques by replaying and reviewing the design.

Figure 18–15 shows the model player. Use the control icons at the top of the dialog box to play, forward, and rewind the model. You can also specify a feature number from which to start playing the model by entering a number in the *Feat #* field. At any time while playing the model, you can click **Feat Info** and **Show Dims** to get additional information on the current feature.

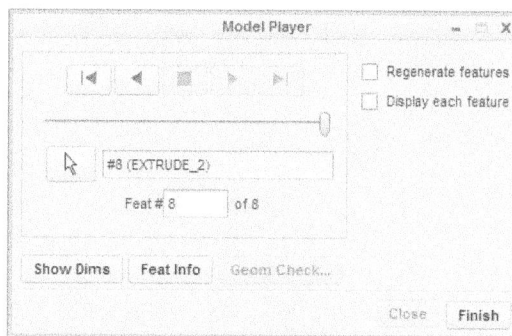

Figure 18–15

The **Regenerate features** option enables you set the model player so that playing the model sequence forces the model to be regenerated instead of just displaying the current feature. The **Display each feature** option repaints the screen after each feature displays. You can use both of these options as required to reduce the replay time for the model, depending on your requirements.

18.4 Changing Parent/Child Relationships

The design intent of the model might change or unwanted relationships might occur as a result of modifying or deleting a parent feature. If the parent feature is modified, the child feature(s) updates with the changes. For example, if a child is dimensioned to an edge of the parent feature and modifying the parent moves this edge, the child feature moves accordingly. If the parent feature is deleted, Creo Parametric no longer has the required references to place the corresponding child feature(s). To avoid affecting the child when deleting the parent, there are methods to change the dependency.

You can change parent/child relationships using the ✎ (Edit Definition) and ✐ (Edit References) options by right-clicking and selecting an option in the contextual menu.

Edit Definition

The ✎ (Edit Definition) option provides you with access to the tab that was used when the feature was created. By defining new references or elements in this dialog box, you can change parent/child relationships.

You can access the ✎ (Edit Definition) option by selecting the feature in the model or in the model tree, or by right-clicking and selecting an option in the contextual menu.

Edit References

The ✐ (Edit References) option can also be used to change parent/child relationships. This option enables you to reroute the existing references to a new reference without displaying the dashboard that was used to create the feature.

The system displays the Edit References dialog box, as shown in Figure 18–16.

You can select a reference in the Original References group in the dialog box, then select a reference to replace it. For example, reference 2 was the RIGHT datum plane, and Reference 4 was a surface on Extrude_1. To change the reference, select it in the dialog box then select the new reference on the model or in the model tree, The dialog box updates to show and updated references as Changed, as shown in Figure 18–17.

Figure 18–16

Figure 18–17

To reset a Changed reference back to the original by selecting it in the list and clicking **Reset**.

By default, you are only changing the current feature's reference to any of the listed references. However, you can change other children of the reference by clicking ⊕ (Child Handling). The current feature will be selected, and any other features using the current reference will also be listed, as shown in Figure 18–18.

This Child Handling option should be used carefully, and requires a detailed understanding of the model's construction.

Figure 18–18

If you want to change the other feature to also use the new reference, select it in the *Update child features* section.

You can use **Roll To** to show the model in a state where the most recent feature from which you can select references is the last regenerated.

Click **Preview** to see the effect of your changes and click **OK** to complete the edit.

18.5 Feature Failure Overview

A feature failure can occur while a feature is being created or while an existing feature is being modified or redefined. Failures can occur for a variety of reasons. Two common examples of failed features are:

- Geometry cannot be created due to invalid or missing references.

- Dimensional changes result in geometry that cannot be calculated.

You can continue working with your model even though there might be failed geometry, but there are limitations to the new geometry that you can create. In addition, it is possible to save a model with failed geometry, but you can set the configuration option **allow_save_failed_model** to either **prompt** or **no**, which will either warn you that you have failed features, or stop you outright from saving until the failures are resolved. Note that there is a legacy environment called *Resolve Mode*. If your company uses Resolve Mode, refer to *Appendix A*.

18.6 Resolving Failures

By default, when a failure is encountered during regeneration, the model continues to regenerate and a warning message displays in the graphics window. In addition, the model tree highlights all of the failed features and impacted child features, as shown in Figure 18–19.

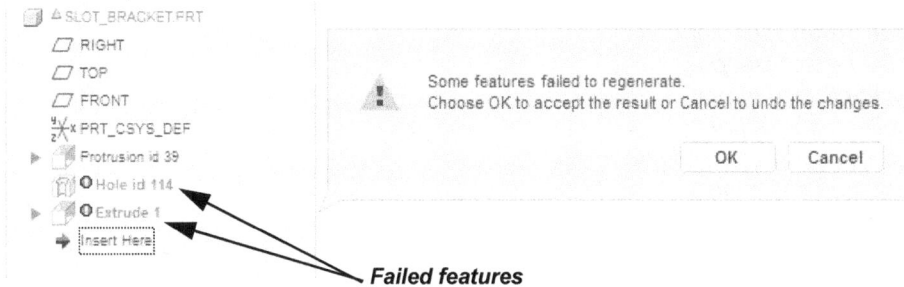

Failed features

Figure 18–19

Click **OK** to continue modeling without correcting the failed features. You can fix the problems at a later time. It is also possible to save a model with failed features, unless the configuration option **allow_save_failed_model** is set to **no**.

Note that some of the operations in the Editing group cannot be used on failed features: **Mirror**, **Copy**, **Paste**, **Paste special**, and **Copy**. You cannot use the **Group** and **Pattern** operations on Failed Features.

Resolving Failures that Occur on Completion of a Feature

When a failure occurs on completion of a feature, the Troubleshooter dialog box might open. The display of the Troubleshooter dialog box depends on the current error. The Troubleshooter provides information on why a feature has failed as shown in Figure 18–20.

The Troubleshooter can also be accessed by right-clicking in any collector field that contains a red or yellow dot, and selecting **What's Wrong***.*

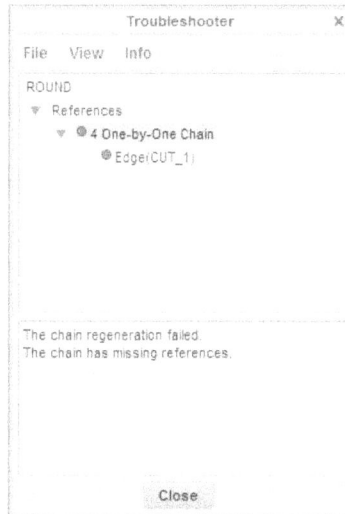

Figure 18–20

The items listed under the feature provide notes that help you determine why the feature could not be created. Select each item one at a time to review the information in the lower frame of the window. Items with yellow dots indicate warnings and items with red dots indicate errors. In general, warnings provide solutions and errors explain why the current combination of references and values has failed.

After diagnosing the problem, click **Close** to return to the feature dashboard.

Resolving Failures that Occur on Regeneration

During regeneration, each feature in the model is recalculated. When a feature fails during regeneration, the Regeneration

Manager can be opened by clicking ⬤ at the bottom of the window. The dialog box opens and can be expanded as shown in Figure 18–21.

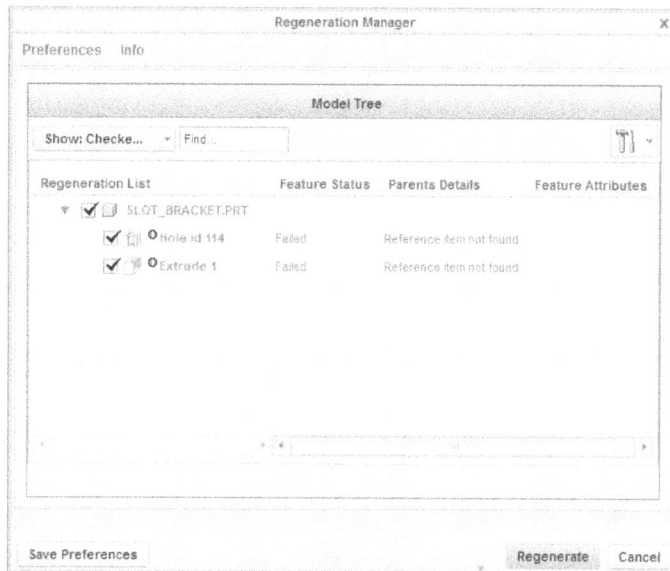

Figure 18–21

The Regeneration Manager displays the status of the features. You can use it to perform the following actions:

- Search for features in the list.

- Apply Tree Filters to show or hide the selected items, cleared items, or both in the Regeneration List.

- Set options similar to those in the model tree.

- Save the Regeneration List as a text file.

- Include or exclude features from the Regeneration List.

- Save the preference modifications.

The Regeneration Manger also enables you to investigate the Reference Viewer. To open the Reference Viewer for a specific feature, right-click on the feature in the Regeneration Manager and select **Reference Viewer**, as shown in Figure 18–22. Once in the Reference Viewer you can investigate and delete unwanted references.

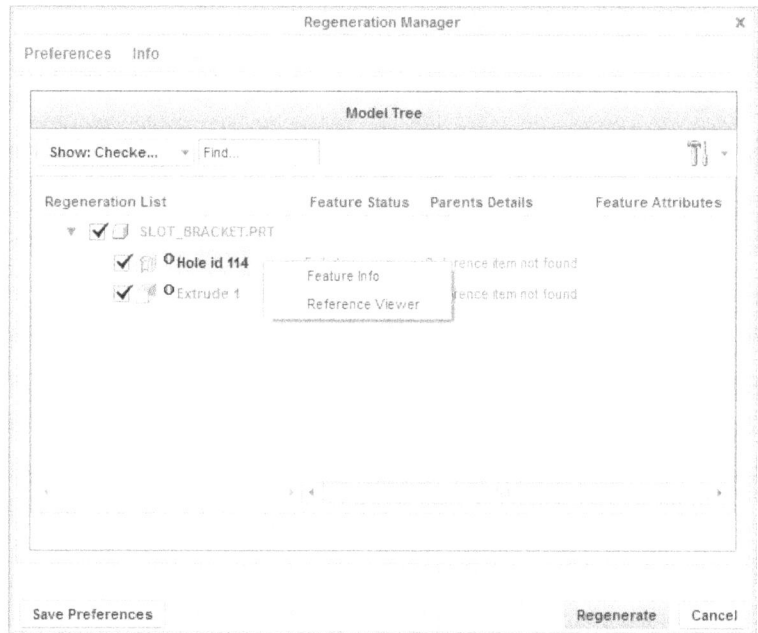

Figure 18–22

Once you have determined which modifications are required to fix the failed feature(s), use Creo Parametric's standard feature editing tools, such as ✎ (Edit Definition), ⌀ (Edit References), and ⊣⊢ (Edit) to fix them.

- **Edit Definition**: Enables you to work on the failed feature using the tab.

- **Edit References**: Enables you to work on the failed feature by changing references.

- **Edit**: Enables you to change dimensions for any feature in the model.

18.7 Case Studies

In the model shown on the left in Figure 18–23, the top linear edge of the model must be changed to an arc.

*The **Replace** option enables you to replace one entity with another so that all references to the original entity are automatically rerouted to the new entity.*

The design intent requires that the linear edge be changed to an arc.

Figure 18–23

The required geometry is shown on the right. To make the change, the original tab used to create the feature displays using the ✎ (Edit Definition) option. Once in Sketcher mode, the linear entity is deleted and an arc is sketched. Answer the following questions:

• Is the base protrusion going to fail on regeneration?

• Are any other features going to fail on regeneration? If so, why?

In the model shown on the left in Figure 18–24, the square cut is created by dimensioning it to a T-shaped cut.

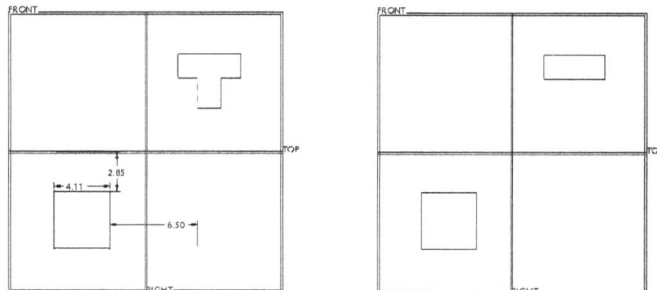

Figure 18–24

A design change is required so that the sketch of the T-shaped cut displays, as shown on the right. Answer the following questions:

- Is the base protrusion going to fail on regeneration?

- Are any other features going to fail on regeneration? If so, why?

Practice 18a	# Changing Parent/Child Relationships

Practice Objectives

- Recognize the possible relationships between features in the model using the Model Player.
- Discover parent/child relationships between features using the Reference Viewer.
- Change an existing parent/child relationship in a model using the editing tools.

In this practice, you will open the model shown on the left in Figure 18–25 and you will delete the hole and chamfer so that the model displays as shown on the right. To delete these features, you have to edit their definition and establish new references in sketched features.

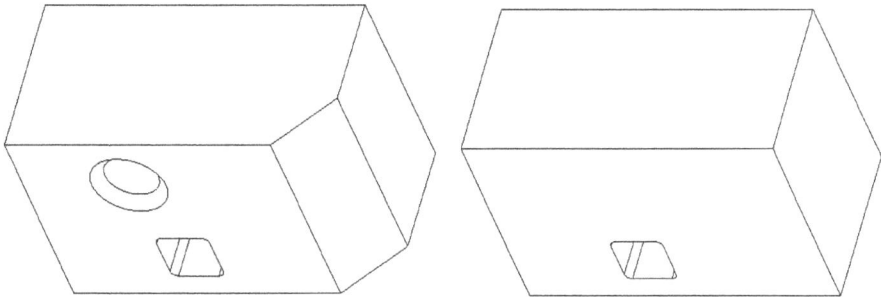

Figure 18–25

Task 1 - Open a part file.

1. Set the working directory to the *Chapter 18\practice 18a* folder.

2. Open **pc01.prt**.

3. Set the model display as follows:

   - ⚹ *(Datum Display Filters)*: All Off

   - ⤳ *(Spin Center)*: Off

   - ◻ *(Display Style)*: ◻ (Shading With Edges)

Task 2 - Investigate the part.

1. Select the *Tools* tab and click ⚊ (Model Player).

2. Click ◁ (Step Backwards) to move to the beginning of the model's feature list. Click ◁ (Step Backwards) to continue until the part is completely regenerated.

3. In the Model Player dialog box, click **Finish**.

4. Select the square cut (**SLOT**), right-click, and select ⟵⟶ (Edit) to display the dimensioning scheme used. The cut is located with respect to the chamfer and the hole.

5. Modify the chamfer dimension to **0.5**. What happens to the square cut? Why is it generally not a good idea to dimension to edges created by features, such as rounds and chamfers?

Task 3 - Redefine the location of the cut.

1. Select **SLOT**, right-click, and select 🖌 (Edit Definition). Right-click and select **Edit Internal Sketch** to activate the *Sketch* tab. Redimension the cut to the right side surface of the base feature, not the chamfer edge.

2. Complete the sketch and the feature.

3. Delete the chamfer. Is **SLOT** affected?

Task 4 - Delete the hole.

1. Select the hole, right-click, and select **Delete**. The Delete dialog box opens indicating that the hole has children, as shown in Figure 18–26. To delete the hole, you must fix the references for the children.

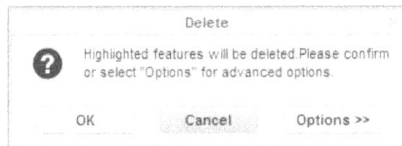

> Delete
>
> ❓ Highlighted features will be deleted. Please confirm or select "Options" for advanced options.
>
> OK   Cancel   Options >>

Figure 18–26

2. Click **Cancel** to cancel the **Delete** action.

3. Select the hole, right-click, and select **Information> Reference Viewer**. The Reference Information Window opens as shown in Figure 18–27, indicating that the **SLOT** and **JHOLE_CHAMFER** are children.

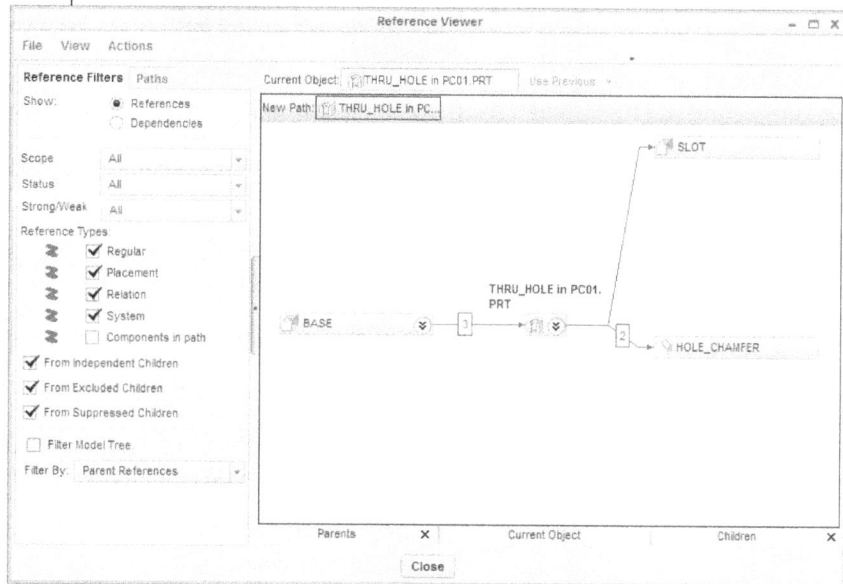

Figure 18–27

4. Right-click on **SLOT** in the Reference Viewer window and select **Display Full Path**. This displays the references used, as shown in Figure 18–28. The hole axis **A_2** was used as a reference for the cut. This must be replaced.

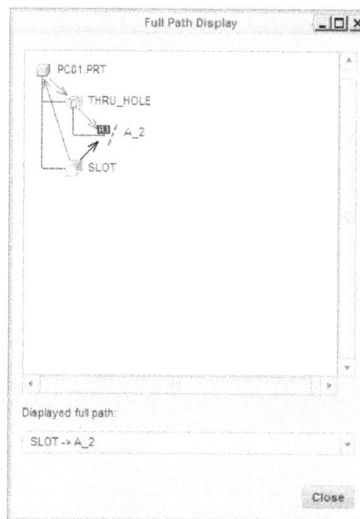

Figure 18–28

5. Close the Full Path Display and Reference Viewer dialog boxes.

6. Select **SLOT**, right-click, and select ✎ (Edit Definition).

7. Right-click and select **Edit Internal Sketch** to activate the *Sketch* tab.

8. Click ▢ (References) to open the References dialog box.

9. In the list of references, select **A_2(AXIS):F6(HOLE)** and delete it.

10. Select Datum Plane **TOP** as a new reference and close the References dialog box.

11. Change the resulting dimension to be strong.

12. Complete the sketch and the feature.

13. Select the hole, right-click, and select **Delete**. The Delete dialog box opens again indicating that the hole has children.

14. The chamfer cannot exist without the hole, click **OK** to delete this feature as well.

15. Save the part and erase it from memory.

Practice 18b | Tooling Jig

Practice Objectives

- Discover parent/child relationships between features using the Reference Viewer.
- Change an existing parent/child relationship in a model using the editing tools.

In this practice, you will incorporate three design changes. You will investigate the features that require changes to see if children will be affected.

Task 1 - Open a part file.

1. Set the working directory to the *Chapter 18\practice 18b* folder.

2. Open **tooling_jig.prt.**

3. Set the model display as follows:

    - $\overset{x/}{\nearrow\!\!\ast}$ *(Datum Display Filters)*: All Off

    - $\overset{\mathcal{S}}{\sim}$ *(Spin Center)*: Off

    - $\square$ *(Display Style)*: $\square$ (Shading With Edges)

Task 2 - Investigate features of the part.

In this task, you are required to delete the **CUT_AWAY** feature due to a design change. Before deleting or incorporating any design change, you should always investigate the part and its features.

1. Display the part and the model tree. Select the **CUT_AWAY** feature to highlight its geometry as shown in Figure 18–29.

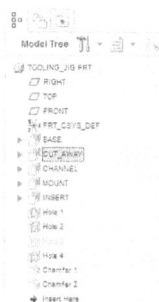

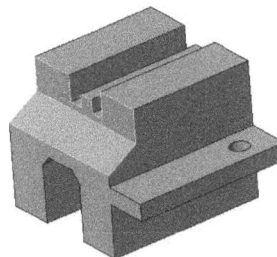

Figure 18–29

2. Determine whether the **CUT_AWAY** feature has any children before deleting it using the Reference Viewer.

3. Toggle off the **System** option.

4. The **CUT_AWAY** feature does have a child (the **CHANNEL** feature), as shown in Figure 18–30.

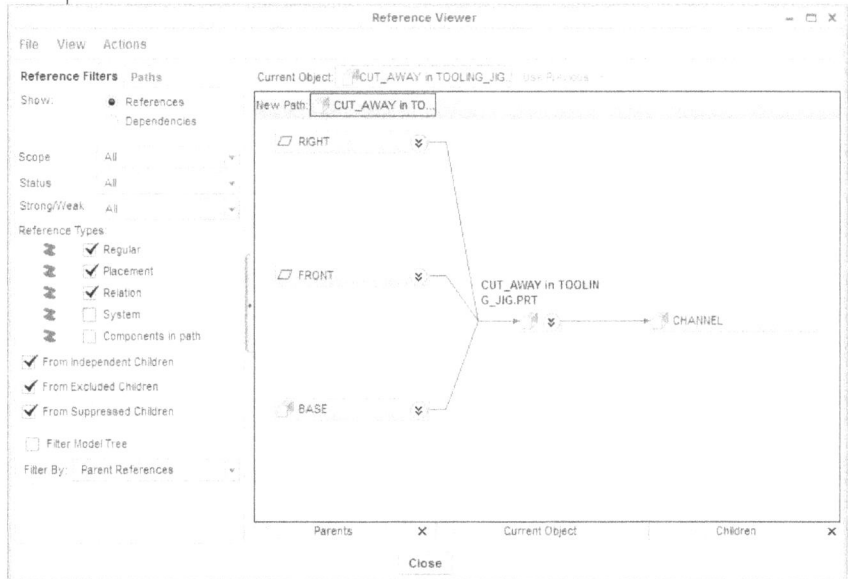

Figure 18–30

5. In the Reference Viewer, expand the **CUT_AWAY** feature to display the reference, as shown in Figure 18–31.

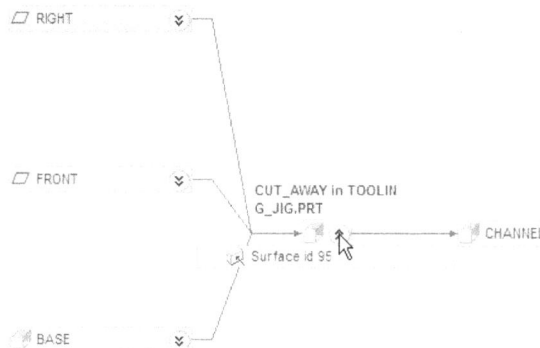

Figure 18–31

6. Select the surface reference to highlight it on the part as shown in Figure 18–32.

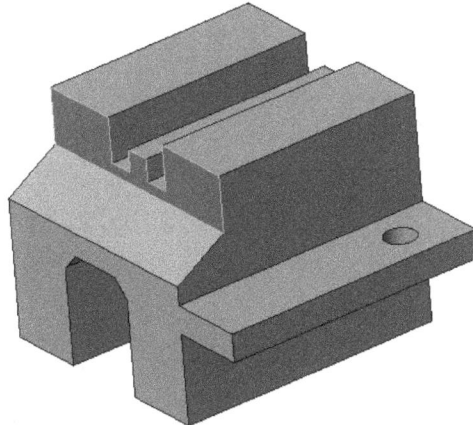

Figure 18–32

7. Close the Reference Viewer.

8. Edit the definition of the child, **CHANNEL**, to break its relationship with the **CUT_AWAY** feature. As shown in Figure 18–33, the **Through Until** depth option resulted in the parent/child relationship.

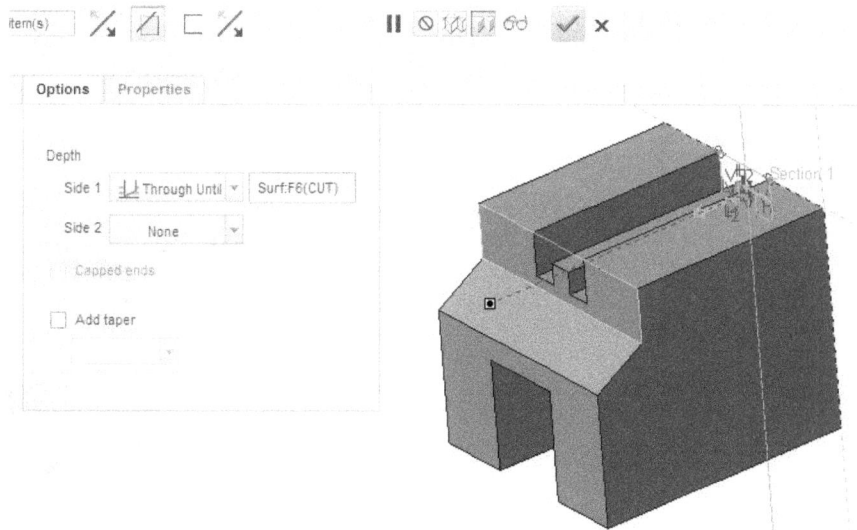

Figure 18–33

9. Change the depth option to **Through All** and complete the definition of the feature.

10. Delete the **CUT_AWAY** feature. The part displays as shown in Figure 18–34.

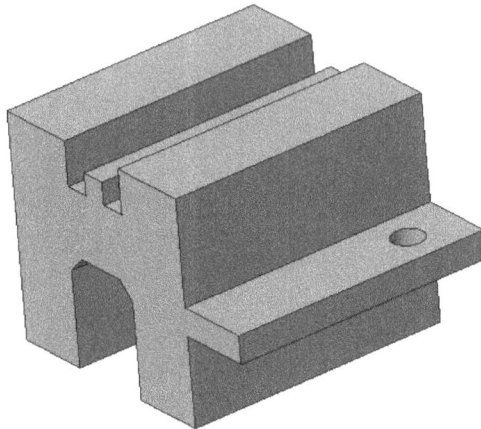

Figure 18–34

Task 3 - Change the design of the part.

Design Considerations

Due to design changes, the part must be changed to display as shown in Figure 18–35. You will not delete and recreate the features. Rather, you will edit the definition of the features, thereby changing the relationships they have with each other.

The MOUNT geometry must be moved to the other side of the part and the Hole must be moved to the top of the part.

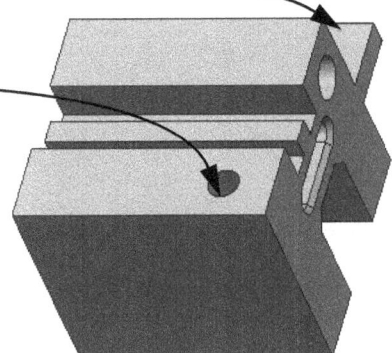

Figure 18–35

1. Edit the definition of the **Hole 1** feature. Its placement references display as shown in Figure 18–36.

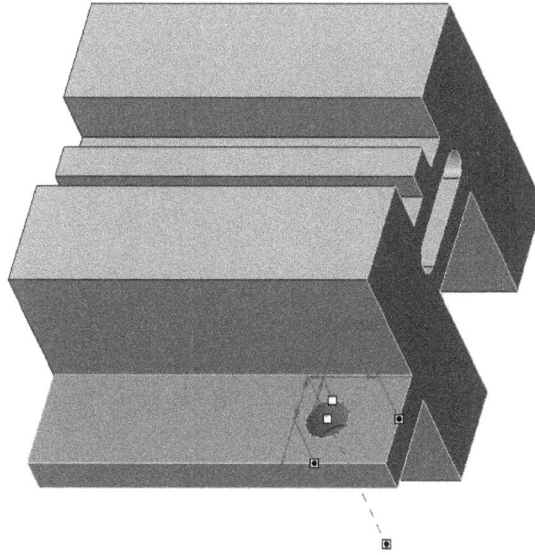

Figure 18–36

2. Change the Placement reference, as shown in Figure 18–37.

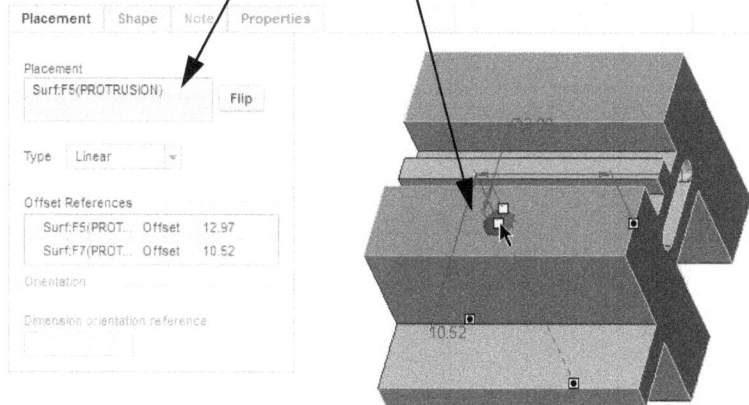

Figure 18–37

3. Select new *Offset References*, as shown in Figure 18–38, and edit the dimensions to the original values of **5** and **3.5**.

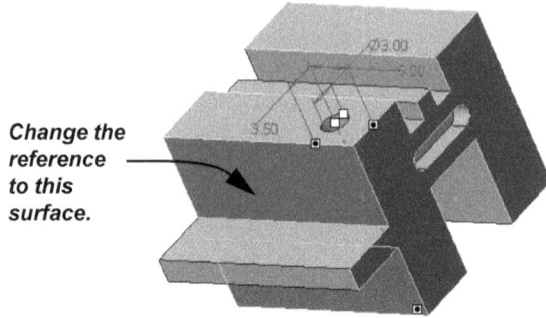

Change the reference to this surface.

Figure 18–38

4. Complete the hole feature. The part displays as shown in Figure 18–39.

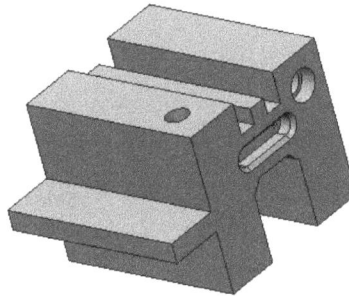

Figure 18–39

Task 4 - Change the location of a sketched feature.

1. Edit the definition of the **MOUNT** feature and access the *Sketch* tab. Click (Sketch View) and the sketch displays as shown in Figure 18–40.

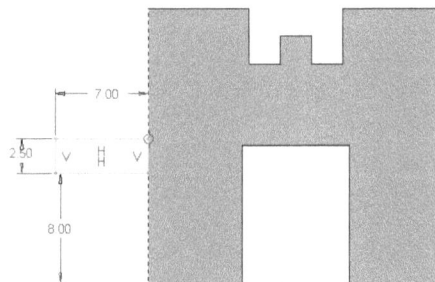

Figure 18–40

2. Click ⌑ (References) and delete the
   Surf:F5(PROTRUSION) reference shown in Figure 18–41.

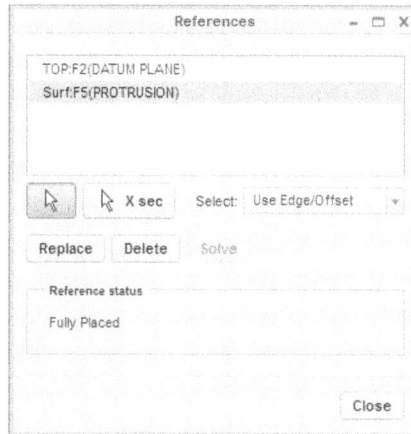

Figure 18–41

3. Add a reference on the opposite side of the part, as shown in
   Figure 18–42.

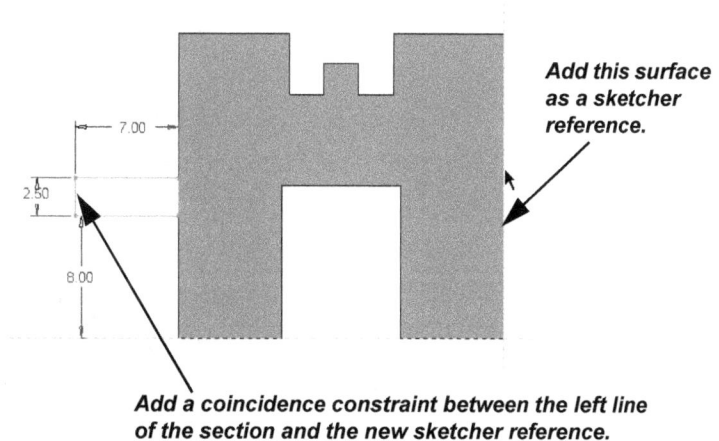

*Add this surface
as a sketcher
reference.*

*Add a coincidence constraint between the left line
of the section and the new sketcher reference.*

Figure 18–42

4. Add a coincidence constraint between the left side of the section and the new sketcher reference. The sketch updates to display as shown in Figure 18–43.

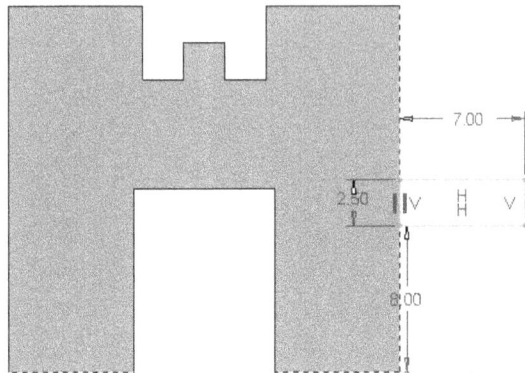

Figure 18–43

5. Complete the feature. The part displays as shown in Figure 18–44.

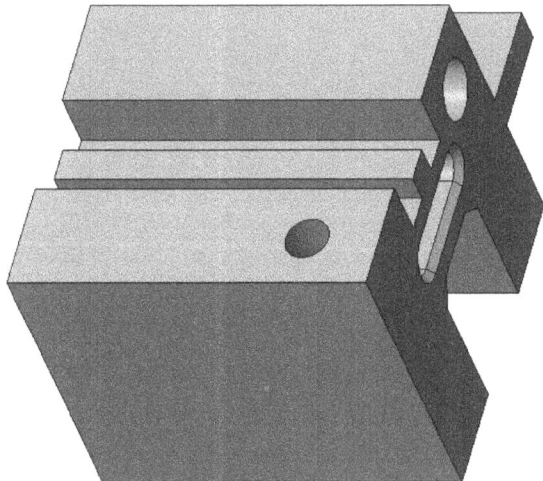

Figure 18–44

6. Save the part and erase it from memory.

Practice 18c

(Optional) Edit References

Practice Objectives

- Discover parent/child relationships between features using the Reference Viewer.
- Change an existing parent/child relationship in a model using the editing tools.

In this practice, you will open the model shown in Figure 18–45 and make changes to the model to reflect a design change. The cut, when originally created, was sketched on a surface of the center protrusion. The design has changed so that the center protrusion is not required.

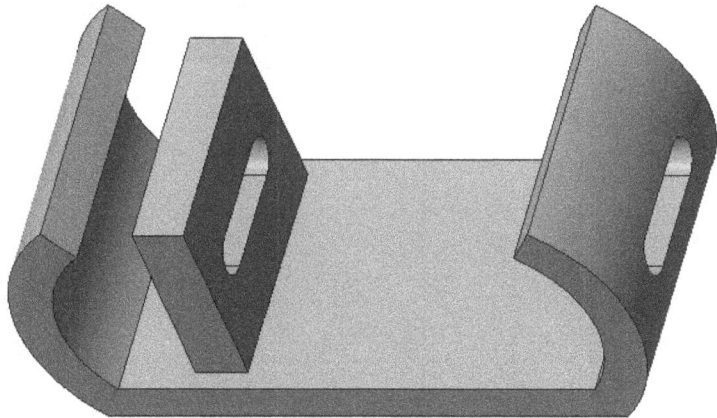

Figure 18–45

Task 1 - Reroute the cut so that the center protrusion can be deleted.

1. Set the working directory to *Chapter 18\practice 18c*.

2. Open **pc02.prt**.

3. Set the model display as follows:

   - ⁀⁎ *(Datum Display Filters)*: All Off

   - ⁀ *(Spin Center)*: Off

   - ⬚ *(Display Style)*: ⬚ (Shading With Edges)

4. Change the cut so the middle protrusion can be deleted without affecting the cut as shown in Figure 18–46. Do not delete and recreate the cut.

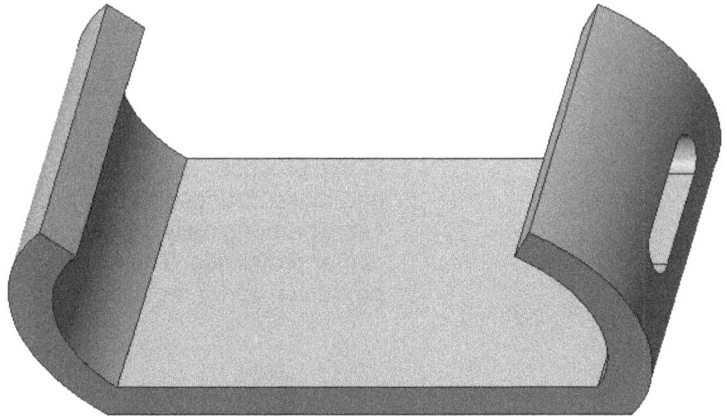

Figure 18–46

5. Save the part and erase it from memory.

Practice 18d | Resolving Failed Features I

Practice Objective

- Diagnose and correct the failures that occur using the appropriate tools.

In this practice, you will open an existing part file that requires a design change. The part is an injection molded part that originally did not require draft due to its small size. The manufacturer has requested that 0.5 degrees of draft be added to the four outside faces. You will incorporate this change.

Task 1 - Open a part file.

1. Set the working directory to the *Chapter 18\practice 18d* folder.

2. Open **no_draft.prt**.

3. Set the model display as follows:

   - *⁺⁄⁺ (Datum Display Filters)*: All Off

   - *⋟ (Spin Center)*: Off

   - *⬚ (Display Style)*: ⬚ (Shading With Edges)

Task 2 - Activate Insert mode.

In this task you will activate Insert mode to insert a draft feature after the base feature because the draft should be created early in the feature list.

1. Drag **Insert Here** up and place it after **Extrude 1**, as shown in Figure 18–47.

Figure 18–47

Task 3 - Add draft to the part.

1. Create a draft feature and select the four outside surfaces shown in Figure 18–48, as the surfaces to which to add the draft.

Shading toggled off for clarity.

Individual Surfaces

Figure 18–48

2. Select the top surface as the draft hinge, as shown in Figure 18–49. Enter **5.0** as the degree of draft (you might need to flip the draft angle direction so that the bottom of the part is larger than the top).

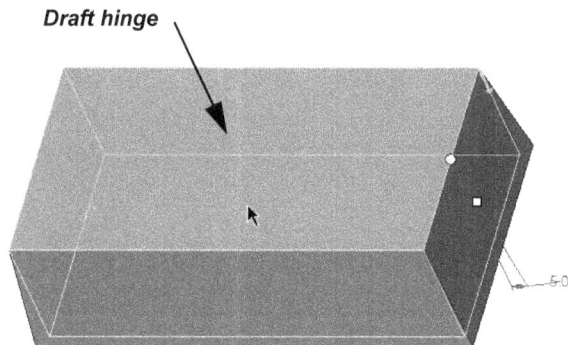

Draft hinge

Figure 18–49

3. Complete the draft feature.

Task 4 - Cancel Insert mode.

1. Drag **Insert Here** down to the bottom of the feature list in the model tree to cancel Insert mode.

2. A failure occurs. In the model tree, **PATTERN_TOP** and **Profile Rib 1** display in red, indicating that there has been a failure as shown in Figure 18–50.

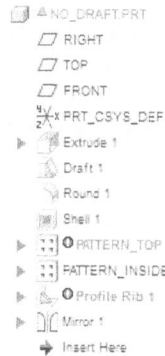

Figure 18–50

3. In the model tree, select **PATTERN_TOP**, right click and select ✍ (Edit Definition) to redefine the pattern. The *Pattern* dashboard opens. Note that the pattern is a Directional pattern. The two planes that were used to define the directions are missing (indicated by the yellow dot next to 1 Plane in the *Reference* fields, as shown in Figure 18–51).

Figure 18–51

4. Select datum plane **RIGHT** as the directional reference for the 1st direction then select in the reference collector for the 2nd direction and select datum plane **FRONT** as the directional reference. The pattern preview displays as shown in Figure 18–52.

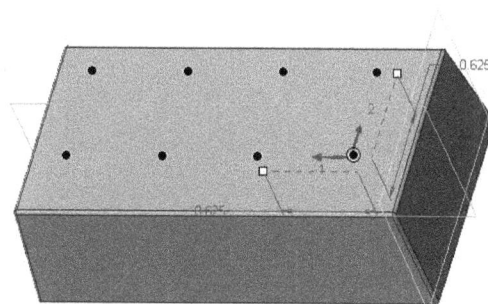

Figure 18–52

5. Complete the pattern.

Task 5 - Fix a failed feature.

1. Once the pattern has regenerated successfully, **Profile Rib 1**
   fails. Click ⬤ (Regeneration Manager) at the bottom of the
   window. The dialog box opens as shown in Figure 18–53.

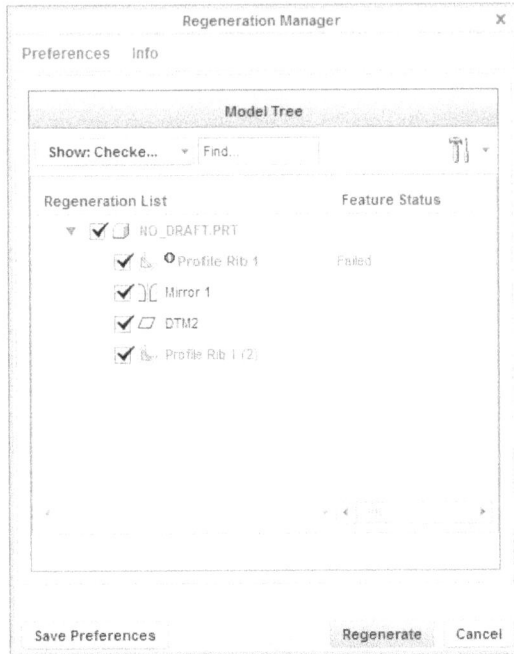

Figure 18–53

2. Right-click on **Profile Rib 1** and select **Reference Viewer**.
   The Reference Viewer shows the parent/child relationship for
   the **Profile Rib 1**.

3. Select the down arrows next to **Shell 1**, as shown in Figure 18–54. The Reference Manager indicates that there are missing references.

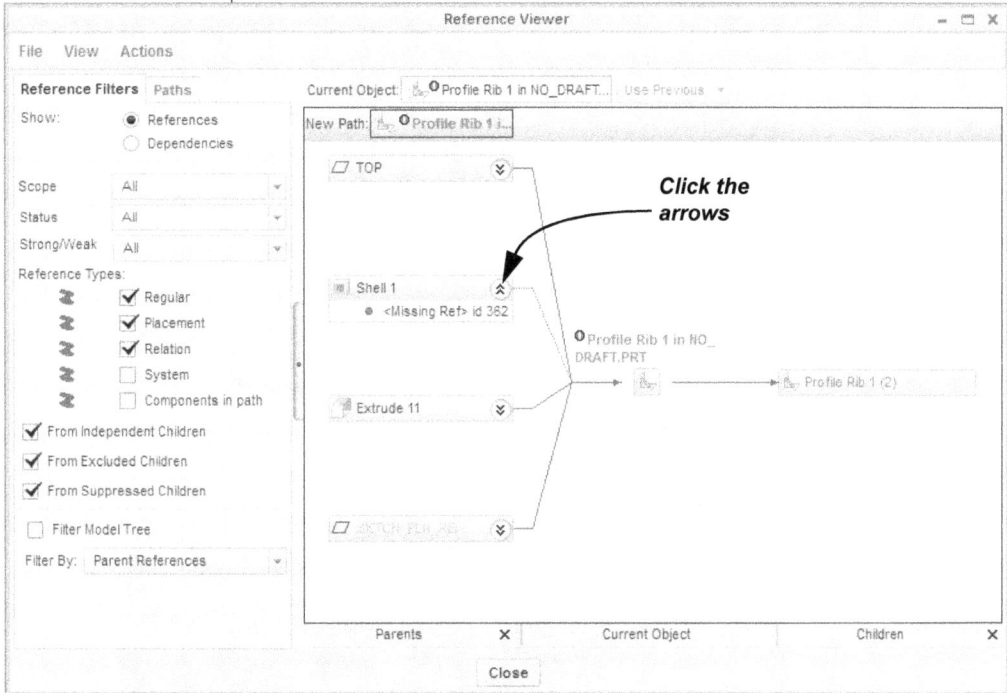

Figure 18–54

4. Click **Close** to close the Reference Viewer dialog box. In the model tree, select the **Profile Rib 1** sketch, right-click and select ✎ (Edit Definition).

5. Right-click and select **Edit Internal Sketch**. Click **Yes** to confirm the message shown in Figure 18–55.

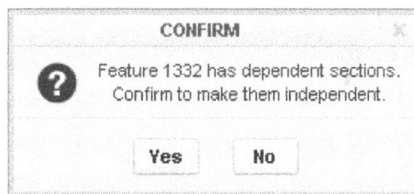

Figure 18–55

6. Select **Surf:F8(SHELL_1)** and click **Replace** to replace the missing reference, as shown in Figure 18–56.

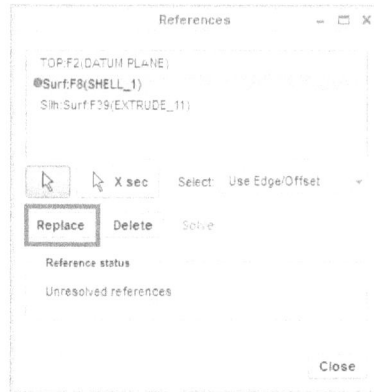

Figure 18–56

7. Select the surface shown in Figure 18–57 as the new reference.

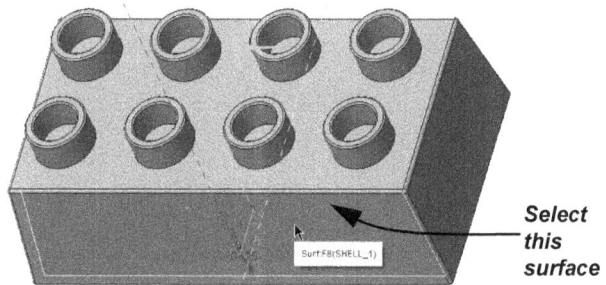

Select this surface

Figure 18–57

8. Click **Solve** in the Reference dialog box. This creates a constraint to the new reference, as shown in Figure 18–58 (there should only be one dimension in this sketch).

Model rotated and shading toggled off for clarity.

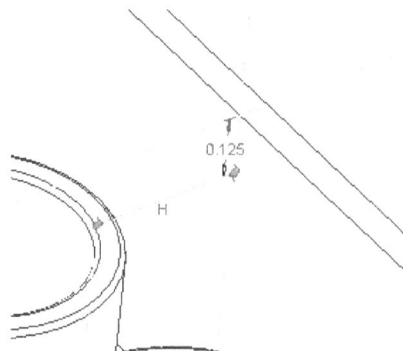

0.125

H

Figure 18–58

9. Close the Reference dialog box.

10. Complete the sketch and complete the rib feature.

11. The mirrored rib fails for the same reason. Although you could use a similar procedure to fix the second rib, it is much quicker to delete and recreate the mirror.

12. Right-click on **Mirror 1** in the model tree and select **Delete**.

13. Select **Profile Rib 1** in the model tree and select 〕〔 (Mirror) from the Editing group in the ribbon.

14. Select datum plane **FRONT** from the model tree and click ✔ (Complete Feature).

15. The completed part displays as shown in Figure 18–59.

Figure 18–59

16. Save the part and erase it from memory.

Practice 18e | Resolving Failed Features II

Practice Objectives

- Diagnose and correct the failures that occur using the appropriate tools.
- Avoid feature failures using the Replace command in the Sketch tab.

In this practice, you will make several modifications to a model. Features that you are modifying will cause failures that must be resolved.

Task 1 - Open a part file.

1. Set the working directory to the *Chapter 18\practice 18e* folder.

2. Open **resolve.prt**.

3. Set the model display as follows:

   - *(Datum Display Filters)*: All Off

   - *(Spin Center)*: Off

   - *(Display Style)*: (Shading With Edges)

Task 2 - Investigate the part.

1. Select the *Tools* tab and click (Model Player).

2. Investigate the model features.

Task 3 - Edit a dimension of a sketch.

Edit **CUT_1** to modify the section height, as shown in Figure 18–60. Set the new value, enter **3**.

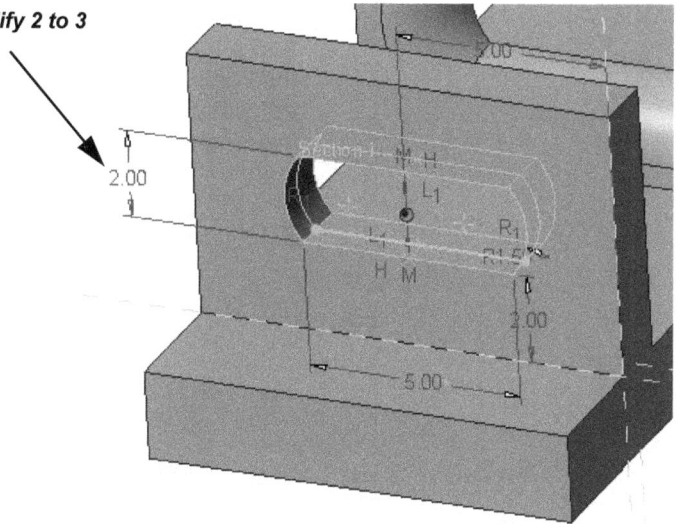

Figure 18–60

The dimension does not update, and a line displays in the message window prompting you that the regeneration has failed because the dimension entered is an incompatible value, as shown in Figure 18–61.

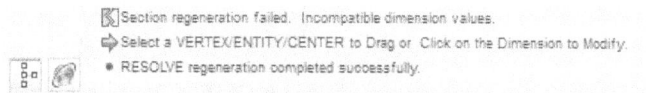

Figure 18–61

The arcs have a radius of **1.5**. This value is incompatible with the section height of **3.0**. If you want to change the section height, you need to modify the arc radii at the same time.

Task 4 - Modify the sketch for an extrude.

1. In the model tree, select **PROTRUSION_1**. Right-click and select 🖌 (Edit Definition). Activate the *Sketch* tab by right-clicking and selecting **Edit Internal Sketch.**

2. Add a horizontal dimension of **1.5** for the top line and delete the vertical constraint on the left side of the sketch. Modify the dimensional values, as shown in Figure 18–62. Do not delete any of the original entities.

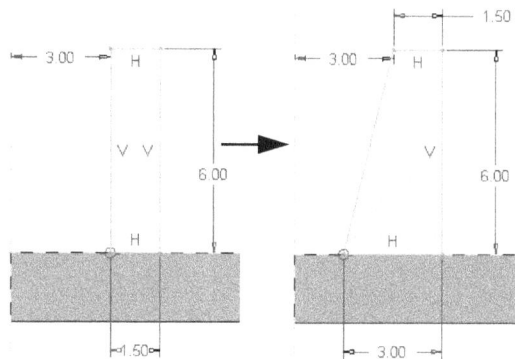

Original   *Modified*

Figure 18–62

3. Complete the feature redefinition.

4. Click OK in the warning message indicating that some features failed to regenerate.

5. The **CUT_1** feature fails because its sketching plane is missing. It was removed by the section modification. To resolve the failure, select **CUT_1** in the model tree, right-click and select ⚭ (Edit References).

6. Select **Surf:F6(PROTRUSION) ID85** in the reference section, then select datum plane **RIGHT** as an alternative sketching plane.

7. Click **OK**. The model displays as shown in Figure 18–63.

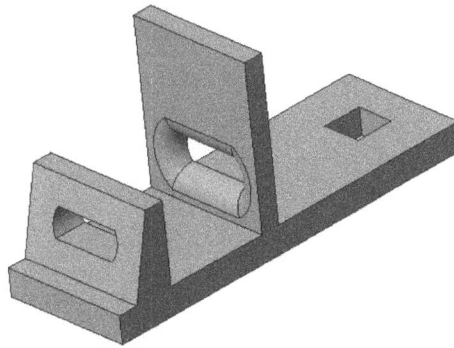

Figure 18–63

Task 5 - Modify the sketch for an extrude.

---

1. In the model tree, expand **CUT_1**. Right-click on sketch **Section 1** and select ✎ (Edit Definition).

2. Modify the feature section as shown in Figure 18–64. Delete the right arc and sketch a vertical line in its place. When prompted to: *This entity is referenced by other feature(s). Continue?*, select **Yes**.

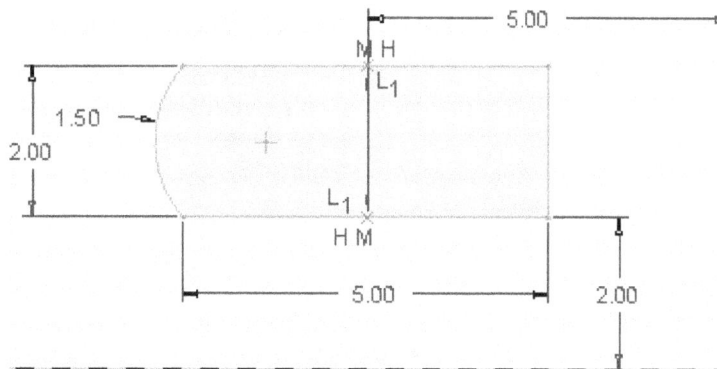

Figure 18–64

3. Complete the sketch.

4. The **ROUND** feature fails because one of its reference edges is missing. It was removed by the section modification. To resolve the failure, right-click and select ✎ (Edit Definition).

---

5. Open the Sets panel and investigate the list of references. There is a red dot next to one of them. Select this reference, right-click, and select **What's wrong** as shown in Figure 18–65. The Troubleshooter window opens.

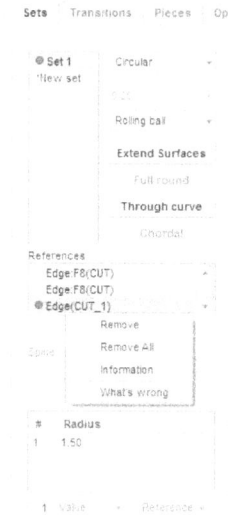

Figure 18–65

6. Read the information in the Troubleshooter window and then close the window.

7. Orient the model to the default view using <Ctrl>+<D>.

8. In the Sets panel, scroll down to the missing edge reference with a red dot in the *References* area, right-click on the failed edge reference, and select **Remove** as shown in Figure 18–66.

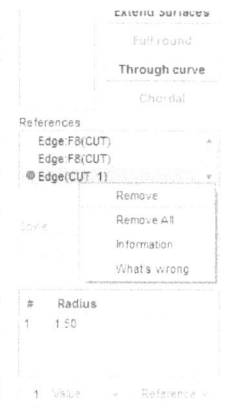

Figure 18–66

9. Press and hold <Ctrl> and select the new straight edge of the cut, as shown in Figure 18–67.

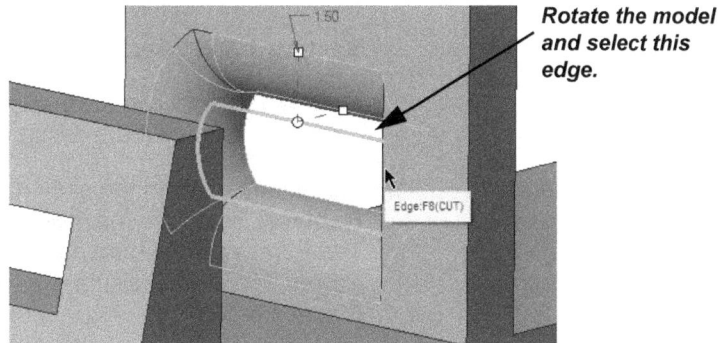

Rotate the model and select this edge.

Edge:F8(CUT)

Figure 18–67

10. Complete the feature. The model displays as shown in Figure 18–68.

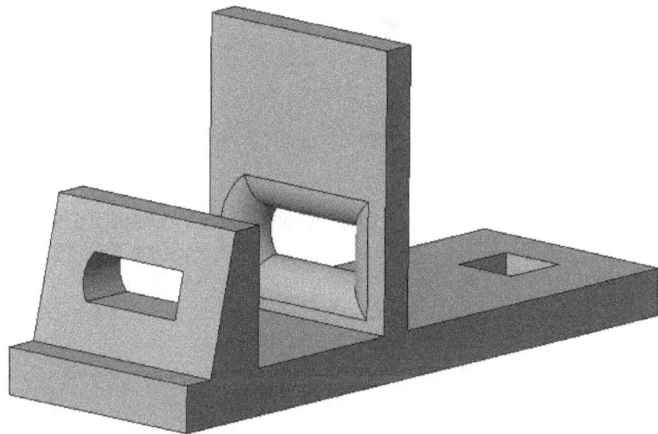

Figure 18–68

Task 6 - Modify the shape of the section for CUT_1.

1. In the model tree, expand **Cut_1**. Right-click on sketch **Section 1** and select ✐ (Edit Definition).

2. Sketch a vertical line as shown on the left in Figure 18–69. This line replaces the existing arc entity.

You can also expand the Operations flyout panel and select **Replace**.

3. Select the arc from the sketch, right-click, and select **Replace**. Select the new vertical line to be replaced. Click **Yes** to remove the dimension and complete the replace action. The sketch displays as shown on the right in Figure 18–69.

Replace this arc with the vertical line.

Sketch this vertical line.

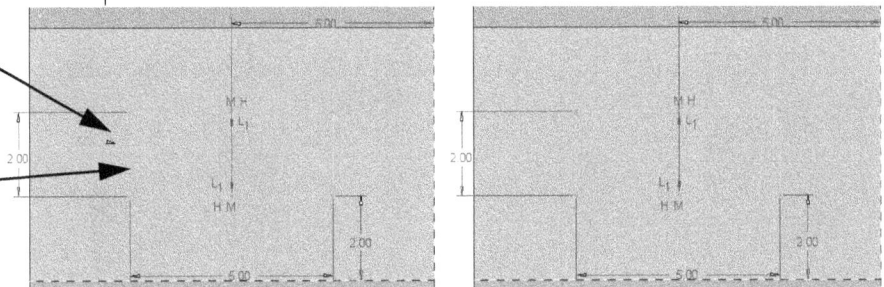

Figure 18–69

4. Complete the feature redefinition. The model displays as shown in Figure 18–70.

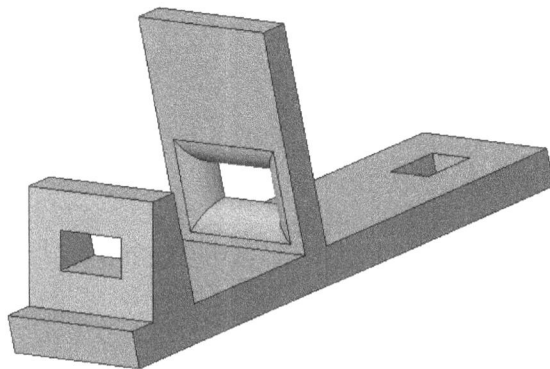

Figure 18–70

The **ROUND** feature has been modified without failure. This is because you replaced the old section entity with the new one.

Task 7 - Modify the shape of the section for the BASE feature.

1. Edit the definition of the **BASE** feature sketch.

2. Modify the sketch as shown in Figure 18–71. Sketch an arc, which will replace the existing vertical line entity. Then, right-click and select **Replace** and follow the system instructions. Click **Yes** to remove the dimension and complete the replace action.

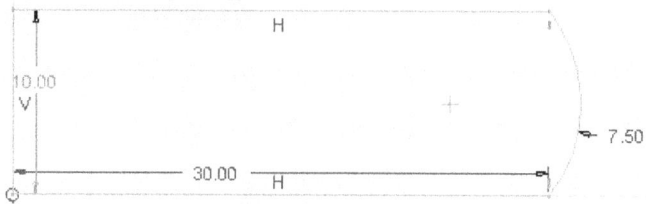

Figure 18–71

3. Complete the feature redefinition.

In the original model, the position of the section of CUT_2 is dimensioned to the right vertical planar surface of the BASE feature.

4. The **CUT_2** feature fails because one of its dimension references is missing. It was removed by the section modification. To resolve the failure, click **OK** in the notification box, right-click **CUT_2**, and select ✎ (Edit Definition).

5. Redefine the feature section. Remove the failed sketcher reference and add a new one. Select the new cylindrical surface from the **BASE** feature as a reference. Modify the feature section as shown in Figure 18–72.

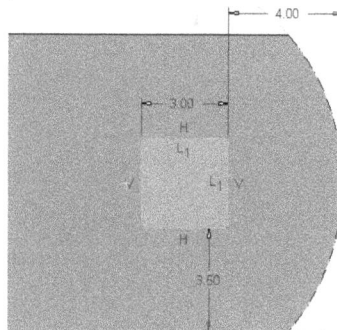

Figure 18–72

6. Complete the feature redefinition.

7. The model displays as shown in Figure 18–73.

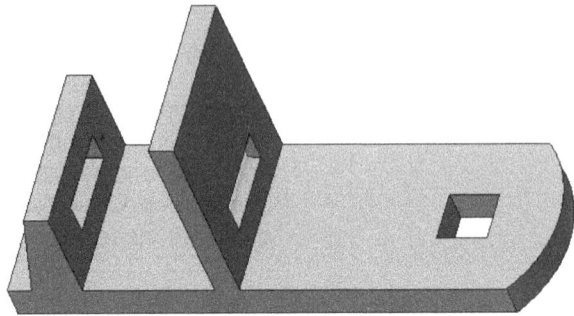

Figure 18–73

8. Save the part and erase it from memory.

Chapter Review Questions

1. A parent/child relationship is established when any solid feature is created in the model.

   a. True

   b. False

2. One Engineering feature can be a parent of another.

   a. True

   b. False

3. Which of the following actions creates a parent/child relationship when sketching a feature? (Select all that apply.)

   a. Selecting the sketching plane.

   b. Selecting the orientation plane.

   c. Maintaining the default orientation plane.

   d. Selecting sketching references.

   e. Creating an offset entity.

   f. Projecting an existing edge to create a new entity.

   g. Dimensioning the length of a line.

   h. Aligning a new entity with an existing entity.

   i. Extruding to a Blind depth.

   j. Extruding through all surfaces.

   k. Extruding to Intersect with a selected surface or plane.

4. Which of the following options can be used to investigate parent/child relationships? (Select all that apply.)

   a. Feature List

   b. Edit References

   c. Reference Viewer

   d. Model Player

5. If a parent feature must be deleted, which of the following options can be used to change the references to the child feature? (Select all that apply.)

    a. Edit

    b. Edit Definition

    c. Edit References

    d. Insert Mode

6. The Delete dialog box opens if you select and delete the hole shown in the Figure 18–74.

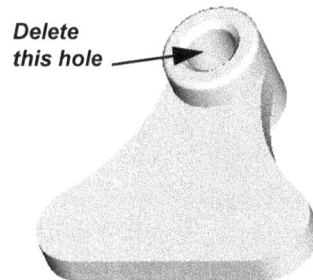

Delete this hole

Figure 18–74

    a. True

    b. False

7. What causes the Delete dialog box to open when you delete a feature?

    a. Parent/child relationships

    b. Feature Failure

    c. Feature is suppressed

    d. Feature is incomplete

8. Investigate the Reference Information Window dialog box shown in Figure 18–75. Which features are children of the current feature? (Select all that apply.)

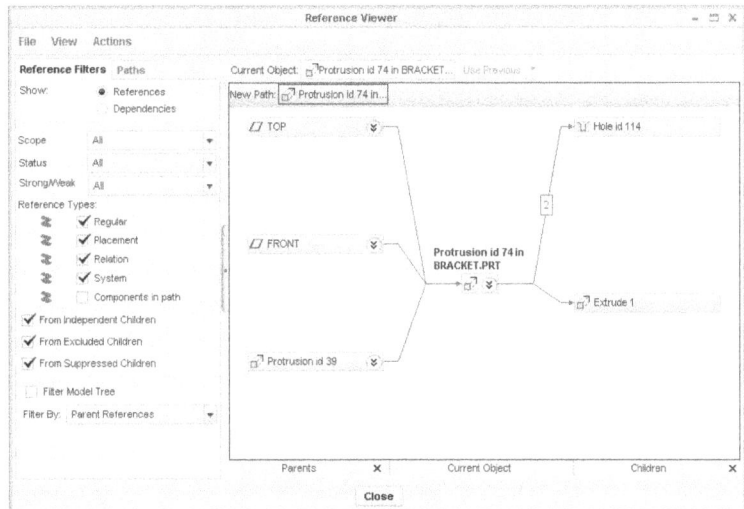

Figure 18–75

a. Hole id 114

b. Extrude 1

c. FRONT

d. Protrusion id 39

9. When a feature fails you can continue to model without fixing the failed feature.

a. True

b. False

10. When a feature fails, the failed feature and all subsequent features are not regenerated and are not displayed in the main window.

a. True

b. False

11. Clicking **Cancel** in the message box shown in Figure 18–76, enables you to fix the failure while maintaining the change that originally caused the failure.

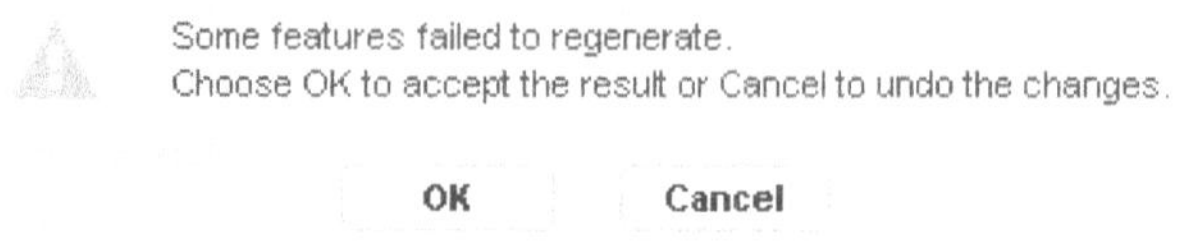

Some features failed to regenerate.
Choose OK to accept the result or Cancel to undo the changes.

OK   Cancel

Figure 18–76

a. True

b. False

Command Summary

Button	Command	Location
	Feature Information	• **Ribbon:** *Tools* tab in the *Investigate* group
	Reference Viewer	• **Ribbon:** *Tools* tab in the *Investigate* group
d=	**Relations**	• **Ribbon:** *Tools* tab in the *Model Intent* group • **Ribbon:** *Model* tab in the Model Intent flyout group
	Model Player	• **Ribbon:** *Tools* tab in the *Investigate* group
	Regeneration Manager	• **Ribbon:** *Model* tab in the *Operations* group

Drawing Basics: View Creation and Detailing

Drawings can be created from the models created in Part or Assembly mode. Drawings are associative, so a change made in the model reflects in the drawing and in turn, a change made in the drawing reflects in the model.

Learning Objectives in this Chapter

- Create a new drawing.
- Add General, Projected, Auxiliary, Detailed, and Section views to create the required documentation of a model.
- Show dimensions on a drawing using the Show Model Annotations dialog box.
- Create additional dimensions and notes in the drawing.
- Manipulate detail items using the contextual menu or the Properties dialog box.
- Add a custom symbol to a drawing.
- Add additional sheets to a drawing, and move objects to it.

19.1 Creating a New Drawing

This section covers the process of creating a basic drawing of your model.

General Steps

Use the following general steps to create a drawing:

1. Create a new drawing.
2. Place the first drawing view.
3. Add views.
4. Modify view properties.
5. Manipulate drawing views, as required.
6. Detail the drawing (e.g., dimensions, notes, tolerances, etc.).
7. Manipulate detail items, as required.
8. Print (or Plot) the drawing.

Step 1 - Create a new drawing.

To create a new drawing, click ⬜ (New) in the Quick Access Toolbar. Select the **Drawing** option in the New dialog box, enter a name, and click **OK**. The New Drawing dialog box opens, as shown in Figure 19–1.

*The default option in the Specify Template area is dependent on whether the **Use default template** option is selected in the New dialog box. If so, the **Use template** option is selected. If not the **Empty** option is selected.*

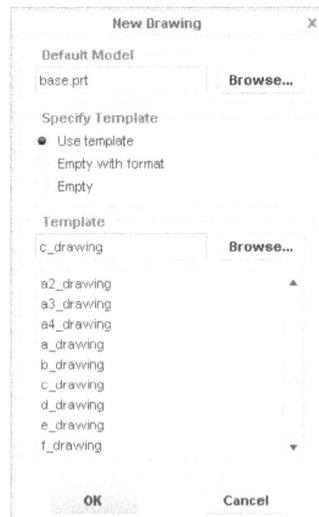

New Drawing

Default Model

base.prt   Browse...

Specify Template
● Use template
  Empty with format
  Empty

Template

c_drawing   Browse...

a2_drawing
a3_drawing
a4_drawing
a_drawing
b_drawing
c_drawing
d_drawing
e_drawing
f_drawing

OK   Cancel

Figure 19–1

If a model is in session, Creo Parametric assigns that model as the default.

The areas in the New Drawing dialog box are described in .

Area	Description
Default Model	Enter the name or click **Browse** to specify the model to be displayed in the drawing.
Specify Template	Select the **Use template**, **Empty with format**, or **Empty** option to specify whether you want to create the drawing with a predefined template, a format, or to leave the drawing empty.
Template	Enter the name or click **Browse** to specify the template that is to be used in the drawing. Only available when the **Use template** option is selected.
Format	Enter the name or click **Browse** to specify the format that is to be used in the drawing. Only available when the **Empty with format** option is selected.
Orientation and Size	Select the appropriate icon to define the orientation of the drawing sheet (portrait, landscape, or variable) and set the sheet size for the drawing. Only available when the **Empty** option is selected.

Templates

A drawing template contains predefined views, sets the view display, creates snap lines, and displays preassigned model dimensions based on the information specified when the template was created. Templates are discussed further in *Creo Parametric: Design Documentation & Detailing*.

Formats

A drawing format can contain standard information that is present in all drawings, such as the title block, company logo, BOM tables, etc. Drawing formats can be used in conjunction with drawing templates.

When you have finished making selections in the New Drawing dialog box, click **OK** to create the drawing.

Step 2 - Place the first drawing view.

Drawings created using a template already contain certain views. Additional views can be added at any time.

The first view placed on the drawing is always a General view. This kind of view is independent of other views. To place the first (General) view, right-click and select **General View** or click

⊟ (General View), in the Model Views group, in the *Layout* tab.

Select **OK** if the Select Combined State dialog box displays. Select a location on the drawing to place the view. The General view is initially placed on the drawing sheet in its default orientation and the Drawing View dialog box opens, as shown in Figure 19–2.

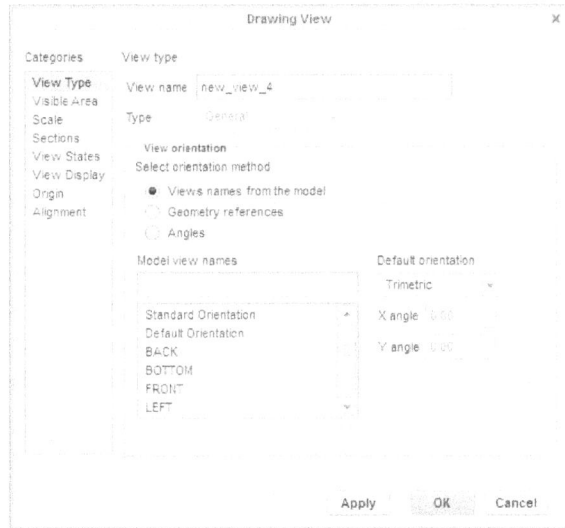

Figure 19–2

By default, the *View Type* category settings display in the Drawing View dialog box. You can enter the View name and change the default view orientation using the options in the *View orientation* area.

To modify the view orientation, you can select one the following methods in the *View orientation* area:

- View names from the model

- Geometry references

- Angles

To apply the new view orientation, click **Apply**.

View Names From the Model

The **View names from the model** option enables you to orient the General view on the drawing, using a predefined view saved from the model. The list of predefined views displays in the Drawing View dialog box, as shown in Figure 19–3.

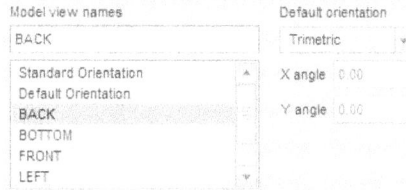

Figure 19–3

Geometry References

The **Geometry references** option enables you to orient the General view using the orientation tools that are used in other 3D models. You must select an orientation (e.g., Front, Top, Right, etc.), and then select a planar surface, datum plane or coordinate system axis as its reference, as shown in Figure 19–4. The two references must be perpendicular to one another to orient the view into 2D.

Using default datum planes to orient the model is recommended. Orientation references can be lost if the selected planar surface references are later deleted.

Figure 19–4

You can click **Default Orientation** to return the view to the default orientation.

Angles

The **Angles** option enables you to orient the General view by selecting a direction and entering angular values to place the view. The available directions are: Normal, Vertical, Horizontal, and Edge/Axis. The Normal, Vertical, and Horizontal directions are relative to the drawing sheet (monitor) and the Edge/Axis direction enables you to select a reference on the model from which to orient. Figure 19–5 shows the *Angles* area. You can add and remove orientation angles as required, using ✚ and ▬.

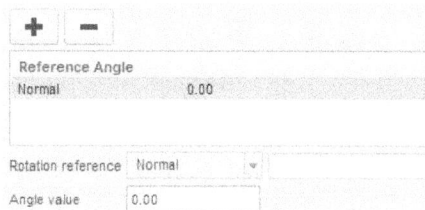

Figure 19–5

For example, the model in Figure 19–6 is oriented to 2D using the **Geometry references** option and by selecting references for the **Front** and **Top** reference options.

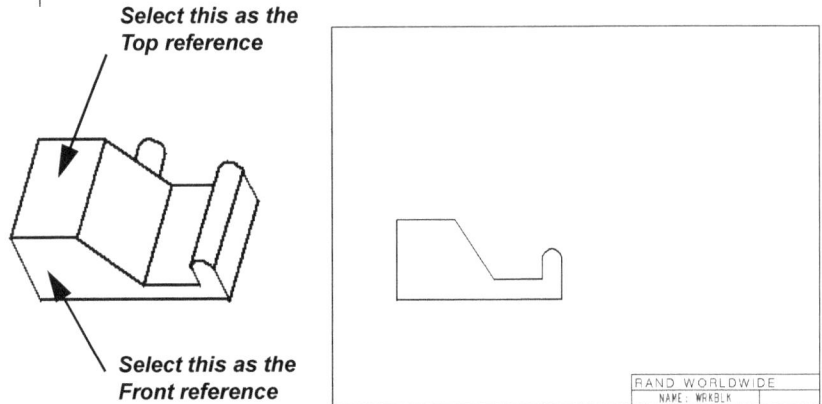

*Select this as the
Top reference*

*Select this as the
Front reference*

RAND WORLDWIDE
NAME: WRKBLK

Figure 19–6

Once the orientation has been defined, click **OK** in the Drawing View dialog box to continue the drawing creation.

Step 3 - Add views.

Additional view types are available after the first general view has been added. To place an additional view, click the icon representing the view you want use in the *Layout* tab, as shown in Figure 15-7.

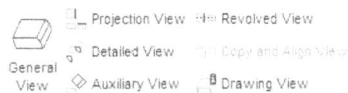

General
View

Projection View   Revolved View
Detailed View   Copy and Align View
Auxiliary View   Drawing View

Figure 19–7

Additional views and options for views can be found in the *Layout* tab.

The available view types are described as follows:

Option	Description
General	A view that is originally displayed in 3D and can be oriented into 2D.
Projection	An orthographic projection of an existing view.
Detailed	A selected portion of an existing view.

Auxiliary	A view projected 90° to a surface, datum, or axis.
Revolved	A cross-section revolved 90° about a cut line.
Copy and Align	A copy of an existing Detailed view with a different boundary defined.

The available view types are dependent on the views that currently exist in the drawing, and whether a view is preselected before you select a view in the View toolbar. If a view is not selected, the system provides a more detailed list that enables you to create new parent views. If a view is preselected, the system assumes that you are creating a child view to the selected view and provides the appropriate view types. Figure 19–8 shows examples of different view types.

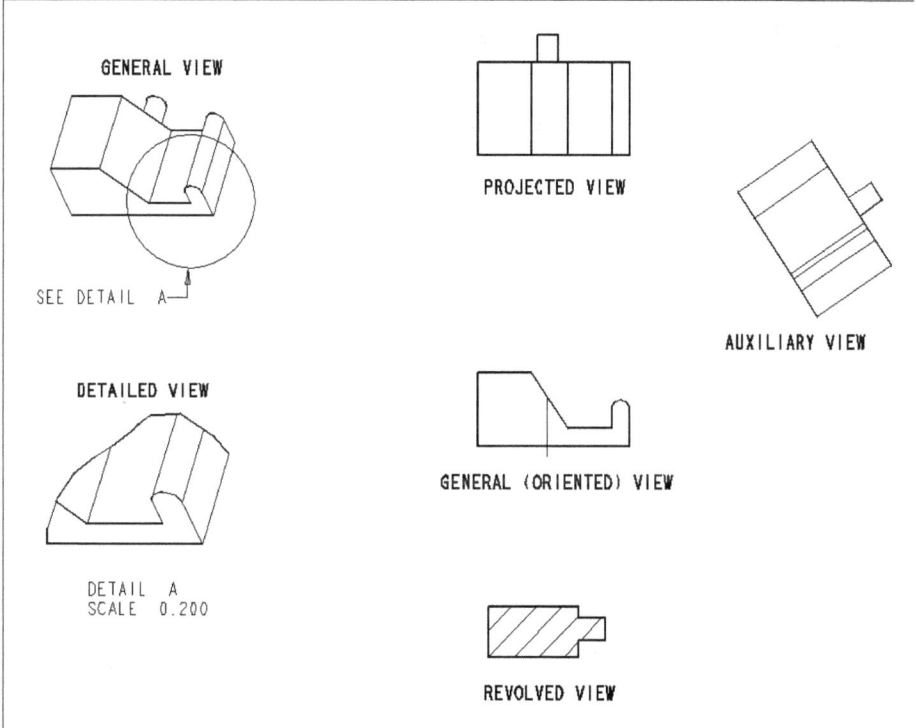

GENERAL VIEW

SEE DETAIL A

DETAILED VIEW

DETAIL A
SCALE 0.200

PROJECTED VIEW

GENERAL (ORIENTED) VIEW

REVOLVED VIEW

AUXILIARY VIEW

Figure 19–8

Shortcuts for General and Projected Views

To quickly create General, Projection, and Auxiliary views, you can right-click and select an option in the contextual menu. To create a General view, right-click and select **General View** and place the view. To create a Projected or Auxiliary view, select the parent view, right-click, and select **Projection View** or **Auxiliary View.** Place the view relative to the parent view.

Step 4 - Modify view properties.

To change the view properties, double click on the view or select the view, right-click, and select **Properties**. The Drawing view dialog box opens. You can now change the properties in individual categories.

View Type

The *View Type* category enables you to change the view type in the Type drop-down list, as shown in Figure 19–9. For example, you can change the General view to a Projection view. Note that the view type modification can be restricted. Some view types might display in gray, indicating that they are not available for selection.

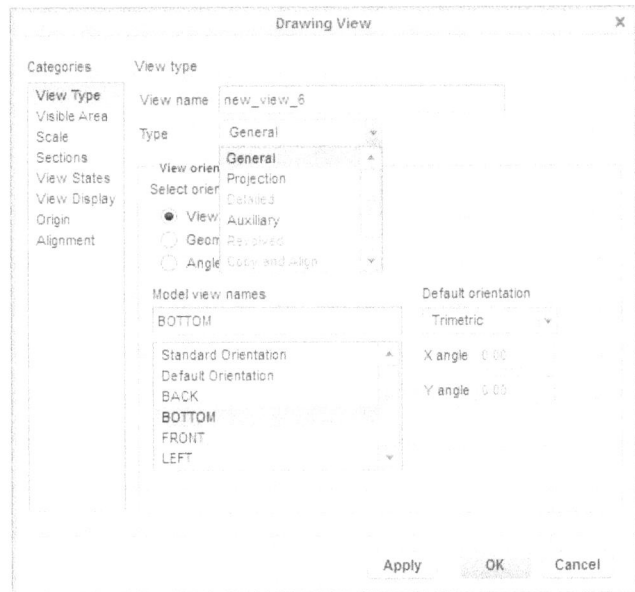

Figure 19–9

The *View Type* category enables you to change the view orientation, using the options in the *View orientation* area. See Step 1 for more detailed information.

When modifying a Detailed view, the *View Type* category enables you to re-sketch the view boundary. Select the *Reference point on parent view* collector and select the new reference point. Select the *Spline boundary on the parent view* collector and sketch the spline representing the view boundary. The options for the *View Type* category are shown in Figure 19–10.

Figure 19–10

Visible Area

The *Visible Area* category enables you to define the portion of the view (visibility) that displays and view clipping options. The options are shown in Figure 19–11.

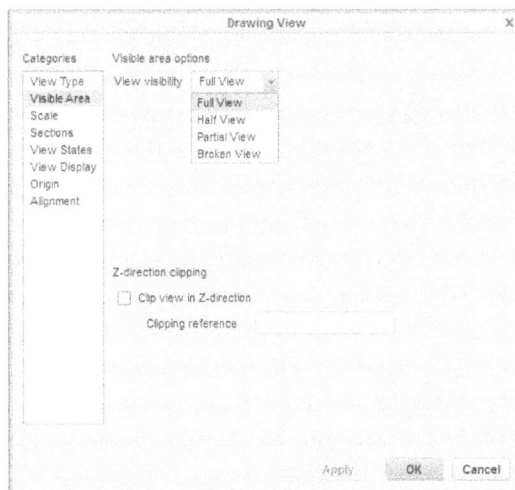

Figure 19–11

The visibility of a view can be defined as Full, Half, Partial, or Broken, as shown in Figure 19–12. Depending on the view type, some visibility options might not be available.

*The **Visible Area** options enable you to highlight key areas of a drawing view.*

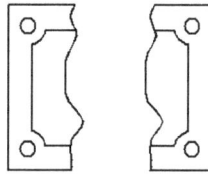

BROKEN VIEW

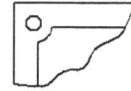

PARTIAL VIEW

FULL VIEW

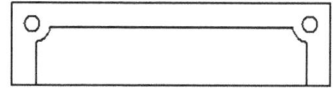

HALF VIEW

Figure 19–12

Scale

The *Scale* category enables you to define whether the view uses the default sheet scale (**Default scale for sheet**) or whether an independent scale is applied (**Custom scale**), as shown in Figure 19–13.

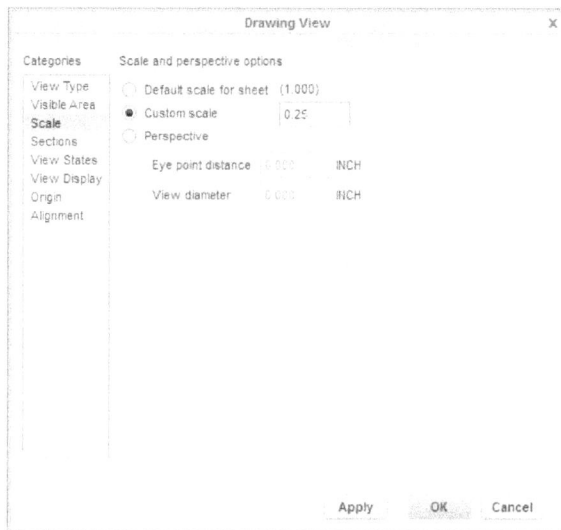

Figure 19–13

Default Scale for Sheet

Select the **Default scale for sheet** option in the Drawing View dialog box to set the default scale for a view. The default drawing scale displays in the lower left corner of the drawing, as shown in Figure 19–14. The scale value is based on sheet and model size, and affects all views in the drawing that are not independently scaled.

SCALE : 1.000   TYPE : PART   NAME : BASE   SIZE : B

⏮ ◀ ▶ ⏭   +   Sheet 1

Figure 19–14

Custom Scale

Select the **Custom scale** option in the Drawing View dialog box to add an independent view scale. The scale value displays directly below the view, as shown in Figure 19–15. Customized scaling is useful when you want views to appear smaller or larger than the default scale permits.

*The scale values associated with individual views can be moved using the standard **Move** tools.*

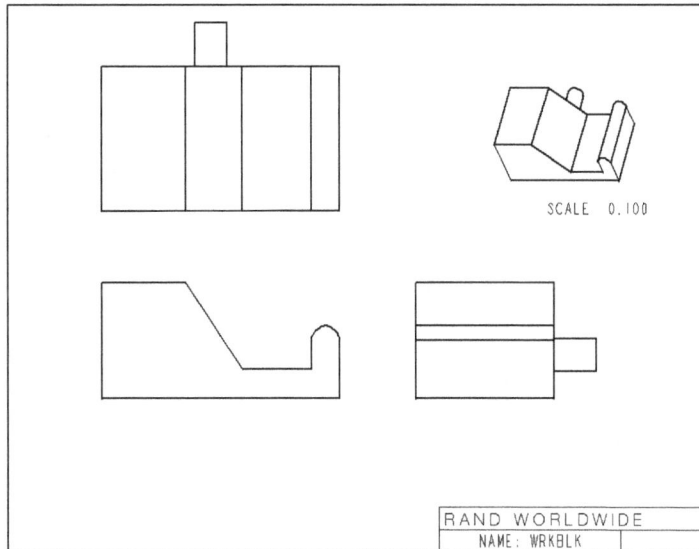

SCALE 0.100

RAND WORLDWIDE
NAME: WRKBLK

Figure 19–15

Sections

The *Sections* category enables you to define whether or not the view contains a cross-section. To add a 2D section created in the model while in Part mode, click ✚, select the cross-section name in the *Name* column, and select an area type in the *Sectioned Area* column, as shown in Figure 19–16. Click ➖ to remove a section from the view. Click ⟋ to flip the material side.

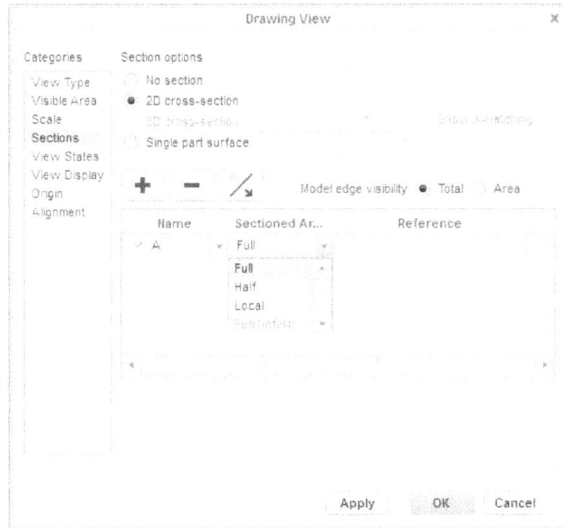

Figure 19–16

Figure 19–17 shows two of the basic cross-section types that can be used. These types are set using the **Model edge visibility** options.

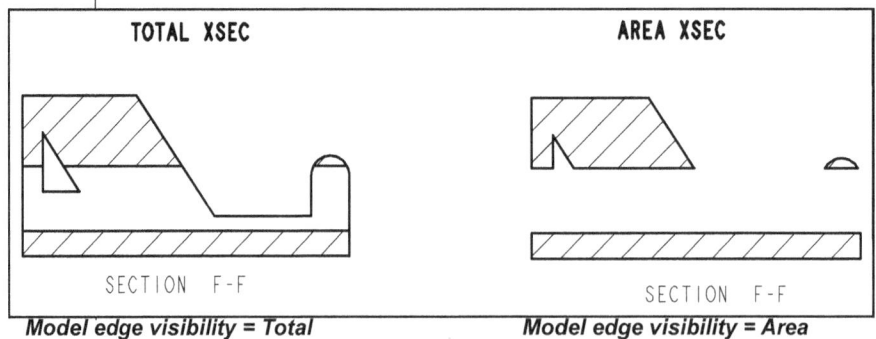

Model edge visibility = Total   *Model edge visibility = Area*

Figure 19–17

View Display

By default, all views display according to the view display icon that is selected in the In-graphics toolbar (⬚ (Wireframe), ⬚ (No Hidden), ⬚ (Hidden Line), ⬚ (Shading) or ⬚ (Shading With Edges)). This setting affects all views in the drawing. The *View Display* category enables you to set the display for each view using the Display style drop-down list as shown in Figure 19–18. Once set, the display for the view is independent of the settings made in the Creo Parametric session.

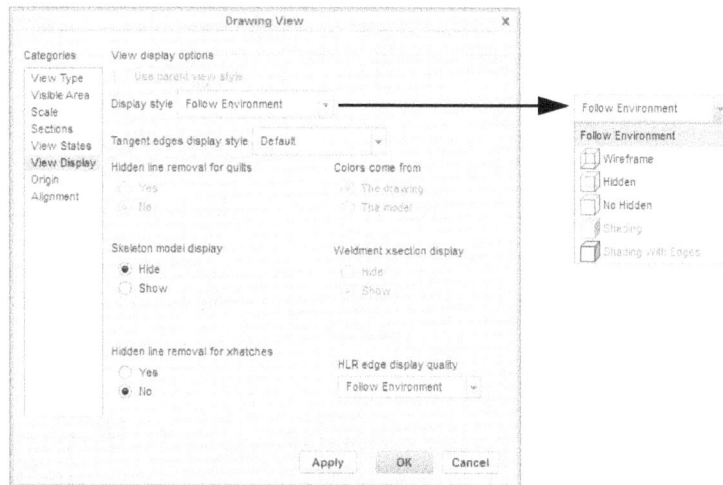

Figure 19–18

Step 5 - Manipulate drawing views, as required.

Once views have been added and modified, some common changes can be made to them including: deleting views, moving views, changing scale, and view display.

Delete Views

Deleted views are permanently removed from the drawing.

Views can be deleted from a drawing using any of the following methods.

- Select the view, right-click, and select **Delete**.

- Select the view and press <Delete>.

- Select the view and click ✕ (Delete) in the *Annotate* tab.

- Select the view name in the Drawing Tree, right-click and select **Delete**.

Move Views

Views are automatically locked to the original location at which they were placed. To enable movement of views, clear the checkmark next to **Lock View Movement** in the contextual menu or click ⬛ (Lock View Movement) in the Document group in the *Layout* tab. Once unlocked, you can select the view and drag it as required on the drawing. All dependent views move relative to their parents. Once you finish moving a view, it is recommended that you relock the view movement using the same tool.

Change Scale

To modify the default drawing scale, double-click on the scale value in the lower left corner of the drawing and enter a value at the prompt. Changing this value affects the scale of all but the independently scaled views.

To modify the scale of an independently scaled view, select the note containing the scale value, and double-click on the scale value inside the note. You can also select the note containing the scale value. Select the scale value, right-click, and select **Edit Value**.

Step 6 - Detail the drawing (e.g., dimensions, notes, tolerances, etc.).

When drawing views have been placed on a drawing, you can add dimensions and notes to communicate information to manufacturing. These items are associative and update with changes to other views and modifications to the model. Detail items display in the drawing tree as shown in Figure 19–19.

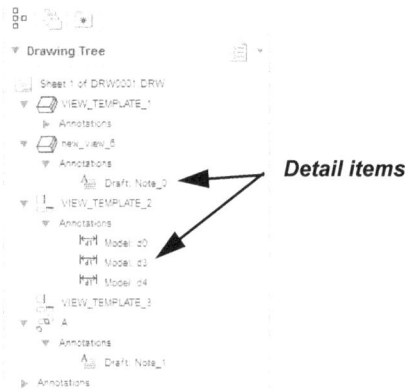

Figure 19–19

Dimensions

Dimensions can be shown or created to provide the required dimensional information for manufacturing the model, as shown in Figure 19–20.

Dimensions can be created in Drawing mode, but these dimensions do not drive the geometry. Only those displayed directly from the model can drive the geometry.

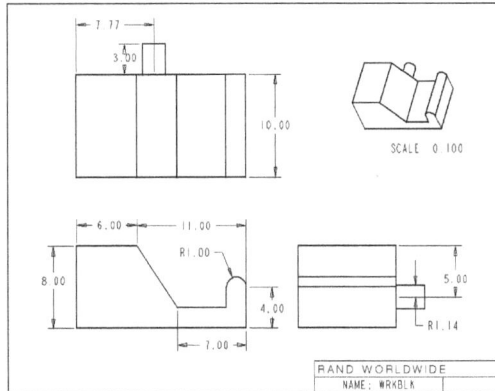

Figure 19–20

Showing Model Annotations

Model dimensions refer to dimensions that are used to create the part model.

How To: Display or Erase Model Dimensions

1. Select the *Annotate* tab.

*Dimensions can also be added by selecting a feature in the model tree, right-clicking and selecting **Show Model Annotation**.*

2. Click ⊞ (Show Model Annotations) in the Annotations group or right-click on the feature in the model tree and select **Show Model Annotations**. The Show Model Annotations dialog box opens as shown in Figure 19–21.

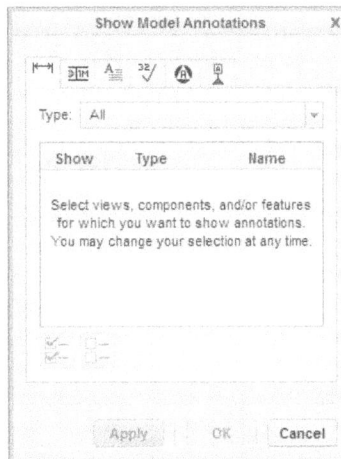

Figure 19–21

3. The *Dimension* tab (⊢⊣) displays by default and the Type drop-down is set to **All**. You can filter your selections as shown in Figure 19–22.

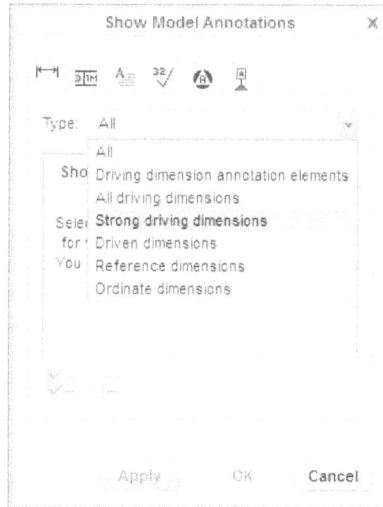

Figure 19–22

4. Select a feature in the view in which you want the dimensions to display in the drawing window. The dimensions display on the view in red and in the dialog box. Select the dimensions that you want to keep for that view as shown in Figure 19–23. They display in black. Use <Ctrl> to select multiple features or views.

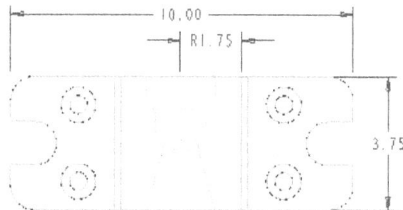

Figure 19–23

5. Click **Apply**.
6. Repeat the procedure to add dimensions to other features in the drawing.

describes additional detail items that can be added to a drawing.

Icon	Description	Icon	Description
⊢—⊣	Dimension	³²/√	Surface Finish
⊐⏢ᴹ	Geometric Tolerance	Ⓐ	Model Symbols
A≡	Note	⚇	Model Datums

Creating Dimensions

When showing dimensions, only those that were created in the model display. If a required dimension does not exist in the model (and therefore is not shown), it can be created. Since created dimensions are driven by the model geometry, their values cannot be modified. However, these values automatically update if the geometry changes in the part. Only displayed dimension values can be modified to change the model.

To create a dimension, click ⊢—⊣ (Dimension) in the *Annotate* tab. Select the references on the drawing view and place the dimension with the middle mouse button. Dimensions created in Drawing mode use the same creation methods as in Sketcher mode.

The following sections describe how to create the various dimension types in your drawing.

Linear Dimensions

To place linear dimensions in sketcher, select the entity(ies) with the left mouse button and place the dimension with the middle mouse button. The following information describes different methods of dimensioning the linear entities shown in Figure 19–24.

Keep the design intent in mind when considering the dimensioning scheme.

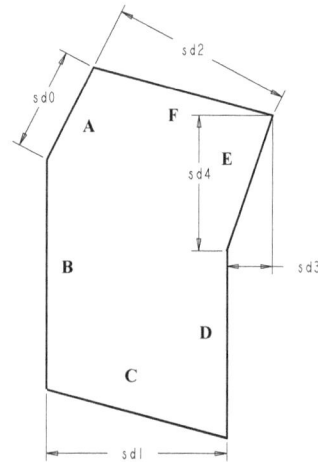

Figure 19–24

How To: Place Dimension sd0

1. Select line **A**.
2. Position the cursor at the location you want to place the dimension, and click the middle mouse button.

How To: Place Dimension sd1

1. Select line **B** and line **D**.
2. Position the cursor at the location you want to place the dimension, and click the middle mouse button.

The placement of the dimension dictates whether it is a horizontal or vertical dimension. In some cases, Pro/ENGINEER prompts to show either horizontal or vertical.

How To: Place Dimension sd2

1. Select line A and the vertex between lines **E** and **F**.
2. Position the cursor at the location you want to place the dimension, and click the middle mouse button.

How To: Place Dimensions sd3 and sd4

1. Select the two vertices at the ends of line **E**.
2. Position the cursor at the location you want to place the dimension, and click the middle mouse button.

Center/ Tangential Dimensions

To dimension the distance between circles and arcs, select the two entities and place the dimension using the middle mouse button. The **Type** menu can display with the **Center** and **Tangent** options, or the **Dim Orientation** menu can display with the **Horiz** and **Vert** options for placing the dimension. These menus can display depending on the location that you choose to place the dimension. To place a slanted dimension, place the dimension at a point along a line that would join the two entities that are being dimensioned.

*Selecting on the arc and circle centers eliminates the **Center** and **Tangent** menu options.*

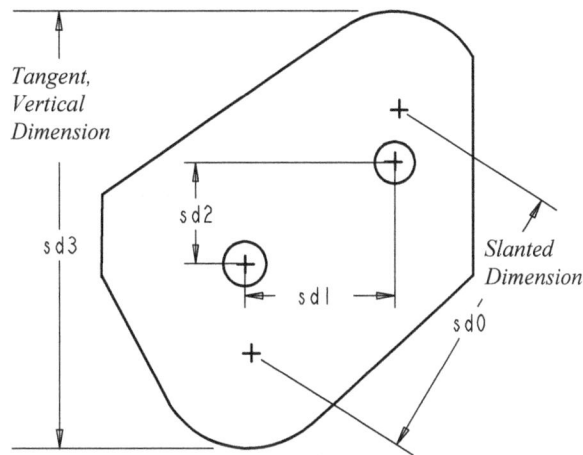

Figure 19–25

Radial / Diameter Dimensions

To create a radius dimension, select on an arc or a circle once and place the dimension using the middle mouse button. To create diameter dimensions, select an arc or circle twice and then place the dimension using the middle mouse button.

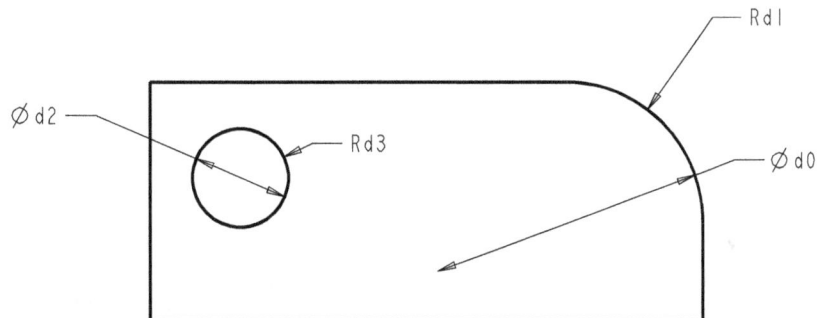

Figure 19–26

Angular Dimensions

For an angular dimension, select lines **A** and **B** and place the dimension using the middle mouse button. The angle is dependent on the placement of the dimension.

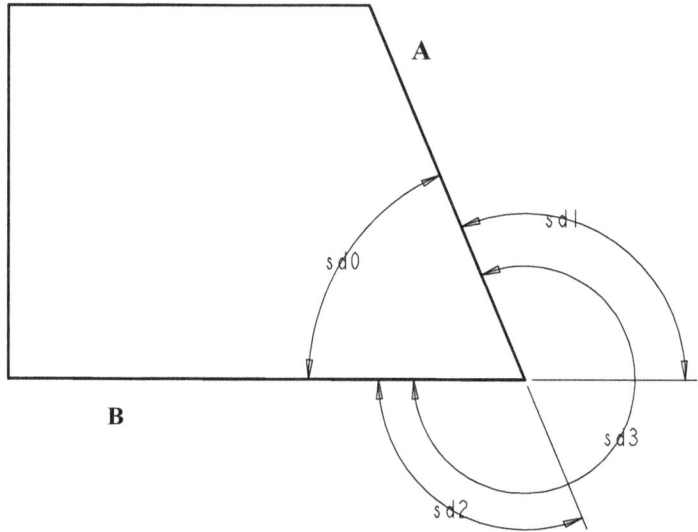

Figure 19–27

Dimensioning arc angles requires three selections. Select the arc (it turns red), then select the two end points, and place the dimension using the middle mouse button, as shown in Figure 19–28.

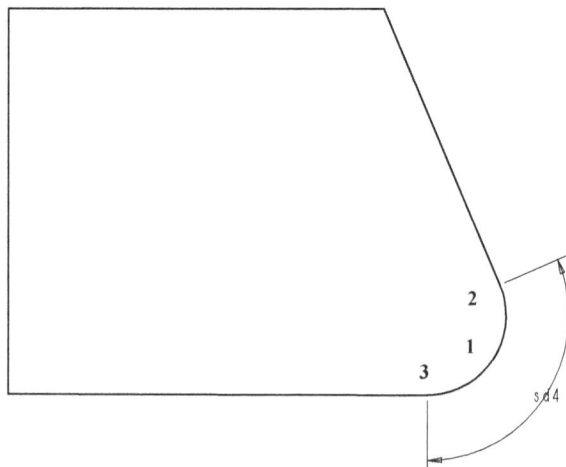

Figure 19–28

Notes

Notes can be added to detail the drawing, as shown in Figure 19–29.

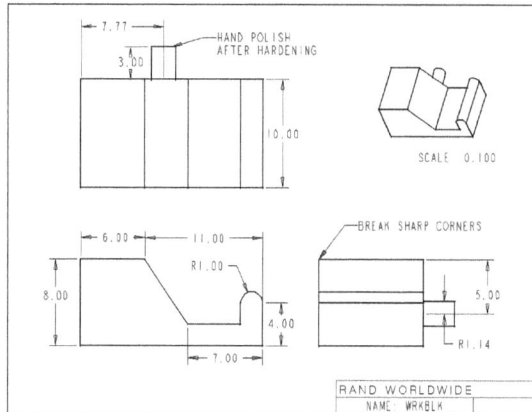

Figure 19–29

Several note types exist, but this course will focus only on unattached and leader notes.

- Unattached notes do not have a leader line, and can be placed freely on the sheet.

- Leader lines are placed with a leader pointing to some aspect of the geometry.

- The other note types are covered in the *Creo Parametric Design Detailing and Drafting* course.

Unattached Note

To create an unattached note, click (Unattached Note) in the *Annotate* tab. The Select Point dialog box opens as shown in Figure 19–30.

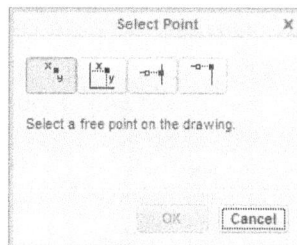

Figure 19–30

Select from the following point options:

- $\overset{x}{}_{\underset{\text{y}}{\blacksquare}}$ (Free Point)

- $\left|\overset{x}{\underset{\text{y}}{\blacksquare}}\right.$ (Absolute Coordinates)

- $\overset{\text{-□-}}{}$ (On Object)

- $\overset{\text{-□-}}{|}$ (On Vertex)

Select the appropriate location to begin creating the note.

Leader Note

To Create a Leader Note, expand the $\overset{A}{\equiv}$ (Note) fly-out in the *Annotate* tab and select $\overset{A}{\diagup}$ (Leader Note). The Select Reference dialog box opens as shown in Figure 19–31.

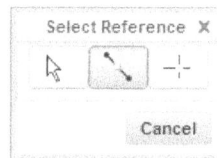

Figure 19–31

Select from the following reference options:

- $\scriptstyle\diagdown$ (Reference)

- $\diagdown$ (Midpoint)

- $\overset{\text{-}}{\underset{\text{-}}{\text{-}|\text{-}}}$ (Intersection)

Select the appropriate reference then click the middle mouse button to place the note.

Regardless of the note type, the *Format* dashboard displays as shown in Figure 19–32, enabling you to define the note details.

Figure 19–32

Once you select the location for the note, the system creates a text entry area for you to enter the note.

You can apply the following:

- The text style (e.g., Bold, Italic, Color, Height, and so on).

- Special symbols.

- Import a note from a file.

- Arrow Style.

Once the options in the *Format* dashboard are defined, click on the screen to complete the note placement.

Notes can incorporate parametric information that updates as the model changes. An ampersand (&) symbol is used to incorporate parametric information. For example, the parametric note shown in Figure 19–33 is entered as **&d23 DRILL- &P0 HOLES**, where the **&d23** and **&P0** reference dimension values are from the model. When you include parametric information, modifications to the size or number of holes in the pattern automatically update in the note.

During note creation,

click 🔲 *(Switch Dimensions) in the Text group to* *display dimensions in their symbolic form.*

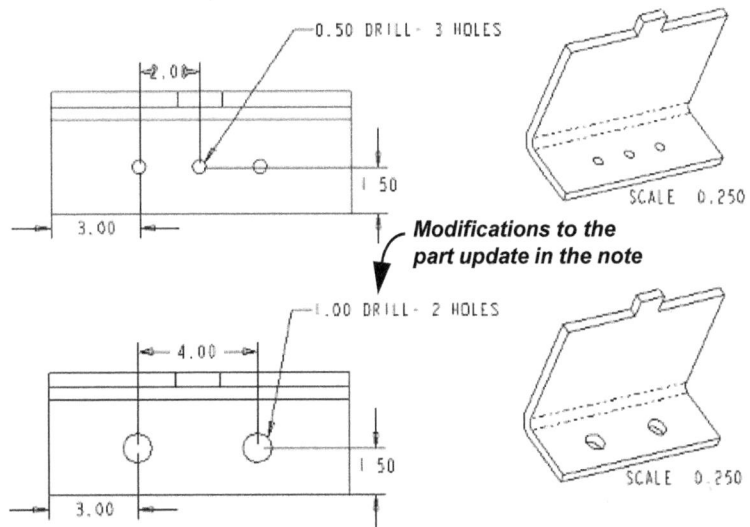

Figure 19–33

Step 7 - Manipulate detail items, as required.

Once detail items have been added to a drawing, changes might be required. Some common changes that can be made to detail items include moving detail items, erasing, editing values, flipping arrows, moving an item to a view, and adding dimensional tolerances.

Move

Select and drag detail items to move them, as required. Detail items can be rotated by selecting the green rotate handle and rotating as shown in .

Use this handle to rotate

Erase

You can erase detail items by selecting the item in the drawing, right-clicking, and selecting **Erase**. The erased annotations still display in the drawing tree as shown in Figure 19–34.

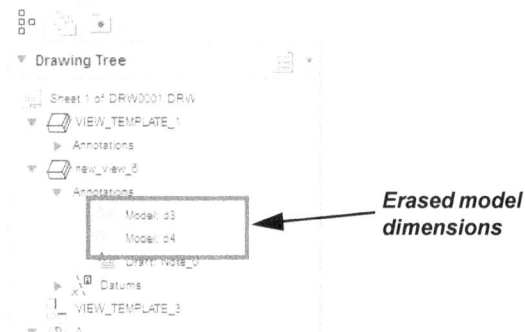

Erased model dimensions

Figure 19–34

Edit Values

The value for a model dimension can be modified directly in Drawing mode by double-clicking it. The change is reflected in the model. You can also modify a dimension value by selecting the dimension, right-clicking, and selecting **Properties**. Created dimensions cannot be modified. However, changes to the model geometry are reflected in the updated dimension value.

Flip Arrows

Right-click and select **Flip Arrows** to change the direction of the dimension arrows.

Move Item to View

When detail items, such as dimensions, display on the drawing, they are not necessarily displayed on the required view. To switch detail items between views, select the dimension(s), right-click, and select **Move to View** as shown in Figure 19–35. Select the new view on which you want the dimension to be displayed. You can select multiple items to be moved by pressing and holding <Ctrl> as you are selecting them.

Figure 19–35

Dimensional Tolerances

To enable dimension tolerances in Drawing mode, the Drawing Options file must have the **tol_display** option set to **yes**. To open the Options dialog box and set the value, select **File> Prepare>Drawing Properties**. The Drawing Properties dialog box opens, as shown in Figure 19–36. Select **change** in the *Detail Options* area.

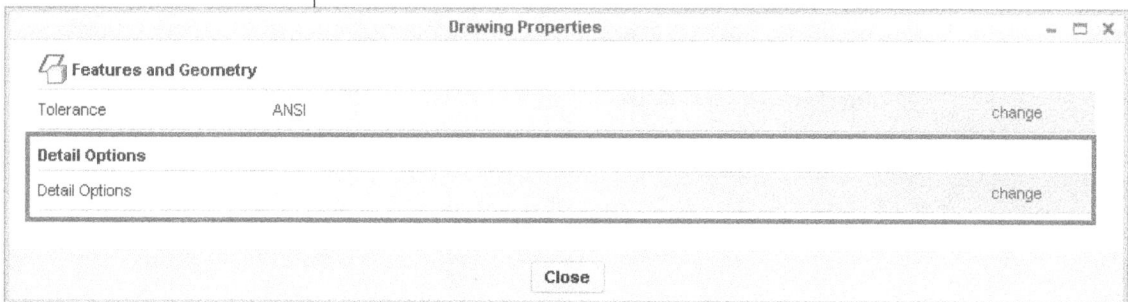

Figure 19–36

To set dimension tolerances, select the dimension(s), right-click, and select **Properties**. You can also double-click on the dimension. The Dimension Properties dialog box opens, as shown in Figure 19–37.

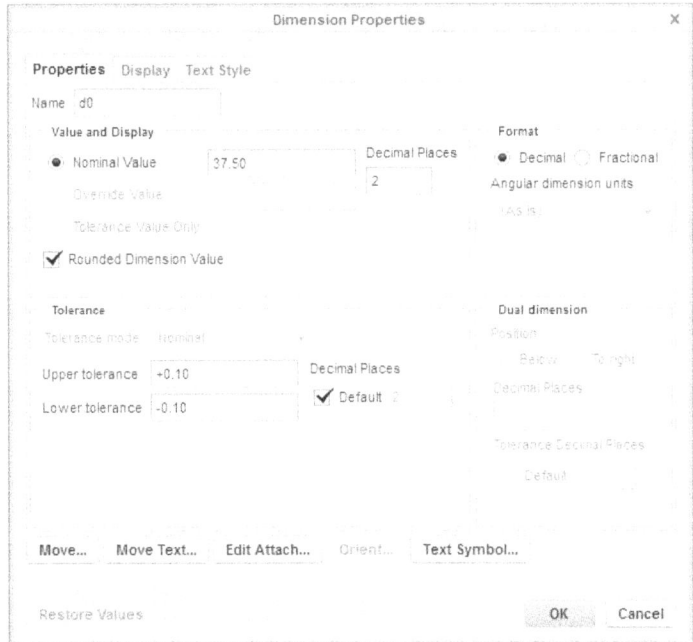

Figure 19–37

The available tolerance modes are listed as follows:

Option	Example
Nominal	1.25
+/- Symmetric	1.25 ± 0.05
Plus-Minus	1.25 $^{+0.05}_{-0.01}$
Limits	1.30 1.20

Step 8 - Print (or Plot) the drawing.

To print or plot the drawing, select **File>Print>Print**. The Printer's dialog box displays, which enables you to print.

Click **Settings** in the Print Preview ribbon to display the Printer Configuration dialog box and all of the plotting options, as shown in Figure 19–38.

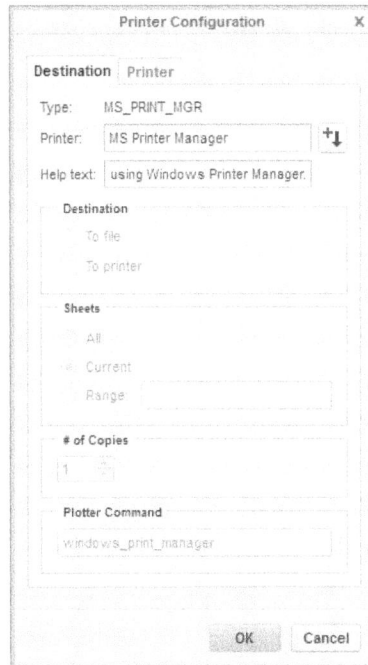

Figure 19–38

To print the file, you must define the destination printer in the drop-down list and configure it, as required. You must also select whether the file is printed to the printer or to a file and the number of copies.

19.2 Placing a Custom Symbol

Your organization will have both standard and custom symbols available for annotating your drawings.

To place a symbol in a drawing, expand ⚛ (Symbol) and click ⚛ (Custom Symbol) or right-click and select **Custom Symbol**. The Custom Drawing Symbol dialog box displays, as shown in Figure 19–39.

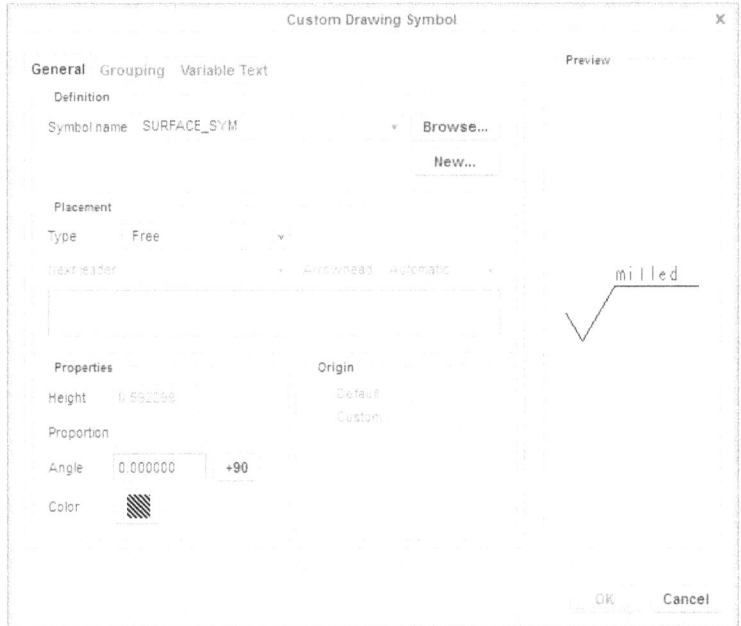

Figure 19–39

Select the symbol in the **Symbol Name** menu or browse to select a symbol that is stored on the system. Only symbols that currently exist in the drawing are listed in the Symbol name drop-down list.

To define symbol placement, select an option in the Type drop-down list, in the *Placement* area, in the *General* tab. The options vary depending on the placement type that was defined when the symbol was created. All of the available placement options are shown in Figure 19–40.

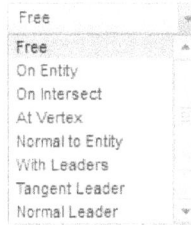

Free

Free
On Entity
On Intersect
At Vertex
Normal to Entity
With Leaders
Tangent Leader
Normal Leader

Figure 19–40

Once a placement option has been defined, move the cursor onto the drawing and place the symbol using the left mouse button. The remaining two areas in the *General* tab enable you to define additional properties for the symbol. If available, you can customize the height, angle of display, and origin. The availability of these options is dependent on how the symbol was originally created.

The *Grouping* tab in the Custom Drawing Symbol dialog box is used to define the group that is placed in the drawing. Figure 19–41 shows a *Grouping* tab for a symbol for which groups have been created. To define the symbol, you must select the groups that you want to include.

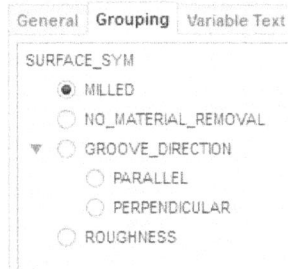

General	**Grouping**	Variable Text

SURFACE_SYM
- ● MILLED
- ○ NO_MATERIAL_REMOVAL
- ▼ ○ GROOVE_DIRECTION
  - ○ PARALLEL
  - ○ PERPENDICULAR
- ○ ROUGHNESS

Figure 19–41

The *Variable Text* tab in the Custom Drawing Symbol dialog box is used to set the variable text values, as shown in Figure 19–42. If options are available for selection, they display in the **value** field.

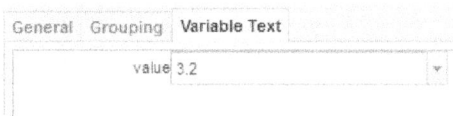

General	Grouping	**Variable Text**

value 3.2

Figure 19–42

To complete symbol placement, click **OK** in the Drawing Symbol dialog box. This button is not available for selection until enough options have been defined to fully locate the symbol in the model.

19.3 Multiple Sheets

Additional sheets can be added to your drawings. You can add a sheet by clicking ⬚ (New Sheet) from the *Document* group in the *Layout* tab of the ribbon. Alternatively, you can click ⁺ (New Sheet) at the bottom of the Creo Parametric window.

As you add sheets, they are listed as tabs at the bottom of the window, as shown in Figure 19–43.

To move between sheets, simply select the applicable tab.

SCALE : 0.800   TYPE : PART   NAME : BASE   SIZE : A   SHEET 3 OF 3

◀◀ ◀ ▶ ▶▶ +   Sheet 1   Sheet 2   Sheet 3

Figure 19–43

Views and detail items can be moved from view to view by right-clicking the object and selecting **Move to Sheet**. If there is only one sheet, the system automatically creates a second sheet and moves the objects.If more than one sheet is already in the drawing, the Select Sheet dialog box displays, as shown in Figure 19–44.

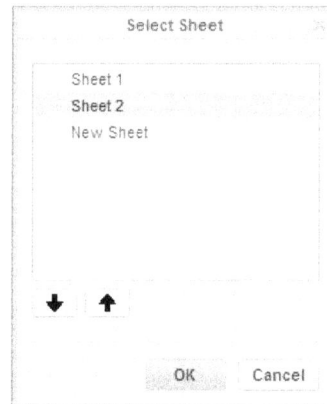

Select Sheet

Sheet 1
Sheet 2
New Sheet

↓   ↑

OK   Cancel

Figure 19–44

In this dialog box, you can select one of the existing sheets or add a New Sheet.

Practice 19a | Create a Drawing

Practice Objectives

- Create a new drawing based on a drawing template.
- Add General, Projected, Section, and Detail views to create a drawing.
- Change the orientation, display style, scale, and add a section using the View dialog box.
- Show dimensions on the drawing using the Show Model Annotations dialog box.
- Create and edit notes in the drawing.
- Add a custom symbol,
- Add a second sheet to the drawing and move a view to it.

In this practice, you will create the two-sheet drawing shown in Figure 19–45, using a predefined format. To complete the drawing, add all of the required views, dimensions, notes and symbols. Manipulate them as required to match the detail shown in Figure 19–45.

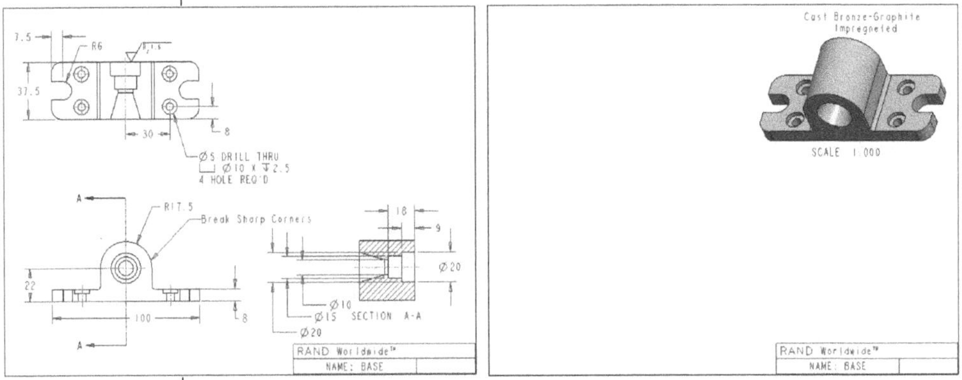

Figure 19–45

Task 1 - Create a drawing and open a format.

1. Set the working directory to the *Chapter 19\practice 19a* folder.

2. Click ☐ (New).

3. In the *Type* area in the New dialog box, select the **Drawing** option.

4. For the drawing name, enter **base**.

5. Clear the **Use default template** option to create the drawing without a template.

6. Click **OK**.

7. Click **Browse** and browse to and select **base.prt**.

8. In the *Specify Template* area in the New Drawing dialog box, select the **Empty with format** option.

9. In the *Format* area, click **Browse**, click ⌣ (Working Directory) in the Common Folders area, and select the **rand.frm** format file. The New Drawing dialog box displays as shown in Figure 19–46.

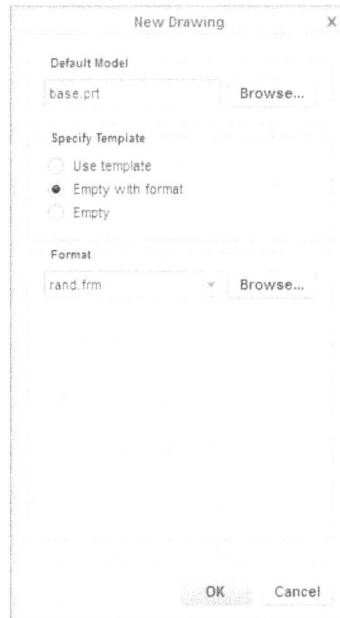

Figure 19–46

10. Click **OK** to finish creating the drawing. A drawing sheet displays in the main window.

11. Select **File>Prepare>Drawing Properties**. Select **change** in the *Detail Options* area, as shown in Figure 19–47.

Figure 19–47

12. In the Option text field, type **tol_display**. Click in the value field, and ensure the *Value* is set to **no**. Click **Add/Change** and close the dialog box. Close the Drawing Properties dialog box.

Task 2 - Add four views to the drawing.

In this task you will create the views shown in Figure 19–48.

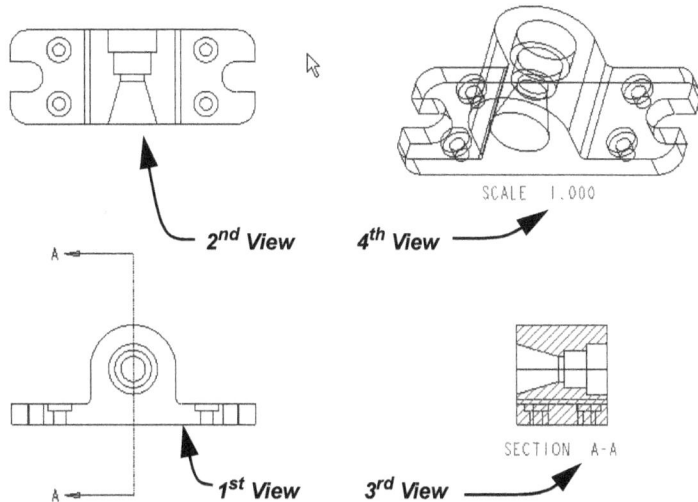

Figure 19–48

13. Set the model display as follows:

- ⁎ *(Datum Display Filters)*: All Off

- ▢ *(Display Style)*: ▢ (Wireframe)

14. Verify that the *Layout* tab is selected. Click ▱ (General View) to add the first view. You can also right-click and select **General View**.

15. If the Select Combined State dialog box opens, select **Do not prompt for combined state** and click **OK**. Select a location on the screen to place the first General view, as shown in Figure 19–49.

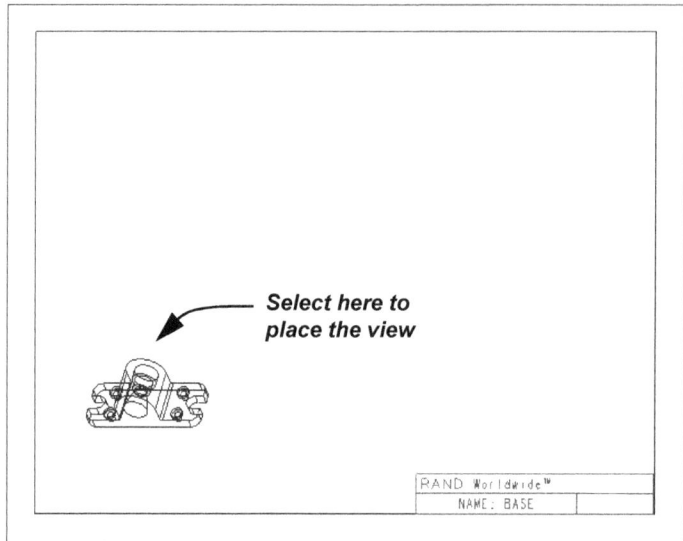

Select here to place the view

RAND Worldwide™
NAME: BASE

Figure 19–49

To reorient the model, you can also select the **Geometry references** *option and select two orthogonal planar references. Use the default datum planes for the orientation references.*

16. Orient the view, as shown in Figure 19–51. In the Drawing View dialog box, the **View names from the model** option is selected, enabling you to select a predefined model view to orient the model. In the *Model view names* area, double-click on the **FRONT** view to reorient the model, as shown in Figure 19–50.

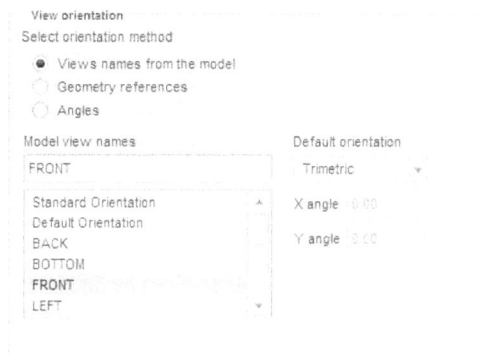

Figure 19–50

17. Click **OK** to complete the view placement. The view displays as shown in Figure 19–51.

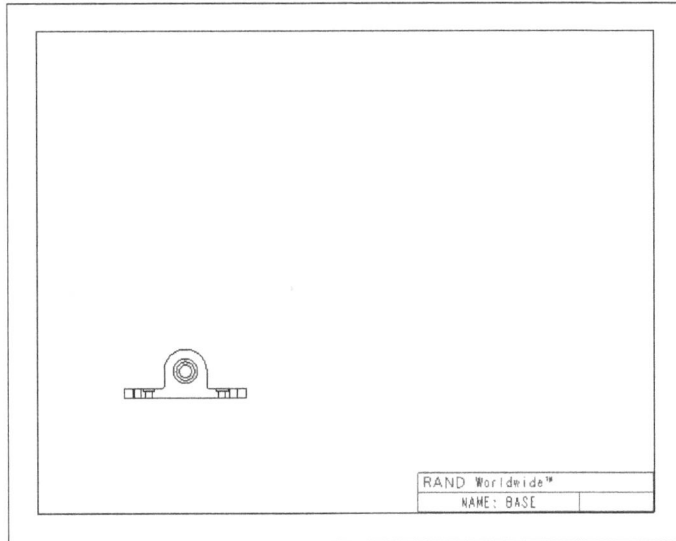

Figure 19–51

You can also click

(Projection View).

A Projected view cannot have an independent scale. It must have the same scale as its parent General view.

18. Select the first view, right-click, and select **Projection View**. Place the second view at the location shown in Figure 19–52.

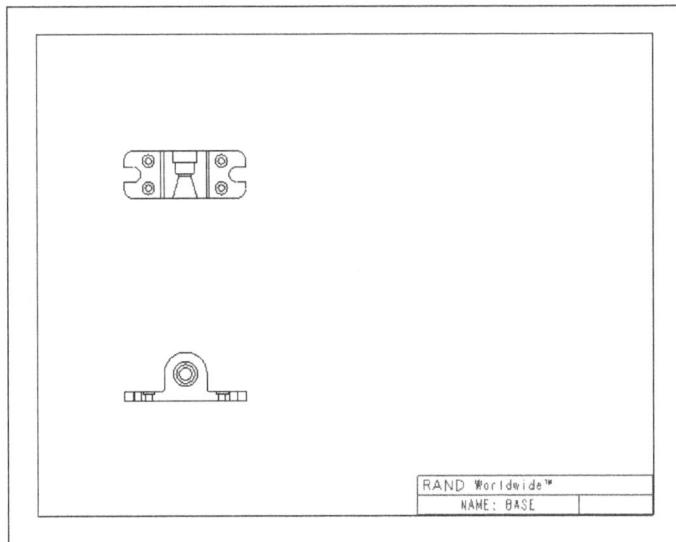

Figure 19–52

19. Select the first view, right-click, and select **Projection View**. Place the third view in the location shown in Figure 19–53.

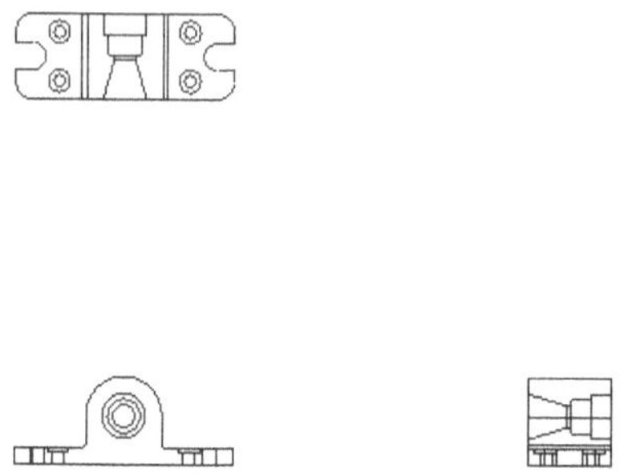

Figure 19–53

20. Select the third view, right-click, and select **Properties**.

21. In the Drawing View dialog box, select the *Sections* category.

22. In the *Section options* area, select the **2D cross-sections** option.

23. Click **+** .

24. In the *Name* column, select cross-section **A**. In the *Sectioned Area* column, select **Full**, as shown in Figure 19–54.

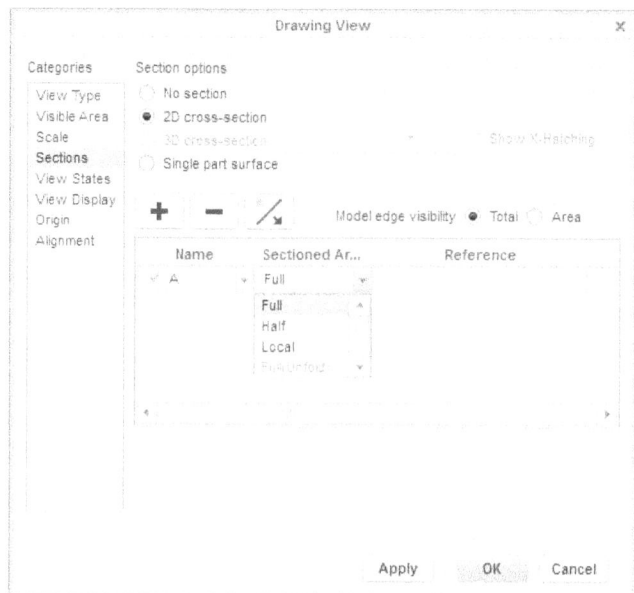

Figure 19–54

You can also open the Drawing View dialog box by double-clicking on the view.

25. Click **OK** to complete the view modification. Select the third view, right-click, and select **Add Arrows**. Select the first view in which to place cross-section arrows. The drawing displays as shown in Figure 19–55.

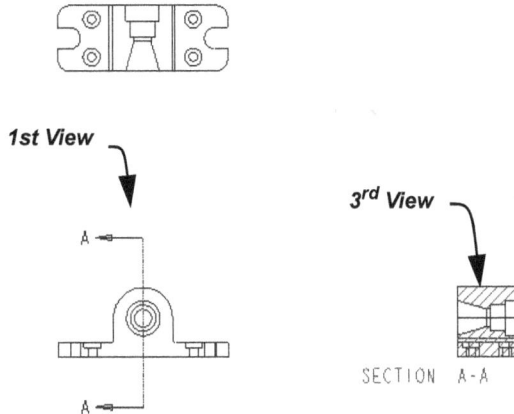

Figure 19–55

26. Right-click and select **General View**, and add the fourth view, as shown in Figure 19–56. Keep the View dialog box open.

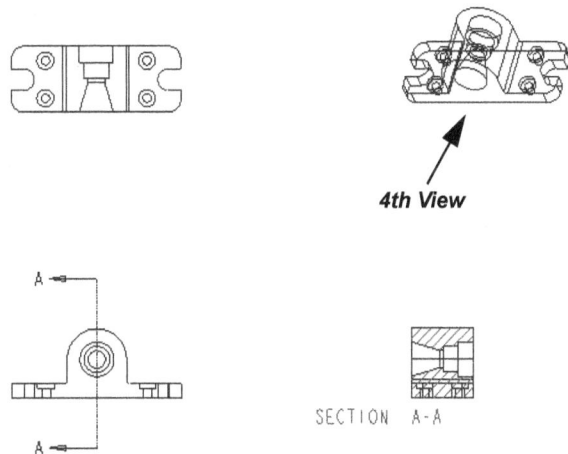

Figure 19–56

27. In the Drawing View dialog box, select the *Scale* category.

28. In the *Scale and perspective options* area, select the **Custom scale** option. Set the *Scale* to **1.0**.

29. Click **Apply** to apply the changes.

30. Click **Close** to close the Drawing View dialog box. The fourth view displays as shown in Figure 19–57.

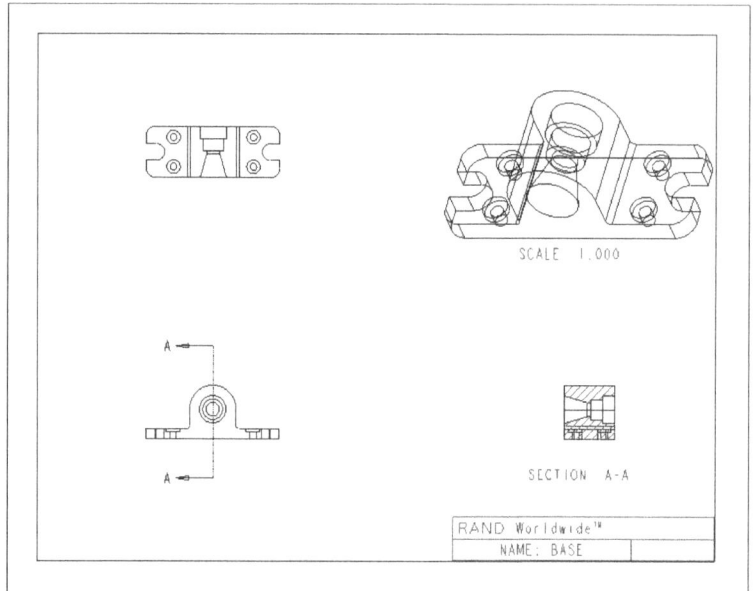

Figure 19–57

Task 3 - Modify the scale of the drawing and move the views.

1. Double-click on the scale value in the lower left corner of the drawing and enter the scale value in the message window, as shown in Figure 19–58.

Figure 19–58

2. Enter **0.8**. The scale of the fourth view remains set at **1.0** because this view has a scale that is independent to the rest of the drawing.

You can also click

⌐ (*Lock View Movement*) *in the Document group in the Layout tab to lock and unlock all of the views.*

3. You can lock or unlock views to prevent them being moved by the mouse. To unlock them, ensure the ⌐ (Lock View Movement) is not selected in the *Layout* tab or in the shortcut menu.

4. Select the views individually and move them, as shown in Figure 19–59. Note how moving a parent view reflects in the placement of dependent views.

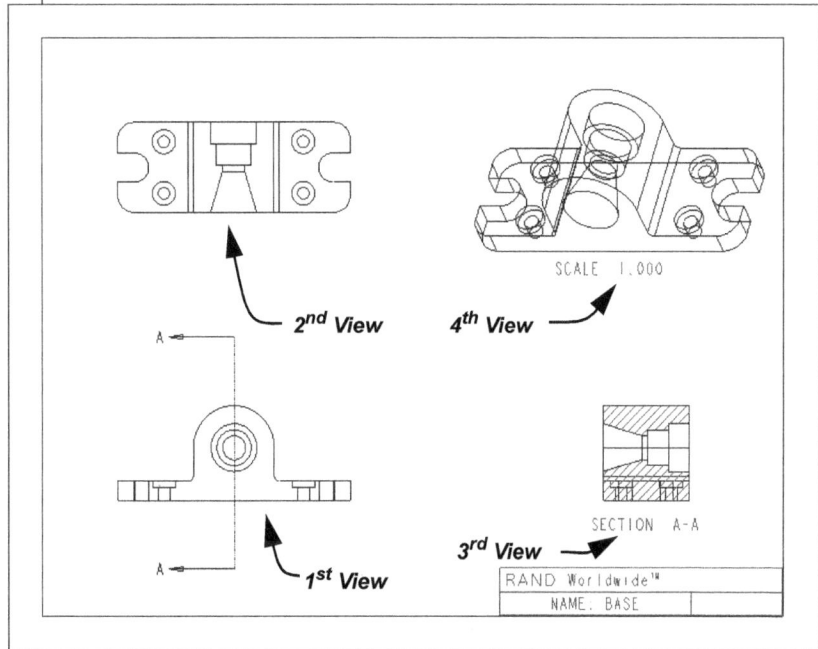

Figure 19–59

Task 4 - Change the view display of the third and fourth views.

---

*You can modify the view display for multiple views at the same time. Press and hold <Ctrl> while selecting the views, right-click, and select **Properties** to open the Drawing View dialog box.*

1. Double-click on the third view.

2. In the Drawing View dialog box, select the *View Display* category.

3. In the Display Style drop-down list, select **No Hidden**.

4. Click **OK** to complete the view modification.

5. Repeat Steps 1 to 3 for the isometric view.

---

6. Move the two view notes to appropriate locations. The drawing displays as shown in Figure 19–60.

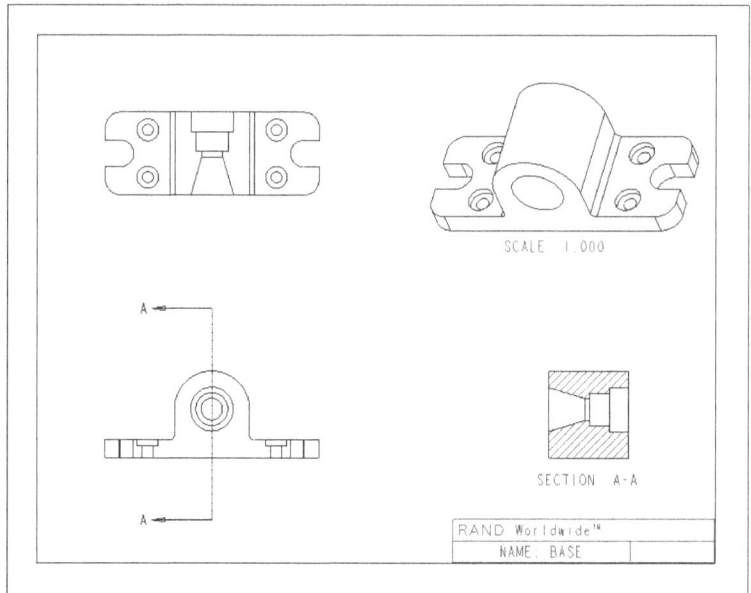

SCALE 1.000

SECTION A-A

RAND Worldwide™

NAME: BASE

Figure 19–60

Task 5 - Change the view display of the fourth view.

1. Double-click on the isometric view.

2. In the Drawing View dialog box, select the *View Display* category.

3. In the Display Style drop-down list, select **Shading With Edges**.

4. Click **OK** to complete the view modification. The drawing displays as shown in Figure 19–61.

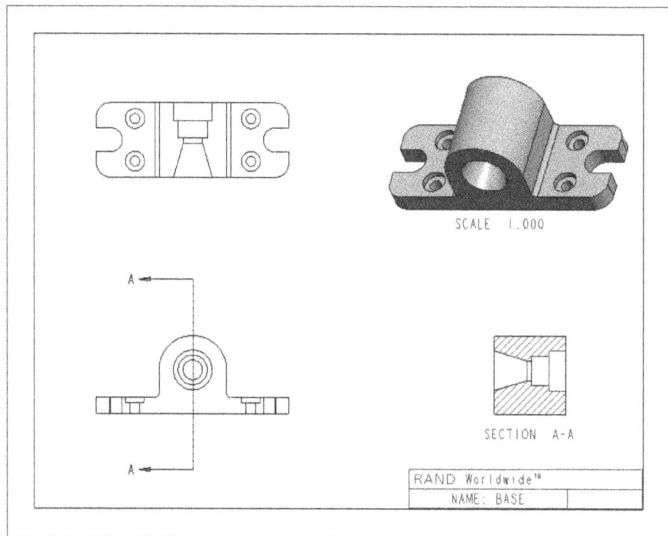

Figure 19–61

Task 6 - Display the dimensions of the base feature.

You can also use the model tree to display dimensions for each feature.

1. Select the *Annotate* tab. Click 🖼 (Show Model Annotations) to open the Show Model Annotations dialog box.

2. Select the *Dimensions* tab (⊢⊣), if required. Verify that the **All** type is selected.

3. In the Top view, select the base feature **(F5(EXTRUDE_1))**.

4. Three dimensions display. In the *Show* column, place a check next to the **37.5** dimension (d0), and click **Apply**, as shown in Figure 19–62.

Figure 19–62

You can select the dimension you want to keep directly on the drawing.

5. In the Front view, select the base feature **(F5(EXTRUDE_1))**. Keep the dimensions shown in Figure 19–63. Click **Apply**.

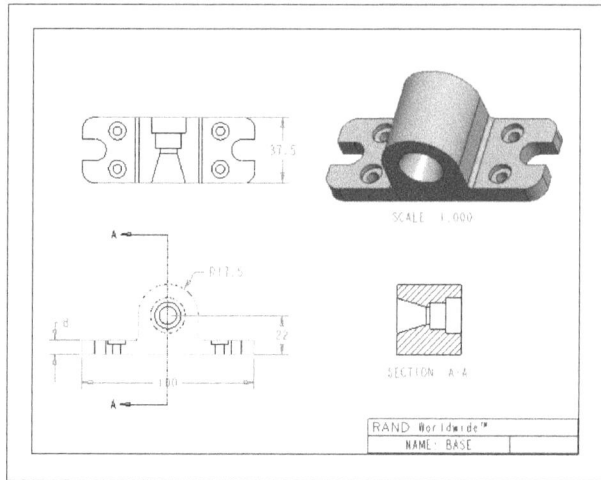

Figure 19–63

Task 7 - Display the dimensions of the U-shaped cut and the hole in the boss.

1. Display and select the dimensions of the U-shaped cut (**F7(NOTCH)**), as shown in Figure 19–64. If the cut was copied, you must select the original cut, which is on the left side of the view.

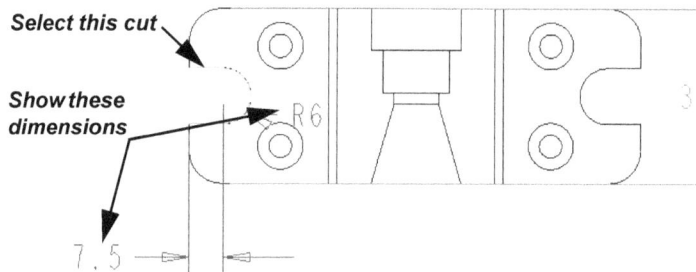

Figure 19–64

2. Click **Apply** in the Show Model Annotations dialog box to keep the dimensions.

3. Display the dimensions for the hole in **F17 (SLOT)** by selecting the feature on the Right (cross-section) view, as shown in Figure 19–65.

4. Click **Apply** in the Show Model Annotations dialog box to keep the dimensions.

*Click ✓– to select all the dimensions. If selecting the hole in the first or third view, right-click and select **Pick From List**.*

5. If required, you can move the dimensions.

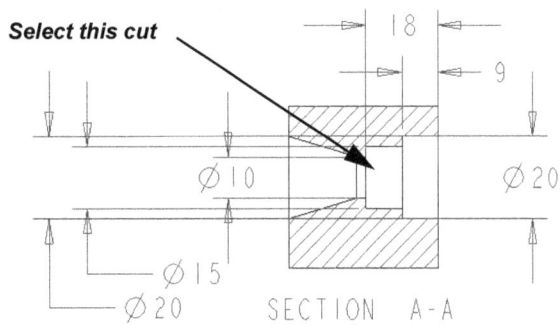

Figure 19–65

6. Click **Cancel** to close the Show Model Annotations dialog box.

Task 8 - Continue selecting features to show dimensions.

---

1. Show dimensions for the remaining features.

2. When all of the dimensions display, close the Show Model Annotations dialog box.

Task 9 - Delete dimensions.

---

1. Select any unwanted dimensions, right-click, and select **Delete** to remove them. Repaint the screen if required.

Task 10 - Arrange the dimensions.

---

1. Select one of the hole dimensions in the Top view, right-click once to flip the arrows, and move the dimension to the location shown in Figure 19–66.

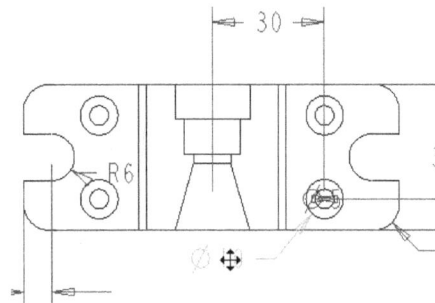

Figure 19–66

2. Move the other hole dimension in the Top view.

3. Select the **20** diameter dimension on the Section view, right-click, and select **Move Item To View**. Select the Top view. The dimension displays as shown in Figure 19–67.

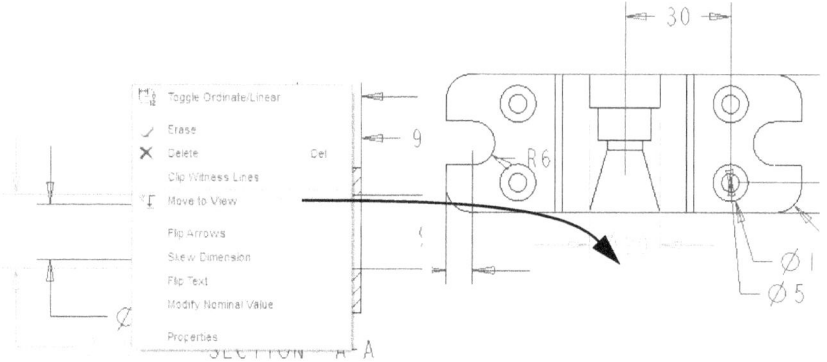

Figure 19–67

4. Undo the previous step.

5. Rearrange the dimensions, as shown in Figure 19–68.

Model dimensions can only be shown once on a drawing.

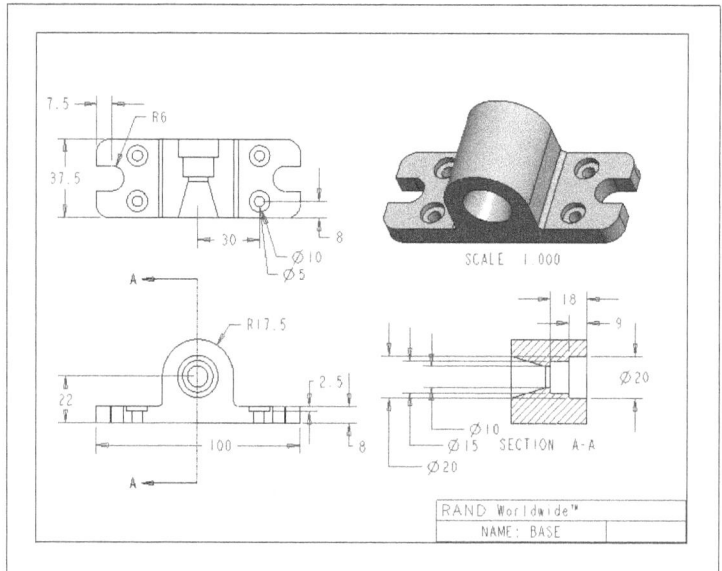

Figure 19–68

Task 11 - Create additional dimensions.

Dimensions are created similar to sketcher dimensions. Created dimensions update with any part changes. However, they cannot be modified to drive part geometry.

1. Click ⊢⊣ (Dimension). The Menu Manager opens. Leave the default options selected.

2. Create some dimensions in the drawing by selecting the entities with the left mouse button and then clicking the middle mouse button to place the dimension. This is similar to creating sketcher dimensions.

Task 12 - Delete some dimensions.

*Alternatively, right-click, and select **Delete**.*

1. Select any of the created dimensions and click ✕ (Delete) or press <Delete>.

Task 13 - Create Note A.

In the following tasks, you will create the three notes shown in Figure 19–69.

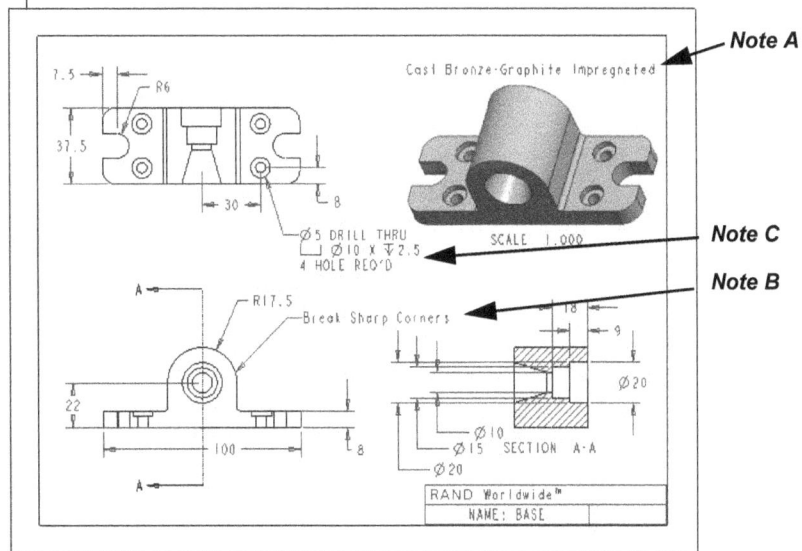

Figure 19–69

1. Select the *Annotate* tab and click ᴬ≡ (Note) to create the first note.

2. Select a location at which to place the note.

3. Enter **Cast Bronze-Graphite Impregnated**.

4. Click on the screen to complete the note. Move it to the appropriate location.

Task 14 - Create Note B.

---

1. Expand the ᴬ≣ (Note) flyout and select ✓ᴬ (Leader Note). Read the message window and select the boss edge, as shown in Figure 19–69.

2. Click the middle mouse button in a location to place the note.

3. For the note, enter **Break Sharp Corners**.

4. Click the screen twice to finish creating the note.

Task 15 - Create Note C.

---

1. Click ✓ᴬ (Leader Note).

2. Select the counterbore hole shown in Figure 19–69.

3. Click the middle mouse button in a location at which to place the note.

As symbols are selected in the palette, they display in the message window.

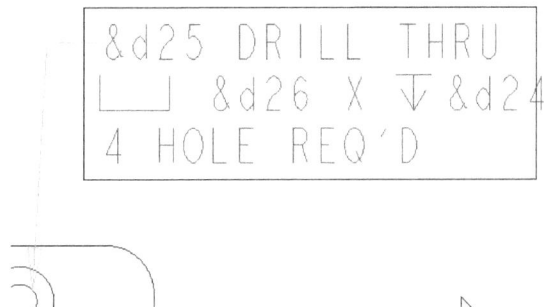

4. Enter the note shown in Figure 19–70. In the *Format* tab, select all of the special symbols from the palette in the Text group, except the diameter symbol and the ampersand (&) symbol. Use the keyboard to enter the ampersand symbol. Press <Enter> once after you complete each of the first two lines.

&d25 DRILL THRU
⌴ &d26 X ↧ &d24
4 HOLE REQ'D

Figure 19–70

5. Click twice on the screen to complete the note.

Task 16 - Modify Note A.

1. Select **Note A**. Select the *Format* tab, if required.

2. Edit the note to be **Center justified**, as shown in Figure 19–71.

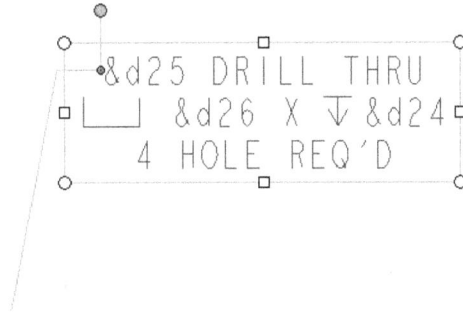

Figure 19–71

Task 17 - Place the symbol in the model.

1. In the *Annotations* group in the ribbon, expand (Symbol) and select **Custom Symbol**.

2. Double-click on **surface_sym.sym** to open it.

3. In the Custom Drawing Symbol dialog box, select the *Grouping* tab and select the *ROUGHNESS* group.

4. Select **On Entity** in the **Type** menu in the *Placement* area.

5. Select the edge shown in Figure 19–72.

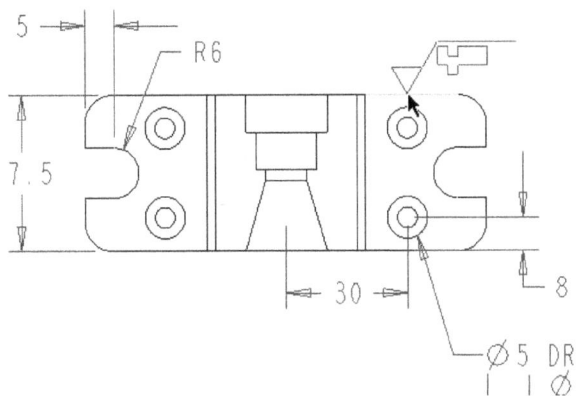

Figure 19–72

6. The Custom Drawing Symbol dialog box displays as shown in Figure 19–73.

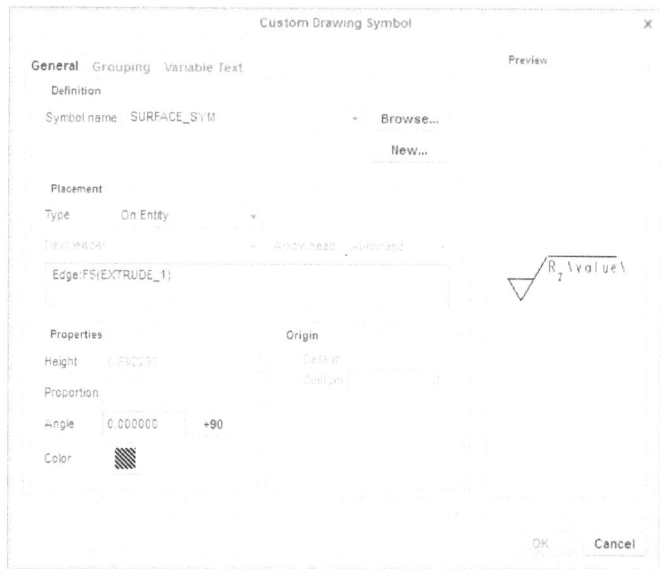

Figure 19–73

7. Place the symbol, as shown in Figure 19–74.

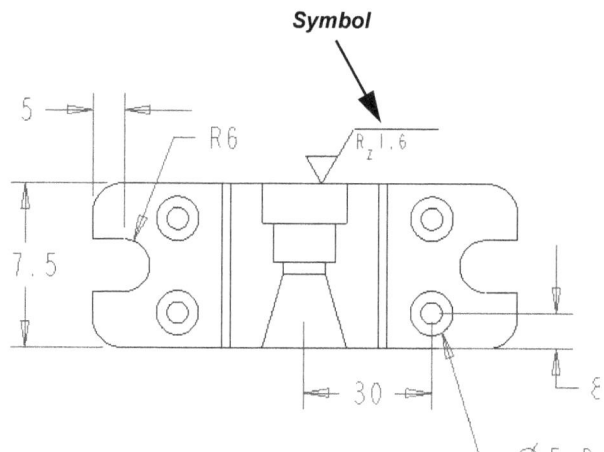

Figure 19–74

8. Click the middle mouse button to complete the symbol placement.

9. Click **OK** to close the Custom Drawing Symbol dialog box.

Task 18 - Move the isometric view to another sheet.

1. Select the isometric view.

2. Press and hold the right mouse button, and select **Move to Sheet**.

3. Creo Parametric automatically creates a second sheet, and moves the view as shown in Figure 19–75.

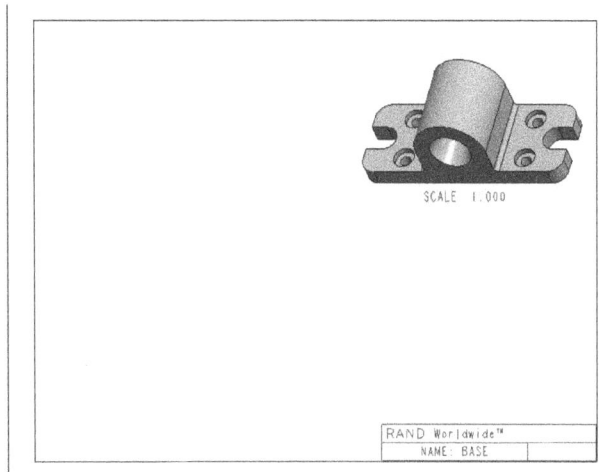

SCALE 1.000

RAND Worldwide™
NAME: BASE

Figure 19–75

4. Select the *Sheet 1* tab in the lower left of the Creo Parametric window to return to the first sheet.

5. Select the **Cast Bronze-Graphite Impregnated** note, right-click and select Move to Sheet.

6. In the Select Sheet dialog box, select **Sheet 2**, as shown in Figure 19–76.

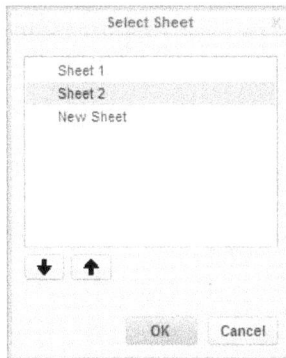

Select Sheet

Sheet 1
Sheet 2
New Sheet

OK   Cancel

Figure 19–76

7. Click **OK**.

8. **Sheet 2** updates as shown in Figure 19–77.

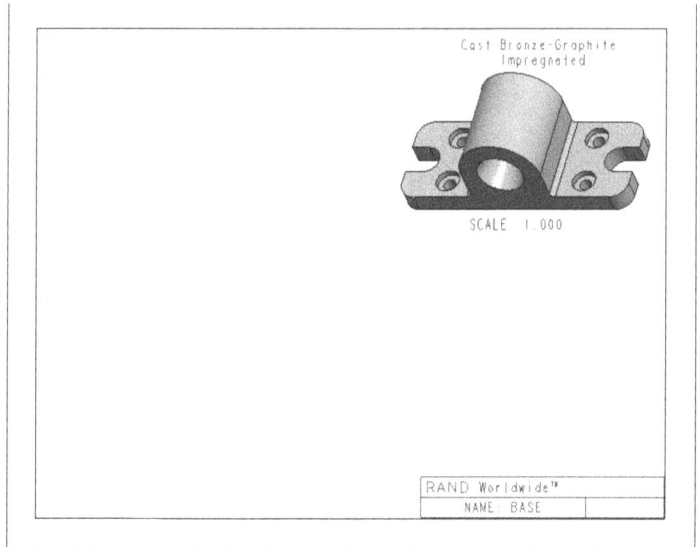

Figure 19–77

Task 19 - Display axes in the views on the first sheet.

1. Select the *Sheet 1* tab at the bottom of the Creo Parametric window.

2. Select the *Annotate* tab in the ribbon.

3. In the Annotations group, click ⬚ (Show Model Annotations).

4. Select the ⬚ (Show Model Datums) tab in Show Model annotations dialog box.

5. Press and hold <Ctrl> and select the holes shown in Figure 19–78.

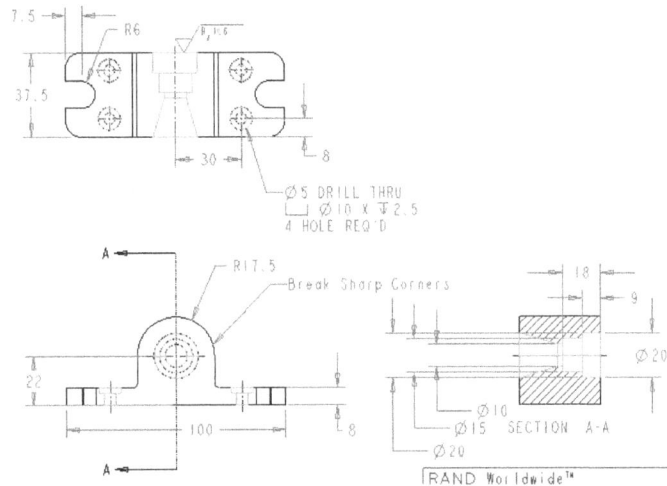

Figure 19–78

6. Click ⊻– (Select All) and click **OK**.

7. Click on the screen to clear any selected entities and the drawing displays as shown in Figure 19–79.

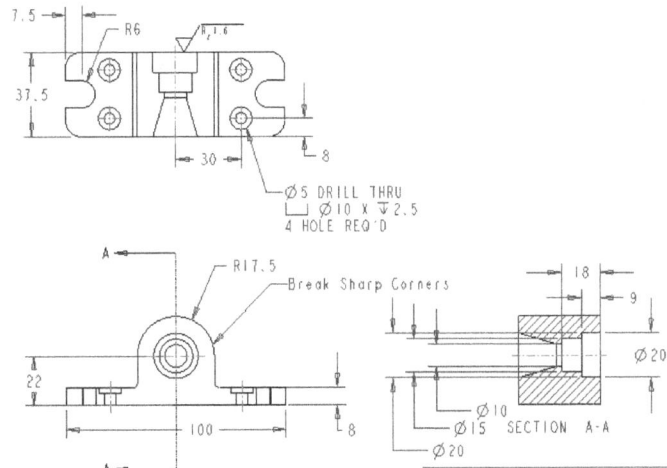

Figure 19–79

Task 20 - Arrange any remaining detail items and save the drawing.

1. Arrange any detail items or views that need to be organized.

2. Save the drawing and erase all of the files from memory.

| Practice 19b | # Create a Drawing using Additional Tools |

Practice Objective

- Create a new drawing, add views, and show dimensions.

In this practice, you will use drawing tools to create the drawing shown in Figure 19–81. Tips are provided for you to create the radial circle of dimensions for the pattern of holes.

Task 1 - Open a part file.

1. Set the working directory to the *Chapter 19\practice 19b* folder.

2. Open **end_cap.prt**.

3. Set the model display as follows:

   - ⁂ *(Datum Display Filters)*: All Off
   - ⸾ *(Spin Center)*: Off
   - ⬚ *(Display Style)*: ⬚ (Hidden Line)

   The part displays as shown in Figure 19–80.

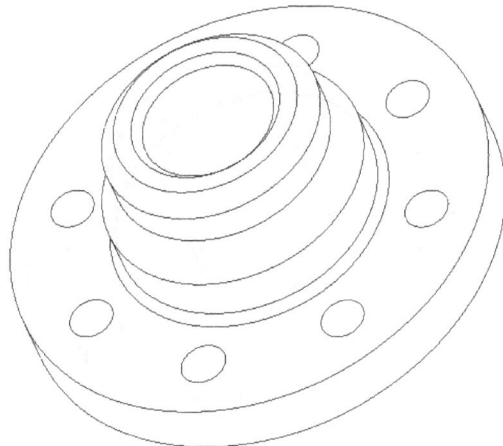

Figure 19–80

4. Review the part and its features.

Task 2 - Create a drawing with limited instruction.

1. Create the drawing shown in Figure 19–81. Set the drawing scale to **0.050**.

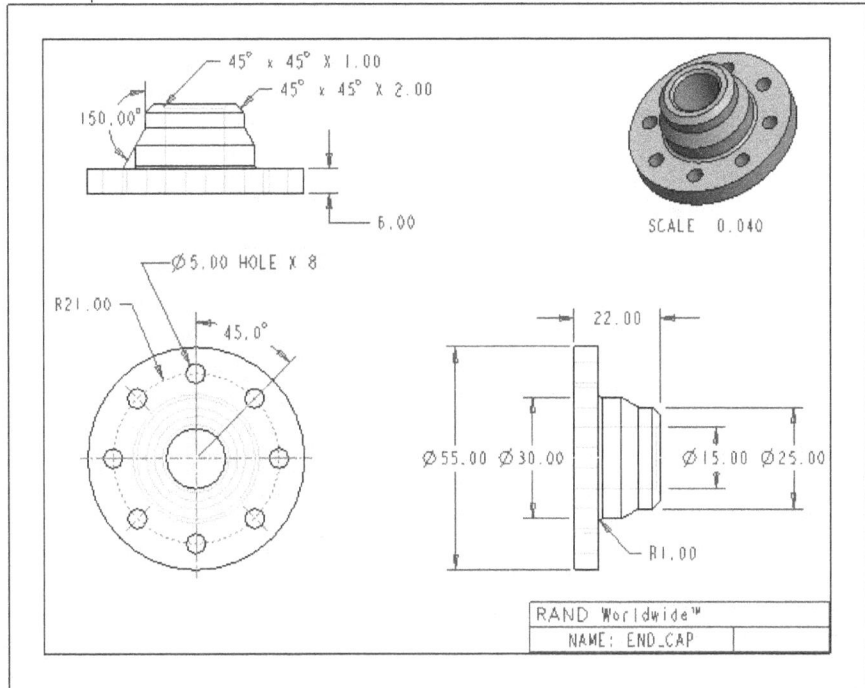

Figure 19–81

Use the following information to help you create the radial circle for the pattern:

- In the drawing setup file, edit an option. Select **File> Prepare>Drawing Properties** and select **change** in the Detail Options dialog box. Edit the **radial_pattern_axis_circle** option, and set it to **Yes**.

- Select the view, right-click and select **Show Model Annotation**.

2. Save the drawing and erase the files from memory.

Chapter Review Questions

1. Which of the following **Specify Template** options enables you to define the orientation of the drawing sheet and set the sheet size for the drawing?

   a. Use template

   b. Empty with format

   c. Empty

2. Which of the following view types must be the first view in a drawing?

   a. Projection

   b. Auxiliary

   c. General

   d. Detailed

3. Which of the following view types enables you to create a 3D view in its default orientation?

   a. Projection

   b. Auxiliary

   c. General

   d. Detailed

4. An independent view scale enables you to ensure that a view maintains the same scale value as the drawing.

   a. True

   b. False

5. Which of the following references can be selected when orienting a view? (Select all that apply.)

   a. Datum planes

   b. Datum axis

   c. Planar surfaces

   d. Cylindrical surfaces

   e. Coordinate system axis

6. Views are automatically locked to the original location at which they were placed. Which of the following options or icons enables you to unlock the view movement?

   a. Click ⊢⊣ in the toolbar.

   b. Click ⁄ in the toolbar.

   c. Right-click and select **Unlock**.

   d. Right-click and ensure that **Lock View Movement** is not selected.

7. Which of the following categories in the Drawing View dialog box enables you to redefine a Projected view as a General view?

   a. View Type

   b. Visible Area

   c. Sections

   d. View Display

8. Which of the following icons enables you to display model dimensions in a drawing?

   a. ⊻

   b. ⊢⊣

   c. A≡

   d. ⊕

Command Summary

Button	Command	Location
	General View	• **Ribbon:** *Layout* tab in the *Model Views* group • **Contextual menu:** Nothing selected
	Projection View	• **Ribbon:** *Layout* tab in the *Model Views* group • **Contextual menu:** Select a view
	Detailed View	• **Ribbon:** *Layout* tab in the *Model Views* group • **Contextual menu:** Nothing selected
	Show Model Annotations	• **Ribbon:** *Annotate* tab in the *Annotate* group • **Contextual Menu:** Select a feature or view in model or model tree
	Dimension	• **Ribbon:** *Annotate* tab in the *Annotate* group • **Contextual menu:** Nothing selected
	Note	• **Ribbon:** *Annotate* tab in the *Annotate* group
	Lock View Movement	• **Ribbon:** *Layout* tab in the *Document* group • **Contextual menu:** Select a view

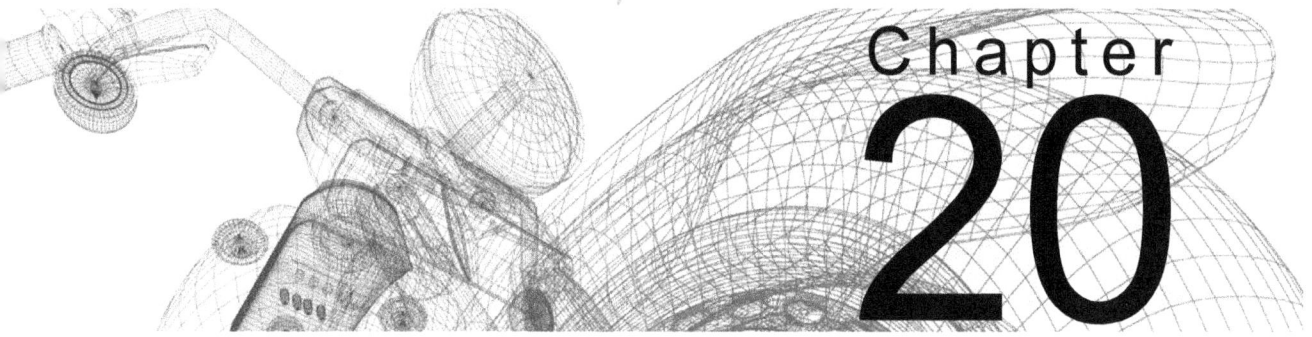

Assembly Mode

Just as features are added to one another to create a part, parts can be assembled to one another to create an assembly. The parts can be assembled individually or as members of a sub-assembly to create a higher level assembly. The parts and sub-assemblies are referred to as components.

Learning Objectives in this Chapter

- Learn how to insert components in an assembly.
- Locate the components in an assembly based on selected constraint type and references using the Component Placement tab.
- Make dimensional, constraint, or reference changes to an existing component using Edit Definition.
- Learn how to use the constraint types in the different examples provided.
- Open and locate components and features in an assembly using the model tree.

20.1 Assembling Components

To create an assembly, components are inserted and constrained using the available Creo Parametric constraints. These are specified to locate components parametrically with respect to existing components and assembly features. Similar to the interdependencies between features in a part, parent/child relationships also exist in an assembly. Any references made to other components when assembling a new component create parent/child relationships.

General Steps

Use the following general steps to insert a component into an assembly:

1. Insert a component.
2. Select a constraint to parametrically place the component.
3. Select the appropriate references on the assembly and component.
4. Assign an offset value, if required.
5. Repeat Steps 2 to 4 until the component is fully constrained.
6. Redefine the component placement, as required.

Step 1 - Insert a component.

To insert a component into an assembly, click (Assemble) in the *Component* group in the *Model* tab. In the Open dialog box, select the component to insert, and click **Open**. The *Component Placement* dashboard displays as shown in Figure 20–1. You can also drag a component into the assembly window from the file browser.

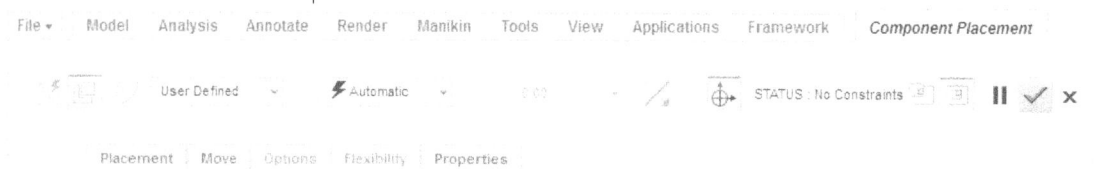

File ▾   Model   Analysis   Annotate   Render   Manikin   Tools   View   Applications   Framework   *Component Placement*

User Defined   ⚡Automatic   STATUS : No Constraints   ‖ ✓ ✗

Placement   Move   Options   Flexibility   Properties

Figure 20–1

The dashboard is the control center for the assembly process. It displays each time you assemble a new component, or redefine the placement of an existing component, and remains open throughout the placement process.

The dashboard contains multiple panels, but this training guide only discusses the options for the Placement panel. The Move panel contains options for placing components non-parametrically. These are discussed in the Creo Parametric: Advanced Assembly Design and Management training guide.

(Separate Window) and (In Window) at the right side of the dashboard enable you to determine whether you want the component that is being assembled to be displayed in a separate window or in the main window, respectively. By default, components are assembled in the main window. The choice should be made based on the convenience of selecting references.

Step 2 - Select a constraint to parametrically place the component.

Constraints locate components parametrically with respect to existing components or features. Constraints are assigned using the Constraint Type drop-down list in the tab or from the Placement panel, as shown in Figure 20–2.

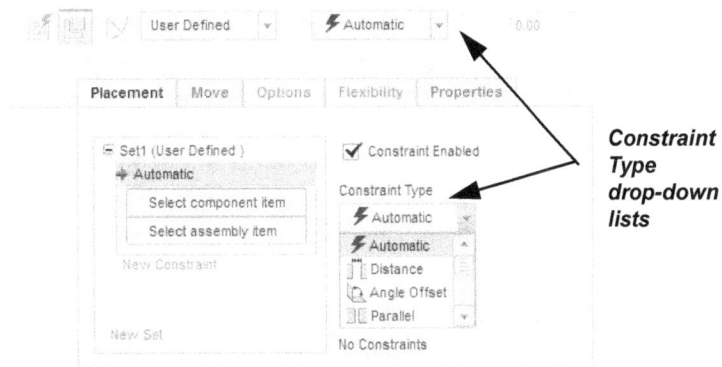

Figure 20–2

The available placement constraints are described as follows:

Options	Description
Automatic (default)	The system assigns an appropriate constraint type based on the references selected from the assembly and component.
Distance	Selected planar surfaces, edges, or points are constrained with an offset value. You can either drag the model using a square handle displayed on the model or enter the offset value in the Component Placement tab. The Offset value changes automatically during the dragging action.

Angle Offset	Selected planar surfaces face the same or opposite direction with an angular offset value. Specifies the rotation of a cylindrical component between two planar surfaces. You can also select lines or edges.
Parallel	Selected planer surfaces are oriented parallel. You can also select lines or edges.
Coincident	Selected planer surfaces edges face the same or opposite directions and are coplanar. Selected revolved surfaces or axes are coaxial. Selected coordinate system's axis are aligned and the origins are mated.
Normal	Selected planer surfaces are oriented perpendicular.
Coplanar	Selected planer surfaces, edges, or axis are oriented coplanar.
Centered	Selected coordinate systems are aligned.
Tangent	Selected surfaces are tangent. Surface normals face each other.
Fix	The Fix constraint fully constrains a component in its current location.
Default	The Default constraint fully constrains a component using its default coordinate system and aligns it to the assembly's default coordinate system.

As constraints are added, the menu updates to only display the remaining possible options. For example, the Default constraint is no longer available after a Coincident constraint is added.

Step 3 - Select the appropriate references on the assembly and component.

A reference to both the component and assembly are required for each constraint. Additionally, each constraint requires its own set of placement references. For example, a Parallel constraint requires a surface or datum plane to be selected on both the component and assembly. Additional constraints are also required to fully place the component.

To display the details of the reference selection, open the Placement panel before you make any selection, as shown in Figure 20–3.

Both selection collectors are active. Therefore, you can select the component and assembly references in any order.

Figure 20–3

By default, you can select component and assembly references in any order. Their status displays in the Placement panel, as shown in Figure 20–3.

You can specify the model for which you are selecting the reference (component or assembly) by selecting the required collector in the Placement panel. Alternatively, you can right-click and select **Select component item** or **Select assembly item** as shown in Figure 20–4, and then select the appropriate reference.

*The **Move Component** option enables you to move the new component to a more convenient position. You can also use the 3D dragger or press <Ctrl>+<Alt> simultaneously and use the mouse to reorient or move the new component.*

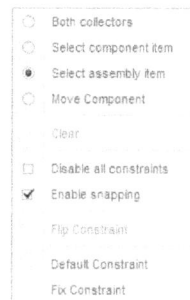

Figure 20–4

Once you have selected the constraint references, additional options might display. For example, when using the Coincident constraint, additional icons display in the Placement panel (**Flip**) and in the dashboard ( ). These enable you to flip the orientation of the component.

To change a selected reference, select the constraint in the Placement panel, select the required reference collector, and select a new reference.

*Use the **Clear** option to remove both the component and assembly references.*

Alternatively, you can change a constraint reference in the graphics window. To change a selected reference in the graphics window, select its name tag, move the cursor away from the selected name tag, right-click and select an option in the contextual menu.

The offset value can be defined before or after you have selected the constraint references.

Step 4 - Assign an offset value, if required.

Distance and Angle Offset constraints require you to define an offset value once the references have been selected. Offset can be defined in the Placement panel or in the dashboard, as shown in Figure 20–5.

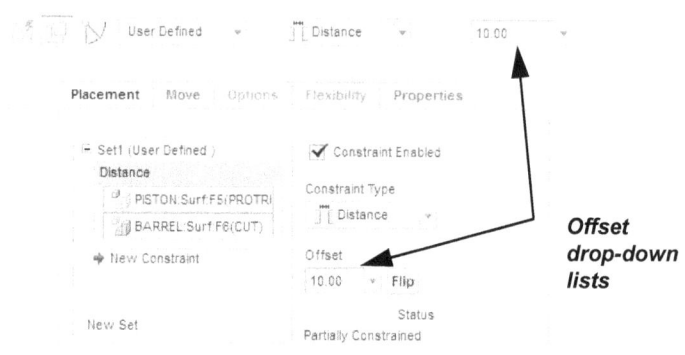

Offset drop-down lists

Figure 20–5

Step 5 - Repeat Steps 2 to 4 until the component is fully constrained.

Before you define the first constraint, the default status of the new component is **No Constraints**, as shown in Figure 20–6. The component displays in the View window in purple until the status indicates that the component is fully constrained or the **Allow Assumptions** option is selected.

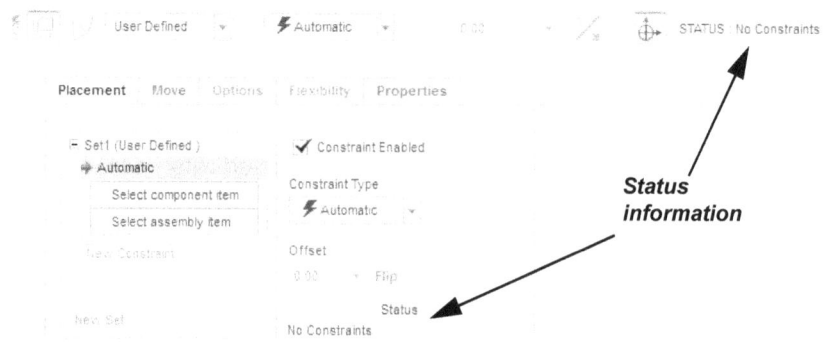

Status information

Figure 20–6

As constraints are added, the status changes to **Partially Constrained**. Finally, the status changes to **Fully Constrained** indicating that enough constraints have been defined to successfully place the component into the existing assembly. If the part or subassembly is fully constrained, the color changes from purple to orange. If you add conflicting constraints, the status changes to **Constraints Invalid**.

Adding Constraints

When constraining a component, you can accept the Automatic constraint default option, or select your own constraints for the new component.

When using automatic constraining, the prompt: *Select any reference for auto type constraining* displays in the *Message* area. Select the assembly and component references to constrain the component. Creo Parametric automatically assigns the appropriate constraint type and adds each new constraint to the Placement panel.

You can also select the constraint type in the tab or in the Placement panel. In this case, Creo Parametric knows which constraint you want to create and prompts you to select the appropriate references. Once you have finished defining a constraint, Creo Parametric activates the automatic constraining again. To add another constraint, select **New Constraint** in the Placement panel, as shown in Figure 20–7.

*You can also right-click and select **New Constraint**.*

Click New Constraint to add a new constraint.

Figure 20–7

If the Placement panel is closed, right-click and select **New Constraint**.

Component placement are not always in the required orientation because Creo Parametric makes assumptions. You can prevent this by clearing the **Allow Assumptions** option, as shown in Figure 20–8. The option is toggled on by default.

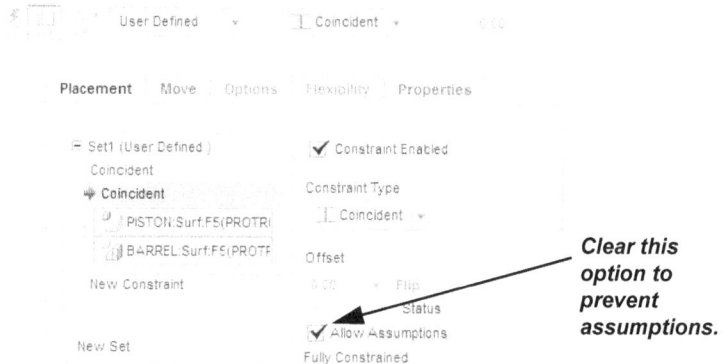

Figure 20–8

Deleting Constraints

To delete a constraint, select it in the Placement panel, right-click, and select **Delete**.

You can also delete a constraint by selecting its name tag in the graphics window, right-clicking, and selecting **Delete**.

Step 6 - Redefine the component placement, as required.

The placement of a component can be redefined by selecting it, right-clicking, and selecting ✏ (Edit Definition). The *Component Placement* dashboard displays. In the Placement panel, all of the constraints used to place the component display. The constraint type, component references, and assembly references can be changed or removed. As each constraint is selected in the Placement panel, the corresponding assembly and component references highlight on the model. To differentiate between the assembly and component references, hover the cursor over the reference's collector. The reference is pre-highlighted on the model.

20.2 Assembly Examples

The following four examples use different combinations of constraints and references to create four different assemblies. The components to be placed are shown in Figure 20–9.

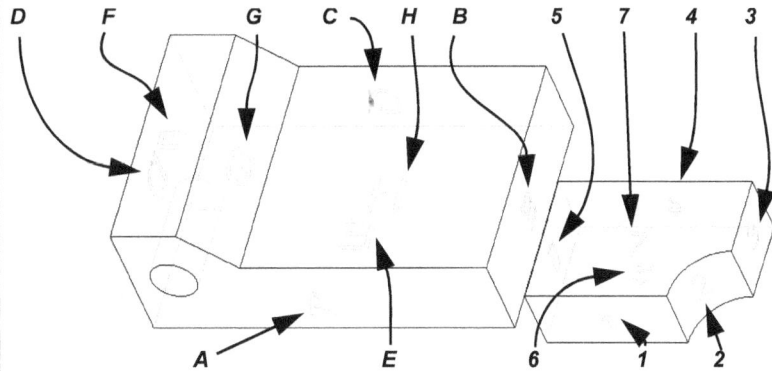

Figure 20–9

Example 1: Coincident

The combination of constraints and references listed below are used to create the assembly shown in Figure 20–10.

Constraint	References
Coincident	Surfaces 7 and H
Coincident	Surfaces 5 and A
Coincident	Surfaces 4 and B

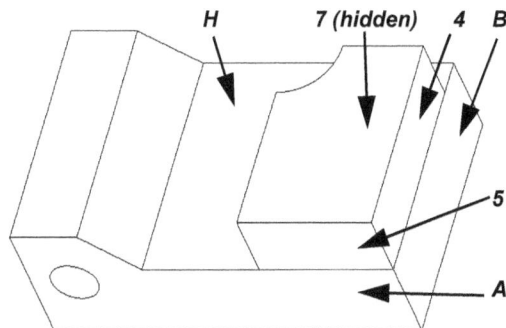

Figure 20–10

Example 2: Distance and Coincident

The combination of constraints and references listed below are used to create the assembly shown in Figure 20–11.

Constraint	References
Distance	Surfaces 7 and H
Coincident	Surfaces 5 and A
Coincident	Surfaces 4 and B

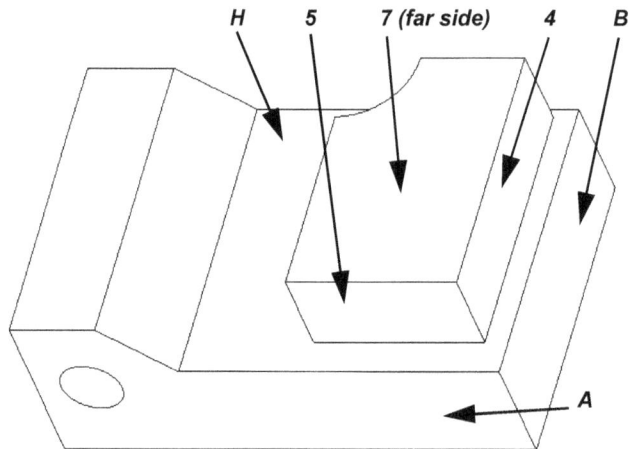

Figure 20–11

Example 3: Coincident

The combination of constraints and references listed below are used to create the assembly shown in Figure 20–12.

Constraint	References
Coincident	Surfaces 6 and H
Coincident	Surfaces 5 and B
Coincident	Surfaces 4 and A

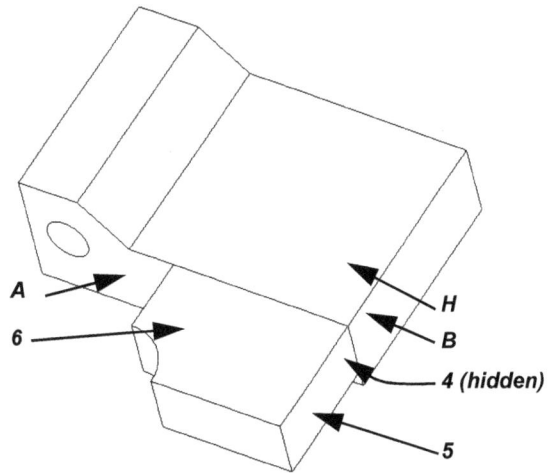

Figure 20–12

Example 4: Distance and Coincident

The combination of constraints and references listed below are used to create the assembly shown in Figure 20–13.

Constraint	References
Distance	Surfaces 5 and B
Coincident	Surfaces 6 and H
Coincident	Surfaces 4 and A

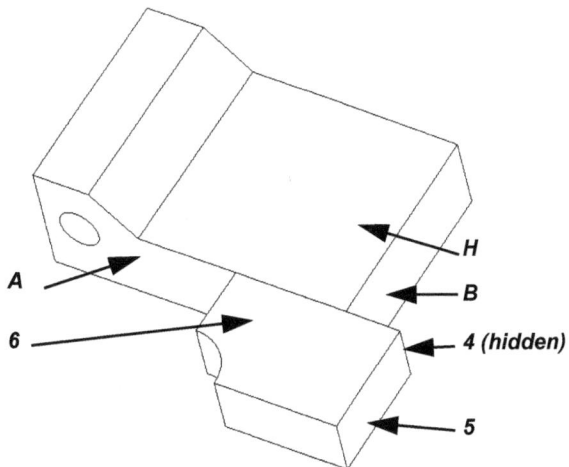

Figure 20–13

Example 5: Coincident

Examples 5 and 6 use different combinations of constraints to create the same assembly. The components to be placed are shown in Figure 20–14.

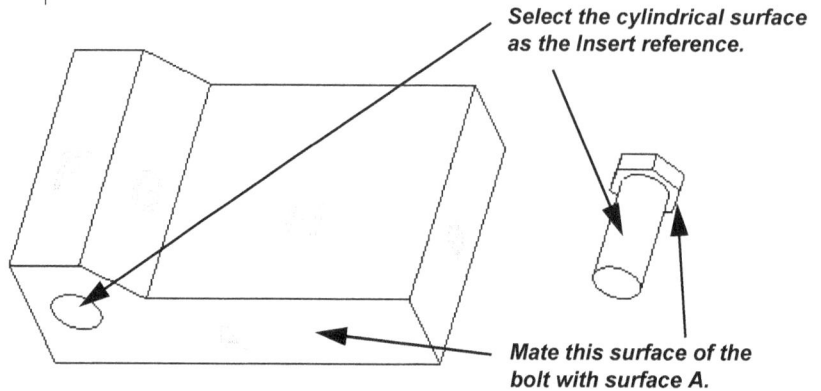

Select the cylindrical surface as the Insert reference.

Mate this surface of the bolt with surface A.

Figure 20–14

The combination of constraints and references listed below are used the create the assembly shown in Figure 20–15.

Constraint	References
Coincident	The cylindrical surface of the bolt and the cylindrical surface created by the hole.
Coincident	The bottom surface of the bolt head and surface A.

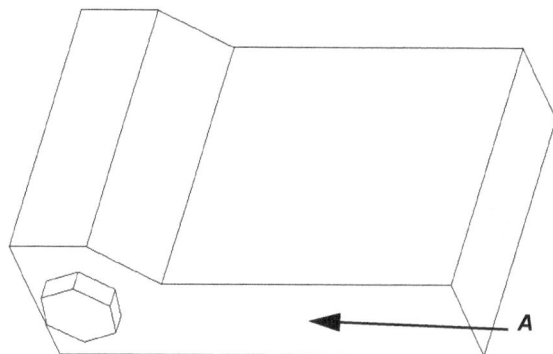

A

Figure 20–15

Example 6: Coincident and Parallel

The combination of constraints and references listed below can be used to create the same assembly, as shown in Figure 20–16.

Constraint	References
Coincident	The cylindrical surface of the bolt and the cylindrical surface created by the hole.
Coincident	The bottom surface of the bolt head and surface A.
Parallel	Surface X of the bolt and surface B.

The first two constraints fully define the placement. However, Parallel is used to define the orientation of the bolt. You could also use Align Angle.

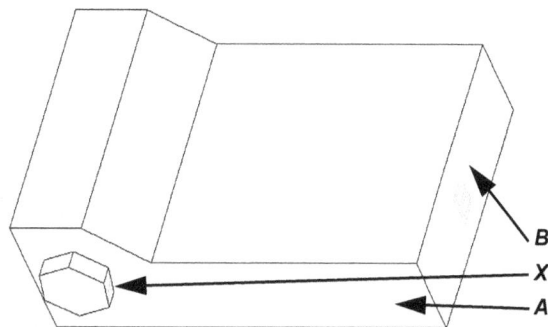

Figure 20–16

Example 7: Tangent and Coincident

Examples 7 and 8 show that using two different combinations of constraints can make a difference in the resulting assembly. The components to be placed are shown in Figure 20–17.

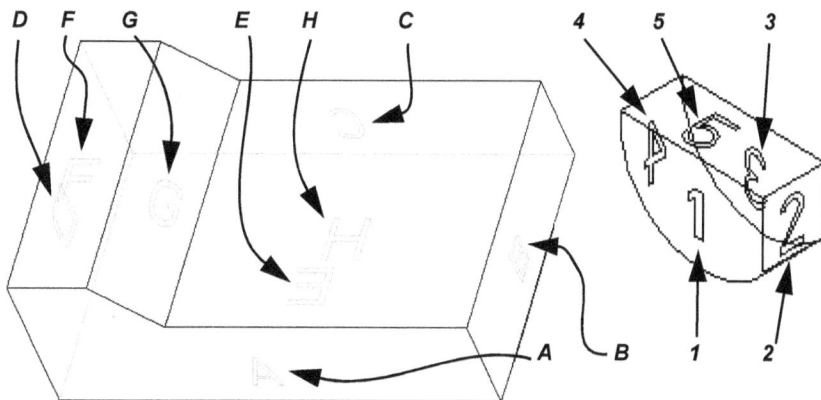

Figure 20–17

The combination of constraints and references listed below are used to create the assembly shown in Figure 20–18.

Constraint	References
Tangent	Surfaces G and 4
Parallel	Surfaces B and 2
Coincident	Surfaces A and 1
Tangent	Surfaces H and 4

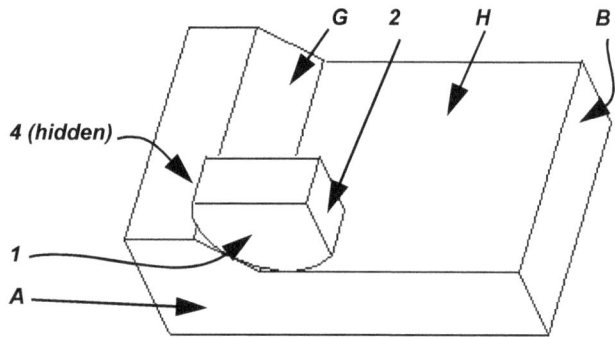

Figure 20–18

Example 8: Tangent, Parallel and Coincident

The combination of constraints and references listed below are used to create the assembly shown in Figure 20–19.

Constraint	References
Coincident	Surface H and Edge 4-2
Tangent	Surfaces G and 4
Coincident	Surfaces A and 1
Parallel	Surfaces G and 5

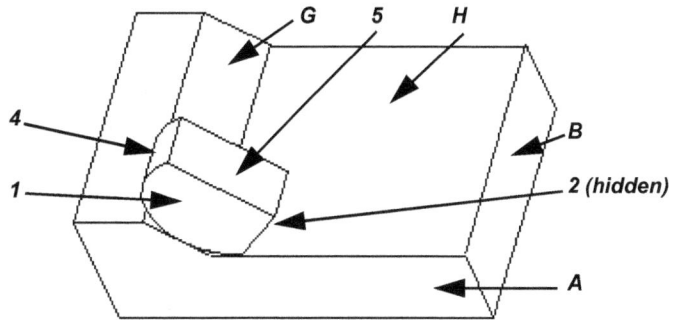

Figure 20–19

Example 9: Default or Centered

As shown in the previous examples, more than one constraint must be used to fully define how components are to be assembled. However, the Default constraint can be used alone. The following example uses the Default constraints listed below, to place the components shown in Figure 20–20. The resulting assembly displays as shown in Figure 20–21.

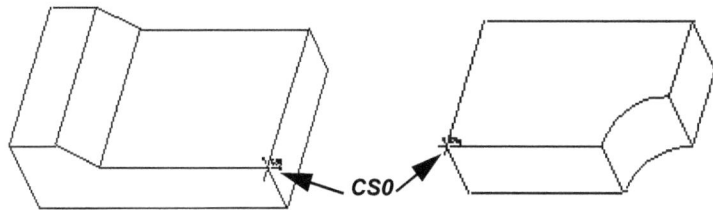

Figure 20–20

Constraint	References
Default	CS0 & CS0

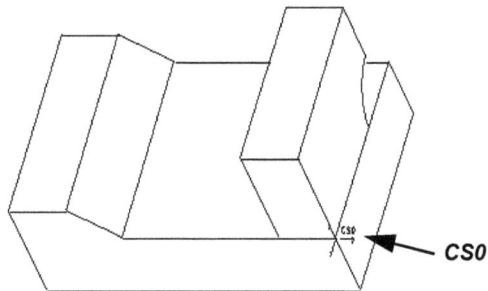

Figure 20–21

20.3 Model Tree

The model tree lists all of the parts and sub-assemblies that combine to create an assembly. You can manipulate parts directly in the model tree (e.g., **Open** or **Edit**). To open a component of an assembly, select it in the model tree, right-click, and select **Open**. The part or sub-assembly opens in a separate window.

To expand the tree and display the components of a sub-assembly, select the plus ( ) symbol next to the assembly name. To compress the expanded section, select the minus ( ) symbol, as shown in Figure 20–22.

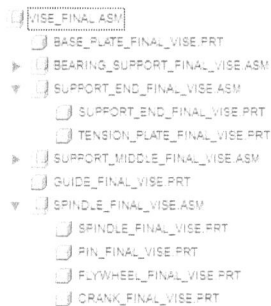

Figure 20–22

Click (Settings) and **Tree Filters** in the model tree and select **Features** in the *Display* area in the Model Tree Items dialog box to see the assembly and part features in the model tree, as shown in Figure 20–23.

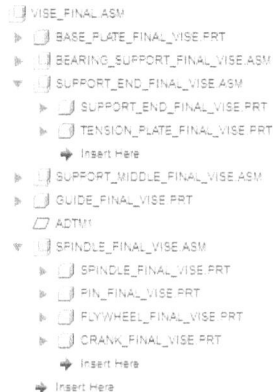

Figure 20–23

Click ⊤ ▼ (Settings)>**Tree Filters** in the model tree. In the
Model Tree Items dialog box, in the *Display* area, select
Placement Folder to see the assembly constraints in the model
tree, as shown in Figure 20–24.

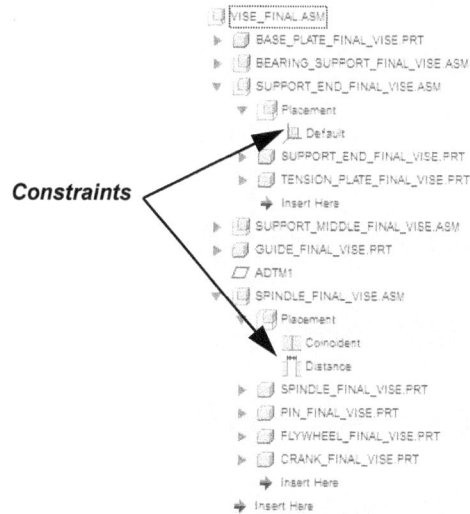

Figure 20–24

Practice 20a | Assembly Basics I

Practice Objectives

- Insert components in an assembly.
- Locate components in an assembly based on selected constraint type and references using the Component Placement tab.
- Make dimensional, constraint, or reference changes on an existing component using Edit Definition.

In this practice, you will open the existing assembly shown in Figure 20–25 and assemble additional components. The following tasks and steps for the assembly constraints reference the lettered and numbered sides on the components. Add and remove constraints as required to reach the required design intent. In addition, redefine the original constraints and references and make modifications to the assembly dimensions.

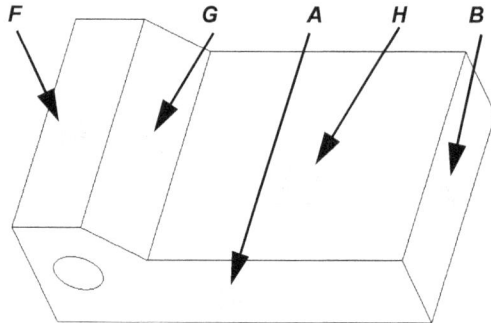

Figure 20–25

Task 1 - Change the working directory and open an assembly file.

1. Set the working directory to the *Chapter 20\practice 20a* folder.

2. Open **practice.asm**.

3. Set the model display as follows:

   - ⁺⁺⁺ *(Datum Display Filters)*: All Off

   - ⟩⟩ *(Spin Center)*: Off

   - ⌐ *(Display Style)*: ⬚ (Shading With Edges)

Task 2 - Assemble the part named bblock.prt.

1. The component will be assembled as shown in Figure 20–26.

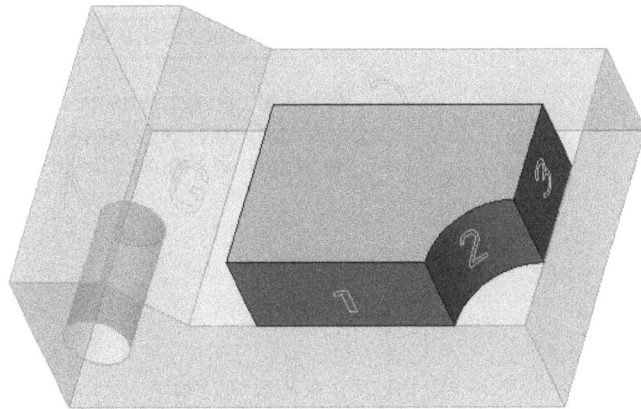

Figure 20–26

2. In the Component group in the *Model* tab, click
   (Assemble).

3. In the Open dialog box, select **bblock.prt**, and click **Open**.
   The *Component Placement* dashboard displays. The new
   component displays in the main window because (In
   Window) is activated by default.

You can also move the component using <Ctrl>+ <Alt> and the mouse to orient the component. Click and hold the right mouse button to pan the component, or click and hold the middle mouse button to spin the component.

4. The component displays in the main window along with the
   3D dragger as shown in Figure 20–27. Note that the color of
   the added component is purple. Drag the centerpoint of the
   3D dragger to freely move the component.

Drag the center to move the component

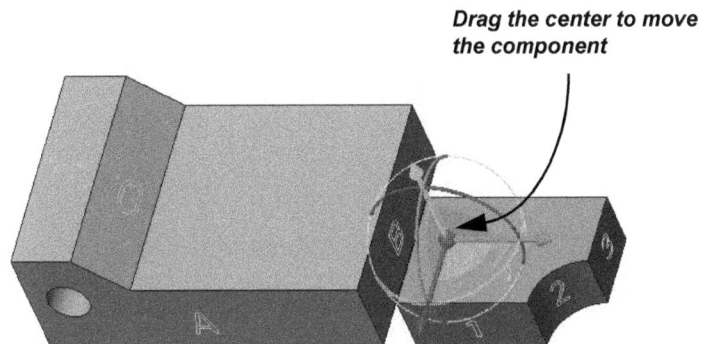

Figure 20–27

5. Drag an arrow to translate the component along the axis.

6. Select a rotation arc to rotate the component.

7. Open the Placement panel and leave it open during the assembly process.

Task 3 - Define the first constraint.

The first constraint is coincident to mate surface 6 on **bblock.prt** and surface **H** on **ablock.prt** (which is already in **practice.asm**), as shown in Figure 20–28.

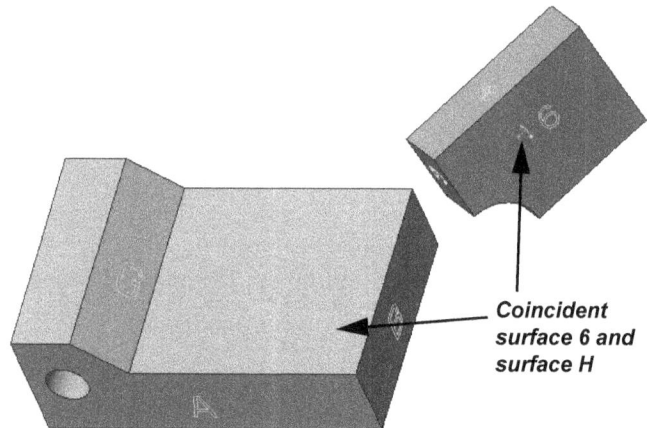

Coincident
surface 6 and
surface H

Figure 20–28

The 3D dragger can be toggled off by clicking

⊕ *(3D Dragger) in the Component Placement tab.*

1. In the Constraint Type drop-down list, scroll down and select **Coincident** as shown in Figure 20–29.

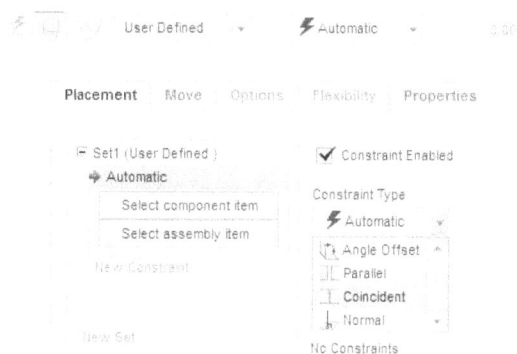

Figure 20–29

Note that your
component may not be
in the exact same
orientation as shown in
Figure 20–28 and
Figure 20–30. The
important thing is to
select the appropriate
surfaces.

2. In **bblock.prt**, select surface **6**.

3. In **ablock.prt**, select surface **H**.

4. Note that the green axis on the 3D dragger displays in gray
    indicating that the model can no longer move in that direction.
    Look at the *Component Placement* tab. The *STATUS* now
    displays as **Partially Constrained**. The first constraint has
    been added and the second can now be defined.

5. Surface **6** and surface **H** should be facing one another. If the
    surfaces are facing the same direction, click **Flip** in the
    Component Placement tab, to flip the part.

Task 4 - Define a second constraint.

The second constraint uses coincident to align surface **3** on
bblock.prt and surface **B** on **ablock.prt**, as shown in
Figure 20–30.

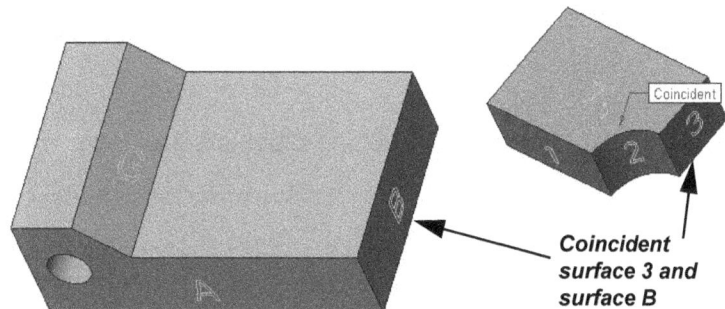

*Coincident
surface 3 and
surface B*

Figure 20–30

1. Right-click and select **New Constraint**.

2. In the Constraint Type drop-down list, select **Coincident**.

3. In **bblock.prt**, select surface **3**.

4. In **ablock.prt**, select surface **B**.

5. Look at the *Component Placement* tab. The *STATUS* still
    displays as **Partially Constrained**. With the current
    constraints, **bblock.prt** can still lie anywhere on surface **H**
    while remaining aligned to surface **B**. A third constraint is
    required to fully constrain the part.

Task 5 - Define a third constraint.

The third constraint uses coincident to align surface **1** on **bblock.prt** and surface **A** on **ablock.prt**, as shown in Figure 20–31.

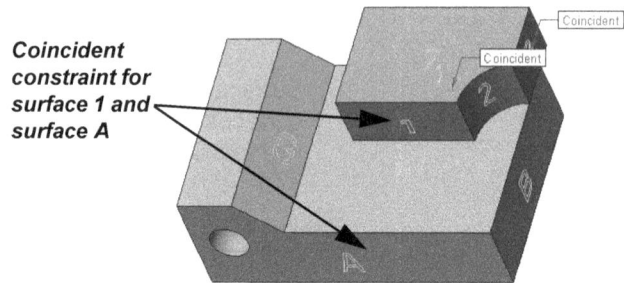

Coincident constraint for surface 1 and surface A

Figure 20–31

1. If the assembly does not display as shown in Figure 20–31, click **Flip** in the Placement panel.

2. Right-click and select **New Constraint**.

3. In the Constraint Type drop-down list, select **Coincident**.

4. In **bblock.prt**, select surface **1**.

5. In **ablock.prt**, select surface **A**.

6. Look at the *Component Placement* tab. The *STATUS* now displays as **Fully Constrained**.

Task 6 - Check the placement of the component in the assembly.

1. Check the placement of **bblock.prt** in the assembly. It must correspond to Figure 20–32.

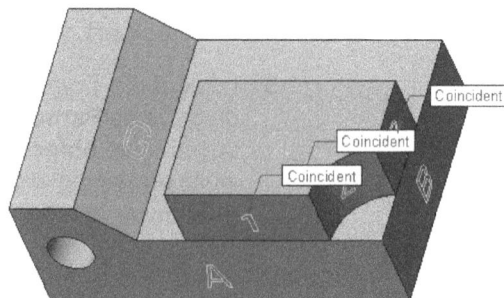

Figure 20–32

2. If the component does not display as expected, click
   ✕ (Cancel Feature) and repeat the previous steps. If the
   placement is correct, click ✓ (Complete Feature).

Task 7 - Assemble bblock.prt a second time. Use the Automatic constraint to assemble the block.

The second Assembled **bblock.prt** is shown in Figure 20–33.

Figure 20–33

1. In the Open dialog box, click 🗁 (Assemble) and double-click
   bblock.prt.

2. Leave the *Placement* panel in the dashboard closed.

3. Click ⊕ (3D Dragger), if required, to enable the 3D Dragger.

4. Click and drag the red rotation arc to orient the block as
   shown in Figure 20–34.

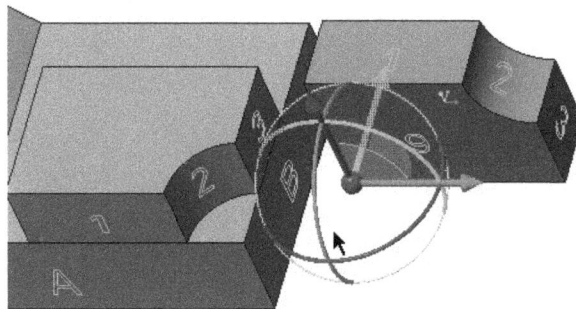

Figure 20–34

---

5. Right-click on surface **6**, then left-click when surface **4** highlights, as shown in Figure 20–35.

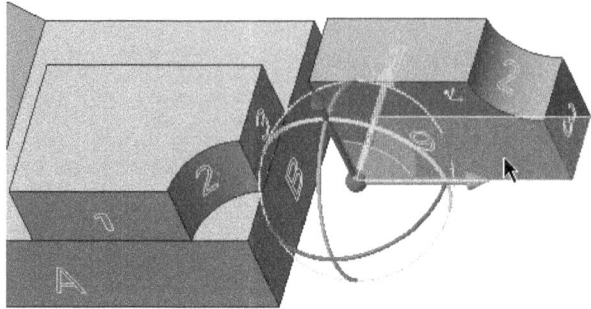

Figure 20–35

6. Select Surface **H**, as shown in Figure 20–36.

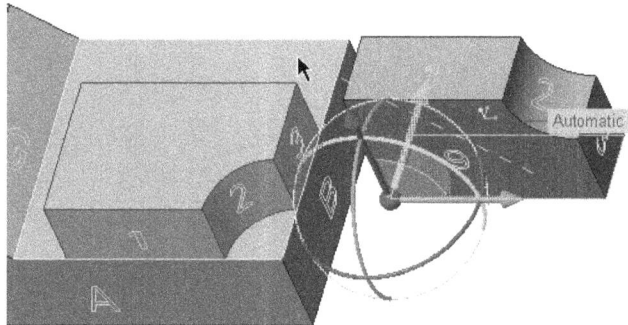

Figure 20–36

7. The constraint automatically changes to **Coincident**, as shown in Figure 20–37

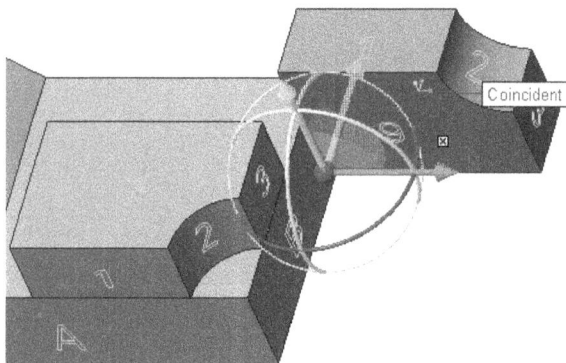

Figure 20–37

8. Select Surface **6** on the bblock you are assembling as shown in Figure 20–38.

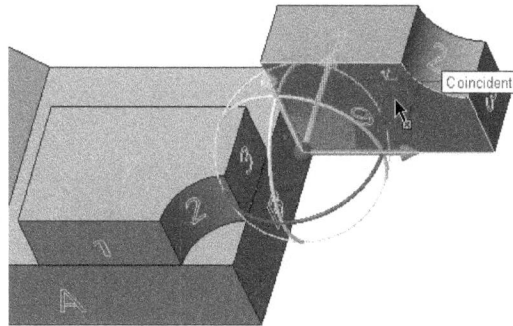

Figure 20–38

9. Right-click on surface **7** of the already assembled bblock, right-click and select surface **4** when it highlights, as shown in Figure 20–39.

The constraint will automatically be set to Coincident again.

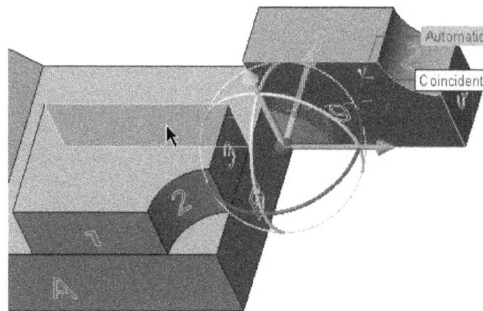

Figure 20–39

10. Select surface **3** on the bblock you are assembling and surface **B**.

11. The constraint is set to **Distance**, as shown in Figure 20–40.

The Distance constraint accounts for the offset of surface 3 and B.

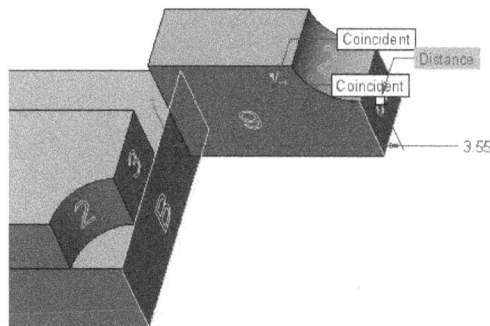

Figure 20–40

12. Right-click on the Distance constraint and select **Coincident** from the menu, as shown in Figure 20–41.

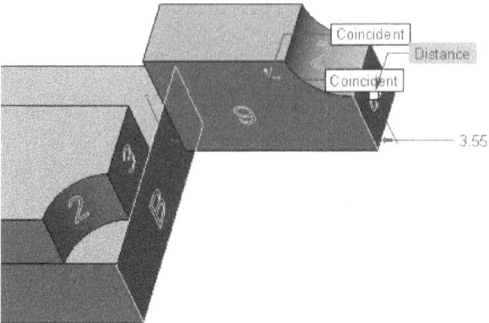

Figure 20–41

13. The assembly updates and the *STATUS* in the dashboard shows **Fully Constrained**, as shown in Figure 20–42,

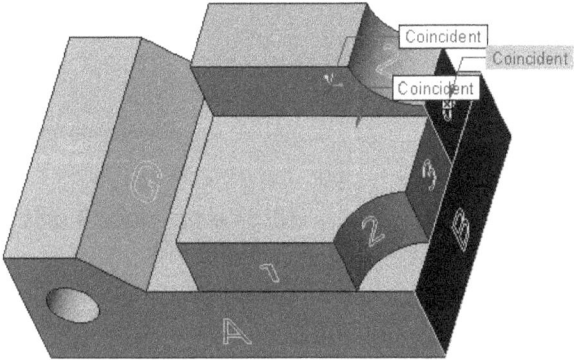

Figure 20–42

14. Click ✔ (Complete Feature) to finish the placing the component.

Task 8 - Assemble the pin.prt part.

1. Click (Assemble) and select **pin.prt** as the component to be assembled.

2. Before you start assembling, use the 3D Dragger to orient the bolt as shown in Figure 20–43.

*If the parallel constraint is your third constraint, you might need to clear the **Allow Assumptions** option in the Placement panel to be able to add this constraint. This is because the first two constraints are sufficient to place the component and the orientation of Surface X is assumed by the system. Although the assumption might be correct, you can add the final constraint to ensure that the surfaces remain oriented regardless of changes that might be made to the models.*

Coincident to insert the cylindrical surface of the pin into the cylindrical surface of the hole

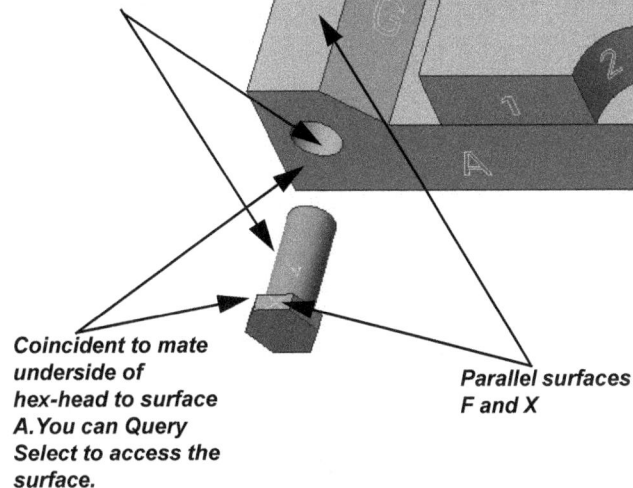

Coincident to mate underside of hex-head to surface A. You can Query Select to access the surface.

Parallel surfaces F and X

Figure 20–43

The assembled component is shown in Figure 20–44.

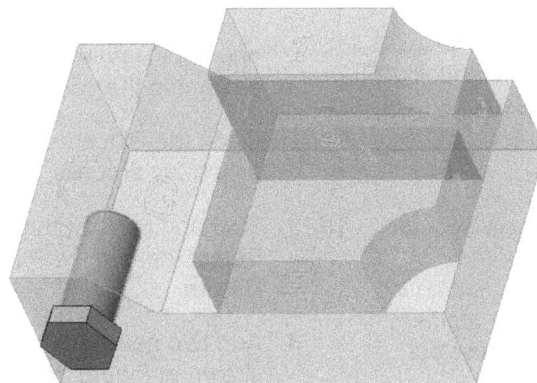

Figure 20–44

Task 9 - Assemble additional instances of ablock.prt and bblock.prt.

1. Assemble the two additional instances of **ablock.prt** and **bblock.prt**, as shown in Figure 20–45.

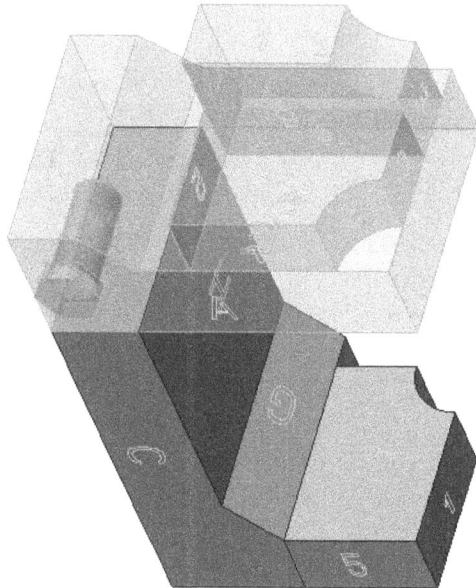

Figure 20–45

Task 10 - Edit the definition of the second instance of ablock.prt in the assembly.

*To easily select the model in the main window, select **Parts** in the filter at the bottom of the main assembly window.*

1. Select the second instance of **ablock.prt** in the model tree or in the model. Right-click and select ✎ (Edit Definition). The original *Component Placement* tab that was used to assemble the component displays.

2. Open the Placement panel and leave it open during the assembly process.

*You can also select the name tags of the Coincident constraints directly on the model, right-click, and select **Delete**.*

3. Find and remove the appropriate two Coincident constraints. Select them in the Placement panel, right-click, and select **Delete**.

4. Add two new constraints to position the component, as shown in Figure 20–46.

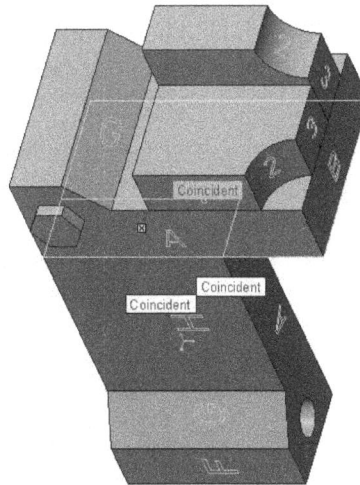

Figure 20–46

5. Click ✓ (Complete Feature) to complete the redefinition of the assembly. The **bblock.prt** component updates relative to the new location for **bblock.prt** because of its placement references.

Task 11 - Obtain information on component placement.

1. Select the *Tools* tab and click 🖳 (Component Information).

In more complicated assemblies, select ***Parts*** *in the selection filter at the bottom of the main assembly window to make the selection of part objects easier.*

2. Select **pin.prt** in the model tree or on the model. An expanded Component Constraints dialog box opens as shown in Figure 20–47. The constraints displays in the order in which you added them.

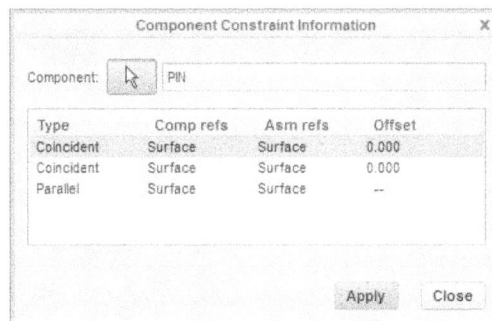

Figure 20–47

3. Select each constraint listed in the dialog box. As you do, note that it highlights the reference surfaces on the model.

4. Click **Apply**. The browser window opens with additional information about the component. The information is written to a text file named **pin.memb**, which is stored in the current working directory.

5. Close both the browser window and Component Constraints dialog box.

Task 12 - Delete all components except for the base component.

---

1. Delete all of the components except the first instance of **ablock.prt**. Remember that parent/child relationships exist. For example, you cannot delete the second instance of **ablock.prt** without the Delete dialog box opening indicating that a child must also be considered.

Task 13 - Assemble bblock.prt using the Align offset.

You can drag the component to the appropriate position before you enter the exact offset value, using the 3D dragger or by pressing <Ctrl>+<Alt> simultaneously and using the mouse to orient it.

1. Assemble **bblock.prt** using a two coincident constraints and a *Distance* constraint with a value of **1.0** between surfaces **6** and **A**, as shown in Figure 20–48. You might need to use an offset of **-1.0** to change the offset direction.

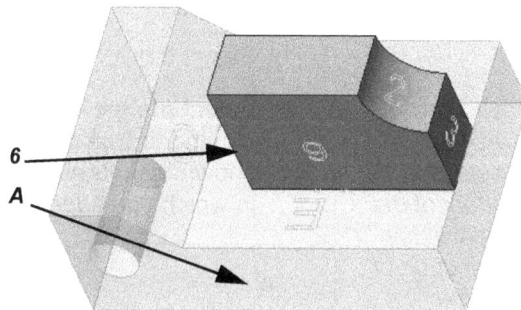

Figure 20–48

Task 14 - Modify the offset value of bblock.prt.

---

1. Select **bblock.prt** in the model tree or on the model. Right-click and select ⊩⟶⊣ (Edit).

2. Select the offset dimension and enter **2**.

3. Click ⬚ (Regenerate) to regenerate the model.

4. Save the assembly and erase all of the models from memory.

Practice 20b | Motor Frame

Practice Objectives

- Insert components in an assembly.
- Locate components in an assembly based on selected constraint type and references using the Component Placement tab.
- Make dimensional, constraint or reference changes on an existing component using Edit Definition.

In this practice, you will open an existing assembly and assemble a subassembly. You will then continue assembling components to complete the top-level assembly. The completed assembly is shown in Figure 20–49.

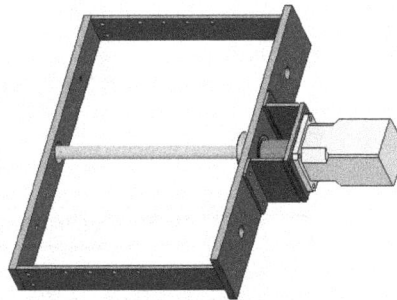

Figure 20–49

Task 1 - Change the working directory and open an assembly file.

1. Set the working directory to the *Chapter 20\practice 20b* folder.

2. Open **motor_frame.asm**.

3. Set the model display as follows:

   - ⁛ *(Datum Display Filters)*: All Off

   - ⟩ *(Spin Center)*: Off

   - ▢ *(Display Style)*: ▱ (Shading With Edges)

Task 2 - Assemble a subassembly.

1. In the *Model* tab, click ⬚ (Assemble).

2. Select **motor_mount.asm** as the file to assemble.

3. Click ⊕ (3D Dragger) to toggle on the 3D dragger, if required.

4. Drag the component to the approximate position shown in Figure 20–50.

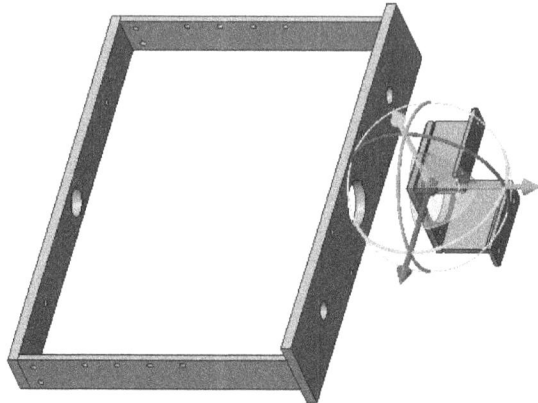

Figure 20–50

Task 3 - Define the first constraint.

1. Select the two circular surfaces shown in Figure 20–51. Ensure that **Coincident** is the type of constraint being used.

3D Dragger is toggled off in this image for clarity.

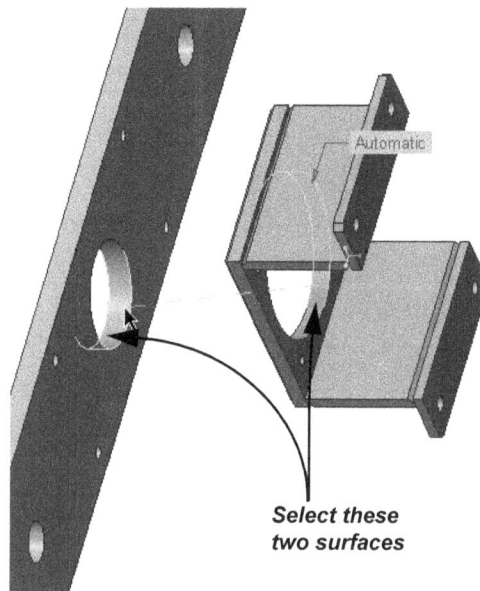

Select these two surfaces

Figure 20–51

Task 4 - Define the second constraint.

1. Select the two surfaces shown in Figure 20–52.

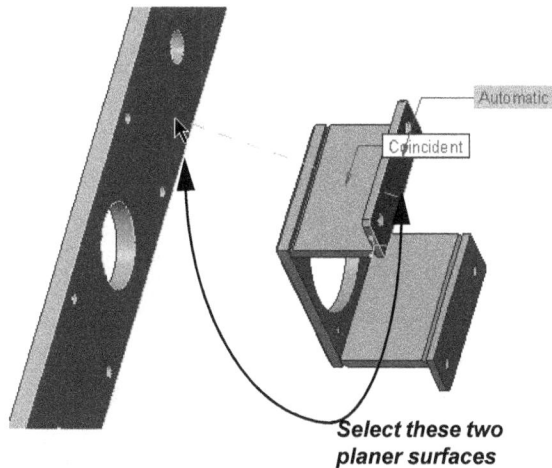

Select these two
planer surfaces

Figure 20–52

2. Ensure that Coincident is the type of constraint being used. The model updates to displays as shown in Figure 20–53.

    Click ⚹ (Change Constraint Orientation) in the *Component Placement* dashboard, if required.

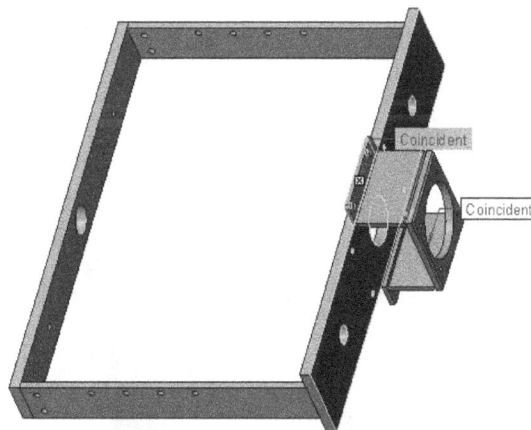

Figure 20–53

Task 5 - Define a third constraint.

1. Right-click and select **New Constraint**.

2. Select the two bolt hole surfaces shown in Figure 20–54. Edit the constraint type to **Coincident** if required.

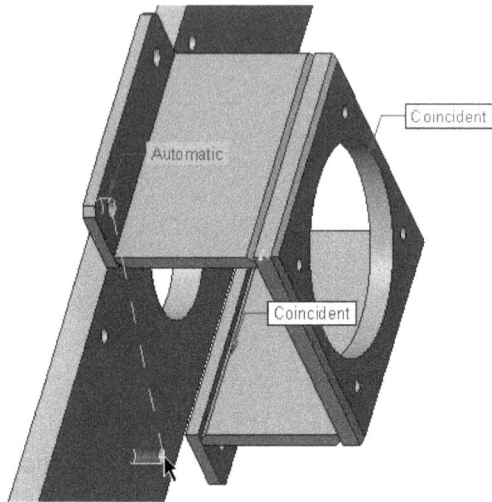

Figure 20–54

3. Look at the *Component Placement* tab. The *STATUS* now displays as **Fully Constrained**. Click ✓ (Complete Feature) to complete the component placement, as shown in Figure 20–55.

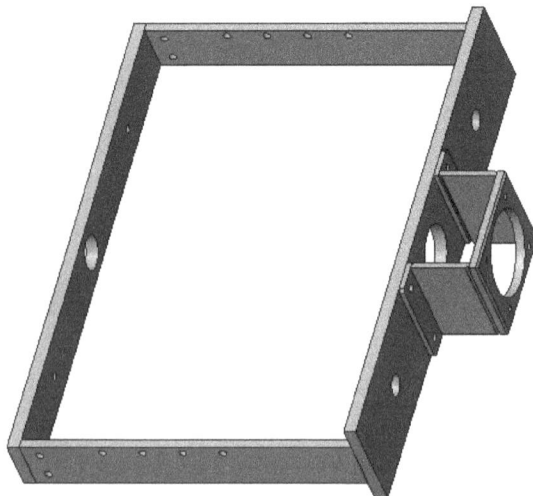

Figure 20–55

Task 6 - Assemble the electric motor part.

1. Assemble **motor.prt**.

2. Before you add constraints, use the 3D dragger to reorient the component to a more appropriate position, as shown in Figure 20–56.

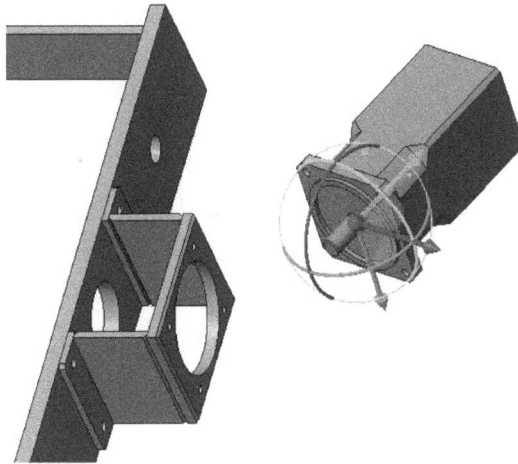

Figure 20–56

3. Create a Coincident constraint and select the two cylindrical surfaces, as shown in Figure 20–57.

3D Dragger toggled off for clarity.

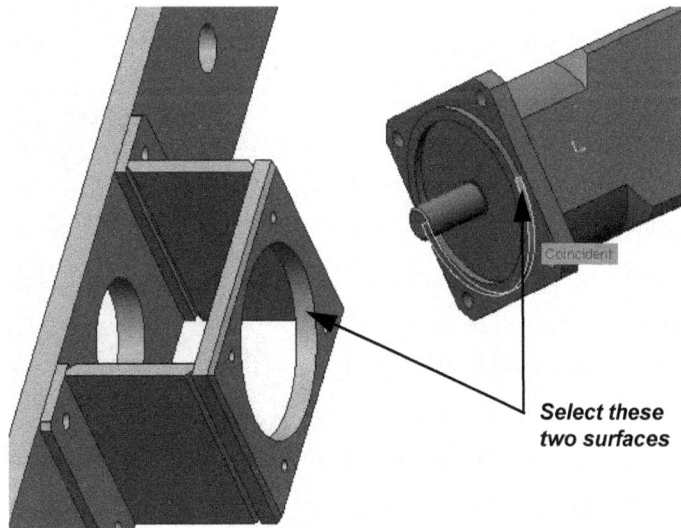

Select these two surfaces

Figure 20–57

4. Apply a Coincident constraint and pick the two planer surfaces, as shown in Figure 20–58.

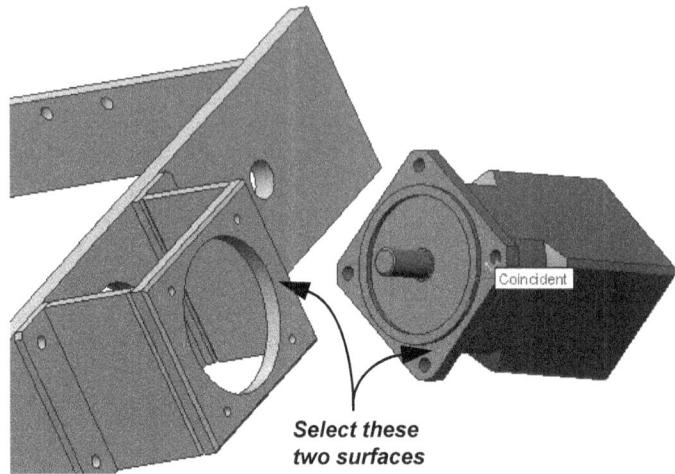

Figure 20–58

5. Right-click and select **New Constraint**.

6. Create a Coincident constraint as shown in Figure 20–59.

*The **Oriented** constraint will also work.*

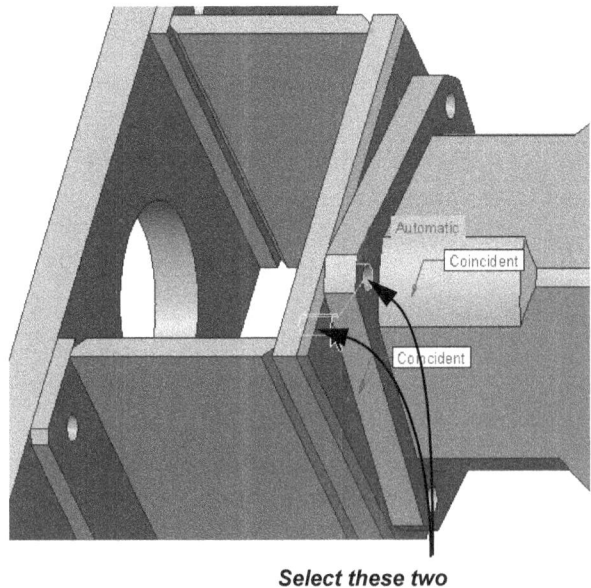

Figure 20–59

The motor part is fully constrained, as shown in Figure 20–60.

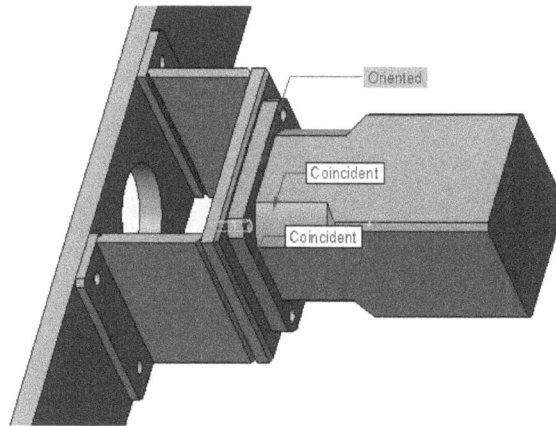

Figure 20–60

7. Click ✓ (Complete Feature) to complete the component placement.

Task 7 - Assemble the bearing housing part.

1. Assemble **bearing_housing.prt**. Use a Coincident constraint to align the cylindrical surfaces. Use a second Coincident constraint to mate the small surface of the bearing housing part to the surface of the frame, as shown in Figure 20–61.

   The constrained bearing housing part displays as shown in Figure 20–62.

Select the small surface of the bearing housing part and the surface of the frame.

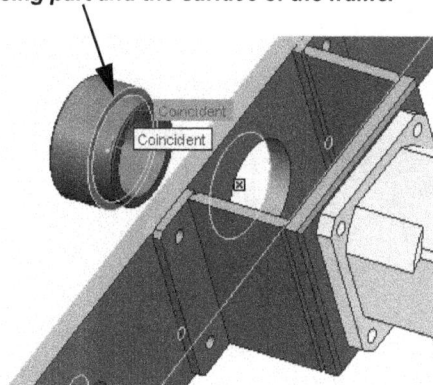

Figure 20–61

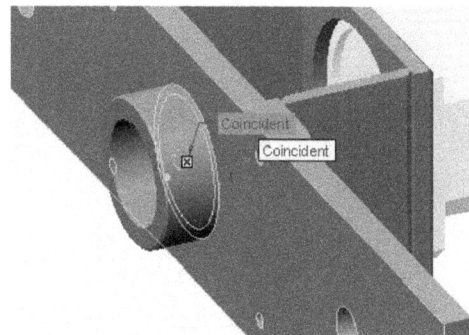

Figure 20–62

2. Complete the component placement.

Task 8 - Assemble the bearing part.

1. Assemble **bearing.prt** as shown in Figure 20–63. Add a
    Coincident constraint to align the surfaces. Add a second
    Coincident constraint to insert the cylindrical surface.

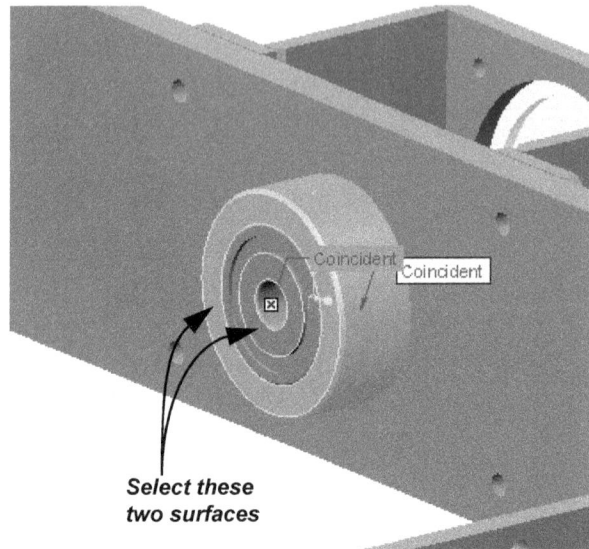

*Select these
two surfaces*

Figure 20–63

Task 9 - Assemble the shaft part.

1. Assemble **shaft.prt** using a Coincident constraint, as shown
    in Figure 20–64.

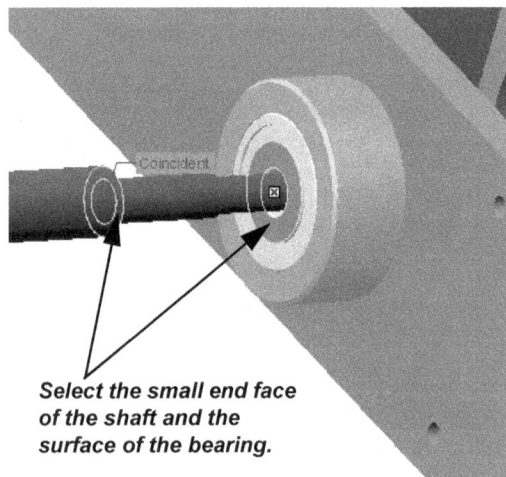

*Select the small end face
of the shaft and the
surface of the bearing.*

Figure 20–64

2. Add a second coincident constrain and select the two cylindrical surfaces to fully constrain the components. The constrained shaft displays as shown in Figure 20–65.

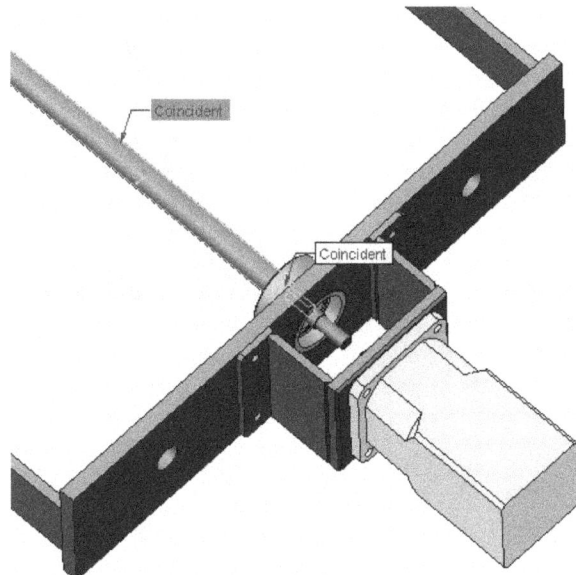

Figure 20–65

Task 10 - Assemble the coupling part.

1. Assemble **coupling.prt** using two Coincident constraints, as shown in Figure 20–66.

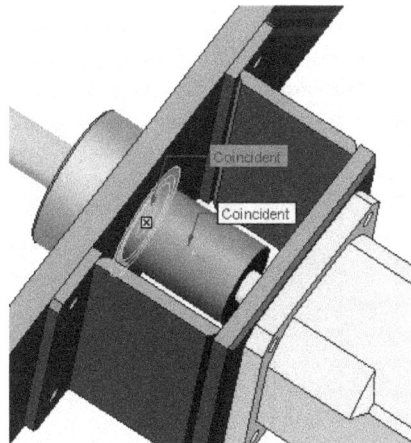

Figure 20–66

The completed assembly displays as shown in Figure 20–67.

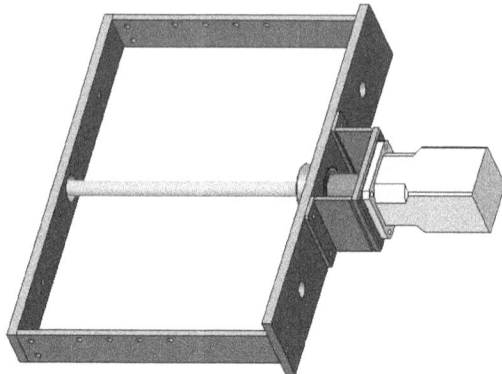

Figure 20–67

2. Save the assembly and erase it from memory.

Practice 20c | (Optional) Subassemblies

Practice Objectives

- Insert subassemblies in an assembly.
- Locate subassemblies in an assembly based on selected constraint type and references using the Component Placement tab.

In this practice, you will create an assembly by assembling parts and assemblies, and then assemble it into a top-level assembly.

Task 1 - Change the working directory and open an assembly file.

1. Set the working directory to the *Chapter 20\practice 20c* folder.

2. Open **rod.asm.**

3. Set the model display as follows:

   - ⁑ *(Datum Display Filters)*: All Off

   - ⌁ *(Spin Center)*: Off

   - ▯ *(Display Style)*: ▱ (Shading With Edges)

Task 2 - Assemble a subassembly.

1. Assemble **piston.asm** as shown in Figure 20–68.

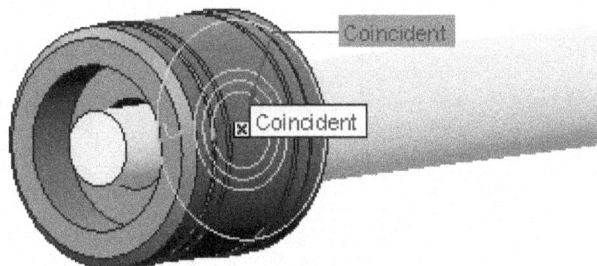

Figure 20–68

2. Assemble **washer.prt** as shown in Figure 20–69.

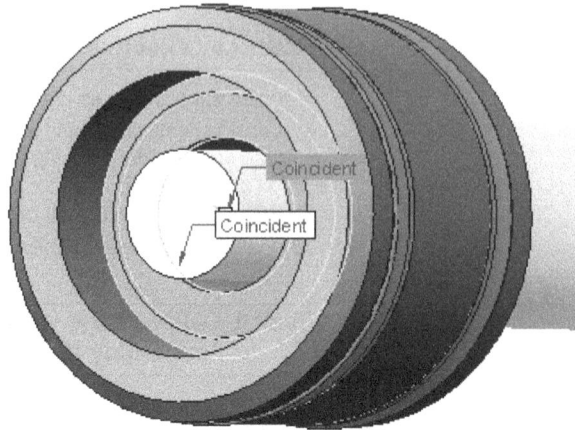

Figure 20–69

3. Assemble **nut.prt** as shown in Figure 20–70.

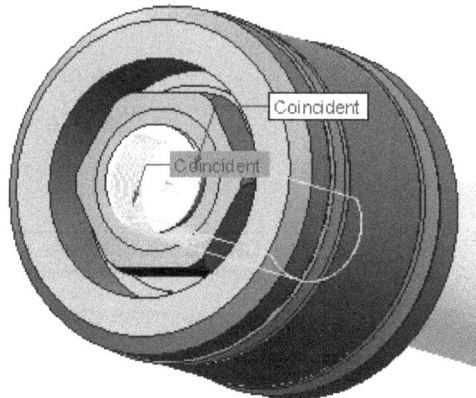

Figure 20–70

4. Assemble **gland.asm** as shown in Figure 20–71.

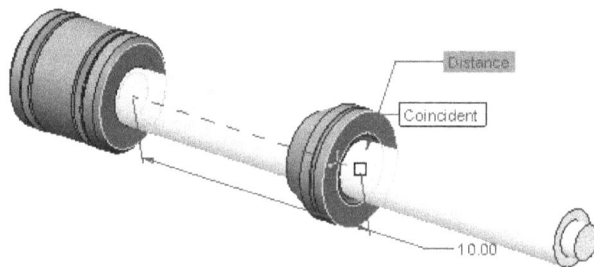

Figure 20–71

5. Save the assembly.

Task 3 - Open the top-level assembly.

1. Open **cylinder.asm**. The assembly has a base component assembled, as shown in Figure 20–72.

Figure 20–72

2. Assemble the **rod.asm** that you just created into **cylinder.asm**, as shown in Figure 20–73.

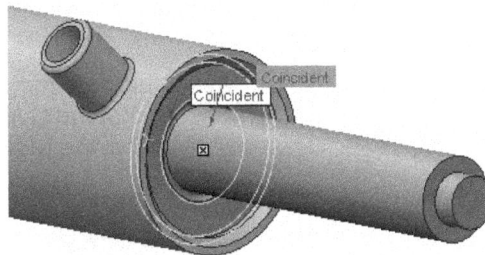

Figure 20–73

Ensure that the Coincident constraint references the front face of the gland part and the aft face of the groove in the barrel part, as shown in Figure 20–74.

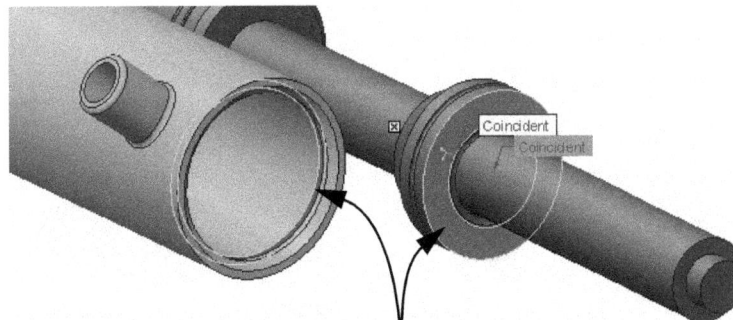

Align these two faces

Figure 20–74

3. Assemble **clevis.prt** as shown in Figure 20–75.

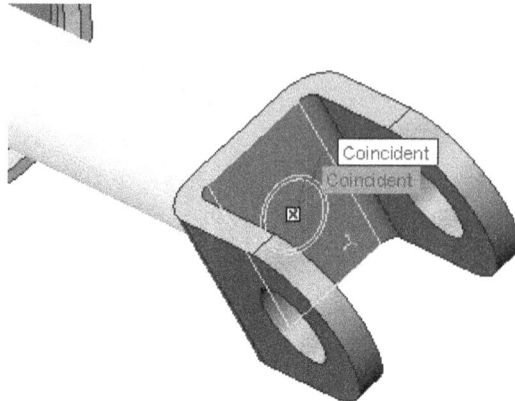

Figure 20–75

4. Assemble **retaining_ring.prt** as shown in Figure 20–76. Ensure that the Coincident constraint references the outside diameter of the retaining ring and the surface of the groove.

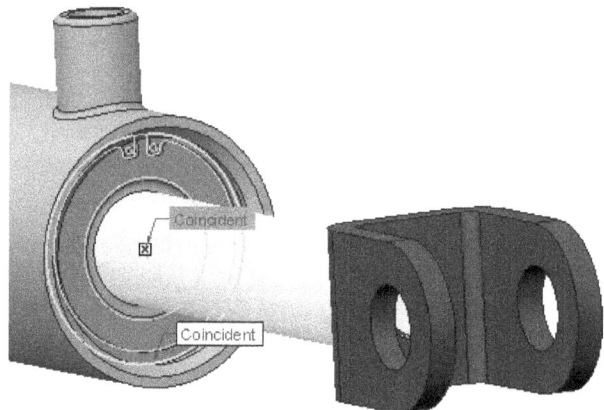

Figure 20–76

The completed assembly displays as shown in Figure 20–77.

Figure 20–77

5. Save the assembly and erase it from memory.

Chapter Review Questions

1. Parent/child relationships cannot exist between components in an assembly.

   a. True

   b. False

2. Which of the following icons enables you to assemble a component into an assembly?

   a.

   b.

   c.

   d.

3. In the *Component Placement* dashboard, which of the following icons enables you to assemble a new component while remaining in the main assembly window?

   a.

   b.

   c.

   d.

4. Which of the following are valid constraint types that can be used to assemble components into an assembly? (Select all that apply.)

   a. Coincident

   b. Distance

   c. Tangent

   d. Tangent to Pnt

5. What is the minimum number of constraints that can be used to parametrically locate a component in an assembly?

   a. 0

   b. 1

   c. 3

   d. 4

6. Which of the following constraint options enable you to constrain a component so that two surfaces are aligned but you still maintain the flexibility of entering an offset value if the design intent changes?

   a. Distance

   b. Parallel

   c. Coincident

7. The *Assembly item* collector in the Placement panel in the *Component Placement* dashboard enables you to define the reference for the component that is being assembled into the assembly.

   a. True

   b. False

8. Which of the following statements are true when you use the Coincident constraint for two planar surfaces? (Select all that apply.)

   a. The surface normals point in the same direction.

   b. Constraining two surfaces to be Coincident is equivalent to using the Distance constraint with a value of 0.

   c. The surface normals point in opposite directions.

   d. Equivalent to using the Normal constraint.

9. Which of the assemblies shown in Figure 20–78 could have used the Parallel constraint to constrain surfaces **C** and **2** and surfaces **A** and **3**?

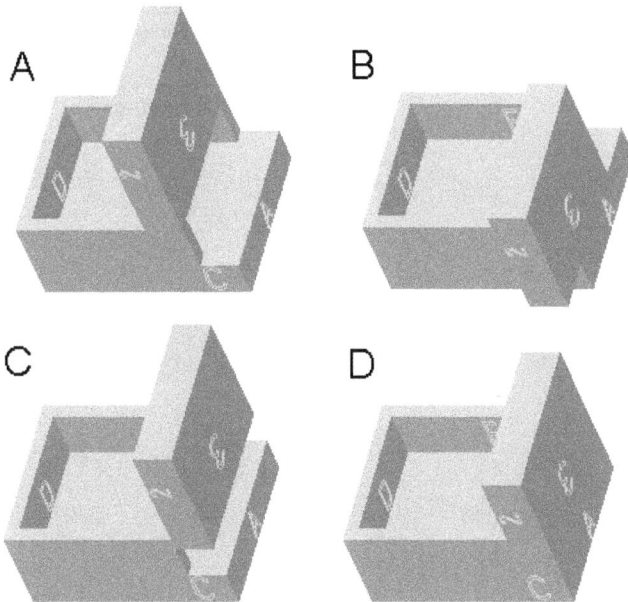

Figure 20–78

a. A

b. B

c. C

d. D

Command Summary

Button	Command	Location
	Assemble	• **Ribbon:** *Model* tab in the *Component* group
	Settings	• Model Tree

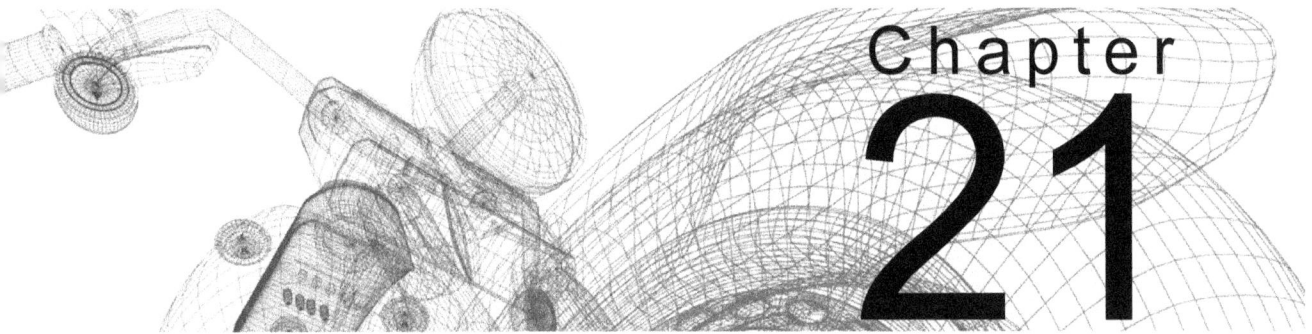

Assembly Tools

In the previous chapter, you learned that components are constrained to one another to form assemblies. The constraints that you use result in parent/child relationships between the components. In this chapter, you learn to assemble components using datum planes as references; this technique avoids unwanted parent/child relationships. You also learn a number of other tools that can be used while in Assembly mode to evaluate and review the entire assembly.

Learning Objectives in this Chapter

- Locate components in an assembly using the datum planes and axis as constraint references.
- Edit existing components in an assembly using correct editing tools.
- Customize and create exploded views using the View Manager dialog box.
- Check for interference between the components of the assembly using the Global Interference Analysis command.
- Generate a bill of materials for the assembly to determine what components are used and how often.
- Hide, unhide, and isolate layers using the layer tree in an assembly.

21.1 Assembly with Datum Planes

As with new parts, new assemblies should start with default datum planes. Using default datum planes makes the assembly more robust. They enable you to easily perform operations, such as patterning and reordering components.

Default datum planes are provided with all standard assembly templates. They can also be created as the first features in the assembly by clicking ▱ (Plane) in the Datum group in the *Model* tab. Default datum planes created using the default template are named **ASM_RIGHT**, **ASM_TOP**, and **ASM_FRONT**, as shown in Figure 21–1.

By default, the datum names, referred to as datum tags, are not visible, but can be displayed by clicking

◻ (Plane Tag Display) in the View tab.

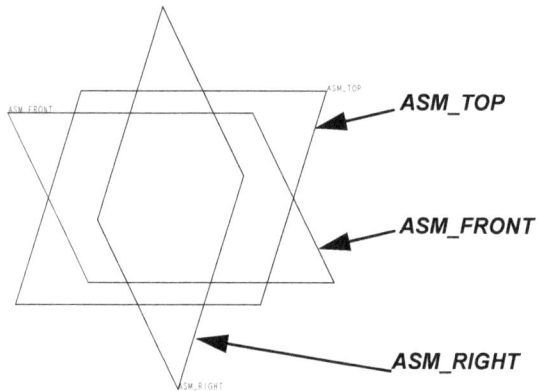

Figure 21–1

However, default datum planes created in the assembly model are named **ADTM1**, **ADTM2**, and **ADTM3**.

Datum planes can be used as constraint references when defining component placements. When a datum plane is selected as a reference, you can click ⤢ (Change Constraint Orientation) in the *Component Placement* dashboard or click **Flip** in the Placement panel to flip the component into the correct orientation if the default is not acceptable. When a datum plane is selected, the action is applied to its dominant (brown) side by default.

In the example in Figure 21–2, the bracket part shown on the right is assembled to the assembly's default datum planes (shown on the left), using the selected constraints.

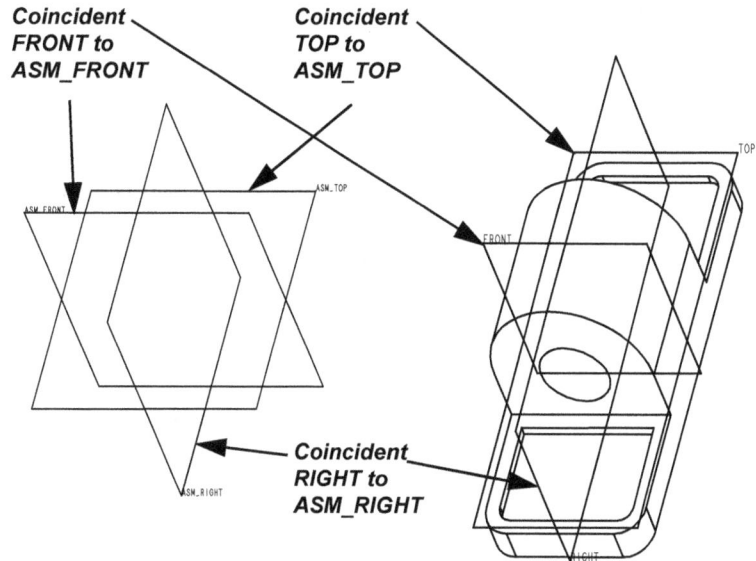

Coincident FRONT to ASM_FRONT

Coincident TOP to ASM_TOP

Coincident RIGHT to ASM_RIGHT

Figure 21–2

*You can also use the **Default** constraint or the **Centered** constraint option to place the component in the same location. This option constrains the default coordinate system of the part to the default coordinate system of the assembly.*

To create this assembly, datum plane **RIGHT** is constrained to datum plane **ASM_RIGHT** of the assembly using Coincident. This forces datum planes **RIGHT** and **ASM_RIGHT** to be coplanar and face the same direction. Likewise, datum plane **TOP** is constrained to datum plane **ASM_TOP**, and datum plane **FRONT** is constrained to **ASM_FRONT** using Coincident. These three constraints are sufficient to fully constrain the part on the assembly's default datum planes, as shown in Figure 21–3.

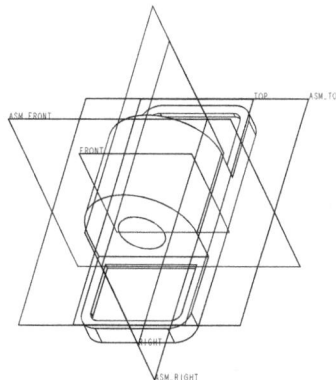

Figure 21–3

Next the pin part is assembled, as shown in Figure 21–4. The following three constraints are used:

- Coincident is used to constrain axis **A_1** of the pin to axis **A_1** of the bracket.

- Coincident is used to constrain datum plane **FRONT** of the pin to datum plane **ASM_FRONT** of the assembly.

- Parallel is used to constrain datum plane **TOP** of the pin to datum plane **ASM_TOP** of the assembly.

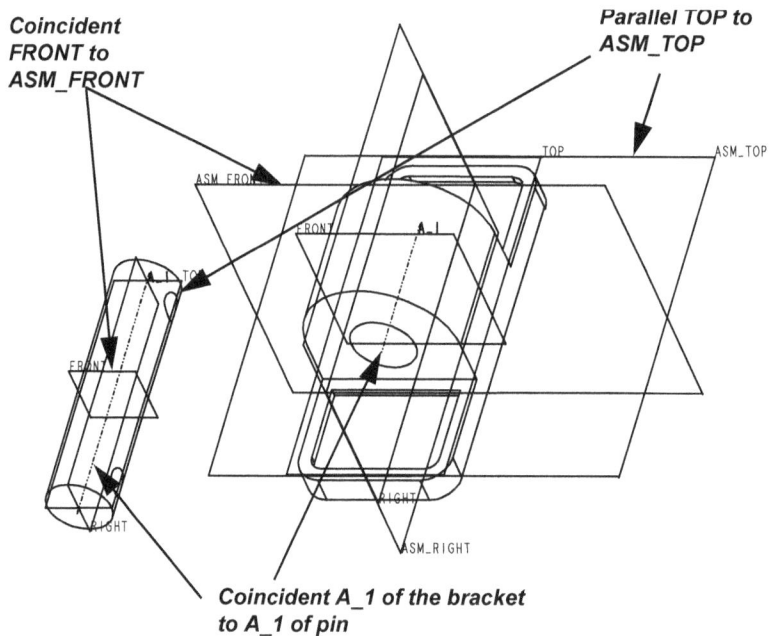

Coincident FRONT to ASM_FRONT

Parallel TOP to ASM_TOP

Coincident A_1 of the bracket to A_1 of pin

Figure 21–4

The pin can then be placed, as shown in Figure 21–5.

The pin is a child of the bracket because the datum axis of the pin to the datum axis of the bracket are constrained. Both components are children of the assembly's default datum planes.

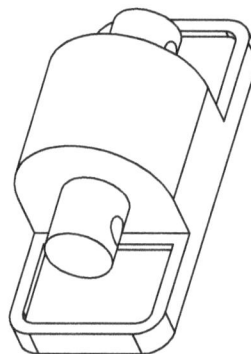

Figure 21–5

Finally, the U-hook part is assembled, as shown in Figure 21–6. The following three constraints are used:

- Coincident is used to constrain datum plane **RIGHT** of the U-hook to datum plane **ASM_FRONT** of the assembly.

- Coincident is used to constrain datum plane **TOP** of the U-hook to datum plane **ASM_RIGHT** of the assembly.

- Coincident is used to constrain axis **A_2** of the U-hook to axis **A_1** of the bracket.

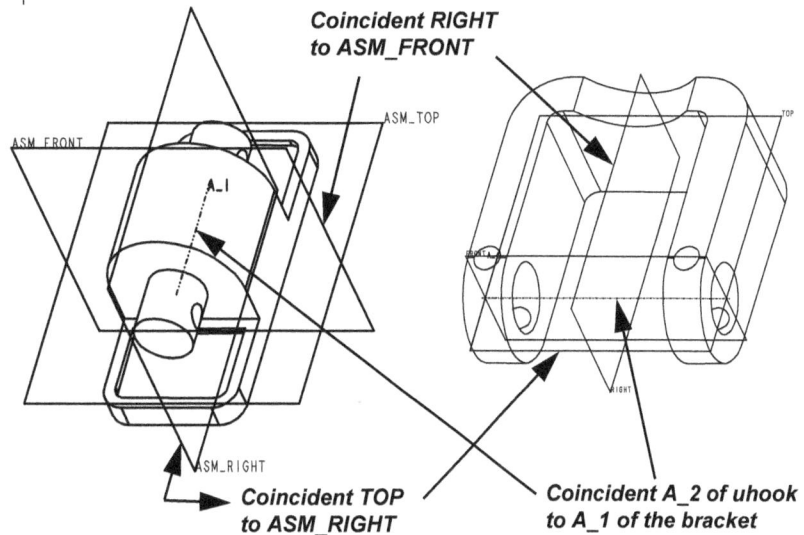

Figure 21–6

The U-hook can then be placed, as shown in Figure 21–7.

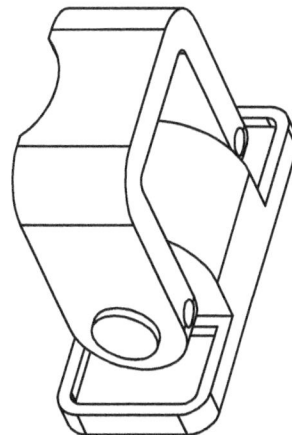

Figure 21–7

Axis **A_2** of the U-hook could have been constrained to axis **A_1** of the pin instead of axis **A_1** of the bracket. Which axis to select would depend on the design intent. Remember that assembly constraints result in parent/child relationships. Consider the following scenarios:

Case 1

A variety of pin parts could be used with this assembly. In each case, the U-hook and bracket parts would remain the same. If the axis of the U-hook was constrained to the axis of the pin, you would need to use the ✏️ (Edit Definition) or ⚙️ (Edit References) option if the pin component was deleted. This is because the U-hook would be a child of the pin. In this situation, it would be better to constrain the axis of the U-hook to the axis of the bracket.

Case 2

Again, a variety of different pin parts could be used with this assembly. However, this time there is a corresponding U-hook for each pin. If the pin was deleted, you would also need to delete the U-hook. In this situation, you would want to have the U-hook as a child of the pin so that they could be deleted together easily.

21.2 Editing an Assembly and its Components

Several options can be used to make changes to an assembly and its components. These include the following:

- To make changes to an assembly you can use the ⊢━┪ᵈ¹ (Edit), ✍ (Edit Definition), and ⚯ (Edit References) options found in the menu bar or in contextual menu. These options enable you to make changes to the dimension values, constraints, and references, respectively.

*Click ⫶ ˅ (Settings)> **Tree Filters** in the Navigator window and select **Features** in the Display area in the Model Tree Items dialog box to display the assembly and part features in the model tree.*

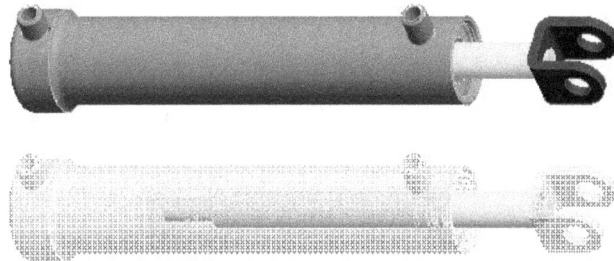

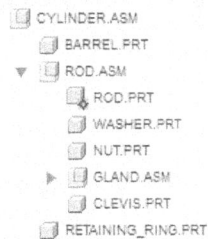

- To make changes to a component while in Assembly mode, you must first activate the component. You can select it in the model tree or directly on the model, right-click, and select **Activate**. This option activates the Part mode options and tabs so that you can make changes to the assembly component while still in Assembly mode. Once a component is activated, the model tree and main window update, as shown in Figure 21–8.

CYLINDER.ASM
  BARREL.PRT
▼ ROD.ASM
    ROD.PRT
    WASHER.PRT
    NUT.PRT
  ▶ GLAND.ASM
    CLEVIS.PRT
  RETAINING_RING.PRT

Figure 21–8

21.3 Exploded Views

Creo Parametric enables you to create exploded views of assemblies. By customizing the exploded positions of the components, you can create a view that can be used in a drawing to indicate an assembly procedure.

To create a customized explode click ⬛ (Manage Views) in the Model Display group in the *Model* tab or in the In-graphics toolbar and then select the *Explode* tab, as shown in Figure 21–9.

To create a temporary explode, click 🔲 *(Exploded View) in the Model Display group in the Model tab. The model displays in its default exploded position and can be modified by dynamically dragging components to new positions in the view. Click the icon again to revert the assembly back to its assembled state.*

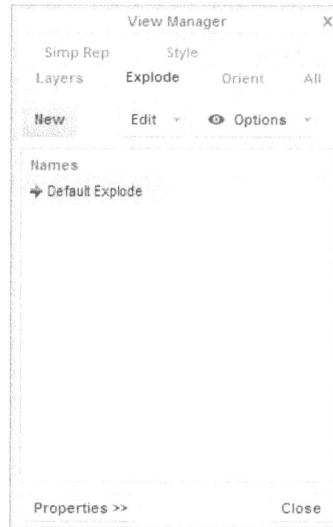

Figure 21–9

General Steps

Use the following general steps to create a customized exploded view:

1. Enter a name for the explode state.
2. Customize the explode position of the components.
3. Define the offset lines, as required.
4. Toggle the explode status of the components, as required.
5. Update the explode state.

Step 1 - Enter a name for the explode state.

Click **New** in the *Explode* area in the View Manager dialog box. Enter a name for the explode and press <Enter>. The new explode is now active, as indicated by the green arrow.

Step 2 - Customize the explode position of the components.

Click **Properties** to define the view properties. The View Manager dialog box opens, as shown in Figure 21–10.

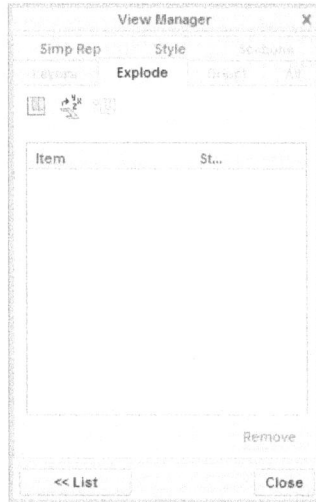

Figure 21–10

Click ⬚ (Edit Position) to open the *Explode Tool* dashboard, as shown in Figure 21–11. Use the options in the dialog box to define the component positions or use the arrows in the view window to move the component in the required direction.

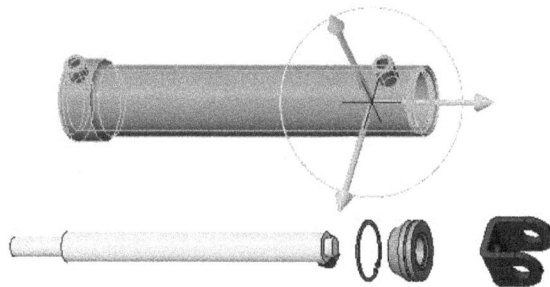

Figure 21–11

For example, a planar surface can be selected as the motion reference when repositioning a component in an exploded assembly view. The component is then restricted to move in a direction that is parallel to the planar motion reference.

How To: Modify the Position of Components

1. Select the *References* tab to open the Reference panel. Activate the *Movement Reference* area and select an **Axis** or **Straight Edge** as the motion reference.

2. Click ⬚↳ (Translation), ↺ (Rotation), or ⬚↳ (View Plane) for the type of movement you want. You can also use the arrows in the view window to drag the component.

3. Select the component to move. A 3D Dragger displays.

4. Use the left mouse button to drag an arrow handle and place the component, as required.

5. Click ✓ (Apply Changes) to close the *Explode Tool* dashboard once all of the components have been moved.

   The View Manager dialog box opens as shown in Figure 21–12, displaying a list of exploded components.

Figure 21–12

6. Select a component in the View Manager dialog box and click **Remove** to unexplode only the selection. Repeat this step, as required.

Step 3 - Define the offset lines, as required.

Offset lines enable you to display exploding lines when the assembly is in the explode state. The lines help to explain how the assembly components are assembled to one another.

To create offset lines, click ⬚ (Edit Position). In the Edit Position tab, click ⬚ (Offset Lines) and select two references to define the extent of the line. The references can be an axis, surface normal, or edge/curve. Once created, you can modify, delete, or change the line style for the line.

Step 4 - Toggle the explode status of the components, as required.

Click ⬚ (Exploded View) and ⬚ (Unexplode) along the top of the View Manager dialog box to toggle the position of the selected components between the exploded and unexploded states.

Click ⬚ (Toggle Status) to only unexplode a selected component. Alternatively, you can remove the component from the explode state.

Step 5 - Update the explode state.

Click **List** to return to the explode listing. The current explode (indicated by the arrow) is temporarily modified with the new settings and displays with a plus (+) symbol appended to the end of its name. For example, A (+) indicates that the A explode was displayed and that it has been changed.

Explode can also be updated by clicking **Edit** *and selecting* **Save**.

To update the changes in the model, right-click and select **Save**. The Save Display Elements dialog box opens as shown in Figure 21–13. Click **OK** to finish the save action.

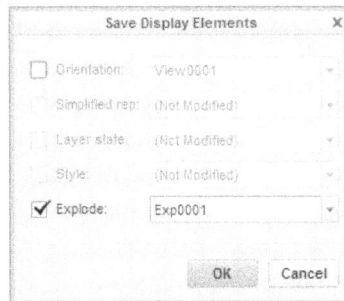

Figure 21–13

You can also click **Edit** *and clear the checkmark next to the* **Explode State** *option.*

To unexplode the view, right-click in the View Manager dialog box and disable the **Explode option** or click ⬚ (Exploded View) in the Model Display group in the *Model* tab.

21.4 Interference Checks

Creo Parametric can check for interference between all of the components in your assembly. It reports the parts involved and the volume of interference. This information is used for ensuring that once a model is manufactured, costly interference conflicts do not occur.

How To: Conduct an Interference Check on an Assembly

1. To conduct a global interference check, click ⌐ (Global Interference) in the Inspect Geometry group in the *Analysis* tab. The Global Interference dialog box opens as shown in Figure 21–14.
2. To conduct the analysis using the default options, click **Preview**. This performs a global interference check between parts in the assembly.

   Otherwise, select options in the *Analysis* tab shown in Figure 21–15, to refine the check.

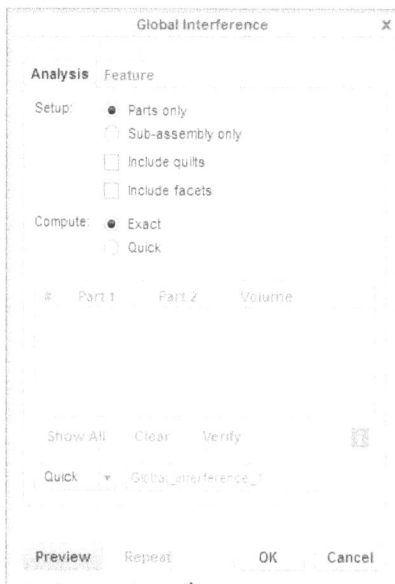

Figure 21–14

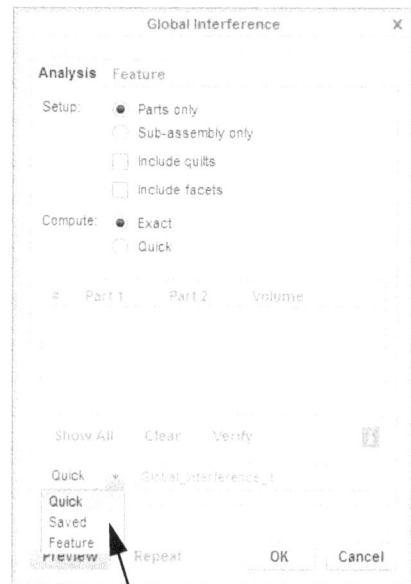

Save options

Figure 21–15

3. Once **Preview** has been selected, any interfering parts are identified in the *Results* area in the Global Interference dialog box. In addition, the interfering parts are highlighted in the main window, as shown in Figure 21–16.

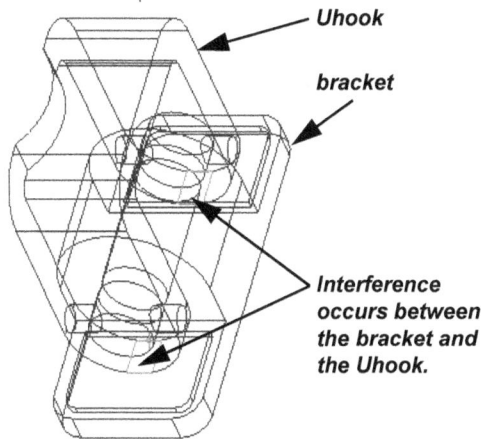

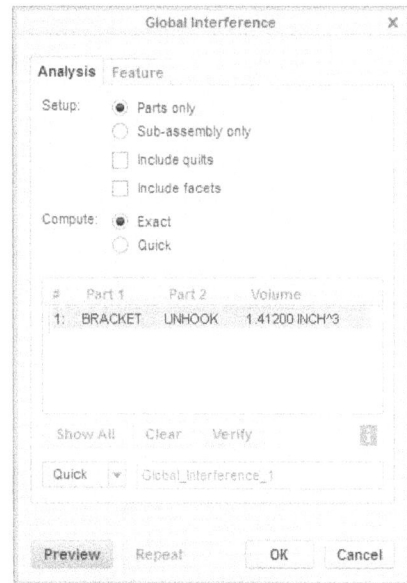

Figure 21–16

4. Resolve any conflicts and reanalyze the assembly, as required. To resolve any interference conflicts, activate one of the components listed in the *Results* area and use the

   ⟶ (Edit) or 🥄 (Edit Definition) options to make the required changes. Once you have modified the components, conduct another global interference check to ensure that all of the conflicts have been resolved.

21.5 Bill of Materials

A Bill of Materials (BOM) can be generated quickly to display a complete list of all of the components in the assembly.

How To: Create a Bill of Materials for an Assembly

1. To create a Bill of Materials, click (Bill of Materials) in the Investigate group in the *Tools* tab, to open the BOM dialog box, as shown in Figure 21–17.

Figure 21–17

2. Click **OK** to display the default Bill of Materials for the top-level assembly in the Browser Window, as shown in Figure 21–18.
3. Investigate the Bill of Materials report. The Bill of Materials for the U-hook assembly shown at the top of Figure 21–18 displays as shown in Figure 21–18.

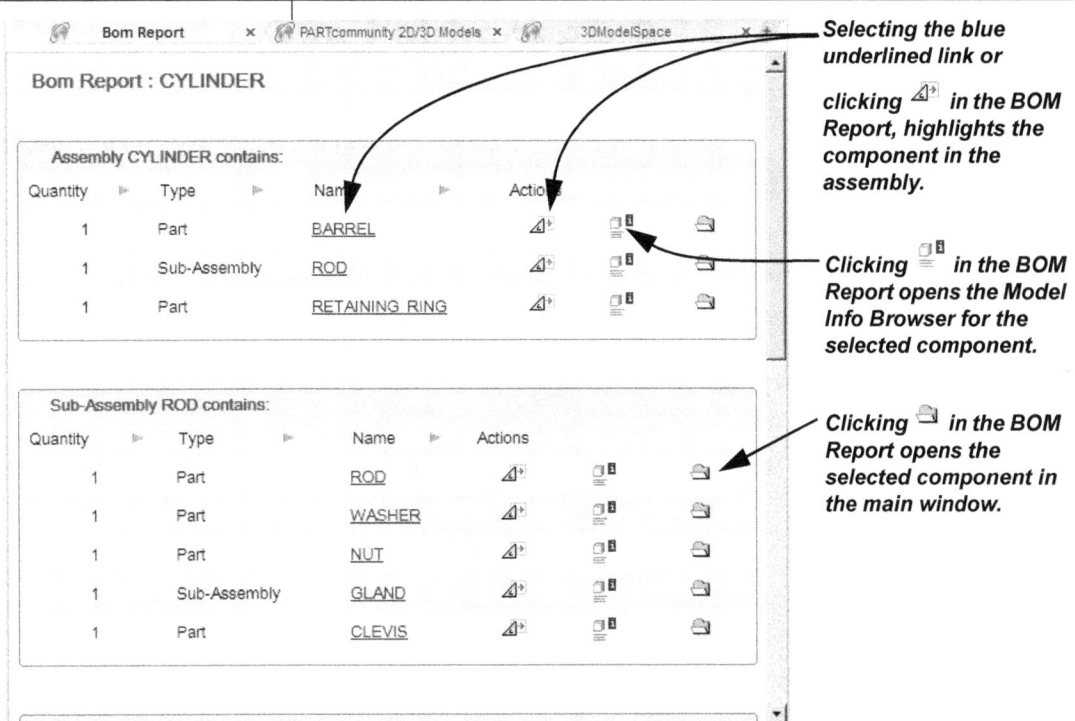

Selecting the blue underlined link or clicking ⊿▸ in the BOM Report, highlights the component in the assembly.

Clicking ▣▯ in the BOM Report opens the Model Info Browser for the selected component.

Clicking ▤ in the BOM Report opens the selected component in the main window.

Figure 21–18

Creo Parametric automatically saves the file with a .BOM extension (e.g., u_hook.bom.1), containing the BOM in plain text format.

Once the BOM Report displays, you can review it in the Browser window or you can save or print it.

• To save the report in HTML format, click ▥ (Save to File) at the top of the Browser window.

• To print the report, click ▣ (Print) at the top of the Browser window.

21.6 Assembly Layers

The Graphics and Layer dialog boxes in Figure 21–19 show items that were added to layers in the assembly and the display status that was set for the layers.

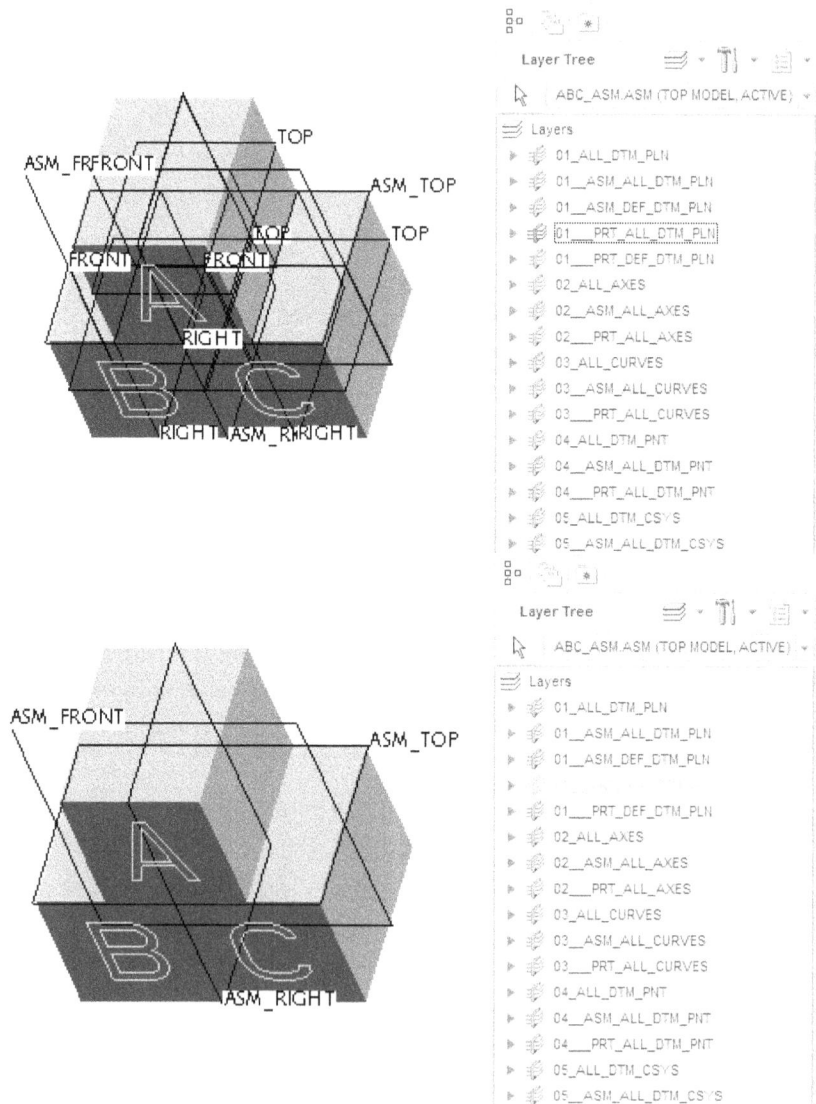

Figure 21–19

Practice 21a | Datum Plane Assembly

Practice Objectives

- Locate components in an assembly using the datum planes and axis as constraint references.
- Edit existing components in an assembly using the correct editing tools.
- Check for interference between the components of the assembly using the Global Interference Analysis command.
- Generate a bill of materials for the assembly to determine what components are used and how often.
- Learn how to use the layer tree in an assembly to hide and unhide entities.

In this practice, you will assemble three components to create the assembly shown in Figure 21–20. For clarity, the datum planes are not shown in this graphic. Once they are assembled, conduct a global interference check, and fix any interferences that are found. Also, activate the handle component and create a feature on it while working in Assembly mode. To complete the practice, generate the Bill of Materials for the assembly, explode it, and make dimensional changes to the assembly constraints to move components.

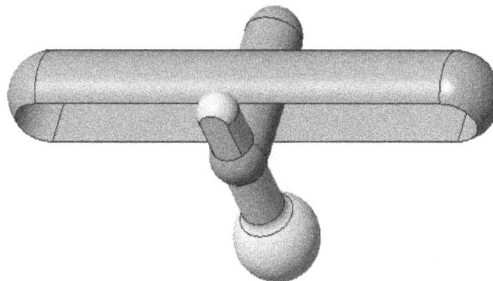

Figure 21–20

Task 1 - Create a new assembly.

1. Change the working directory to the *Chapter 21/practice 21a* folder.

2. In the Quick Access Toolbar, click ⬜ (New) and select **Assembly** in the New dialog box. Name the assembly **slider** and use the default template.

3. Set the model display as follows:

   - ⁺⧭ *(Datum Display Filters)*: Only ⬜ (Plane Display)

- ⟩ *(Spin Center)*: Off
- ◟ *(Display Style)*: ⬜ (Shading With Edges)

4. Select 𝕋 ˅ (Settings)>**Tree Filters**.

5. Click **Features** to enable it, if required and click **OK** in the Model Tree items dialog box.

Task 2 - Assemble the base component.

1. Assemble **guide.prt**. Apply a Default constraint.

Use ╱ (Change Constraint Orientation) in the Component Placement dashboard to flip the component if the orientation is not correct.

2. Click ✔ (Apply Changes). The assembly displays as shown in Figure 21–21.

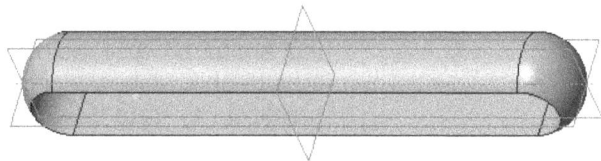

Figure 21–21

Task 3 - Assemble a part using datum planes.

1. Click ▤ ˅ (Show)>**Layer Tree** to display the layer tree.

2. Expand the **01__PRT_DEF_DTM_PLN** layer.

You want to assemble to the assembly default datum planes, so hide them in the Guide part.

3. Select **in GUIDE.PRT**, right-click and select **Hide**, as shown in Figure 21–22.

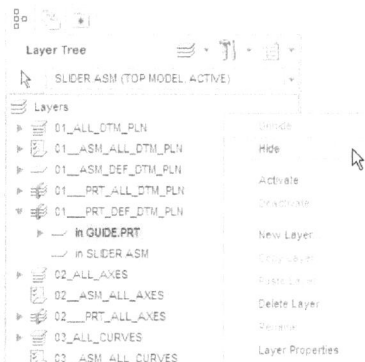

Figure 21–22

4. Click ▤ ˅ (Show)>**Model Tree**.

We will use the Plane Tags in this practice.

5. Select the *View* tab.

6. In the Show group, click ⬚ (Plane Tag Display).

7. Select the *Model* tab.

8. Assemble **bar.prt**.

9. Assign a Distance constraint to datum plane **RIGHT** of the component with datum plane **ASM_RIGHT** of the assembly. Enter an offset value of **5**. Use **-5** if you need to flip the new component to the opposite side of datum plane **ASM_RIGHT**.

10. Assign a Coincident constraint to datum plane **TOP** of the component to datum plane **ASM_TOP** of the assembly.

11. Assign a Coincident constraint to datum plane **FRONT** of the component to datum plane **ASM_FRONT** on the assembly.

12. Click ✔ (Apply Changes) and the assembly displays as shown in Figure 21–23.

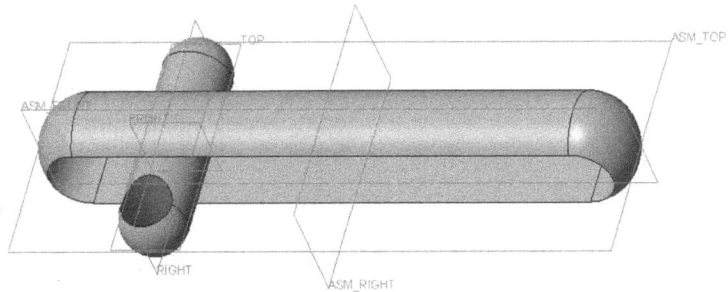

Figure 21–23

Task 4 - Assemble the handle.prt part.

---

1. Click ▤ ▾ (Show)>**Layer Tree**.

2. Expand the **01__PRT_DEF_DTM_PLN** layer, select **in BAR.PRT**, right-click and select **Hide**.

3. Click ▤ ▾ (Show)>**Model Tree**.

4. In the In-graphics toolbar, expand ⚹ (Datum Display Filters) and select ⟋⊙ (Axis Display) to enable the display of axes.

5. Select the *View* tab.

6. In the Show group, click 🔍 (Axis Tag Display).

7. Select the *Model* tab.

8. Assemble **handle.prt**.

9. Assign a Coincident constraint to axis **A_1** of the handle with axis **A_4** of the shaft, as shown in Figure 21–24.

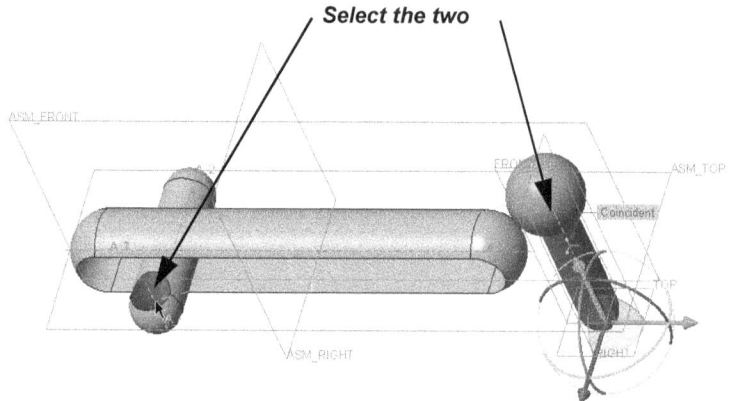

Select the two

Figure 21–24

10. Assign a Distance constraint to datum plane **TOP** of the component with datum plane **ASM_TOP** of the assembly. Enter an offset value of **3**.

11. Right-click and select **New Constraint**.

If required, click

✏ (Change Constraint Orientation) in the Component Placement dashboard.

12. Assign a Parallel constraint to the planar surface on the handle with datum plane **ASM_FRONT** on the assembly, as shown in Figure 21–25.

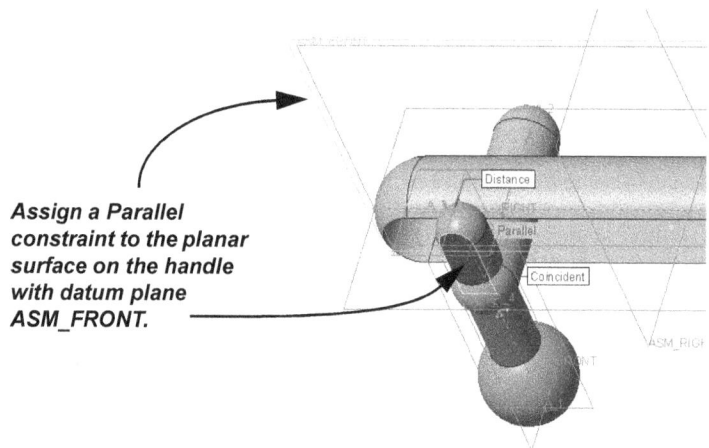

Assign a Parallel constraint to the planar surface on the handle with datum plane ASM_FRONT.

Figure 21–25

13. Click ✓ (Apply Changes).

Task 5 - Perform an interference check on the assembly.

1. Select the *Analysis* tab. Click 🗺 (Global Interference) in the Inspect Geometry group.

2. Accept the default selections and click **Preview**. The *Results* area in the dialog box should indicate an interference between the bar and the handle.

3. Click 🛈. The Information window identifies the interfering parts and the volume of interference.

4. Close the Information window and the Global Interference dialog box.

Task 6 - Modify the diameter of the handle.

1. Select the handle component in the model tree.

When a component is activated from

Assembly mode, ⬚ *displays next to its name.*

2. Right-click and select **Activate**.

3. In the model tree, expand **HANDLE.PRT**. Select **Revolve 1** in the handle, right-click, and select 'd1' (Edit) to display its dimensions.

4. Double-click the **1.55** diameter dimension and enter **1.49**.

5. Click ⬚ (Regenerate) to regenerate the model.

6. In the model tree, select **SLIDER.ASM**, right-click, and select **Activate** to reactivate the assembly.

7. Do another interference check. Are there any other interferences?

Task 7 - Create a round on the handle without leaving Assembly mode.

1. Click ⬚ ▾ (Show)>**Layer Tree** to display the layer tree.

2. Hold <Ctrl>, select the **01_ASM_DEF_DTM_PLN** layer, **01__PRT_DEF_DTM_PLN**, **02__PRT_ALL_AXES** layers, right-click and select **Hide**.

3. Click ▤ ▾ (Show)>**Model Tree**.

4. Select the handle, right-click and select **Activate**.

5. Select the edge shown in Figure 21–26, right-click and select **Round**.

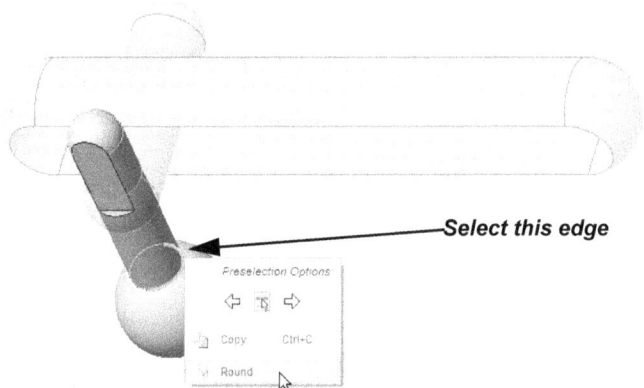

Figure 21–26

6. Edit the round *Radius* to **0.5**. Complete the feature.

7. In the model tree, select **SLIDER.ASM**, right-click, and select **Activate** to reactivate the assembly.

8. Select **HANDLE.PRT** in the model tree, right-click and select **Open**.

Although it was created while in Assembly mode, the round is a feature of the handle part, as shown in Figure 21–27.

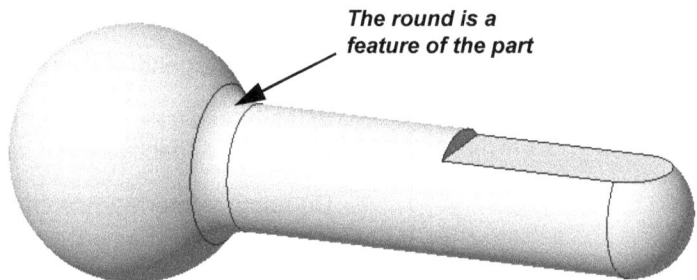

The round is a feature of the part

Figure 21–27

9. Close the part window. Click in the assembly window and it becomes active.

Task 8 - Create a Bill of Materials.

1. Select the *Tools* tab from the Investigate group and click
   📄 (Bill of Materials).

2. Note that the **Top Level** option is selected and click **OK** in the
   BOM dialog box. The Bill of Materials displays in the
   Information window.

3. Click 💾 (Save to File) in the browser and save the BOM
   report as an HTML file.

4. Close the Browser Window.

Task 9 - Modify a dimension to move components in the assembly.

1. Select the *Model* tab.

2. Double-click on the bar component in the main window.
   Select the offset dimension that displays and change it to **0**.

3. Click ⬚ (Regenerate) to regenerate the assembly. The
   assembly displays as shown in Figure 21–28.

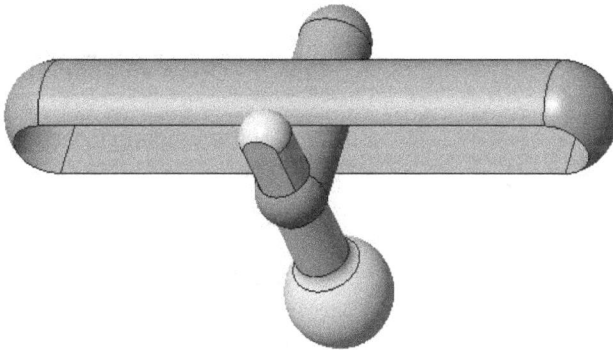

Figure 21–28

4. Save the assembly and erase it from memory.

Practice 21b | Explode Assembly

Practice Objectives

- Learn to use the View Manager and create an exploded view.
- Learn to move one or multiple components and create snap lines for the exploded view.

In this practice, you will explode components of the assembly shown in Figure 21–29.

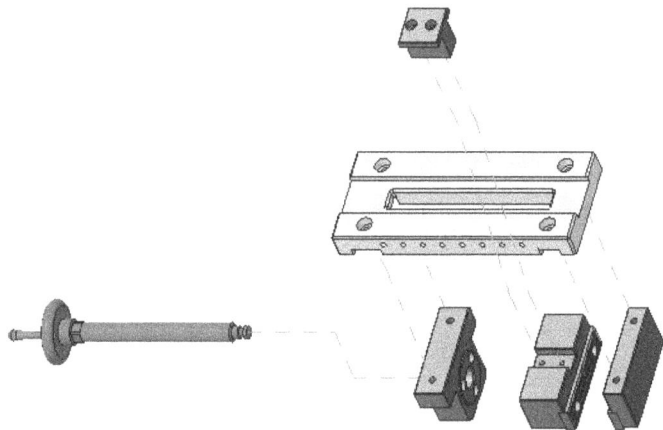

Figure 21–29

Task 1 - Open an assembly file.

1. Set the working directory to the *Chapter 21\practice 21b* folder.

2. Open the **vise_final.asm** assembly.

3. Set the model display as follows:

- *(Datum Display Filters)*: None
- *(Spin Center)*: Off
- *(Display Style)*: (Shading With Edges)

Task 2 - Explode the assembly.

You can also click the
(View Manager) icon
in the In-graphics
toolbar.

1. Select the *Model* tab and expand (Manage Views) if required, and select (View Manager) in the Model Display group. The View Manager dialog box opens as shown in Figure 21–30.

2. Select the *Explode* tab, as shown in Figure 21–31.

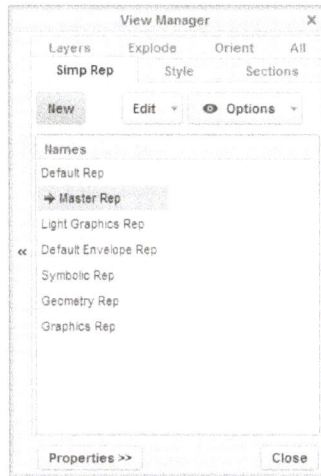

View Manager	×
Layers	Explode	Orient	All
Simp Rep	Style	Sections

New | Edit ▾ | ● Options ▾

Names
Default Rep
➔ Master Rep
Light Graphics Rep
« Default Envelope Rep
Symbolic Rep
Geometry Rep
Graphics Rep

Properties >> | Close

Figure 21–30

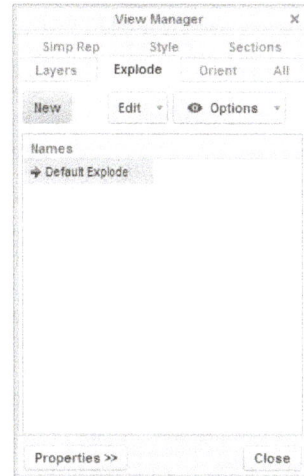

View Manager	×
Simp Rep	Style	Sections
Layers	**Explode**	Orient	All

New | Edit ▾ | ● Options ▾

Names
➔ Default Explode

Properties >> | Close

Figure 21–31

3. In the *Explode* tab in the View Manager dialog box, click **New**.

4. Type **explode1** for the name and press <Enter>. The new explode is now active as indicated by the arrow.

5. Click **Properties** to define the view properties.

Task 3 - Modify the position of the components in the exploded view.

1. Click (Edit Position) to define the component positions in the *Explode Tool* dashboard, as shown in Figure 21–32.

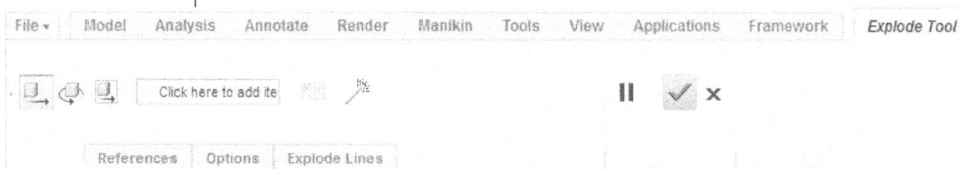

File ▾ | Model | Analysis | Annotate | Render | Manikin | Tools | View | Applications | Framework | *Explode Tool*

Click here to add ite | ‖ ✓ ✕

References | Options | Explode Lines

Figure 21–32

2. Select **SPINDLE_FINAL_VISE.ASM** in the model tree. Drag the axis to the location shown in Figure 21–33.

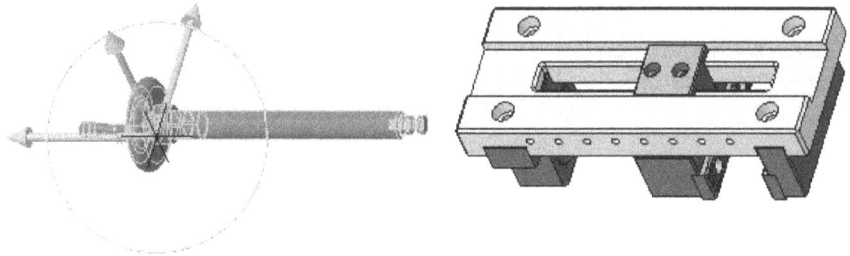

Figure 21–33

Be careful to select a subassembly when it makes sense to do so. Use Query Selection or the model tree.

3. Select the component shown in Figure 21–34 and move it to the location shown.

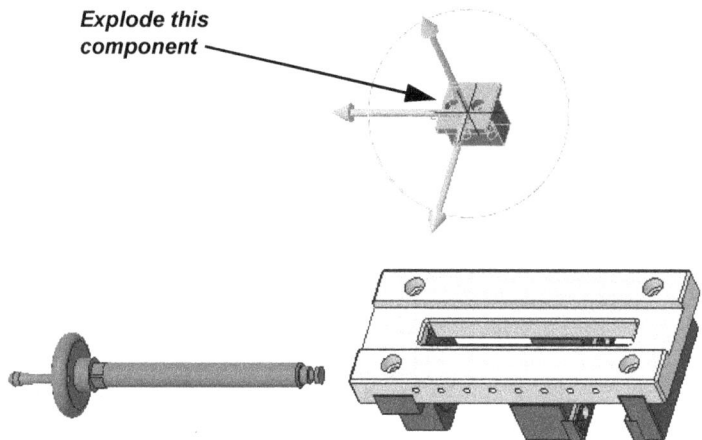

Explode this component

Figure 21–34

4. In the model tree, press <Ctrl> and select the three subassemblies listed:

• **Bearing_Support_Final_Vise.asm**
• **Support_End_Final_Vise.asm**
• **Support_Middle_Final_Vise.asm**

You can also select the appropriate *Movement Reference* in the References panel.

If you are not satisfied with the position of the components, you can click ⬚⬚ (Toggle Explode) in the Explode Tool dashboard to return the component to its original position.

5. Use the left mouse button to drag and place the components, as required. You can select the axis on the drag handle in the direction in which you want the component to move as shown in Figure 21–35.

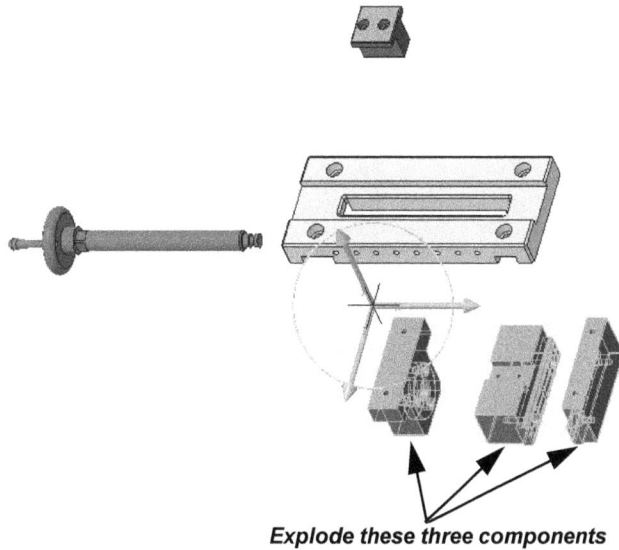

Explode these three components

Figure 21–35

6. Click ✔ (Apply Changes) in the *Explode Tool* dashboard. The View Manager dialog box displays as shown in Figure 21–36.

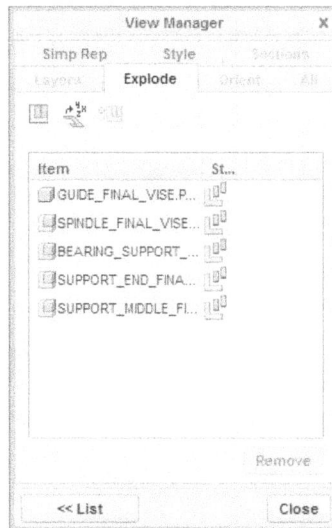

Figure 21–36

---

7. Click ⚏ (Edit Position).

8. Click ╱ (Offset Lines) to create explode lines. The Cosmetic Offset Line dialog box opens as shown in Figure 21–37.

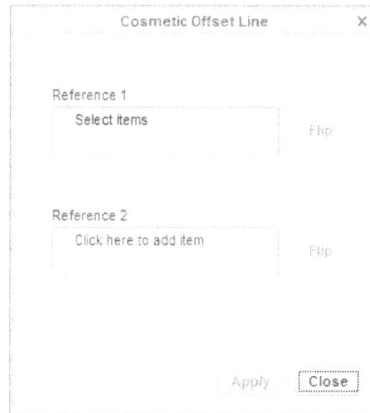

Figure 21–37

9. In the In-graphics toolbar, expand ⚏ (Datum Display Filters) and select ⚏ (Axis Display) to enable the display of axes.

10. Select the axes of the appropriate holes or cylinders to define the explode offset lines and click **Apply** after each selection. Continue creating explode lines. Adjust the component positions until the assembly displays approximately as shown in Figure 21–38.

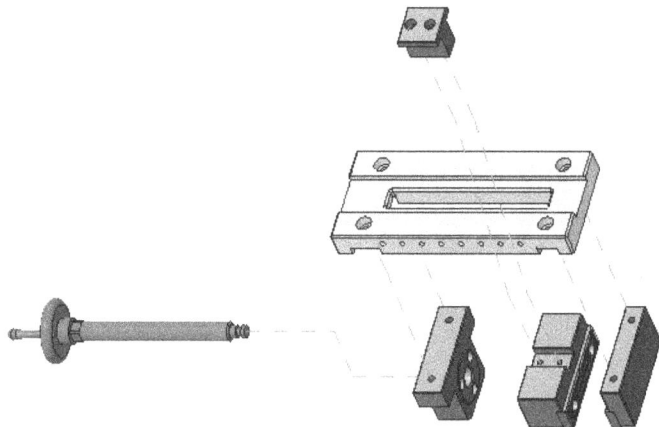

Figure 21–38

11. Click **Close**. This returns you to the *Explode Tool* dashboard.

12. Use the Explode Lines panel in the tab to manipulate the existing explode lines. Select a existing explode line and select an option in the Explode Lines panel, as shown in Figure 21–39.

Figure 21–39

13. Click ✓ (Complete Feature).

14. Click List in the **View Manager** to return to the listing of the explode. The current explode, is temporarily modified with the new settings and displayed with a plus (+) symbol appended to the end of its name.

15. Right-click **Explode1(+)** and select **Save**. The Save Display Elements dialog box opens.

16. Click **OK** to finish the Save action.

17. Close the View Manager dialog box.

18. Save the assembly and close all of the windows.

19. Erase all the files.

Practice 21c

Using Layers in Large Assemblies

Practice Objectives

- Hide, unhide, and isolate layers using the layer tree in an assembly.
- Select components in the assembly using the layer tree.

In this practice, you will open an existing assembly and use the Layers tools to control the display of components in the model. You will also use layers to quickly select components to suppress, resume, and delete.

Task 1 - Open an assembly file.

Ensure that all of the files have been erased from memory before opening this assembly.

1. Set the working directory to the *Chapter 21\practice 21c* folder.

2. Open **sorter.asm**.

3. Set the model display as follows:

    - $\overset{x'}{\nearrow_*}$ *(Datum Display Filters)*: All On

    - $\nearrow$ *(Spin Center)*: Off

    - $\mathbb{I}$ *(Display Style)*: $\square$ (Shading With Edges)

Task 2 - Investigate the assembly.

1. In the model tree, select **CASING.ASM**, right-click, and select **Open** to open the assembly in a new window. Review the components that exist in this assembly.

The window is activated just by switching to it. Alternatively, you can select the window itself it its visible on your screen.

2. In the Quick Access Toolbar, click $\overset{}{\boxminus}$ $\cdot$ (Windows) and select **SORTER.ASM** to switch to that window.

3. Open the **BASKET.ASM** and **DRIVER.ASM** subassemblies in separate windows for further investigation.

4. Close the **CASING.ASM**, **BASKET.ASM**, and **DRIVER.ASM** windows once you are familiar with them.

Task 3 - Hide existing layers.

1. Click ▤ ▾ (Show)>**Layer Tree** to display the list of model layers.

2. Select the first layer, press <Shift> and select the last layer. All of the layers in the layer tree are selected.

3. Right-click and select **Hide** to hide all of the layers.

4. Click ▨ (Repaint) to update the display, if required. Only the components shown in Figure 21–40 should be displayed. These components are not included in any layer.

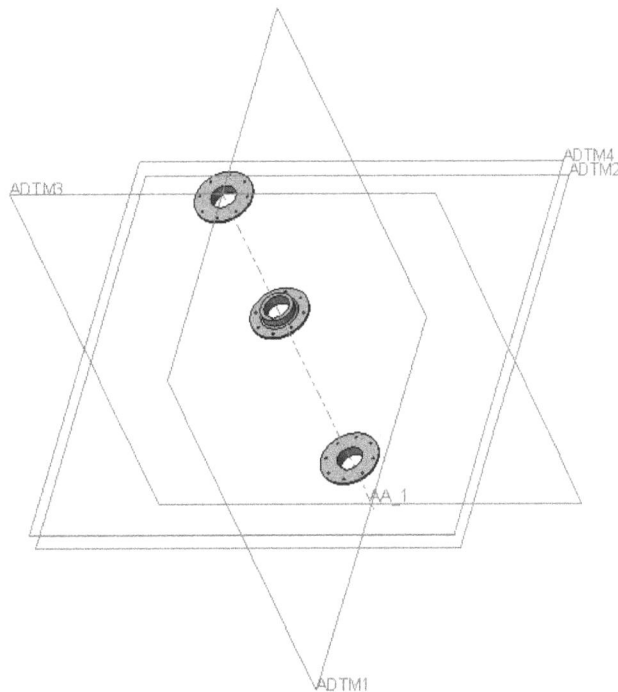

Figure 21–40

5. Click ▤ ▾ (Show)>**Model Tree** to return to the model tree display.

6. The layer status for each component can be displayed in the model tree. Click 🔧 ▾ (Settings)>**Tree Columns**. The Model Tree Columns dialog box opens.

7. In the Type drop-down list, select **Layer** as shown in Figure 21–41.

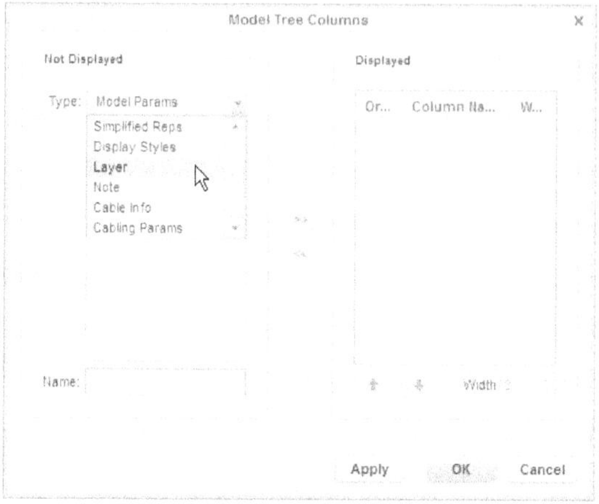

Figure 21–41

8. In the field below the Type drop-down list, select **Layer Status** and click ≫ (Add Column) to add Layer Status to the *Displayed* column.

9. Click **OK**. The model tree displays as shown in Figure 21–42. Flanges are the only displayed components. Expand the list for the patterned components in the top-level assembly. Note that they also have **Hidden** listed as their Layer Status.

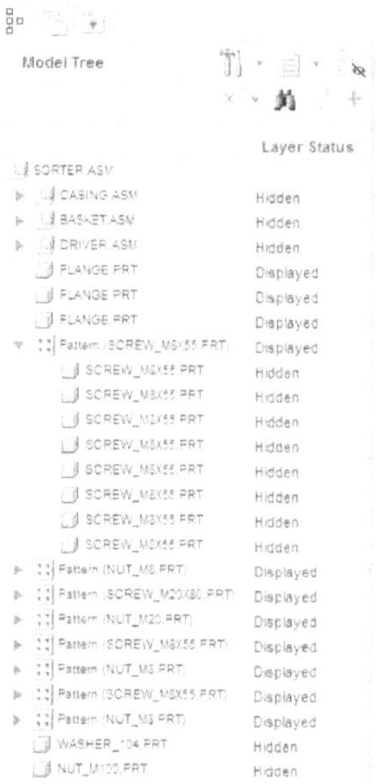

Figure 21–42

Task 4 - Create a new layer.

1. Click ☰ ▼ (Show)>**Layer Tree** to return to the layer tree display.

2. Right-click and select **New Layer**.

3. For the layer name in the Layer Properties dialog box, type **flanges**. DO NOT press <Enter>.

4. Click ☰ ▼ (Show)>**Model Tree**.

5. In the model tree, select the three **FLANGE.PRT** components. The Layer Properties dialog box updates as shown in Figure 21–43.

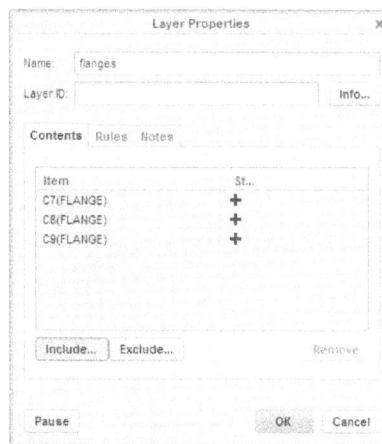

Figure 21–43

6. Click **OK**.

7. Return to the layer tree display and note that this layer is the only one that is not hidden, as indicated by the ▱ symbol.

Task 5 - Determine the content of all of the layers.

1. To determine the contents of each layer, select any layer name in the layer tree, right-click, and select **Layer Info**. An Information window opens, displaying the current display status of the layer, and a list of all of the items contained on the layer. Close the Information window when you have finished reviewing its content.

*Layer items are highlighted if the **Highlight Geometry** option (accessible through the 📄 ▾ (Show) flyout) is selected.*

2. Select any layer names in the layer tree and note that the items on the layer highlight.

3. Select the **FLANGES** layer in the layers tree.

4. Select the **DRIVER** layer in the layers tree. All components on the layer highlight, even if they are hidden, as shown in Figure 21–44.

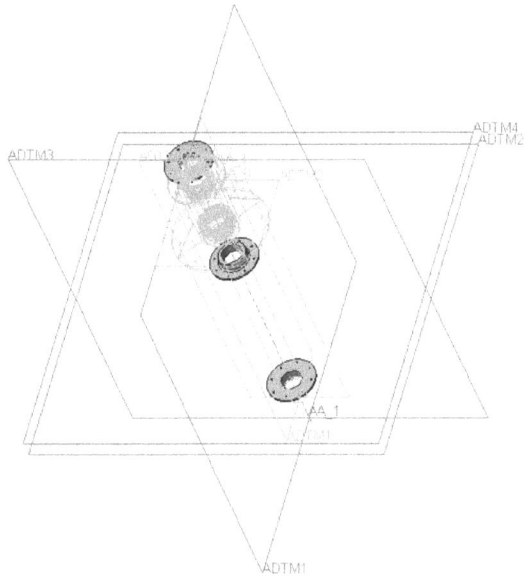

Figure 21–44

Task 6 - Isolate the DRIVER layer.

1. In the In-graphics toolbar, expand ✳ (Datum Display Filters) and toggle off all datum display filters.

2. Right-click on Layers at the top of the layer tree and click **Select Layers**.

3. All of the layers are selected. so right-click, and select **Unhide**. All of the components are returned to the display.

4. Select the **DRIVER** layer in the layer tree. Click 📄 ▾ (Layer) and select **Isolate**. Repaint the screen. The assembly displays as shown in Figure 21–45.

When a large number of layers exists and you want to display the contents of a single layer, it is faster to Isolate the single layer than to hide all of the others.

Figure 21–45

5. Create a layer named **test**.

6. Click ▶ next to the **DRIVER** layer to expand it. The only item on this layer is the driver assembly.

7. Select the **DRIVER** assembly in the **DRIVER** layer. It is added to the **TEST** layer that you just created.

8. Click **OK** to complete the layer.

9. Hide the **TEST** layer. Why does the model remain unchanged?

10. Right-click on Layers at the top of the layer tree and select **Select Layers**.

11. Right-click on any layer in the tree and select **Unhide**. All of the layers are now visible.

Task 7 - Use layers as a selection tool.

1. Suppressing all of the screws and nuts individually can be time-consuming. All of these components are contained on the **JOINTS** layer. Therefore, they can be quickly suppressed by selecting the layer. Select the **JOINTS** layer in the layer tree.

2. All of the components highlight on the screen. However, they are not actually selected. Right-click and select **Select Items**.

3. Return to the model tree display, right-click, and select **Suppress** and confirm the suppression of these components from the model.

4. Note that the model tree updates with the items removed, as shown in Figure 21–46.

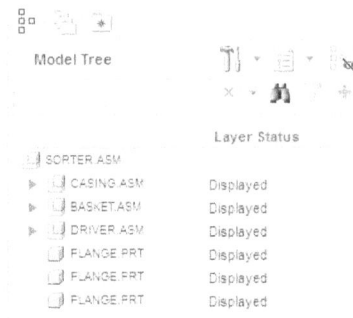

Model Tree

Layer Status

SORTER.ASM	
▶ CASING.ASM	Displayed
▶ BASKET.ASM	Displayed
▶ DRIVER.ASM	Displayed
FLANGE.PRT	Displayed
FLANGE.PRT	Displayed
FLANGE.PRT	Displayed

Figure 21–46

Suppressed features and components can be displayed in the model tree by clicking 🗍 ˅ *(Settings)>Tree Filters>Suppressed Objects. Suppressed items have a black square next to their names.*

5. Use the same technique to suppress the **BASKET** layer. Some of the components in this layer have children. Suppress them as well.

6. To resume all suppressed components, select the *Model tab* and select **Operations>Resume>Resume All**.

7. Save the assembly.

8. Close all windows and erase from memory.

Chapter Review Questions

1. By default, components that reference datum planes are assembled on the dominant brown side of the datum plane. Which of the following icons do you select to flip a component's orientation direction?

   a.

   b.

   c.

   d.

2. Datum planes can be used as constraint references when defining component placements.

   a. True

   b. False

3. Which of the following statements are true regarding making changes to components while in Assembly mode? (Select all that apply.)

   a. Features cannot be added to a component of an assembly while in Assembly mode.

   b. To make changes to an offset assembly constraint value, you can use the $\overleftrightarrow{\text{d1}}$ (Edit) option.

   c. To make changes to constraint references, you can use the $\overleftrightarrow{\text{d1}}$ (Edit) option.

   d. To change a feature dimension associated with a component in an assembly, select the component in the model tree, right-click, and select **Activate**.

4. A Bill of Materials report generates a complete list of all of the components in an assembly.

   a. True

   b. False

5. Which of the following icons, when viewed in the model tree, indicates that an assembly component is active?

   a.

   b.

   c.

   d.

6. Which of the following statements are true regarding exploding assemblies? (Select all that apply.)

   a. To explode an assembly, click (Manage Views) in the *Model* tab, and select the *Explode* tab.

   b. The default explode position for assembly components is based on the constraints that were used to assemble the components.

   c. A planar surface can be selected as the motion reference when repositioning a component in an exploded assembly view.

   d. A straight edge can be selected as a motion reference.

7. Which of the following items are reported in a Global Interference check? (Select all that apply.)

   a. Component names.

   b. Volume of interference.

   c. Interfering material is highlighted in red.

   d. Interfering components are highlighted in the model.

Command Summary

Button	Command	Location
	Manage Views	• **Ribbon:** *Model* tab in the *Model Display* group • **Ribbon:** *View* tab in the *Model Display* group • Graphics toolbar
	Toggle Status	• **Ribbon:** *Model* tab in the *Model Display* group • **Ribbon:** *View* tab in the *Model Display* group
	Exploded View	• **Ribbon:** *Model* tab in the *Model Display* group • **Ribbon:** *View* tab in the *Model Display* group
	Bill of Materials	• **Ribbon:** *Tools* tab in the *Investigate* group
	Global Interference	• **Ribbon:** *Analysis* tab in the *Inspect Geometry* group

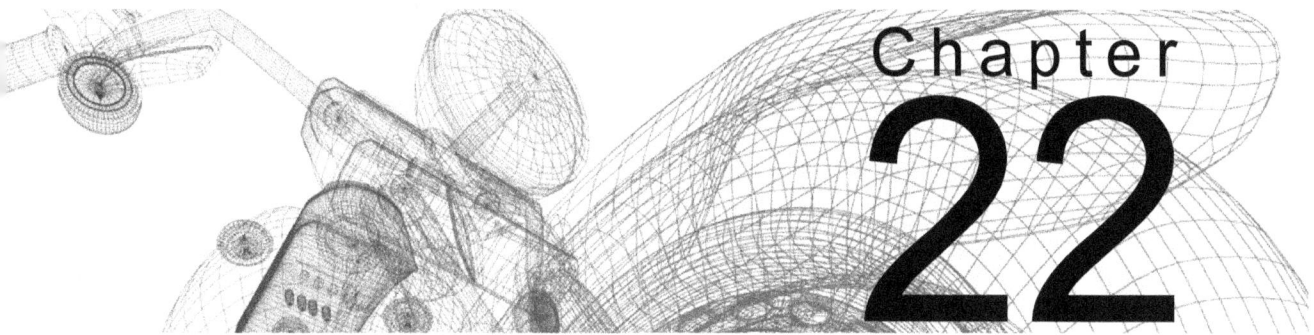

Model Information

Creo Parametric provides you with several tools that can be used to obtain information about a part's measurements and mass properties. Cross-sections can also be created to further analyze a model.

Learning Objectives in this Chapter

- Learn how to efficiently access the measurement tools using the Ribbon.
- Measure the distance between geometry using the Distance command.
- Learn how to save or create a feature for the measurement.
- Learn how to efficiently access the mass properties tool using the Ribbon.
- Set the type and run the analysis.
- Create a cross-section using one of the two methods.
- Create the cross-section using options in the Section tab.
- Activate, deactivate, or show the cross-section using the model tree or the View Manager dialog box.
- Set, create, and change the model units using the Model Properties dialog box.
- Assign material to the model.

22.1 Measure Analysis

Select the *Analysis* tab to access options to measure specific parameters in your model, as shown in Figure 22–1.

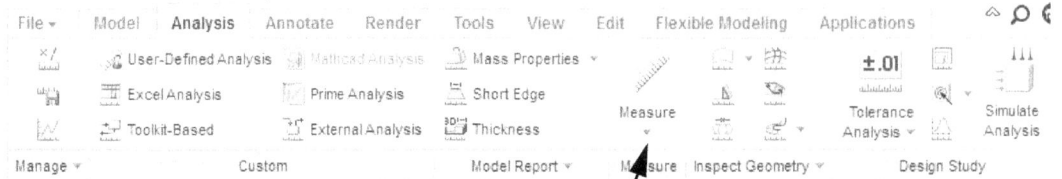

Measure options ⸺

Figure 22–1

The process to perform each of the measurement options is similar.

To perform a distance analysis, in the *Analysis* tab, expand (Measure) and select (Distance). The Distance dialog box opens as shown in Figure 22–2.

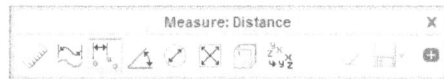

Figure 22–2

You can toggle and select a different type of measurement command in the Measure dialog box.

The dialog box can be expanded to display additional options by clicking (Expand The Dialog) as shown in Figure 22–3.

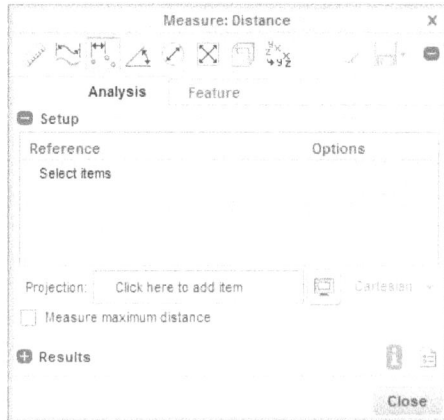

Figure 22–3

Select the required references to measure the distance between the entities. The distance is calculated and displayed in the view window and in the *Results* area in the *Measure dialog box*, as shown in Figure 22–4. The measurement can be expanded or collapsed in the View window.

Use the Measure dialog box to review or change the references, as shown in Figure 22–4.

**Click to collapse the
measurement display.**

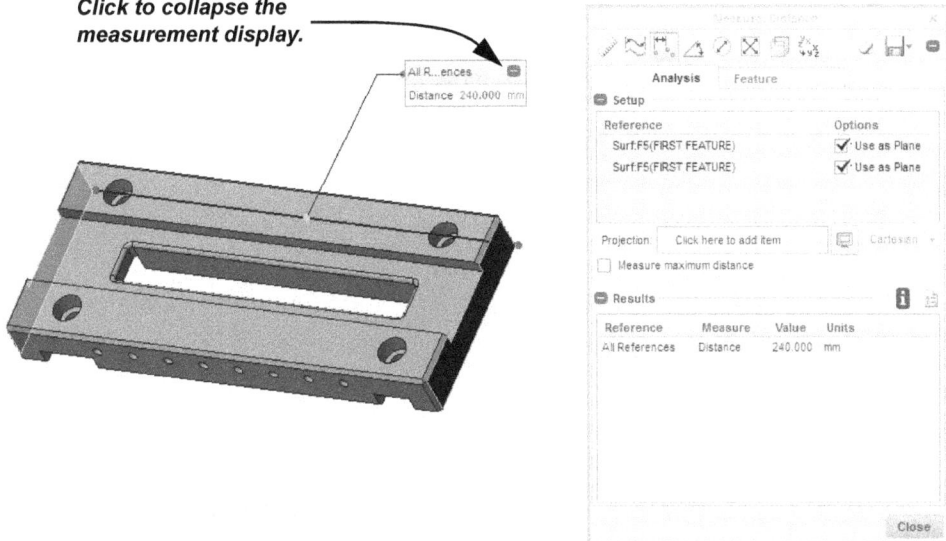

Figure 22–4

In the Setup area, the selected references are listed in the References column of the dialog box. Depending on the selected reference, there are several options available in the Options column.

- **Use as Plane** - Extends the selected surface or plane infinitely in both directions so you can measure normal to that reference entity. The extension does not physically extend the entity, as it is only for the measurement you are making.

- **Use as Line** - Extends the selected straight edge or curve infinitely in both directions so you can measure normal to that reference entity. The extension does not physically extend the entity, as it is only for the measurement you are making.

- **Use as Center** - Measures the distance from the center of a circle or an arc-shaped curve or edge. Clear this option to measure from the edge instead of the center.

- **Use as Axis** - Measures the distance from the central axis of the cylindrical surface. Clear this option to measure from the surface instead of the axis.

You can select the **Measure maximum distance** check box to determine the maximum distance between the two selected entities. For entities that are parallel, this option has no impact on the result.

Once the measurement has been created, click ⊟ (Save Analysis) to save, name, or create the measurement as a feature, as shown in Figure 22–5.

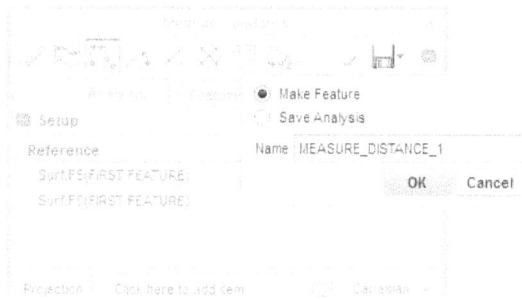

Figure 22–5

22.2 Mass Properties

The model report options, shown in Figure 22–6, are different in Assembly and Part modes. One of the most common calculations performed is to determine mass properties.

Figure 22–6

Click (Mass Properties) in the *Analysis* tab to calculate the assembly or part mass properties. The Mass Properties dialog box opens as shown in Figure 22–7.

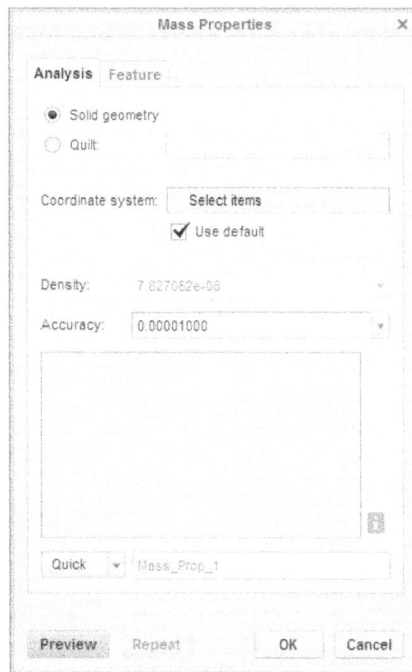

Figure 22–7

If the model does not have an assigned density, Creo Parametric prompts you to set it before the calculation starts.

By default, the analysis type is set to **Quick**. You can change the type of analysis using the *Analysis* tab. The three types of analysis are described as follows. In this example, a Quick analysis is performed.

Type	Description
Quick	The analysis is calculated and the result displayed in the dialog box.
Saved	The analysis is calculated and the result displayed in the dialog box and graphics window. The definition of the analysis is saved in the model and automatically recalculated when the model changes. To access a saved analysis, click (Saved Analysis) in the Manage group in the *Analysis* tab.
Feature	The analysis is calculated and the result displayed in the dialog box. Additionally, an analysis feature is created and shown in the model tree. This option enables you to create feature parameters and datum features based on the analysis.

Keep **Use default** enabled, or select a coordinate system on the model.

The mass properties of the model are calculated and displayed in the *Results* area in the *Analysis* tab, as shown in Figure 22–8. It is important to note that the calculation does not include information on suppressed features or components.

Figure 22–8

22.3 Creating Cross-sections

A cross-section defines a slice through a model as shown in Figure 22–9. Cross-sections can be created in parts and assemblies. Two methods can be used to create cross-sections.

- The first method requires you to expand 📄 (Section) in the *View* tab and select the type of cross-section you want to create.

- The second method uses the View Manager dialog box to create a cross-section by selecting the *Section* tab. The types of cross-sections that can be created using either method. are described as follows:

Option	Description
Planar	A planar cross-section is created using a datum plane in the location of the required slice, as shown on the left in Figure 22–9.
X Direction	A X Direction cross-section is created in the X direction. The location can be changed by entering a value or by dragging the arrow.
Y Direction	A Y Direction cross-section is created in the Y direction. The location can be changed by entering a value or by dragging the arrow.
Z Direction	A Z Direction cross-section is created in the Z direction. The location can be changed by entering a value or by dragging the arrow.
Offset	An offset cross-section is created by sketching a *cut line* to define the required cross-section, as shown on the right in Figure 22–9.
Zone	Zones enable you to divide a component into geometric work regions that can be used to define a condition for rule-driven simplified representations.

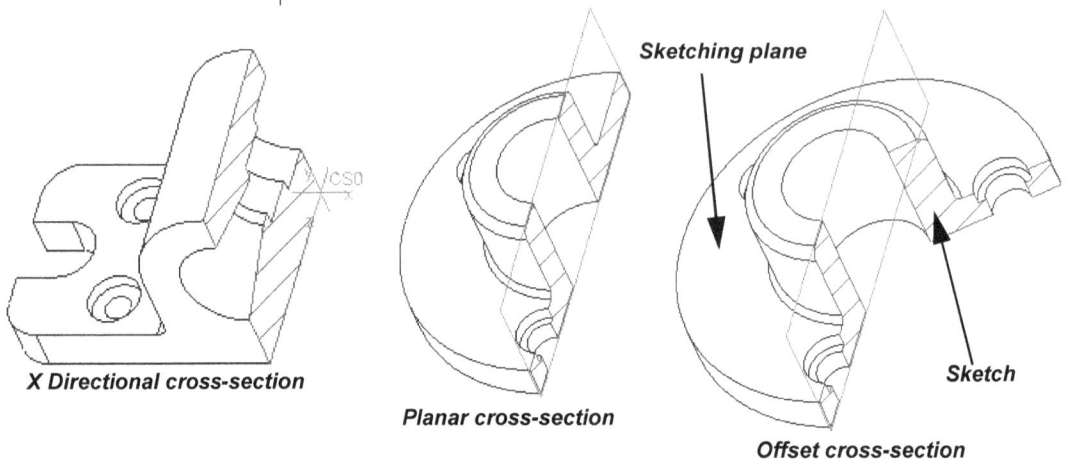

X Directional cross-section

Planar cross-section

Sketching plane

Sketch

Offset cross-section

Figure 22–9

General Steps

Use the following general steps to create a cross-section:

1. Start the creation of a cross-section.
2. Create the cross-section.
3. Select the options for the cross-section.
4. Finalize the cross-section.
5. Modify the cross-hatching.
6. Manage the visibility of the cross-section.

Step 1 - Start the creation of a cross-section.

Method 1

To start the creation of a cross-section, expand ⬚ (Section) and select the type of section in the *View* tab, as shown in Figure 22–10.

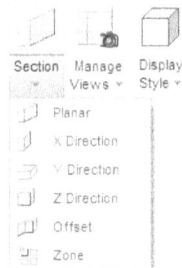

Figure 22–10

You can also click  (Manage Views) in the View tab to open the View Manager, then select the Section tab.

The View Manager tabs vary depending on the current mode in which you are working. In Part mode there are four tabs and in Assembly mode there are six.

Method 2

1. To start the creation of a cross-section, click  (View Manager) in the In-graphics toolbar, and the View Manager dialog box opens. Select the *Sections* tab, as shown in Figure 22–11.
2. Click **New** and select a type of cross-section, as shown in Figure 22–12. Enter a name for the cross-section and press <Enter>.

Figure 22–11

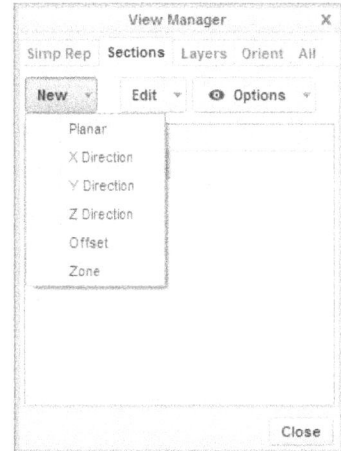

Figure 22–12

Step 2 - Create the cross-section.

The cross-section definition varies depending on its type.

Planar Cross-section

Select a datum plane or planar surface that defines the location of the cross-section. The *Section* dashboard activates as shown in Figure 22–13.

Figure 22–13

You can also change the offset value in the Section tab.

Once the *Section* dashboard is active, you can dynamically change the offset plane by using the mouse to drag the arrow, as shown in Figure 22–14. You can also toggle on the 3D dragger to dynamically translate and rotate the section.

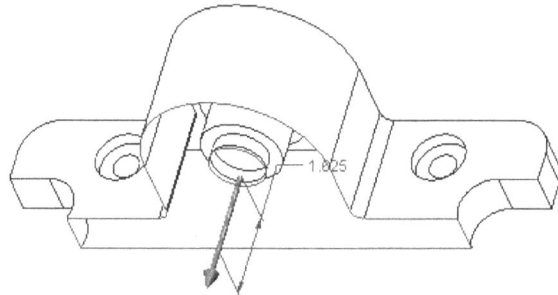

Drag the arrow to change the offset value.

Figure 22–14

Directional Cross-section

The directional cross-section does not require a selection. The location of the cross-section is dependent on the type, default coordinate system, and offset value in the *Section* dashboard. Once the *Section* dashboard is active, you can dynamically change the offset plane by using the mouse to drag the arrow, as shown in Figure 22–15. You can also toggle on the 3D dragger to dynamically translate and rotate the section.

Section created in the X-direction

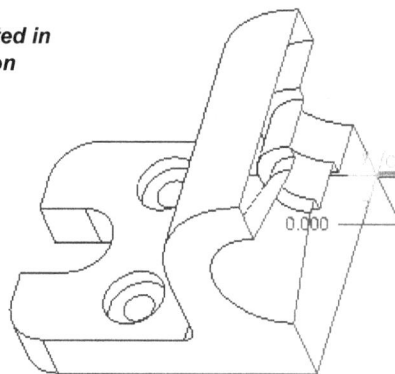

Drag the arrow to change the offset value.

Figure 22–15

Offset Cross-section

The Offset cross-section option enables you to sketch the section using the tools in the *Sketch* tab. The *Section* dashboard activates once the Offset type has been selected, as shown in Figure 22–16.

Figure 22–16

Select a sketching plane on which you can sketch the cut line for the offset cross-section. Sketch the required cut line as shown in Figure 22–17.

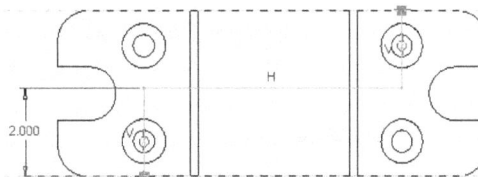

Figure 22–17

Step 3 - Select the options for the cross-section.

The commands and options in the *Section* tab are described as follows:

Option	Description
	Flips the clipping direction.
	Caps the surface of the cross-section.
	Opens the section color palette.
	Displays the hatching pattern.
	Toggles on the 3D dragger to dynamically rotate or translate the cross-section.
	Displays a separate window of the 2D view.
	Previews the cross-section without clipping.
	Previews the cross-section with clipping.

You can also dynamically detect any component interference using the **Show Interference** option in the Options panel, as shown in Figure 22–18.

Components can be excluded from the section by selecting the Models panel, as shown in Figure 22–19.

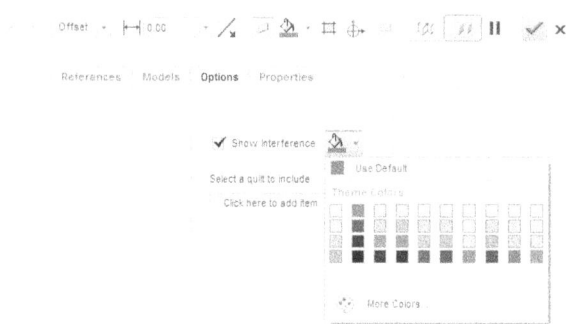

Figure 22–18   **Figure 22–19**

Step 4 - Finalize the cross-section.

Click ✔ (Complete Feature) to complete the cross-section. Cross-sections display in the model tree, as shown in Figure 22–20.

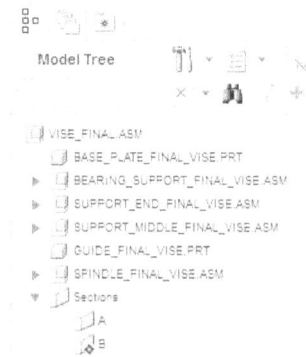

Figure 22–20

Step 5 - Modify the cross-hatching.

When you show the cross-section, it displays with the default line spacing and line angle for the cross-hatching, as shown in Figure 22–21.

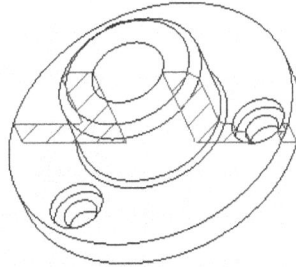

Figure 22–21

*You can also expand **Edit** and select the **Edit Hatching** option in the View Manager.*

To modify the default cross-hatching, select the cross-section in the model tree, right-click, and select ▨ (Edit Hatching). The Edit Hatching dialog box opens as shown in Figure 22–22.

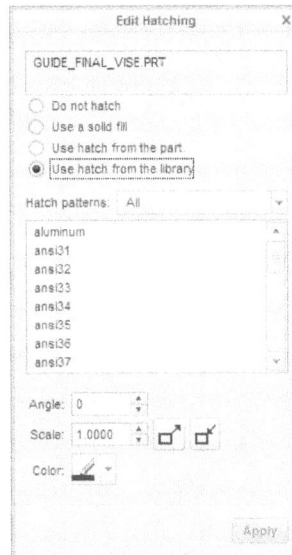

Figure 22–22

You can select from the hatch library or create your own by setting the angle and scale values. You can also click ⊿ (Double Spacing) or click ⊿ (Halve Spacing) to change the spacing between the hatching lines. Expand ✎ (Set Color) to specify the hatching color.

Step 6 - Manage the visibility of the cross-section.

The tool does not actually cut the geometry, it is for visualization purposes only

When you finalize the cross-section, it is automatically active and cuts the model. The active cross-section displays as shown in Figure 22–23.

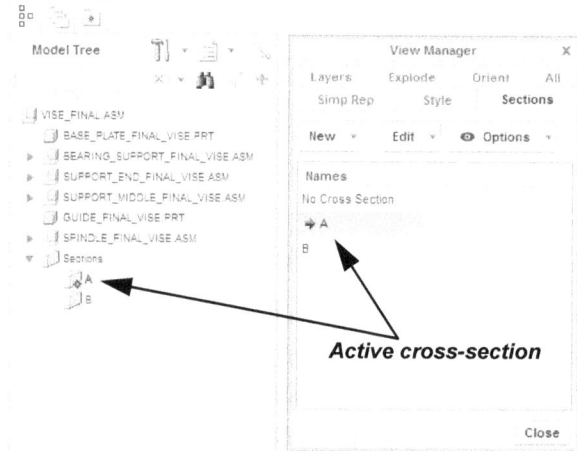

Figure 22–23

Right-click in the model tree and select **Deactivate** to disable the cross-section. You can enable a different cross-section by right-clicking on the section in the model tree or View Manager, and selecting **Activate**, as shown in Figure 22–24. Only one cross-section can be set as active.

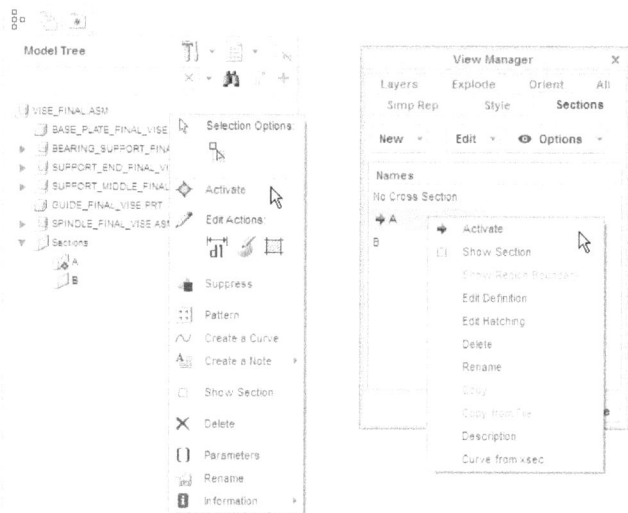

Figure 22–24

You can display the cross-hatching lines, as shown in
Figure 22–25, by right-clicking on the section and selecting
Show Section in the model tree or in the View Manager dialog
box. Note that the symbol in the model tree changes, as shown
in Figure 22–25.

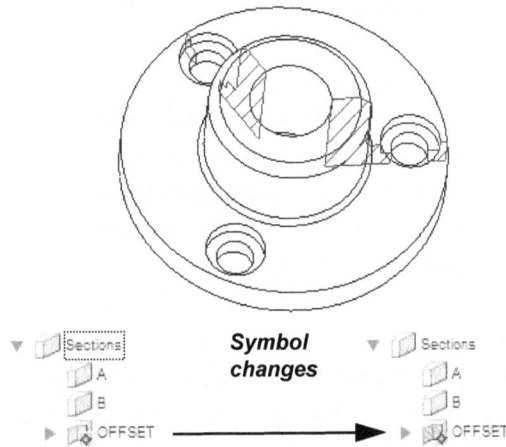

Figure 22–25

22.4 Changing Model Units and Material

Occasionally, the part units in your models might need to be modified. When modifying the part units, you can convert the existing units to the new system of units or you can maintain the current values in the new system.

How To: Change Part Units

1. To change the units of your model, select **File>Prepare> Model Properties** to open the Model Properties dialog box as shown in Figure 22–26.

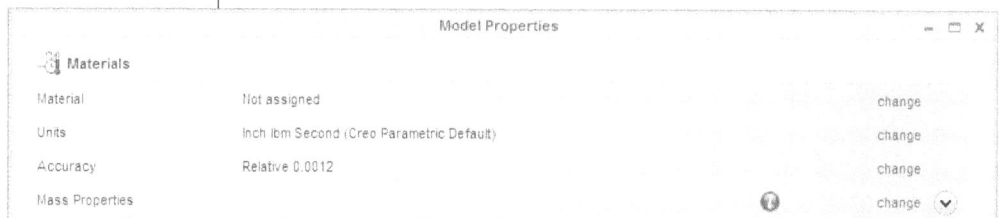

Model Properties			— ☐ ✕
🔩 Materials			
Material	Not assigned		change
Units	Inch lbm Second (Creo Parametric Default)		change
Accuracy	Relative 0.0012		change
Mass Properties		🛈	change ⌄

Figure 22–26

2. Click **change** beside Units in the *Materials* area in the dialog box. The Units Manager dialog box opens as shown in Figure 22–27.

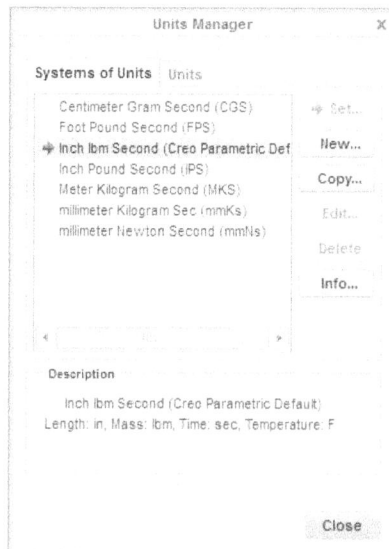

Units Manager	✕
Systems of Units	Units
Centimeter Gram Second (CGS)	➡ Set...
Foot Pound Second (FPS)	
➡ Inch lbm Second (Creo Parametric Def	New...
Inch Pound Second (IPS)	Copy...
Meter Kilogram Second (MKS)	
millimeter Kilogram Sec (mmKs)	Edit...
millimeter Newton Second (mmNs)	Delete
	Info...

Description

Inch lbm Second (Creo Parametric Default)
Length: in, Mass: lbm, Time: sec, Temperature: F

Close

Figure 22–27

3. To define a new system of units, you can select from the list of predefined systems or create a new one. A description of the predefined units is listed at the bottom of the Units Manager dialog box. To create a new system of units, click **New**. The System of Units Definition dialog box opens as shown in Figure 22–28.

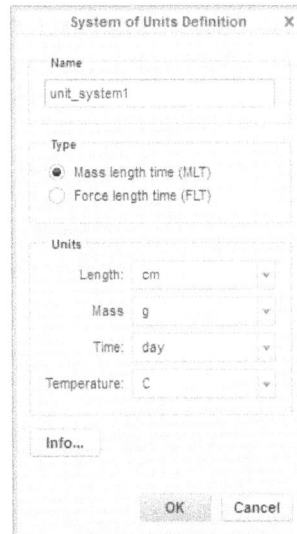

Figure 22–28

To define the new system of units, assign a name and type, and select the required type of units. Click **OK** to complete the definition.

4. Select the new system of units and click **Set** to finalize the change of units. The Changing Model Units dialog box opens as shown in Figure 22–29.

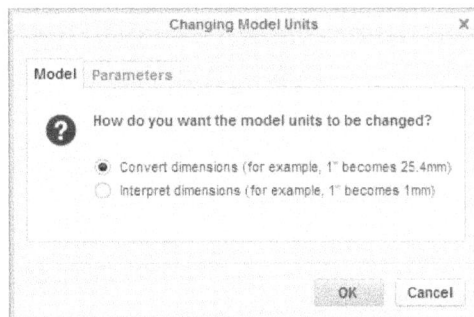

Figure 22–29

- In the *Model* tab, select how the current dimension values are going to change in the model. You must select one of the following:

  - The **Convert Dimensions** option converts the existing dimensions to the new system of units, while maintaining the same size in the resulting model (i.e., 1" becomes 25.4 mm).

  - The **Interpret Dimensions** option keeps the same numeric values in dimensions when changing the system of units (i.e., 1" becomes 1 mm).

- In the *Parameters* tab, select how the parameters change in the model, as shown in Figure 22–30. The *Parameters* tab lists Real number parameters that only have units assigned to them.

*The **Interpret Dimensions** option can be useful if you accidentally design the model using the wrong units.*

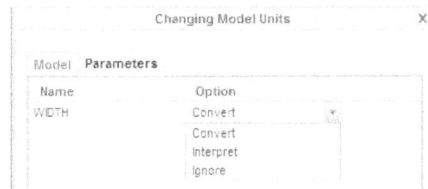

Figure 22–30

5. Click **OK** to complete the change of units and close the Units Manager dialog box.

   You can also assign a material to the model using the Model Properties dialog box. Click change next to Material in the Model Properties dialog box, and the Materials dialog box displays as shown in Figure 22–31.

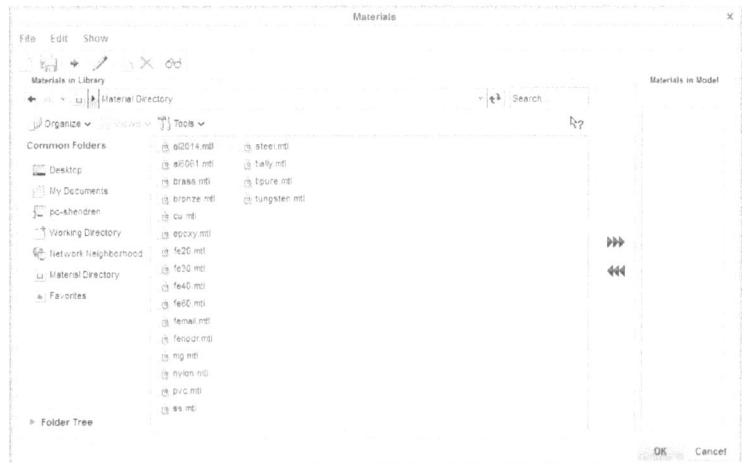

Figure 22–31

6. Select a material from the list, then click ▶▶▶ (Add Material) to assign it to the model, as shown in Figure 22–32.

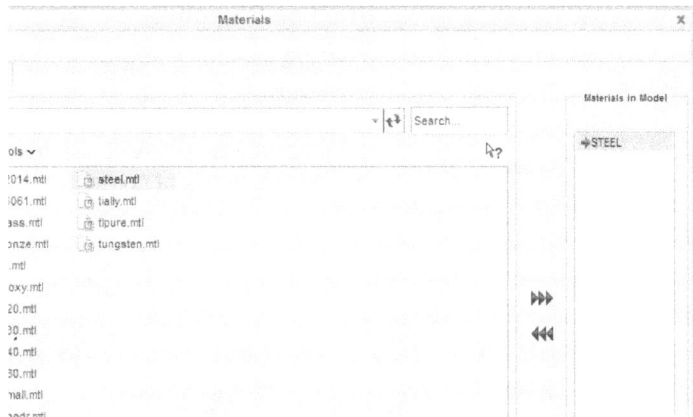

Figure 22–32

To remove the material from the model. select it in the Materials i Model list and click ◀◀◀ (Remove Material).

Practice 22a

Cross-Sections

Practice Objective

- Create a planar and an offset cross-section using the Section command.

In this practice, you will use the View Manager dialog box to create two types of cross-sections, as shown in .

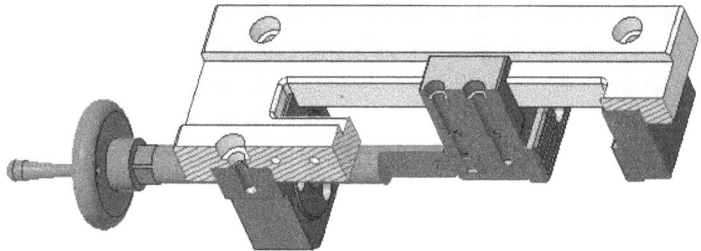

Figure 22–33

Task 1 - Open an assembly file.

1. Set the working directory to the *Chapter 22\practice 22a* folder.

2. Open **vise_final.asm**.

3. Set the model display as follows:

   - *(Datum Display Filters)*: (Axis Display) only

   - *(Spin Center)*: Off

   - *(Display Style)*: (Shading With Edges)

4. Click (Settings)>**Tree Filters** in the model tree.

5. Select **Features** in the *Display* area of the Model Tree Items dialog box.

6. Click **OK**.

Task 2 - Create an assembly datum plane.

Select the Model tab to create a datum plane.

1. Create an assembly datum plane through the two axes, as shown in Figure 22–34. Press <Ctrl> while selecting the axes.

Select these two axes as datum references.

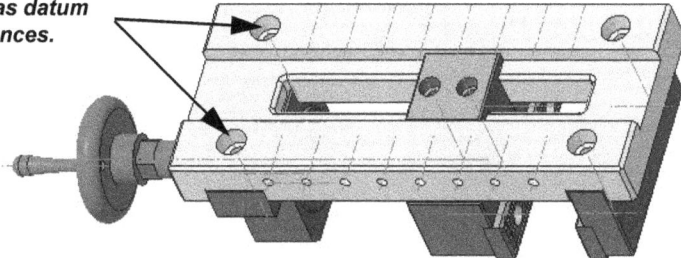

Figure 22–34

2. Select the Properties tab and rename the plane to **SECTION-B**.

3. Click **OK**.

Task 3 - Create a planar cross-section.

You can also select the View tab to create a section.

1. Select the *Model* tab. Expand ☐ (Section) and select **Planar**. The *Section* tab activates as shown in Figure 22–35.

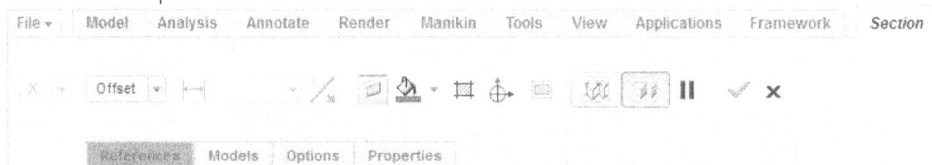

Figure 22–35

2. Select the *Properties* panel and set the *Name* to **B**.

3. Select **SECTION-B** from the model tree.

4. Click ✓ (Complete Feature) to complete the cross-section.

5. In the In-graphics toolbar, click ⅍ (Datum Display Filters) and disable ⌀ (Axis Display).

6. If required, in the model tree right-click on section **B** and select **Activate**. The cross-section displays as shown in Figure 22–36. One side of the cross-section is removed from the display.

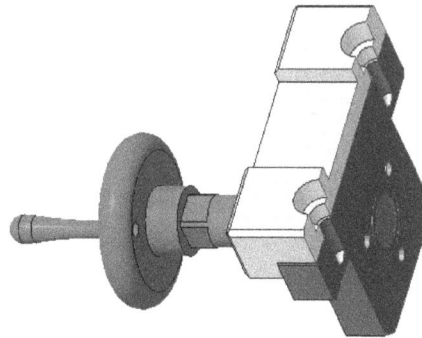

Figure 22–36

7. In the model tree, right-click on section **B** and select **Show Section** to display the cross-hatching for the section. The section displays as shown in Figure 22–37.

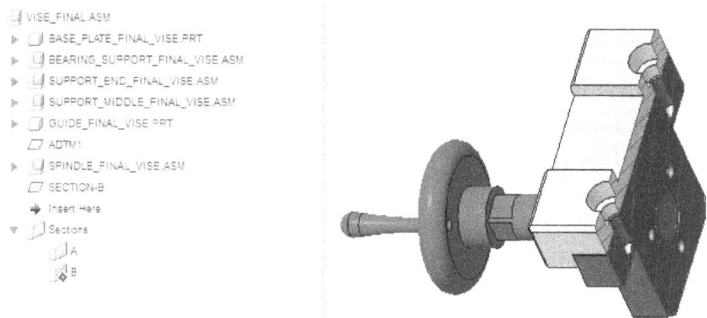

Figure 22–37

8. Toggle off cross-hatching for the section

9. Right-click on the section and select **Deactivate** to return the display to normal.

Task 4 - Create an offset cross-section.

---

1. In the *View* tab, expand ⬚ (Section) and select **Offset**. The *Section* tab activates.

2. In the *Properties* panel, name the cross-section **C**.

3. Select the top-most surface of the assembly as a sketching plane as shown in Figure 22–38.

Select this surface for the sketch plane

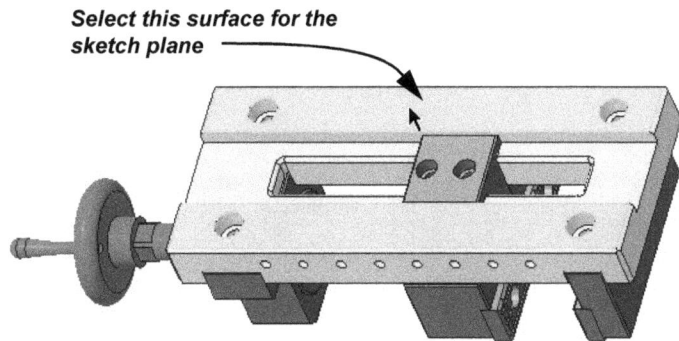

Figure 22–38

4. In the Setup group, click 🔲 (Sketch View).

5. Select the left and right sides of **base_plate_final_vise.prt** as the sketching references. Two vertical dashed lines display. Do not close the Reference dialog box.

6. In the In-graphics toolbar, click ⅍ (Datum Display Filters) and enable ⟋ (Axis Display).

7. Change the selection filter to **Axis** and select one of the axes shown in Figure 22–39. Change the selection filter to **Axis** again and select the other axis.

Shading is toggled off for clarity.

Select these axes

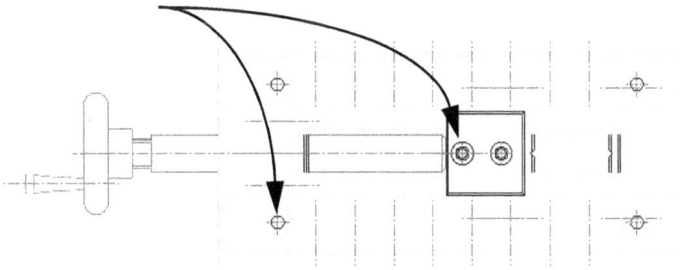

Figure 22–39

8. Close the References dialog box.

9. Disable axis display.

10. Create the sketch shown in Figure 22–40.

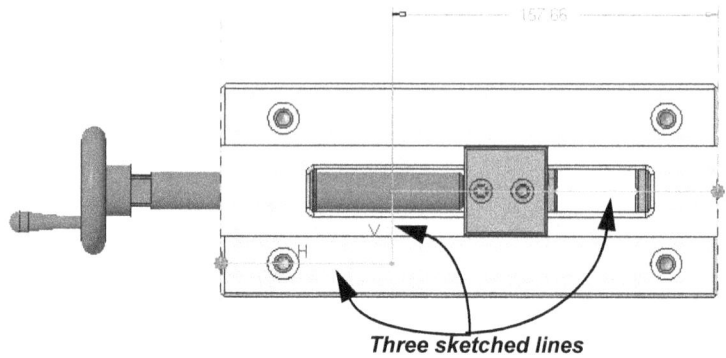

Three sketched lines

Figure 22–40

11. Complete the sketch. The cross-section is complete.

12. Right-click on **C** in the model tree and select **Show Section** to display the cross-hatching for the section. The model should look similar to one shown in Figure 22–41.

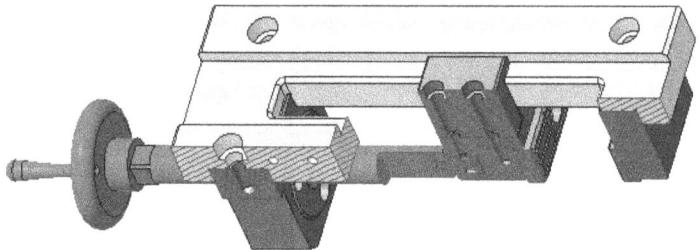

Figure 22–41

13. Save the assembly and erase it from memory.

Practice 22b | Model Measurements

Practice Objective

- Find the length, height, angle, and the distance between entities using the measurement tools.

In this practice, you will use the measurement tools to investigate a model. You will use the measurement tools to verify the distance, area, angle, and diameter of various features in the model.

Task 1 - Open a part file.

1. Set the working directory to the *Chapter 22\practice 22b* folder.

2. Open **pillow_block.prt**.

3. Set the model display as follows:

   - ⁺⁄⁎ *(Datum Display Filters)*: All Off

   - ⊱ *(Spin Center)*: Off

   - ⬚ *(Display Style)*: ⬚ (Shading With Edges)

Task 2 - Measure the overall length.

1. Select the *Analysis* tab and click ⟋ (Measure)> ⊓ (Distance).

2. If required, click ⊕ (Expand The Dialog) to expand the Measure: Distance dialog box as shown in Figure 22–42.

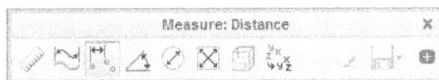

Click to expand the dialog box.

Figure 22–42

3. If required, click ⊕ (Expand The Dialog) next to *Setup* and *Results* to expand the Measure dialog box as shown in Figure 22–43.

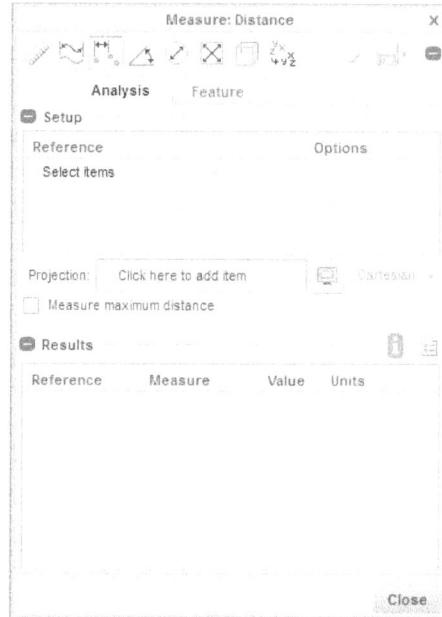

Figure 22–43

4. Select the vertical planar surface on the right side of the model, as shown in Figure 22–44.

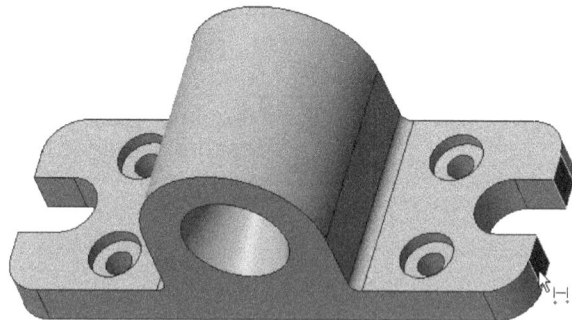

Figure 22–44

5. Hold <Ctrl> and select a similar vertical planar surface on the left side of the model.

6. The information displayed in the *Graphics* window and in the Distance dialog box indicates that the *Distance* = **10.0000** as shown in Figure 22–45.

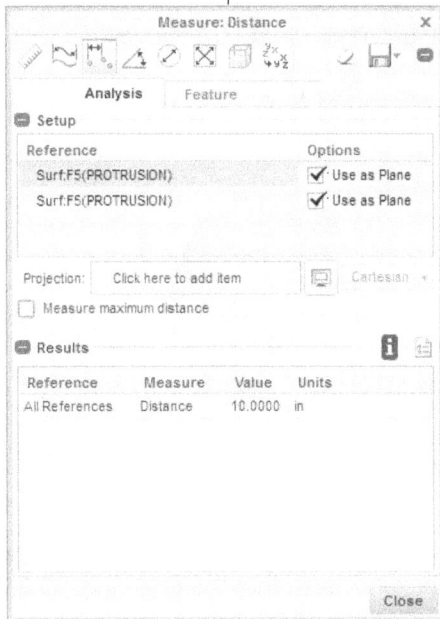

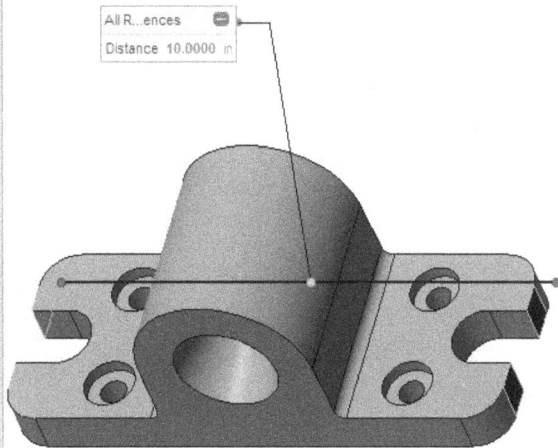

Figure 22–45

7. Do not close the Distance dialog box.

Task 3 - Measure the overall height.

*You can also right-click and select **Remove** to clear the selected references or to select new references.*

1. Click ⌐ (Clear Selections) in the Measure dialog box to clear the selected references.

2. Select the bottom surface of the part as shown in Figure 22–46.

Select the bottom surface

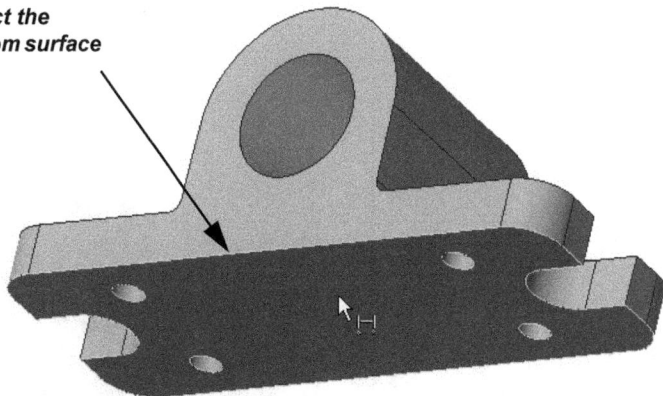

Figure 22–46

3. Hold <Ctrl> and select **DTM2** from the model tree to measure the overall height as shown in Figure 22–47.

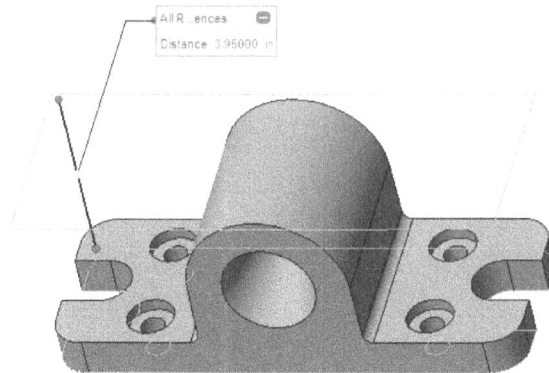

Figure 22–47

4. The information displayed in the Graphics window and in the Distance dialog box indicates that the *Distance* = **3.95000**.

5. Do not close the Distance dialog box.

Task 4 - Measure a distance between the U-shaped cut and the hole.

---

1. Click ✐ (Clear Selections) in the Measure dialog box to clear the selected references.

2. Select the cylindrical surface of the U-shaped cut, as shown in Figure 22–48.

3. Hold <Ctrl> and select the cylindrical surface of the hole, as shown in Figure 22–48.

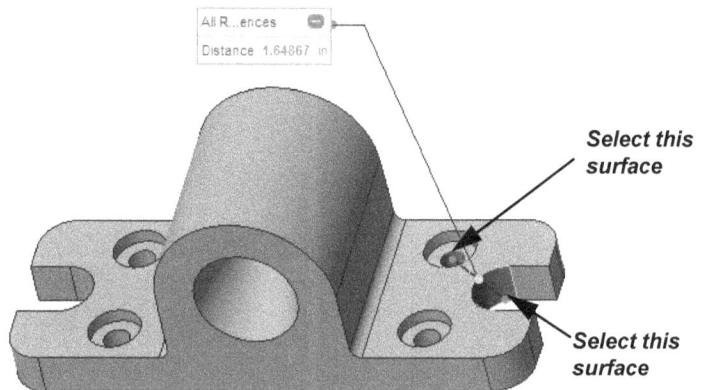

Figure 22–48

4. The information displayed in the Graphics window and in the Distance dialog box indicates that the *Distance* = **1.64867**.

5. Clear **Use as Axis** for both references in the *References* area of the dialog box. The information displayed in the Graphics window and in the Distance dialog box indicates that the *Distance* = **0.80000**.

6. Enable **Use as Axis** for both references in the *References* area of the dialog box.

7. Enable **Measure maximum distance** and the information displayed in the Graphics window and in the Distance dialog box indicates that the *Maximum Distance* = **2.49867**.

As shown in Figure 22–49, the Maximum Distance option measures the distance between the opposing surfaces.

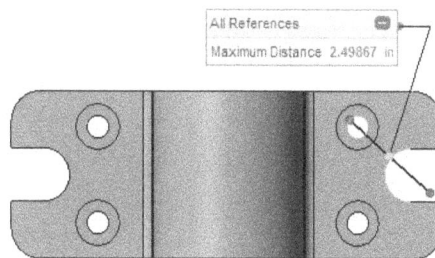

All References

Maximum Distance 2.49867 in

Figure 22–49

Task 5 - Measure the length of an edge.

*You can also right-click and select **Measure> Length**.*

1. Click ⟍ (Clear Selections) in the Measure dialog box to clear the selected references.

2. Click ⟋ (Length) in the dialog box.

3. Select the edge as shown in Figure 22–50.

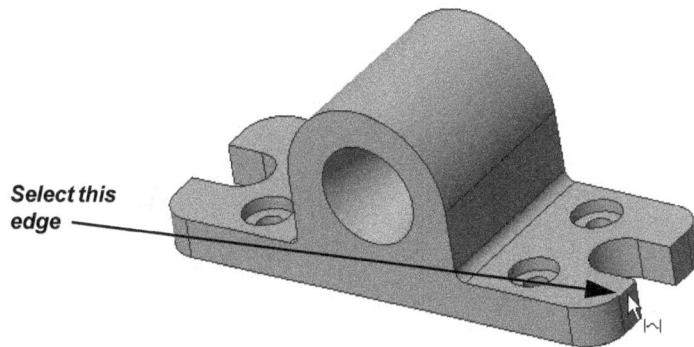

Select this edge

Figure 22–50

4. Right-click in the References collector and select **Use as Chain** as shown in Figure 22–51.

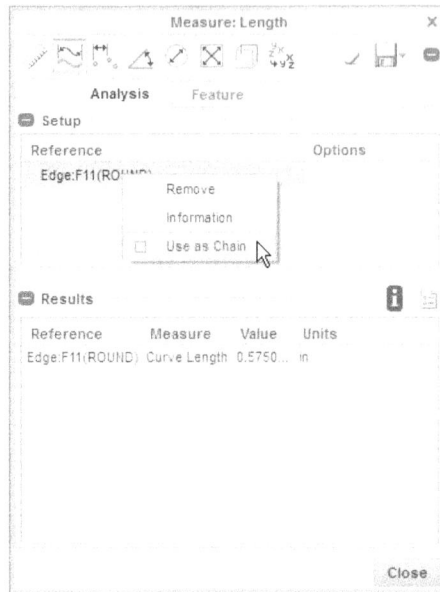

Figure 22–51

5. Select **Rule-based** and ensure that **Tangent** is selected. All of the tangent edges are selected as shown in Figure 22–52.

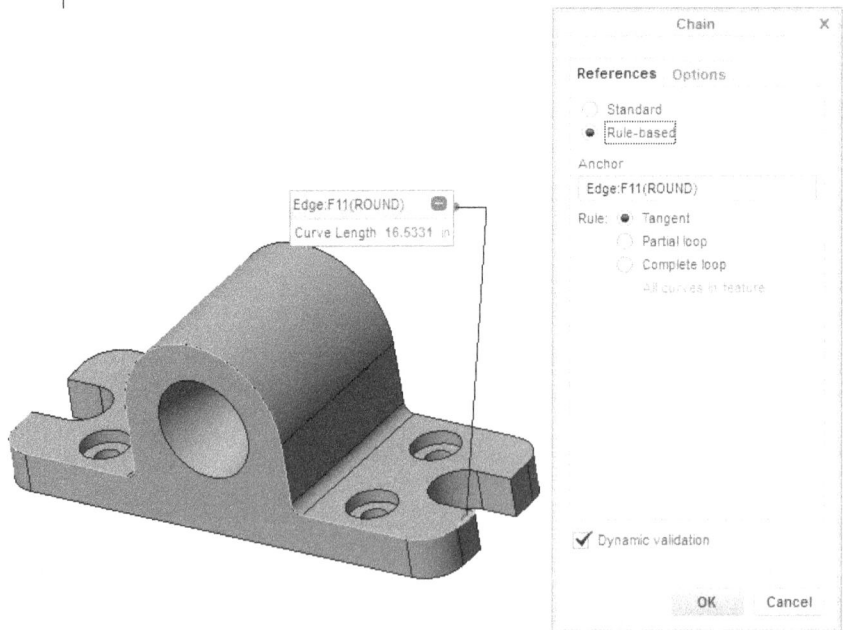

Figure 22–52

6. The information displayed in the Graphics window and in the Length dialog box indicates that the *Length* = **16.5331**.

Task 6 - Measure point to point with a distance measurement.

---

1. Click ✐ (Clear Selections) in the Measure dialog box to clear the selected references.

2. Click ⊓. (Distance) in the Measure dialog box.

3. Select the vertex shown in Figure 22–53.

4. Hold <Ctrl> and select the cylindrical edge shown in Figure 22–54. The centerpoint of the arc is selected by default.

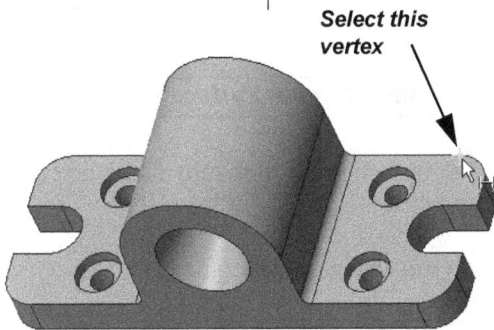

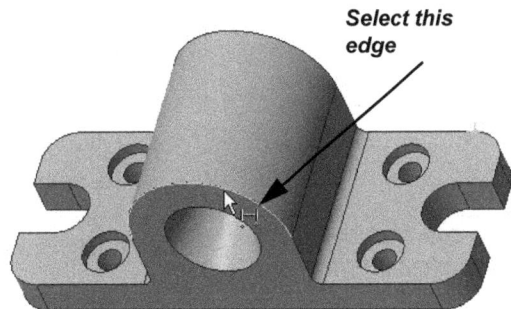

Figure 22–53   **Figure 22–54**

5. Select the **Projection** reference collector in the Measure: Distance dialog box as shown in Figure 22–55.

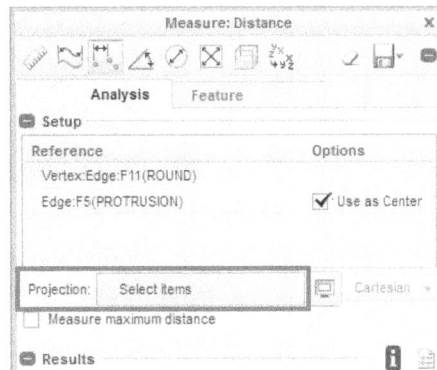

Figure 22–55

---

6. Select the **PRT_CSYS_DEF** coordinate system from the model tree. This projects the measurement to the coordinate system. The measurement displays as shown in Figure 22–56.

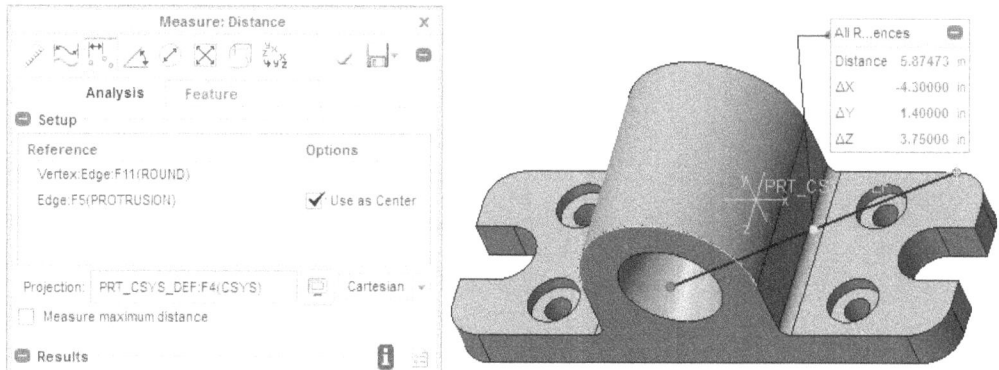

Figure 22–56

Task 7 - Measure an angle between surfaces.

1. Click ⟋ (Clear Selections) in the Measure dialog box to clear the selected references.

*You can also right-click and select **Angle**.*

2. Click ⟁ (Angle) in the Measure dialog box.

3. Select two planar surfaces, as shown in Figure 22–57.

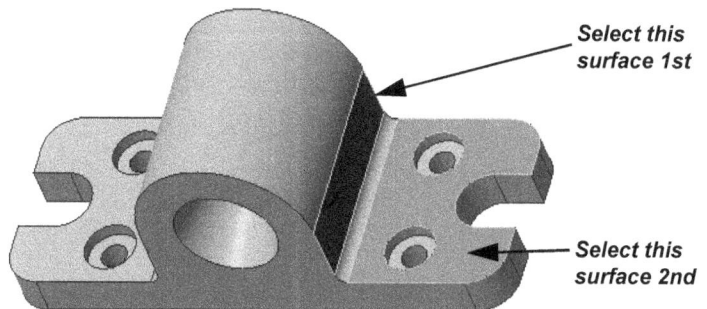

Select this surface 1st

Select this surface 2nd

Figure 22–57

4. The information displayed in the Graphics window and in the Angle dialog box indicates that the *Angle* = **89.0000**.

5. Expand the Angle drop-down list and select **Supplement** in the *Angle* field as shown in Figure 22–58. This changes the angle direction with an *Angle* of **91.0000** degrees.

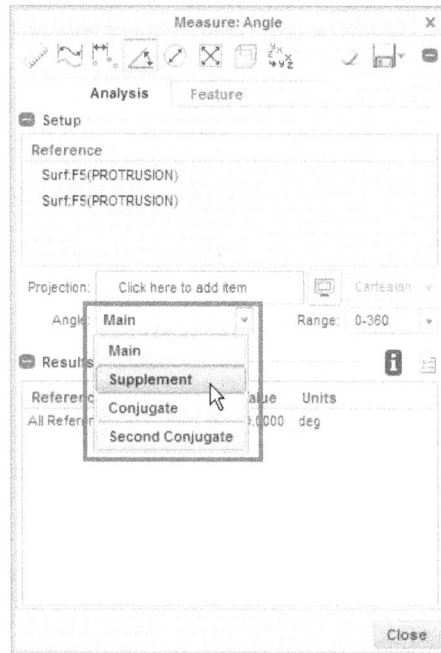

Figure 22–58

6. The information displayed in the Graphics window and in the Angle dialog box indicates that the *Angle* = **91.0000**, as shown in Figure 22–59. This is the correct value.

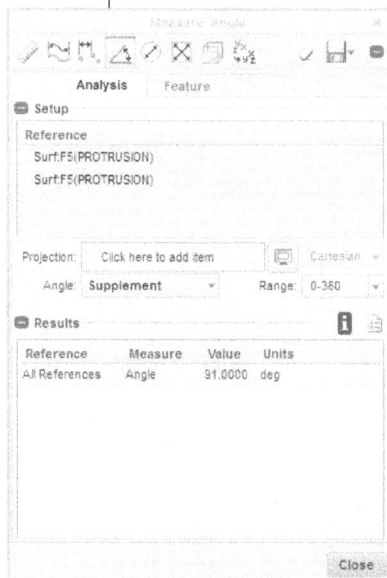

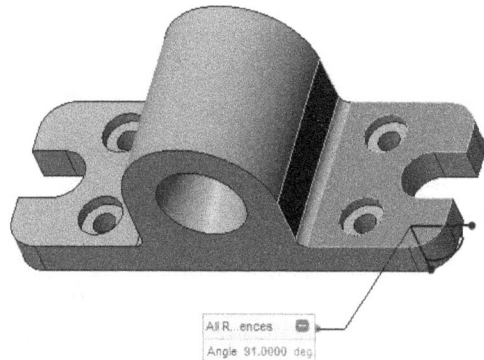

Figure 22–59

Task 8 - Measure the area of a surface.

1. Click ✓ (Clear Selections) in the Measure dialog box to clear the selected references.

2. Click ⊠ (Area) in the Measure dialog box.

3. Select a planar surface as shown in Figure 22–60.

Select this surface

Figure 22–60

4. The information displayed in the Graphics window and in the Area dialog box indicates that the *Area* = **8.1125**.

Task 9 - Measure the diameter of a surface.

1. Click ✓ (Clear Selections) in the Measure dialog box to clear the selected references.

2. Click ⟋ (Diameter) in the Measure dialog box.

3. Select a cylindrical surface as shown in Figure 22–61.

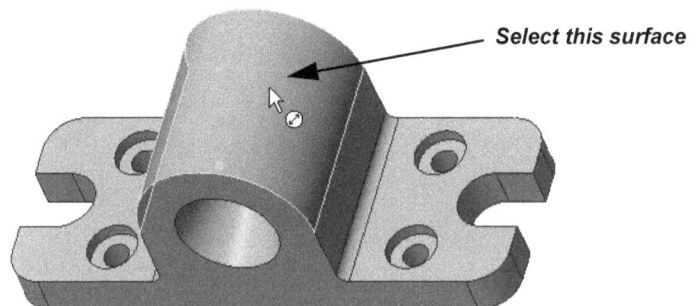

Select this surface

Figure 22–61

4. The information displayed in the Graphics window and in the Diameter dialog box indicates that the *Diameter* = **3.5000** and *Radius* = **1.7500**.

5. Click ✎ (Summary) in the Measure dialog box. Note that the summary displays the area, perimeter, and diameter, as shown in Figure 22–62.

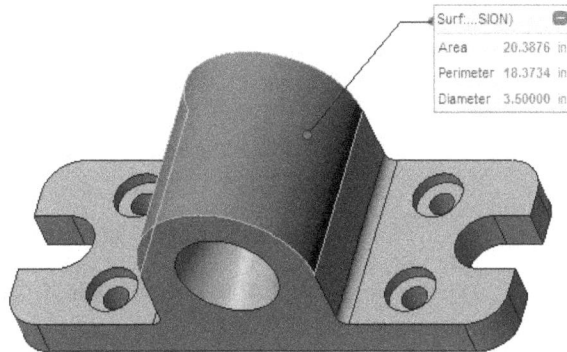

Surf:....SION)	
Area	20.3876 in²
Perimeter	18.3734 in
Diameter	3.50000 in

Figure 22–62

6. Click ⊟▾ (Save Analysis) and select **Save Analysis**.

7. Click **OK**.

8. Close the Measure dialog box.

You can also collapse the measurement in the View window by clicking ⊟ next to the measurement.

9. Click ⊟ (Saved Analysis) in the *Analysis* tab.

10. Expand the **All** drop-down list in the lower right of the Saved Analysis dialog box and select **Hide All** to remove the analysis from the View window.

11. Close the Saved Analysis dialog box.

12. Erase the model from memory.

Practice 22c | (Optional) Model Measurements

Practice Objective

- Compare dimensions in the model using the measurement tools in the Analysis tab.

In this practice, you will take a variety of measurements with little instruction.

Task 1 - Open a part file.

1. Set the working directory to the *Chapter 22\practice 22c* folder.

2. Open **crank_shaft.prt**.

3. Set the model display as follows:

    - ⁎ *(Datum Display Filters)*: *All Off*

    - ⌐ *(Spin Center)*: Off

    - ⬚ *(Display Style)*: ⬚ (Shading With Edges)

4. The model displays as shown in Figure 22–63.

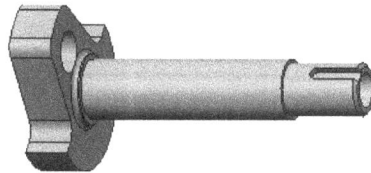

Figure 22–63

Task 2 - Take a variety of measurements.

1. Select the *Analysis* tab and use the icons in the Measure group to take the measurements shown in Figure 22–64. Descriptions of the types of measurements are listed in the table. Compare your results to those listed in the table to ensure that the measurements have been taken correctly.

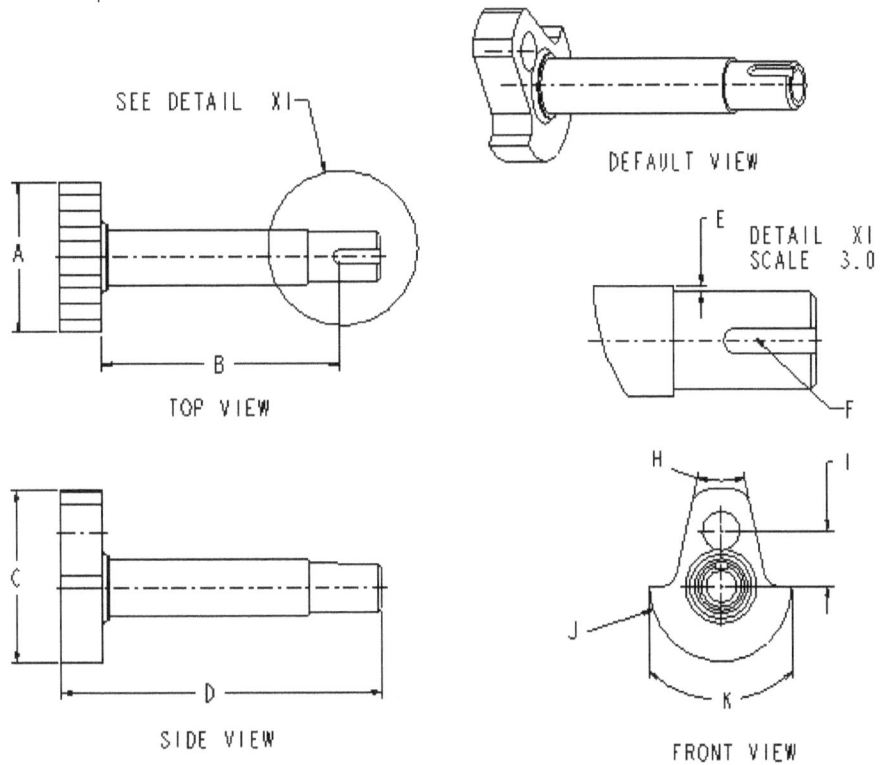

SEE DETAIL XI

DEFAULT VIEW

TOP VIEW

DETAIL XI
SCALE 3.0

SIDE VIEW

FRONT VIEW

Figure 22–64

Dimension	Description	Value
A	Overall width of model.	46.00
B	From face to center of arc on slot.	75.00
C	Overall height of model.	53.00
D	Overall length of model.	101.00
E	Height of step.	1.00
F	Surface area of slot.	58.28
H	Angle	25.46
I	Center to center between shaft and hole.	17.00
J	Diameter	46.00
K	Arc length	72.26

2. Save the part and erase it from memory.

Chapter Review Questions

1. Analysis tools are only available in Assembly Mode.

   a. True

   b. False

2. Which of the following options saves your analysis in the model?

   a. Quick

   b. Saved

   c. Feature

   d. You cannot save an analysis.

3. Which icon enables you to view a saved distance measurement?

   a.

   b.

   c.

   d.

4. Mass Property calculations include information on suppressed features or components.

   a. True

   b. False

5. A _____ cross-section is created using a datum plane in the location of the required slice.

   a. Offset Cross-section

   b. Planar Cross-section

   c. Directional Cross-section

6. Cross-sections physically cut the model.

   a. True

   b. False

7. The _____ option changes existing dimensions to the new system of units (i.e., 1" becomes 25.4 mm).

   a. Convert

   b. Interpret

8. If a model has been created using the wrong units, what is the best conversion method to use?

a. Convert Dimensions

b. Interpret Dimensions

c. You must scale the model.

Command Summary

Button	Command	Location
	Measure	• **Ribbon:** *Analysis* tab in the *Measure* group
	Manage Views	• **Ribbon:** *Model* tab in the *Model Display* group • **Ribbon:** *View* tab in the *Model Display* group • Graphics toolbar
	Mass Properties	• **Ribbon:** *Analysis* tab in the *Model Report* group
	Saved Analysis	• **Ribbon:** *Analysis* tab in the *Manage* group
	Section	• **Ribbon:** *View* tab in the *Model Display* group • **Ribbon:** *Model* tab in the *Model Display* group

Appendix

A

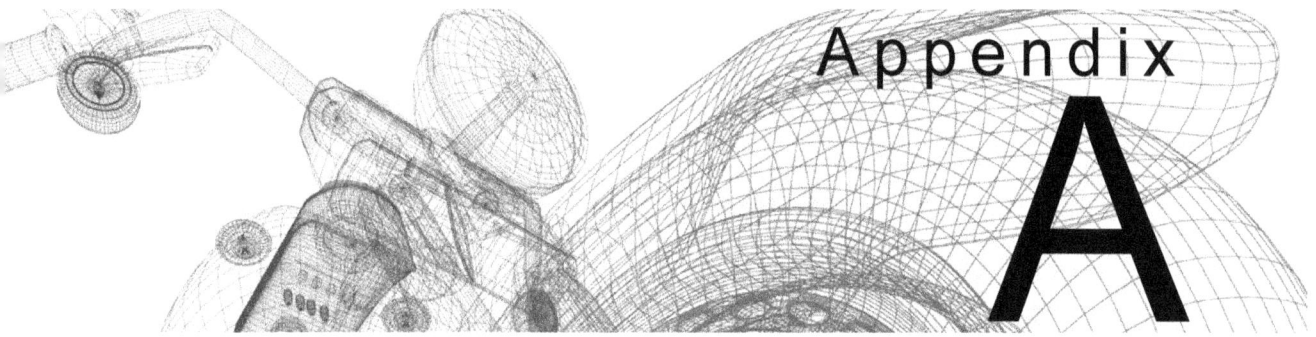

Resolve Environment

Some companies want their users to work with the legacy resolve mode of Creo Parametric. This mode will force you to correct any feature failures before continuing with the model process. If your company uses Resolve Mode, complete this appendix.

Learning Objectives in this Appendix

- Learn to diagnose and correct failures occur using the appropriate tools.
- Learn who to use the Resolve mode to diagnose and correct failures.
- Learn how to avoid feature failures using the Replace command.

A.1 Resolve Environment

You can set the **regen_failure_handling** configuration option to **resolve_mode**, so that the Resolve Environment is used when features fail. If this option is set, you will not be able to continue modeling or save the model until all failures are resolved. This prevents downstream issues as unresolved failures could lead to rework for you or others working on the model.

General Steps

Use the following general steps to resolve failures.

1. Access the resolve environment, if required.
2. Investigate the failure.
3. Undo the previous changes made to the model, as required.
4. Use the **Quick Fix** options to resolve the failure, as required.
5. Use the **Fix Model** options to resolve the failure, as required.
6. Confirm the failure resolution.

Step 1 - Access the resolve environment, if required.

When a feature fails due to regeneration, the Failure Diagnostics window and the **RESOLVE FEAT** menu open immediately, as shown in Figure A–1. The failure must be resolved before you can continue working on the model.

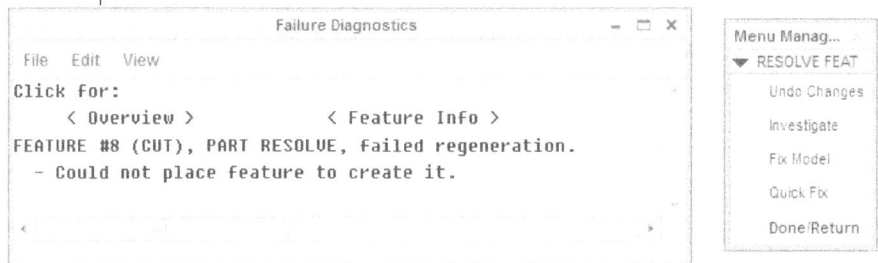

Figure A–1

Once a model has failed and the Resolve Environment is available, many options in the *File* tab are no longer available, as shown in Figure A–2. For example, a model cannot be saved while a feature is in failure resolution.

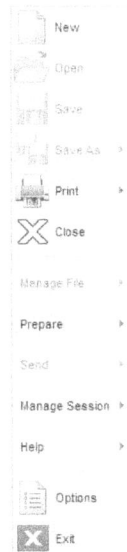

New

Open

Save

Save As

Print

Close

Manage File

Prepare

Send

Manage Session

Help

Options

Exit

Figure A–2

The failed feature and all subsequent features are not regenerated or displayed in the main graphics window. For example, the **Insert Here** arrow in the model tree is placed directly before the failed feature, **Profile Rib 1**, as shown in Figure A–3. Only the features before the **Insert Here** arrow are regenerated.

RESOLVE.PRT
RIGHT
TOP
FRONT
PRT_CSYS_DEF
BASE
PROTRUSION_1
PROTRUSION_2
Insert Here
CUT_1
ROUND
CUT_2

Figure A–3

Step 2 - Investigate the failure.

The failed feature might be the one that was modified or it might be a feature that references it. Changes to parent features can affect child features. To investigate the failed feature, you can use options in both the Failure Diagnostics window and the **RESOLVE FEAT** menu.

Failure Diagnostics Window

The Failure Diagnostics window identifies the feature that has failed regeneration. It is identified by its feature number and type. A short description of why it has failed is displayed at the bottom of the window, as shown in Figure A–4.

Feature # and type for the failed feature   *Description of failure*

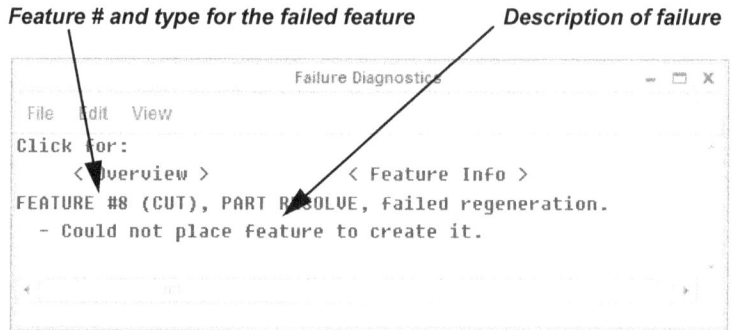

Figure A–4

In addition to the description of the feature you can select the **<Overview>** or **<Feature Info>** options in the Failure Diagnostics window to retrieve additional information about the feature. The **<Overview>** option provides a brief description of the Resolve environment and its available options. The **<Feature Info>** option opens an HTML browser in the Creo Parametric software and enables you to review the details of the failed feature, as shown in Figure A–5.

The commands at the top of the browser are similar to the options available in any standard HTML browser.

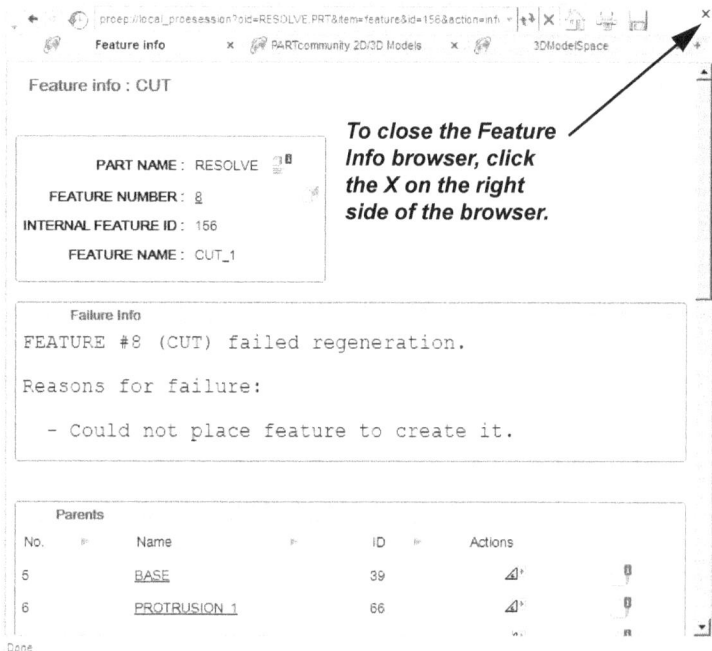

Figure A–5

RESOLVE FEAT
Menu

*The **Diagnostics** option in the **INVESTIGATE** menu enables you to toggle the display of the Failure Diagnostics window on or off.*

The **Investigate** option in the **RESOLVE FEAT** menu shown in Figure A–6, enables you to use options that can help you investigate the failed feature.

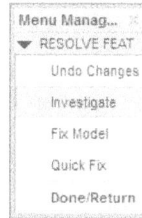

Figure A–6

The options available in the **INVESTIGATE** menu to resolve failures are described as follows:

Option	Description
List Changes	Lists the changes made to the model that caused the failure.
Show Ref	Shows the features that are referenced to the failed feature.
Failed Geom	Shows the failed geometry by highlighting it on the model.
Roll Model	Rolls the model back to one of its features to help review the failure.

Step 3 - Undo the previous changes made to the model, as required.

Once you have investigated the reason for the failure, you must to resolve it. The **Undo Changes** option in the **RESOLVE FEAT** menu shown in Figure A–7, provides you with a basic method for resolving the failure.

Figure A–7

This option undoes all changes made before the regeneration that caused the failure. Using this option undoes all of the changes, even those that did not cause the failure. Once selected, you must confirm the action. The model is then automatically regenerated and returned to its prefailure state.

Step 4 - Use the Quick Fix options to resolve the failure, as required.

In many cases, the change that is made to the model is required and although using the **Undo Changes** option enables you to return to modeling, it does not resolve the underlying problem with the model. The **Quick Fix** option shown Figure A–8, enables you to access several standard options that can be used to fix the failed feature.

Figure A–8

*The **Redefine** and **Reroute** options are equivalent to the*

✎ *(Edit Definition) and*

⚭ *(Edit References) options, respectively.*

Some of the standard options that can be accessed using Quick Fix include the following:

- Redefine

- Reroute

- Delete

Step 5 - Use the Fix Model options to resolve the failure, as required.

The **Quick Fix** option only enables you to work on the failed feature. To make changes to any feature before the failed one you must use the **Fix Model** option in the **RESOLVE FEAT** menu, as shown in Figure A–9.

*The **Fix Model** option is helpful when you must make changes to several features to fix the failure.*

Menu Manag... ✕
▼ RESOLVE FEAT
Undo Changes
Investigate
Fix Model
Quick Fix
Done/Return

Figure A–9

This option opens the **FIX MODEL** menu. The options in this menu enable you to work on any feature that exists before the feature failure. The two options include:

*The **Modify** option is equivalent to the ⊢dī⊣ (Edit) option.*

- **Feature** (open the standard **FEAT** menu)

- Modify

Note that when using **Fix Model** with **Current Modl**, **Quick Fix** can still be used, but **Undo Changes** is no longer available. If **Fix Model** is used with **Backup Modl**, both **Quick Fix** and **Undo Changes** are then available.

Step 6 - Confirm the failure resolution.

Once the failure has been resolved, the **YES/NO** menu displays enabling you to exit the Resolve environment. Once this menu displays, you can save the model before exiting the Resolve environment and select the **No** option to investigate other solutions to the feature failure.

Practice A1

Resolving Failed Features Using the Resolve Environment

Practice Objectives

- Change the configuration option to use the resolve mode to diagnose and correct failures.
- Diagnose and correct the failures that occur using the appropriate tools.
- Avoid feature failures using the Replace command in the Sketch tab.

In this practice, you will make several modifications to a model. Features that you are modifying will cause failures that must be resolved using both **Quick Fix** and **Fix Model**.

Task 1 - Open a part file.

1. Set the working directory to the *Appendix A* folder.

2. Open **resolve.prt**.

3. Set the model display as follows:

    - *(Datum Display Filters)*: All Off

    - *(Spin Center)*: Off

    - *(Display Style)*: ☐ (Shading With Edges)

Task 2 - Toggle on the Resolve Environment.

1. Select **File>Options**. Select **Configuration Editor** in the dialog box as shown in Figure A–10.

Note that the options in your configuration file may differ from those shown in Figure A–10.

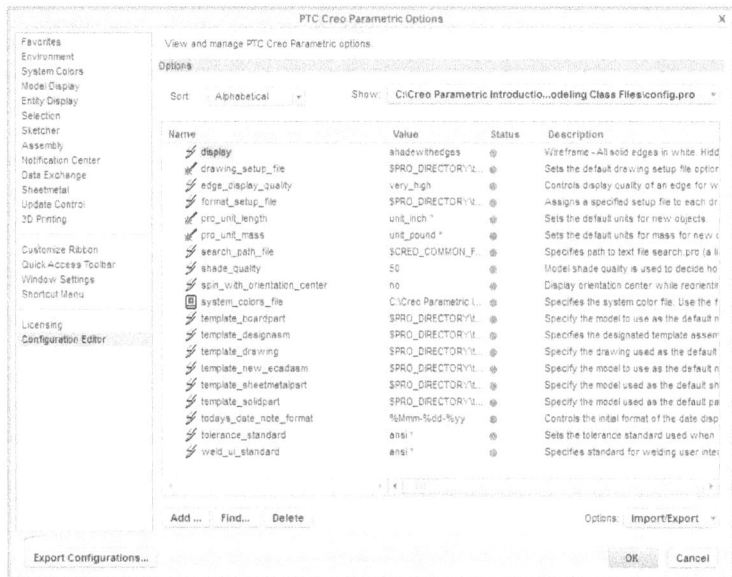

Figure A–10

2. Click **Add** in the Creo Parametric Options dialog box to open the Options dialog box. Set the following, as shown in Figure A–11:

   - *Option name:* **regen_failure_handling**
   - *Option value*: **resolve_mode**

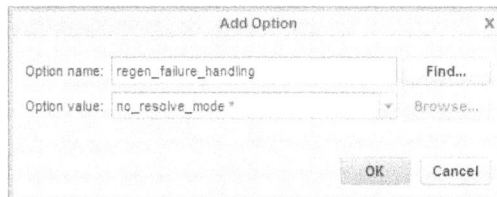

Figure A–11

3. Click **OK** to close the Options dialog box.

4. Click **OK** to close the Creo Parametric Options dialog box.

5. Click **No** when prompted.

Task 3 - Investigate the part.

1. Select the *Tools* tab and click ⋯ (Model Player) and investigate the model features.

Task 4 - Edit a dimension of a sketch.

1. Edit **CUT_1** to modify the section height, as shown in Figure A–12. Set the new *Value* to **3**.

Modify 2 to 3

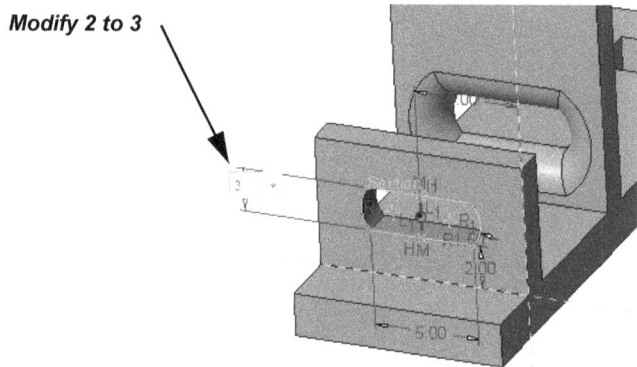

Figure A–12

The dimension does not update, and a line displays in the message window prompting you that the regeneration has failed because the dimension entered is an incompatible value, as shown in Figure A–13.

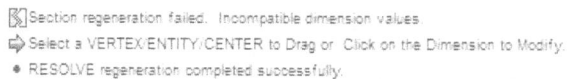

Section regeneration failed. Incompatible dimension values
Select a VERTEX/ENTITY/CENTER to Drag or Click on the Dimension to Modify.
• RESOLVE regeneration completed successfully.

Figure A–13

The arcs have a *Radius* of **1.5**. This value is incompatible with the section eight of 3.0. If you want to change the section height, you need to modify the arc radii at the same time.

Task 5 - Modify the sketch for an extrude.

1. In the model tree, select **Protrusion_1**. Right-click and select ✎ (Edit Definition). Activate the *Sketch* tab by right-clicking and selecting **Edit Internal Sketch.**

2. Add a horizontal dimension of **3.00** for the top line and delete the vertical constraint on the left side of the sketch, as shown in Figure A–14. Modify the dimensional values as shown. Do not delete any of the original entities.

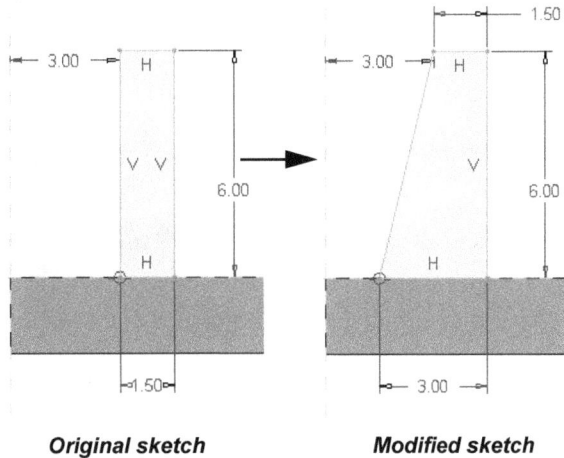

Original sketch   *Modified sketch*

Figure A–14

3. Complete the feature redefinition.

4. The Resolve Environment opens as shown in Figure A–15.

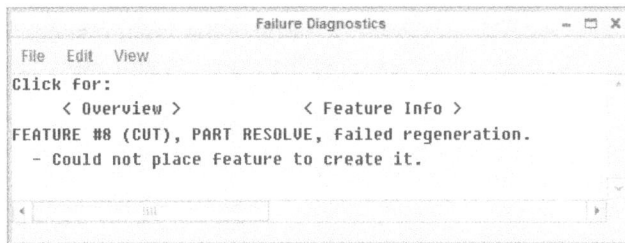

Figure A–15

5. The **CUT_1** feature fails because its sketching plane is missing. It was removed by the section modification. To resolve the failure, select **Quick Fix>Reroute>Confirm** in the Menu Manager.

6. Select datum plane **RIGHT** as an alternative sketching plane and select **Same Ref** for the remaining references.

7. Select **Yes** to exit Resolve mode. The model displays as shown in Figure A–16.

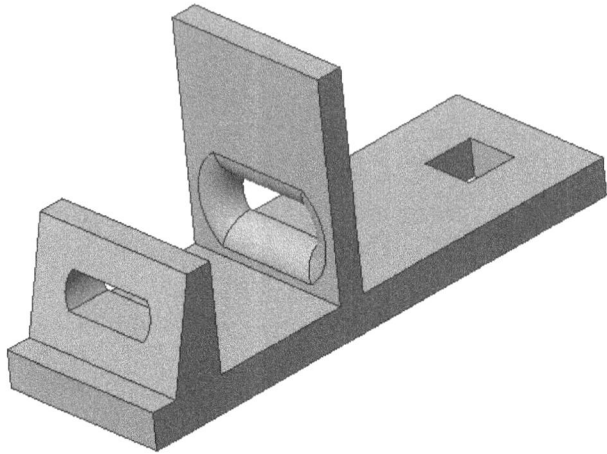

Figure A–16

Task 6 - Modify the sketch for an extrude.

1. In the model tree, expand **CUT_1**. Right-click on sketch Section 1 and select ✎ (Edit Definition).

2. Modify the feature section as shown in Figure A–17. Delete the right arc and sketch a vertical line in its place. At the prompt: *This entity is referenced by other feature(s). Continue?*, select **Yes**.

Shading is toggled off for clarity.

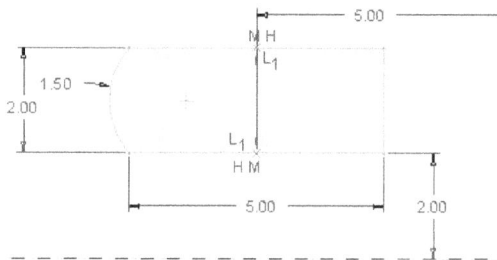

Figure A–17

3. Complete the sketch.

4. The **ROUND** feature fails because one of its reference edges is missing. It was removed by the section modification. To resolve the failure, select **Quick Fix>Redefine>Confirm**.

5. Open the Sets panel and investigate the list of references. There is a red dot next to one of them. Select this reference, right-click, and select **What's wrong**, as shown in Figure A–18. The Troubleshooter window opens.

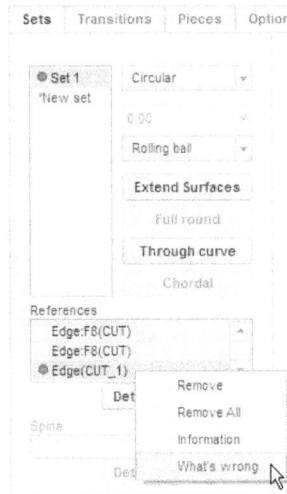

Figure A–18

6. Read the information in the Troubleshooter window and then close the window.

7. Orient the model to the default view using <Ctrl>+<D>.

8. In the *Sets* panel, again select the missing edge reference in the *References* area, right-click and select **Remove** as shown in Figure A–19.

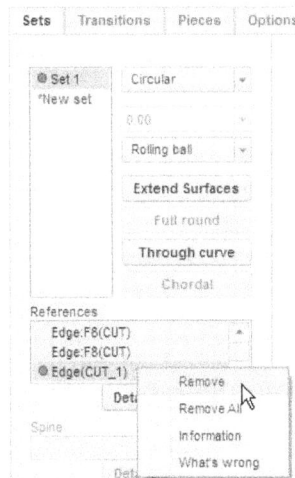

Figure A–19

9. Press and hold <Ctrl> and select the new straight edge of the cut, as shown in Figure A–20.

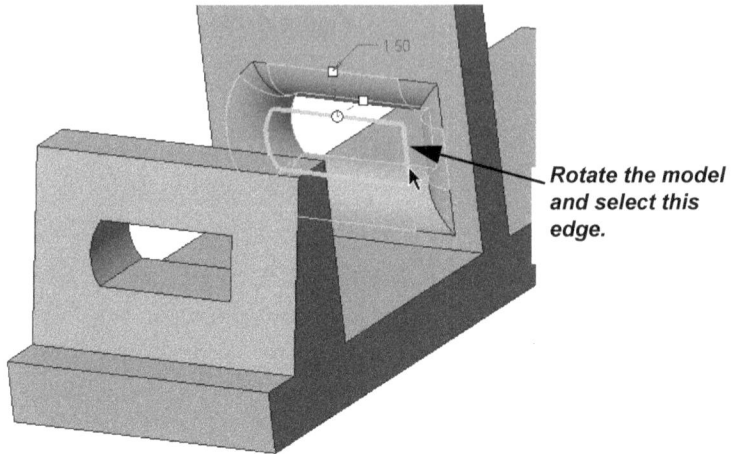

Rotate the model and select this edge.

Figure A–20

10. Complete the feature.

11. Select **Yes** to exit Resolve mode. The model displays as shown in Figure A–21.

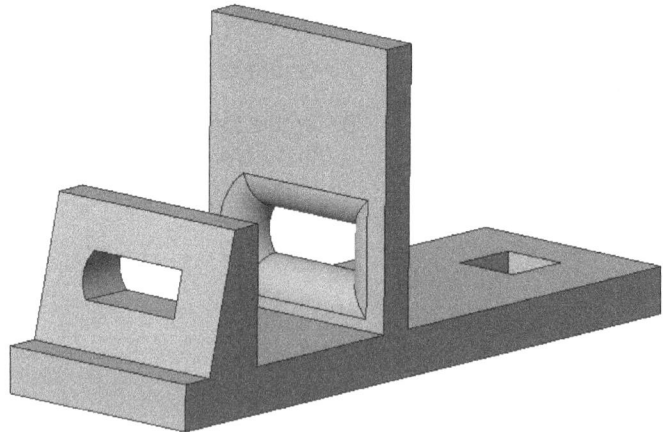

Figure A–21

Task 7 - Modify the shape of the section for CUT_1.

1. In the model tree, expand **Cut_1**. Right-click on sketch **Section 1** and select **Edit Definition**.

2. Sketch a vertical line as shown on the left in Figure A–22. This line replaces the existing arc entity.

You can also expand the Operations flyout panel and select **Replace**.

3. Select the arc from the sketch, right-click, and select **Replace**. Select the new vertical line to be replaced. Click **Yes** to remove the dimension and complete the replace action. The sketch displays as shown on the right in Figure A–22.

Replace this arc with the vertical line.

Sketch this vertical line.

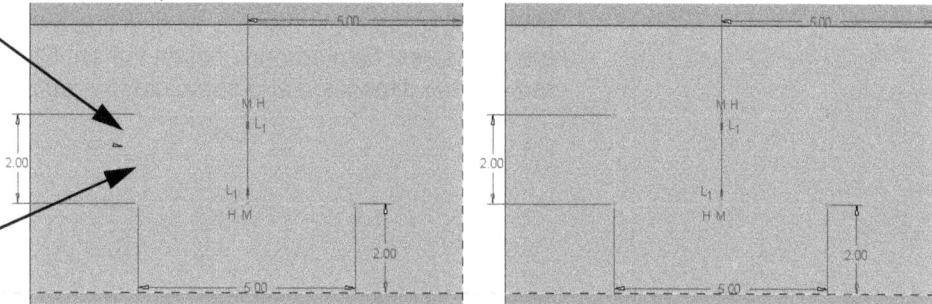

Figure A–22

4. Complete the feature redefinition. The model displays as shown in Figure A–23.

Figure A–23

The **ROUND** feature has been modified without failure. This is because you replaced the old section entity with the new one.

Task 8 - Modify the shape of the section for the BASE feature.

1. Edit the definition of the **BASE** feature sketch.

2. Modify the sketch as shown in Figure A–24. Sketch an arc, which will replace the existing vertical line entity. Right-click the line, select **Replace** and select the arc. Click **Yes** to remove the dimension and complete the replace action.

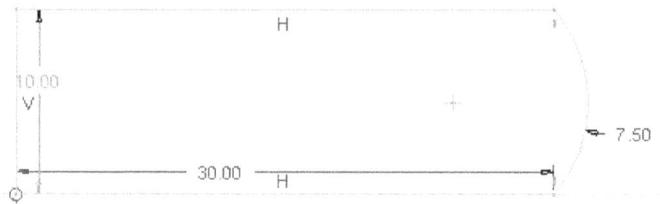

Figure A–24

3. Complete the feature redefinition.

In the original model, the position of the section of CUT_2 is dimensioned to the right vertical planar surface of the BASE feature.

4. The **CUT_2** feature fails because one of its dimension references is missing. It was removed by the section modification. To resolve the failure, select **Quick Fix> Redefine>Confirm**.

5. Right-click and select **Edit Internal Sketch**. Remove the failed sketcher reference and add a new one. Select the new cylindrical surface from the **BASE** feature as a reference. Modify the feature section, as shown in Figure A–25.

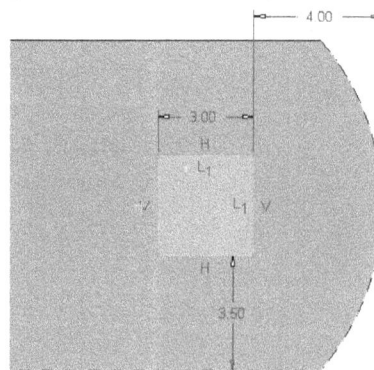

Figure A–25

6. Complete the feature redefinition.

7. Select **Yes** to exit Resolve mode. The model displays as shown in Figure A–26.

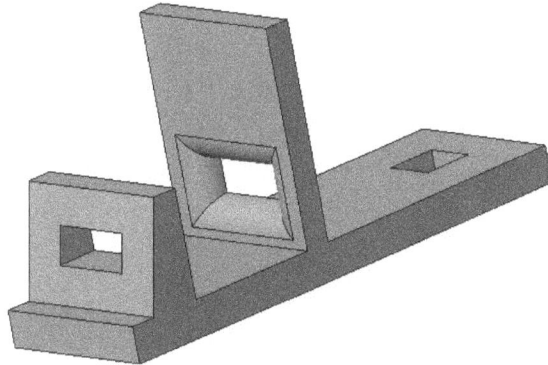

Figure A–26

8. Save the part and erase it from memory.

9. Change the *regen_failure_handling* configuration option back to **no_resolve_mode**.

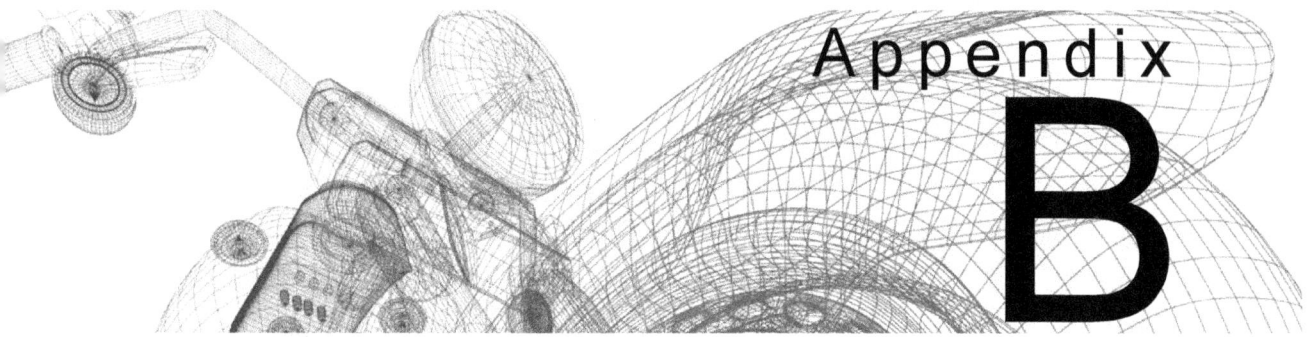

Additional Practices

This appendix provides additional practices that can be used to review some of the topics in this training guide.

Practice B1 | Creating Parts

Practice Objective

- Create new parts and use the appropriate tools to create the geometry.

In this practice, you will create various parts using the appropriate tools available.

1. Set the working directory to the *Appendix B* folder.

2. Create the new part shown in Figure B–1, using the default template.

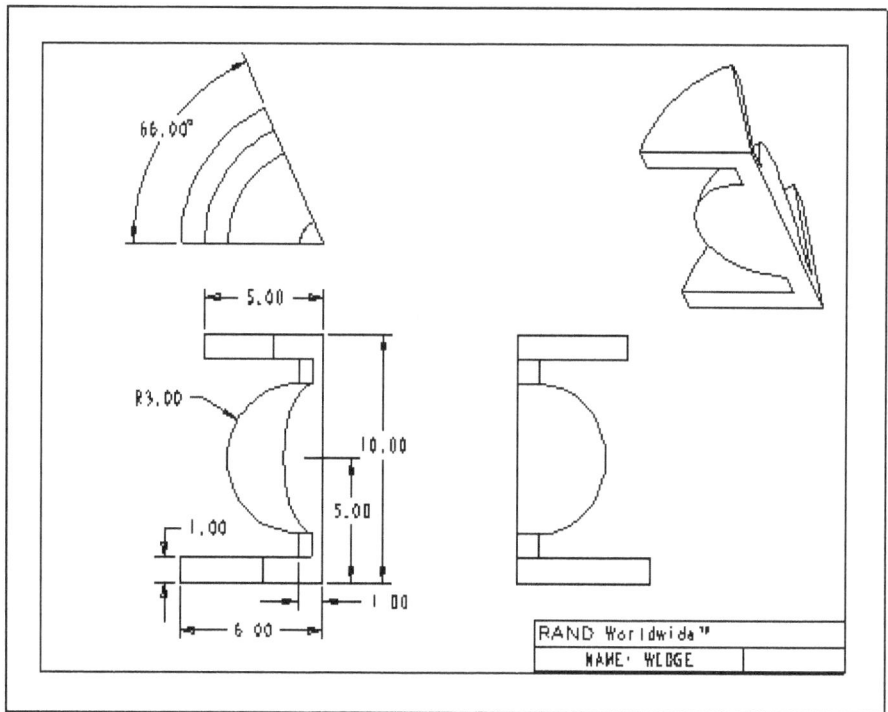

Figure B–1

3. Create the new part shown in Figure B–2, using the default template.

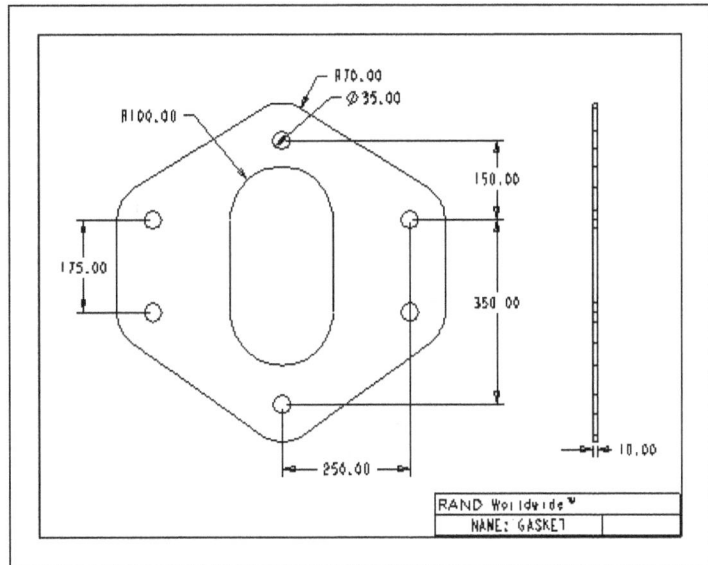

Figure B–2

4. Create the new part shown in Figure B–3, using the default template.

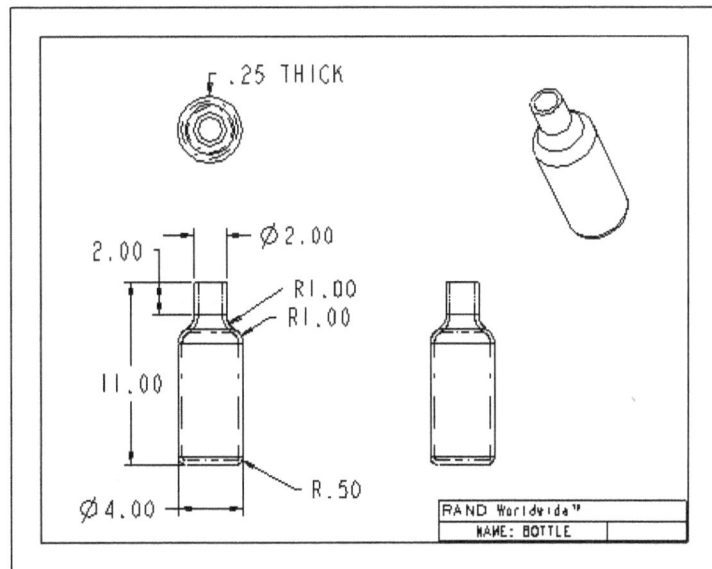

Figure B–3

Practice B2 | Sketched Features

Practice Objective

- Create a new part and use the extrude feature to create the base and secondary features.

In this practice, you will create a new part and protrusions.

1. Set the working directory to the *Appendix B* folder.

2. Create the new part shown in Figure B–4, using the default template.

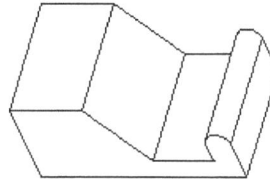

Figure B–4

3. Create the D-shaped and slanted protrusions shown in Figure B–5. For the slanted protrusion use an open section and ensure that the height of the protrusion is not beyond the point at which the slanted surface and vertical surface intersect (the feature fails if this occurs).

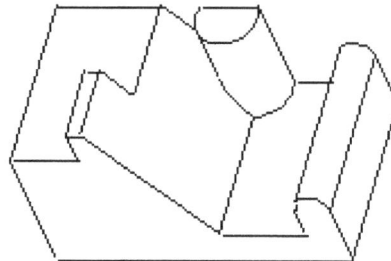

Figure B–5

Practice B3 | Sketched Geometry

Practice Objective

- Create new parts and use the appropriate tools to create the geometry.

In this practice, you will experiment creating the various parts shown.

1. Set the working directory to the *Appendix B* folder.

2. Create the new parts shown in Figure B–6, Figure B–7, Figure B–8, and Figure B–9, using the default template. The dimensions of these parts have been omitted to help you understand that Creo Parametric is a design tool. Once the model has been built, dimensions can be modified to their required values. Build the parts, keeping in mind your design intent for the model.

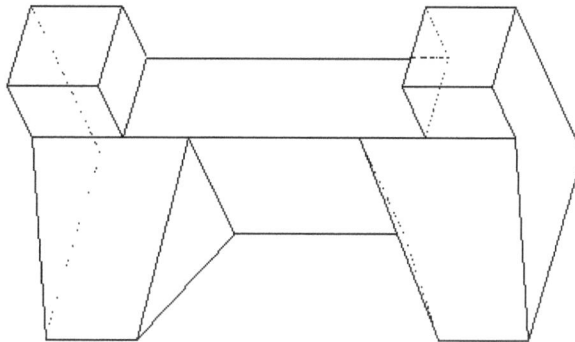

Figure B–6

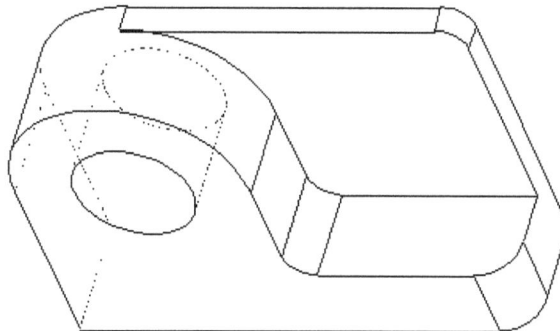

Figure B–7

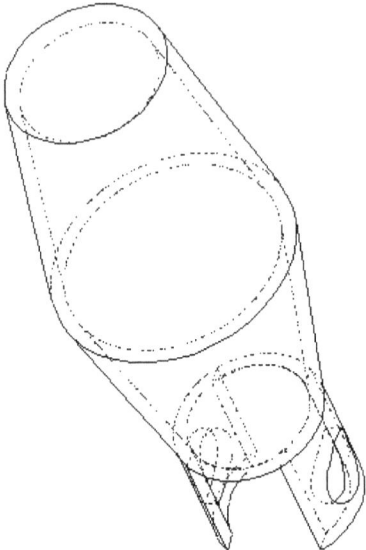

Figure B–8

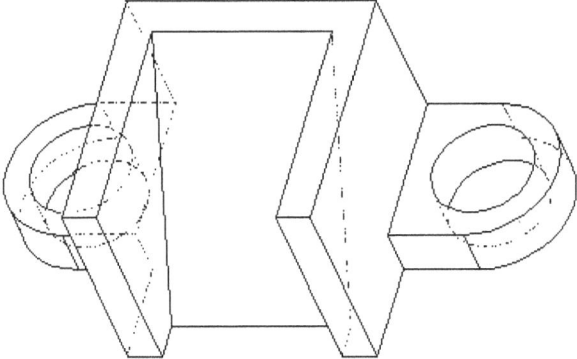

Figure B–9

Practice B4 | Feature Creation

Practice Objectives

- Create a new part and the geometry.
- Create new part and ask question to ensure the geometry meets the design intent.

Task 1 - Create a new part.

1. Set the working directory to the *Appendix B* folder.

2. Using the default template, create a new part called **hubguard**, as shown in Figure B–10. Create the protrusion so that the default view is as shown in the upper right corner in Figure B–10.

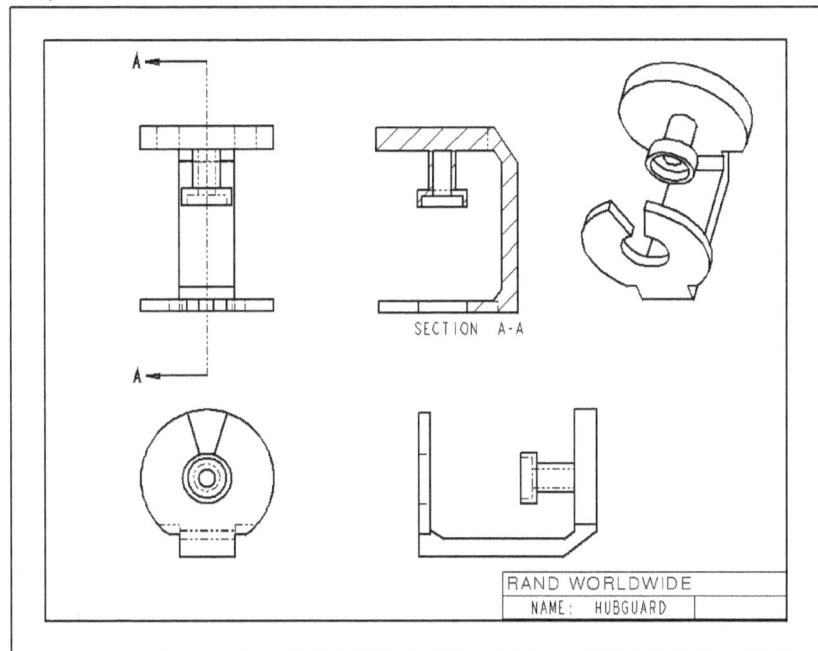

Figure B–10

3. Save the part and close the window.

Task 2 - Create a new part.

1. Using the default template, create the new part called **chamfer.prt** as shown in Figure B–11. Consider the following design intent suggestions when creating parent-child relationships:

   - Should the holes be revolved sketched cuts or holes?
   - Should the holes be created as individual features?
   - Is there an easy duplication technique that can be used to ensure that all holes are dependent on one another?

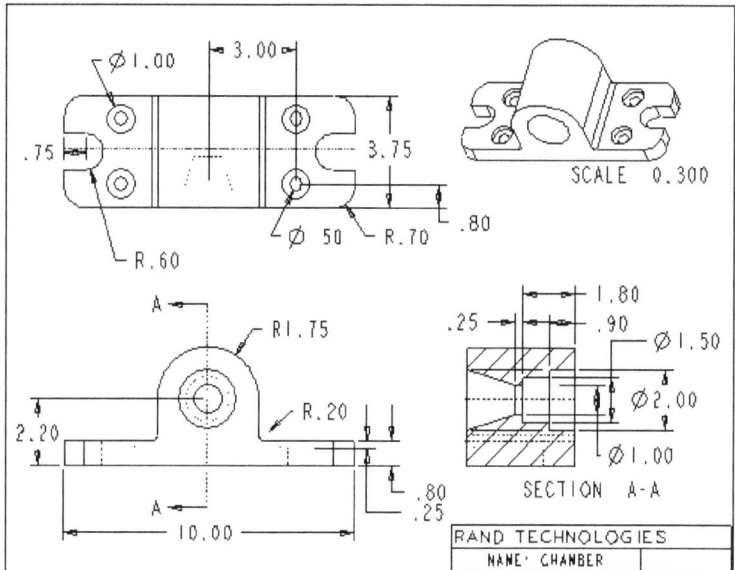

Figure B–11

2. Save the model and close the window.

Practice B5 | Connector

Practice Objective

- Edit the part and fix the failed features using either method.

In this practice, you will resolve feature failures with limited instructions. You will then modify the part to make it more robust and flexible to design changes. To resolve the failure you can use either method. Note that if you intend to use Resolve mode, the **config** option must be set to **resolve_mode.**

Task 1 - Implement a design change.

In this task, you will implement a design change request. The total length of the connector part is 2. The design change calls for a *0.125* change to make the overall length of **2.125**. The overall length is controlled by a datum plane named **CONNECTOR_LENGTH**.

1. Set the working directory to the *Appendix B* folder.

2. Open **connector.prt**.

3. Edit the **CONNECTOR_LENGTH** datum plane and change the offset value from *2* to **2.125**, as shown in Figure B–12.

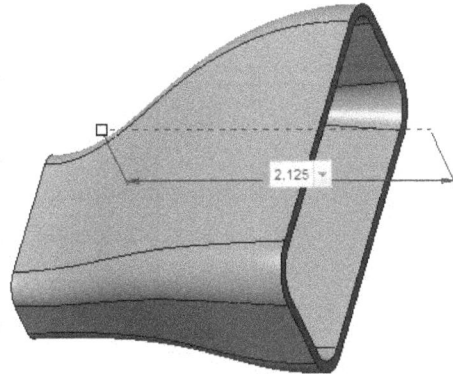

Figure B–12

4. Regenerate the part.

5. Resolve the feature that fails.

Hint: Remove the edge references that no longer exist.

6. Edit the *Depth* of **Cut id 433** to **.625**.

Task 2 - Modify the part to make it more robust.

1. Once the feature failure has been resolved and the part has successfully regenerated, make the required changes so that the original references for **Round 3** can be added, as shown in Figure B–13.

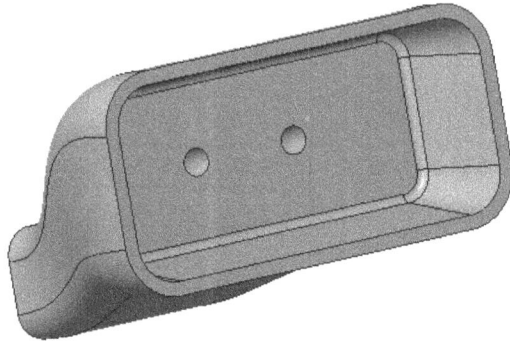

Figure B–13

2. Save the part and erase it from memory.

Practice B6

Place a Section

Practice Objective

- Create a sketch and reuse the sketch to create the geometry using the **File Import** command.

Task 1 - Create a new part.

1. Set the working directory to the *Appendix B* folder.

2. Create a new part using the default template.

3. Sketch the extruded base feature of the part shown in Figure B–14 on the default datum planes. When the sketch has regenerated successfully, save it.

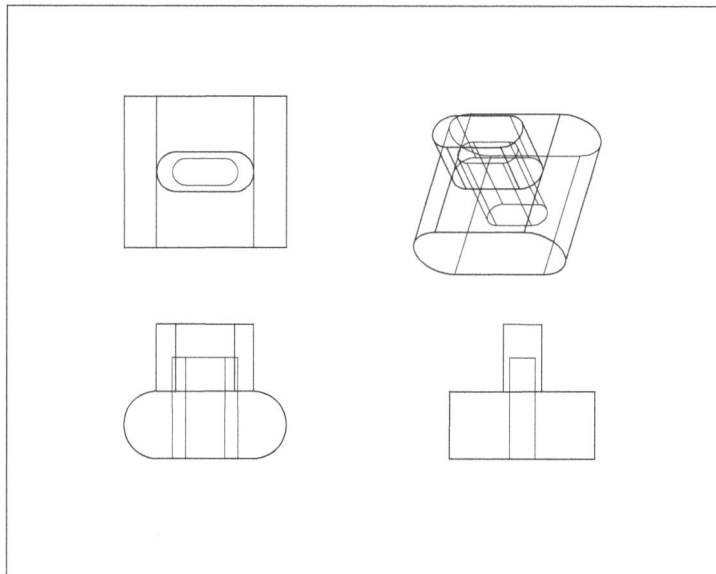

Figure B–14

You can also use the ***Copy*** *and* ***Paste*** *options.*

4. Use the saved sketch to create two additional features, by clicking (File System) in the Get Data group.

5. Save the model and erase it from memory.

Practice B7 | Advanced Geometry

Practice Objective

- Create text using the *Sketch* tab.

In this practice, you will create the part shown in Figure B–15.

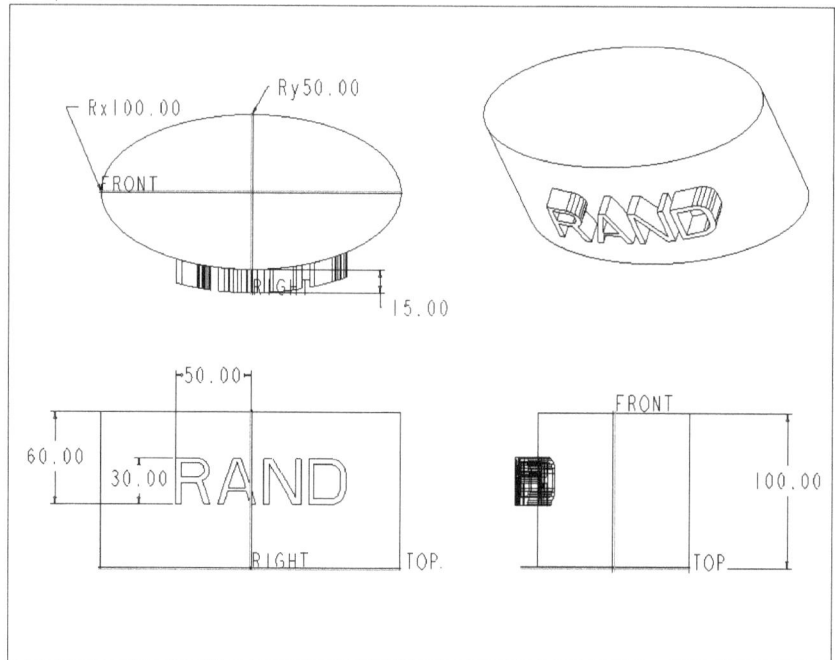

Figure B–15

1. Set the working directory to the *Appendix B* folder.

2. Create a new part using the default template.

3. Create the base extruded protrusion by sketching the ellipse on the default datum planes, as shown in Figure B–15.

4. Create another extruded protrusion. Select datum plane **FRONT** as the sketching plane. Use A (Text) to sketch the text **RAND**. Extrude the text using a blind *Depth* of **75**. This is an arbitrary value to be cut away in the next step.

5. Create a cut to trim the text. Sketch the cut on datum plane **TOP**. In Sketcher mode, use ⌐ (Offset) to create a cut that follows the outline of the base protrusion at an offset of **15**, as shown in Figure B–15. Extrude the cut through all.

Practice B8 | Sweeps

Practice Objective

- Create sweep features using the appropriate options.

In this practice, you will create new parts.

1. Set the working directory to the *Appendix B* folder.

2. Create the parts shown in Figure B–16 and Figure B–17, using swept features where required.

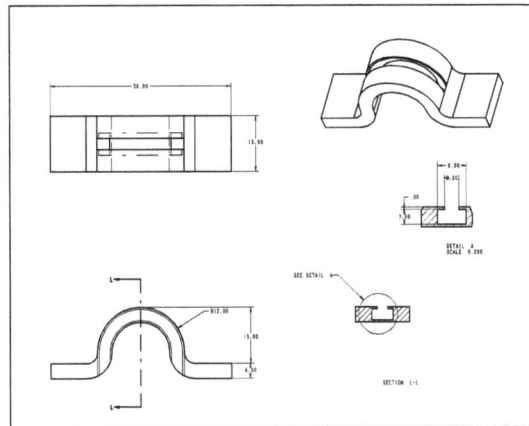

Figure B–16

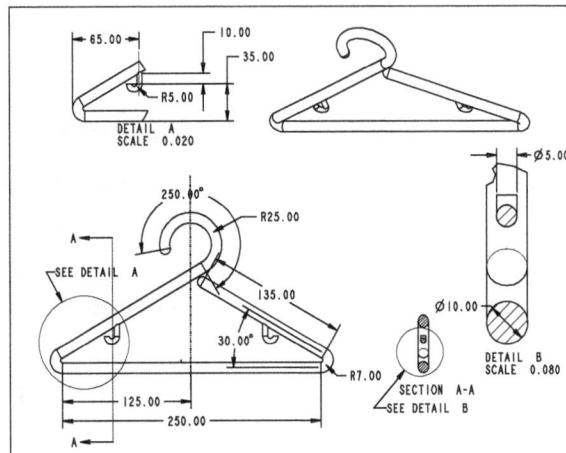

Figure B–17

3. Save the models and erase them from memory.

Practice B9

Create Blend Features

Practice Objective

- Create a blend feature using the appropriate options.

In this practice, you will create the blend feature shown in Figure B–18. This model requires the creation of seven sub-sections, the first of which is a sketcher point.

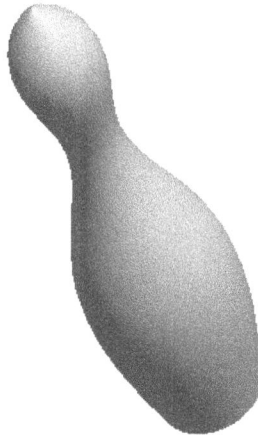

Figure B–18

Task 1 - Create a Blend feature.

1. Set the working directory to the *Appendix B* folder.

2. Create a part called **bowling_pin** using the default template.

3. Select **Shapes>Blend** in the *Model* tab.

4. Select datum plane **TOP** as the sketching plane and accept the direction for the blend feature.

5. Select **Right** as the orientation direction and select datum plane **RIGHT** as the reference.

6. Sketch each section as a circular entity located at the intersection of datum planes **FRONT** and **RIGHT**. Use the diameter values shown below to create sub-sections.

Sub-Section	Diameter
1	1.75
2	2.00
3	2.50
4	1.00
5	1.50
6	0.25

7. For the last section, click ⚹ (Point) to create a sketcher point. Place the point at the intersection of datum planes **FRONT** and **RIGHT**.

8. Enter the depth values for each section when prompted, as shown below.

Sub-Section	Depth
2	0.5
3	3.0
4	3.0
5	2.0
6	1.0
7	0.1

9. Select **Straight** in the Options panel.

10. Complete the blend. The model displays as shown in Figure B–19.

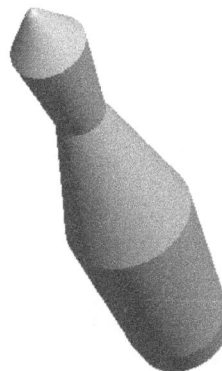

Figure B–19

Task 2 - Edit the definition of the blend.

1. Select the feature, right-click, and select ✐ (Edit Definition). The Blend dialog box opens.

2. Select **Smooth** in the Options panel.

3. Complete the feature. The model displays as shown in Figure B–20.

Figure B–20

4. Select the feature, right-click, and select ⟼dī (Edit). All dimensions that were used to create the model display. Modify some of the values to change the size and depth of the sections.

5. Save the model and erase it from memory.

Practice B10 | Rotational Patterns

Practice Objective

- Create a pattern using the appropriate pattern options.

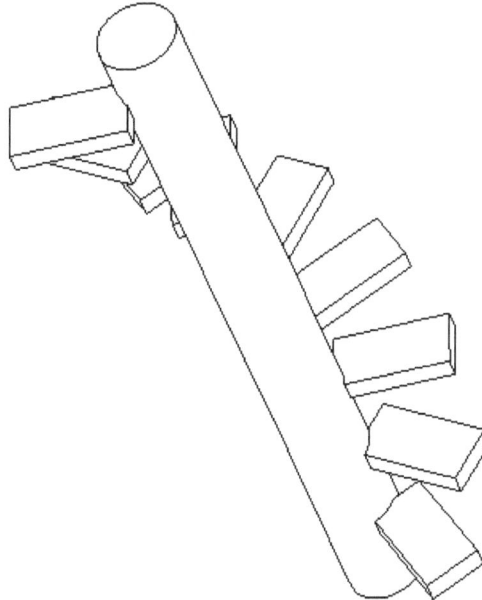

Figure B–21

Task 1 - Create a new part.

1. Set the working directory to the *Appendix B* folder.

2. Create a new part using the default template.

3. Create the base extruded protrusion as a circular section with a diameter of **2**. Extrude the feature to a blind *Depth* of **20**.

Task 2 - Create a rectangular extruded protrusion.

In this task, you will create a rectangular extruded protrusion to be patterned as shown in Figure B–21. The pattern must be driven by both a linear dimension and an angular dimension. To accomplish this, you will create datums on the fly for both the sketch and orientation planes. For the sketching references, only select the axis of the cylinder and the datum on the fly that you created as the orientation plane. DO NOT select the cylinder as the reference.

Task 3 - Pattern the rectangular protrusion.

In this task, you will pattern the rectangular protrusion. Select the linear dimension that was used to create the first datum on the fly (sketching plane), as the first dimension to drive the pattern. Select the angular dimension that was used to create the second datum on the fly (orientation plane) as the second dimension in the first direction to drive the pattern.

Practice B11 | Axial Patterns

Practice Objective

- Create an axial pattern to create the cuts.

In this practice, you will create a radial pattern of an extruded cut. You use an Axis pattern to create the required rotational pattern. The model shown on the left in Figure B–22 represents the original model. Once the cut is created and patterned and the pattern is modified, the model displays as shown on the right in Figure B–22.

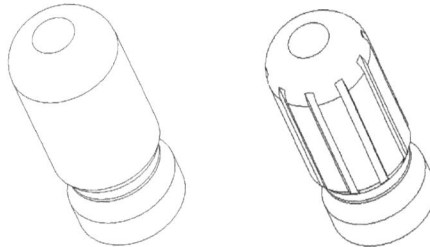

Figure B–22

Task 1 - Create a new part.

1. Set the working directory to the *Appendix B* folder.

2. Using the default template, create a part called **switch.prt**.

3. Sketch the section on the default datum planes as shown in Figure B–23, and create the revolved protrusion.

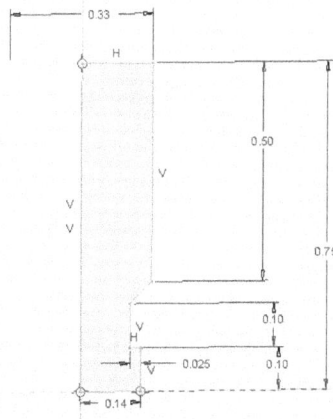

Figure B–23

Task 2 - Create the rounds.

1. Create the rounds shown in Figure B–24.

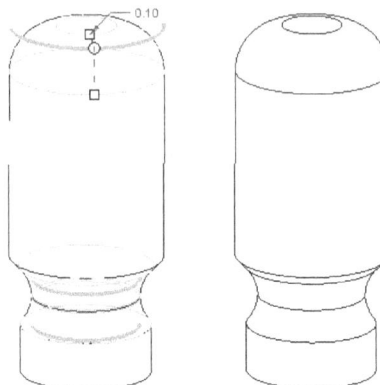

Figure B–24

Task 3 - Create the cut feature to be patterned radially.

1. Click ✏ (Extrude) to create an extruded feature. The *Extrude* tab displays.

2. Select the top surface of the switch as the sketching plane as shown in Figure B–25.

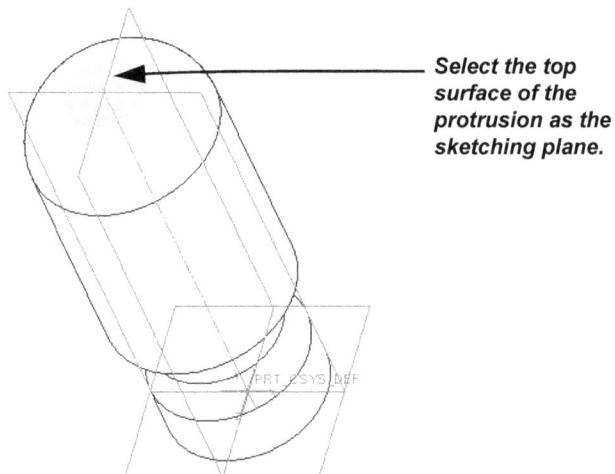

Select the top surface of the protrusion as the sketching plane.

Figure B–25

3. Click ☐ (References) to open the References dialog box.

4. Select datum plane **RIGHT** and the outside surface of the revolved protrusion as references, as shown in Figure B–26.

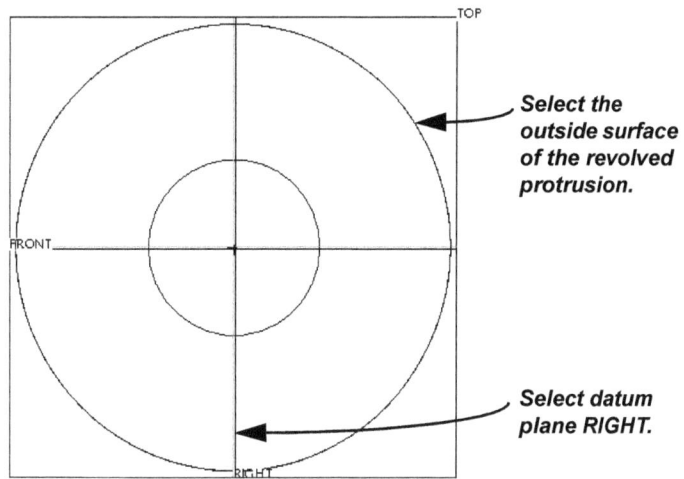

Select the outside surface of the revolved protrusion.

Select datum plane RIGHT.

Figure B–26

5. Close the References dialog box.

6. Sketch the section shown in Figure B–27.

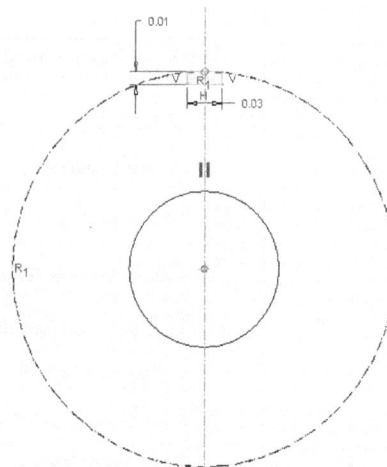

Figure B–27

7. Complete the sketch.

8. Set the **Depth** option to extrude to the next surface using ≝ (To Next).

9. Click ◢ (Remove Material) to set this extruded feature to remove material. Click ⟋ (Change Material Direction) (the one on the left) to flip the direction of the feature creation, if required. Hover the cursor over the icon to display a short help line in the message window.

10. Complete the feature. The model displays as shown in Figure B–28.

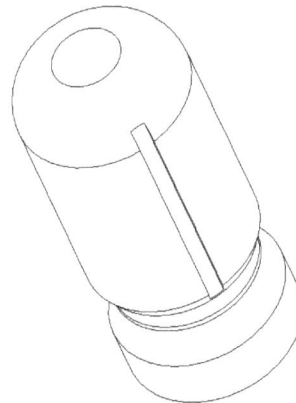

Figure B–28

Task 4 - Radially pattern the extrusion.

1. Select the extruded feature that was just created and click ⠿ (Pattern).

2. In the Pattern Type drop-down list, select **Axis**.

3. For the axis reference to pattern about, select **axis A_2**.

4. Set the following, as shown in Figure B–29:

   • *Number of instances* in the first direction: **20**
   • *Pattern increment* for the first direction: **18**

Enter 20 as the number of instances in this field.   **Enter 18 as the pattern increment in this field.**

Figure B–29

5. Complete the pattern. The model displays as shown in Figure B–30.

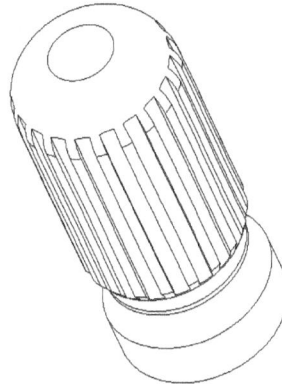

Figure B–30

Task 5 - Modify the pattern.

1. Select the pattern that was just created, right-click, and select **Edit**. All of the dimensions associated with the patterned feature display.

2. Double-click on the **20 Extrudes** dimension. For the new number of cuts, enter **10** and press <Enter>.

3. Regenerate the model. It displays as shown in Figure B–31. Note how the pattern does not update to equally space the cuts around the entire diameter of the model.

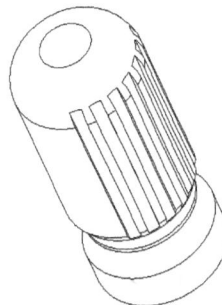

Figure B–31

4. Select the pattern, right-click, and select ✎ (Edit Definition). The tab displays.

5. Click ⊿ (Equal Spacing) next to the *Angular increment* collector (i.e., the 18 value) for the first direction. The tab updates as shown in Figure B–32. Complete the pattern. The model updates because the system has been set to automatically space the number of instances equally, based on the angular extent that is set in the field.

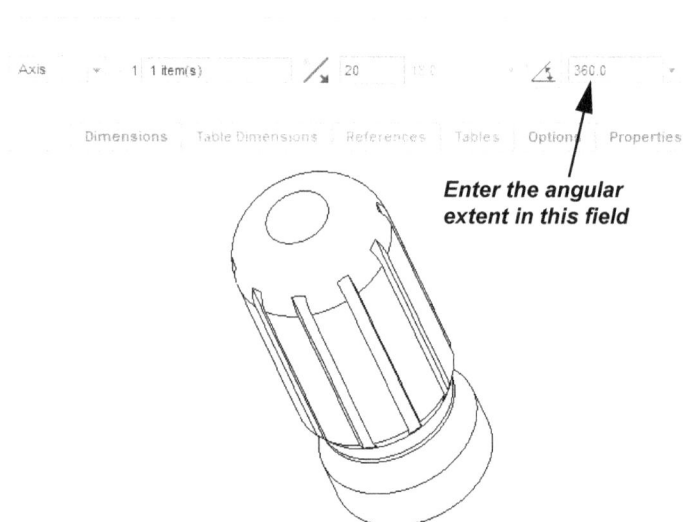

Enter the angular extent in this field

Figure B–32

6. Save the model and erase it from memory.

Practice B12 | Part and Assembly Creation

Practice Objective

- Create and assemble the new parts.

Task 1 - Create the parts.

In this task, you will create the parts that are used during the assembly task as shown in Figure B–33, Figure B–34, Figure B–35, Figure B–36, and Figure B–37.

At the end of this practice, there are tips on creating each part. Try to refer to them only if required.

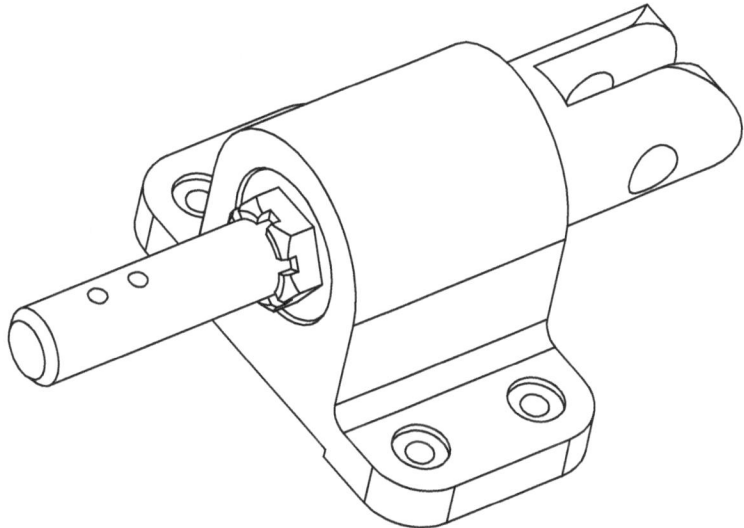

Figure B–33

Yoke

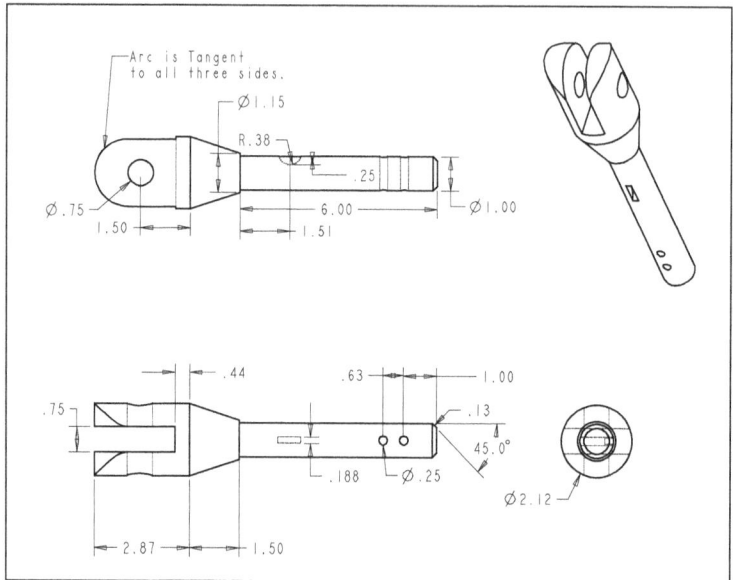

Figure B–34

Collar

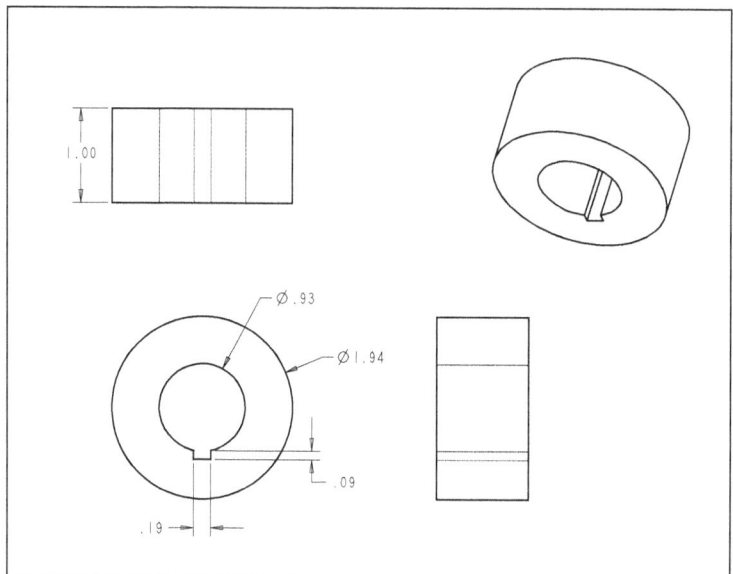

Figure B–35

Nut

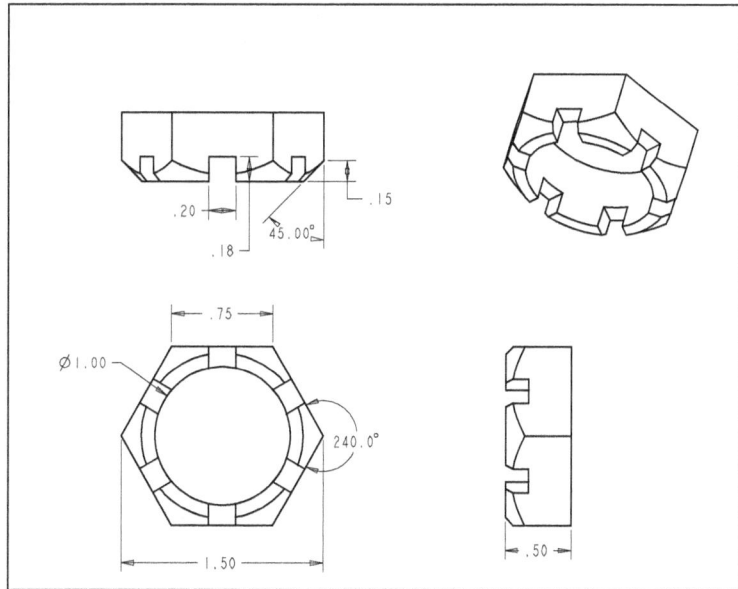

Figure B–36

Base

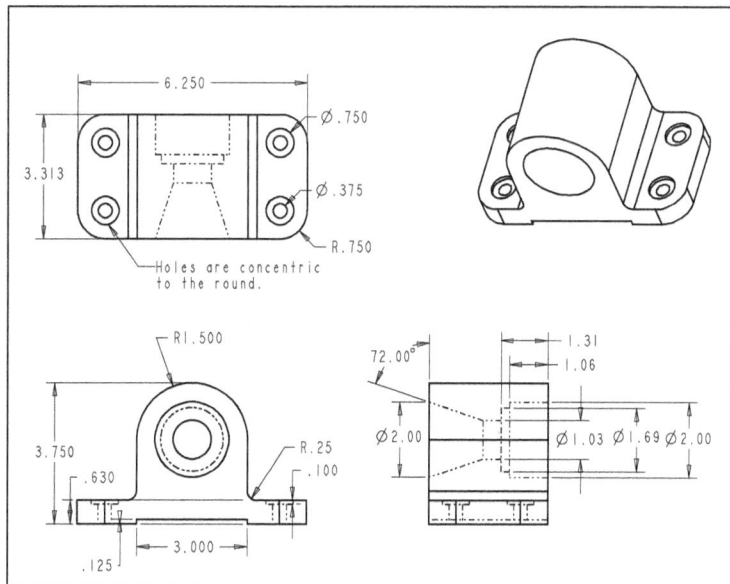

Figure B–37

Task 2 - Create the assembly.

In this task you will create an assembly that should enable the yoke, collar, and nut to be rotated as shown in Figure B–38 and Figure B–39. Check for interference between the components.

Hint: The sloped surfaced on the yoke can be used to mate to the base.

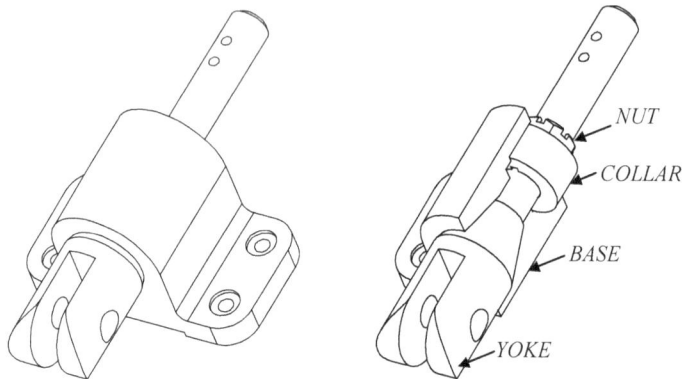

Figure B–38

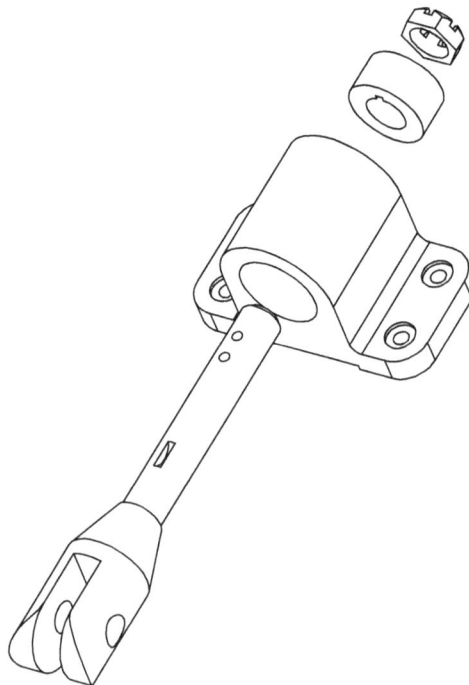

Figure B–39

YOKE

1. Create the model using the default template.

2. Revolve a base feature (the sketch must be closed and a centerline is required as an axis of revolution). Exaggerate the small step where the sloped surface meets the shaft portion; this might eliminate regeneration errors. After a successful regeneration, modify it to the correct value.

3. To create outside diameter dimensions, the following selections are required:

   • Select the edge/endpoint.
   • Select the centerline (required for the axis of revolution).
   • Select the edge/endpoint once again.
   • Place the dimension.

4. Create the large arc cut on both sides of a center datum using the ⊒ ⊨ (Through All) depth option. To create a tangent arc to three sides, sketch centerlines on each of the sides and align them with the part. Then sketch a 3-tangent arc and align the endpoints to the part. The arc is assumed to be tangent to the centerlines (which are aligned to the part).

5. Create the small arc cut on both sides of a center datum using the ⊥ (Blind) depth option. Use a 3-Point arc to sketch the shape. Align the endpoints.

6. Create a 45 x D Edge chamfer on the bottom of the shaft.

7. Create the large hole. Use a Linear hole placed on the center datum dimensioned from the edge and aligned to a center datum. When making the screen selection to locate the hole, select a spot very close to the center datum. The system then enables you to align the hole to the center datum when the center datum is selected as a reference. If the screen selection is not close enough, the alignment prompt is not given, but 0 can be entered as the dimension.

8. Create a small hole similar to Step 7 and pattern the second small hole.

BASE

1. Create the model using the default template.

2. Extrude a base feature on both sides of default datum planes. Sketch the feature so that it is centered on a datum plane (the arc center can then be aligned to the datum). Do not add rounds to the base feature; add them as a separate round feature.

3. Revolve a cut for the hole in the boss.

4. Create the four corner rounds.

5. Create a counterbore hole by placing two coaxial holes on a datum axis. Create a datum axis using the round, it is considered to be cylinder. Copy and mirror the coaxial holes.

6. Create the two edge rounds on the boss.

COLLAR

1. Create the model using the default template.

2. Extrude or revolve a base feature centered on default datum planes.

3. Create a cut.

NUT

1. Create the model using the default template.

2. Extrude a base feature centered on default datum planes. Sketch and regenerate half the sketch, then mirror to complete the sketch.

3. Create the sloped edge by revolving a cut.

Create the square cut and pattern it. This option expands on dimension patterns so that you can simply select the patterning direction. Because you no longer need to select a dimension directly from the pattern leader, this pattern type can help you pattern features that do not explicitly have a dimension for the required pattern.

www.ingramcontent.com/pod-product-compliance
Lightning Source LLC
Chambersburg PA
CBHW080124220326
41598CB00032B/4947